Global Political Transitions

Series Editors
Imtiaz A. Hussain, Independent University of Bangladesh, Dhaka, Bangladesh
Leonard Sebastian, S. Rajaratnam School of International Studies, Nanyang Technological University, Singapore, Singapore

The series publishes books dealing with important political changes within states and in relations between states. The two key questions it seeks to answer are: to what extent are countries becoming more democratic/liberal, and to what extent are inter-state/inter-regional relations creating/demanding new 'governance' arrangements? The series editors encourage submissions which explore local issues (where the local could be a state, society, region) having global consequences (such as regionally, internationally, or multilaterally), or vice versa, global developments (such as terrorism, recession, WTO/IMF rulings, any democratic snowball, like the Third Wave, Fourth Wave, and so forth) triggering local consequences (state responses; fringe group reactions, such as ISIS; and so forth).

More information about this series at
https://link.springer.com/bookseries/15583

Imtiaz A. Hussain
Editor

Global-Local Tradeoffs, Order-Disorder Consequences

'State' No More An Island?

palgrave
macmillan

Editor
Imtiaz A. Hussain
Global Studies and Governance
Independent University
Dhaka, Bangladesh

ISSN 2522-8730 ISSN 2522-8749 (electronic)
Global Political Transitions
ISBN 978-981-16-9418-9 ISBN 978-981-16-9419-6 (eBook)
https://doi.org/10.1007/978-981-16-9419-6

© The Editor(s) (if applicable) and The Author(s), under exclusive license to Springer Nature Singapore Pte Ltd. 2022
This work is subject to copyright. All rights are solely and exclusively licensed by the Publisher, whether the whole or part of the material is concerned, specifically the rights of translation, reprinting, reuse of illustrations, recitation, broadcasting, reproduction on microfilms or in any other physical way, and transmission or information storage and retrieval, electronic adaptation, computer software, or by similar or dissimilar methodology now known or hereafter developed.
The use of general descriptive names, registered names, trademarks, service marks, etc. in this publication does not imply, even in the absence of a specific statement, that such names are exempt from the relevant protective laws and regulations and therefore free for general use.
The publisher, the authors and the editors are safe to assume that the advice and information in this book are believed to be true and accurate at the date of publication. Neither the publisher nor the authors or the editors give a warranty, expressed or implied, with respect to the material contained herein or for any errors or omissions that may have been made. The publisher remains neutral with regard to jurisdictional claims in published maps and institutional affiliations.

Cover credit: Yuri_Arcurs/GettyImages

This Palgrave Macmillan imprint is published by the registered company Springer Nature Singapore Pte Ltd.
The registered company address is: 152 Beach Road, #21-01/04 Gateway East, Singapore 189721, Singapore

Acknowledgments

This volume stemmed from casual conversations among some of us authors about one aspect of unfolding global relations or another. Many of us have a common intellectual background, groomed in International Relations. Nuances enlivened those discussions, based on our individual experiences in different countries or simply by interpreting any given issue with colleagues from other disciplines. Just from crossing boundaries between countries or knowledge-modes exposed so much of a local and global divide that we just fished out an appropriate IR theory to envelop our various interpretations. This, the resultant volume, could also ride on touchstone global developments over the past generation, from the Cold War shift to a neo-liberal order, what the corresponding elevation of laws and order over quarrels and conflicts meant, how refugee-camp experiences evolved into post-camp life, pandemic onset and economic impacts, and a host of others dotting the twenty-first century landscape.

Our primary debts are from each to all other of our colleagues, contributors or not, and to our many students upon whom we played out one hypothesis after another for new sparks. We also thank the meticulously skilled team at Palgrave Macmillan for steering our project to publication.

Ultimately we alone remain responsible for any and all errors of each of our works.

Dhaka, February 2022   Imtiaz A. Hussain

Praise for *Global-Local Tradeoffs, Order-Disorder Consequences*

"This is an innovative look at transformations across the post-Cold War world. Imaginative and easy to read, it tackles a panoply of issues from populism and democratization to education to peace operations to climate change to migration and sweat-shop exports, applying and building upon theoretical insights from Rosenau and others in the post-Cold War era. It asks how globalization and localization dynamics can be institutionalized or not, and how the familiar patterns of International Relations can be thrown into disarray. Highly recommended."
 —Dr. Mark Aspinwall, Visiting Professor, *Dartmouth College, New Hampshire, United States; Professor-Investigador, División de Estudios Internacionales, Centro de Investigación y Docencia Económicas (CIDE), CDMX*

"In an era when transnational challenges like climate change, refuge flows, and pandemics are clashing with the insular ideologies of economic nationalism, xenophobia, and populism, the tension between the forces of fragmentation and integration are likely to grow. This volume dives deep into the diverse and contradictory domestic and international forces that shape the dynamics of and solutions to the world's most pressing problems."
 —Geoffrey Macdonald, Ph.D., *Bangladesh Country Director, International Republican Institute*

CONTENTS

1 Globalization, Localization, and Leaky Umbrellas: Problematic *Pot Pouri*?   1
  Imtiaz A. Hussain

2 Globalization, Governance, and New Institutionalism: Exploring a New "Developing World" Framework   23
  Delwar Hossain

3 The Growth of Populism and Populist Publics: Globalization Under the Gun?   61
  Lailufar Yasmin

4 From Peacekeeping to Peace Enforcement Operations: What Next?   89
  Rashed Uz Zaman and Niloy Ranjan Biswas

5 Spying and Hidden Partnerships in the *Global South*: Bangladesh's Case   111
  A. S. M. Ali Ashraf

6 Climate Change-Induced Displacement and the United Nations   149
  Md Abdul Awal Khan

7	Rwandan Land-Tenure Reforms: Local Socio-Economic Impacts and External Inputs Hossain Ahmed Taufiq	165
8	Ready-Made-Garments: Supply-Chain Management & COVID-19 Impacts Md. Mamun Habib and Ikram Hasan	191
9	Sustainable Democracy, Economy, Youth: Leadership in Local–Global Contexts Ziaur Rahman	217
10	Liberating Education and Awakening Refugee Consciousness: Insights from Rohingya–Syria Comparisons Jessica Tartila Suma	227
11	Globalization, Localization, and the 1990s: "Liberal" Hour Knocking on Mexico's Door Imtiaz A. Hussain and Galia Rosemberg	271
12	Floating Frameworks and Precipitous Posturings: Post-Cold War Anarchy? Imtiaz A. Hussain	313
Index		321

Notes on Contributors

A. S. M. Ali Ashraf is a Professor of International Relations at the University of Dhaka. He holds a Ph.D. in International Security Policy from the University of Pittsburgh, USA. His teaching and research interests are broadly in the fields of security and intelligence studies, international migration, and public policy. He was a recipient of the J. William Fulbright Scholarship and the European Union Center of Excellence Dissertation Award. He has provided consulting services for the United Nations, World Bank, International Organization for Migration, and the International Labour Organization. He often lectures at the Defence Services Command and Staff College, the Foreign Service Academy, and the National Defence College of Bangladesh. He is a member of the International Institute for Strategic Studies, London. He has edited a volume titled *Intelligence, National Security, and Foreign Policy: A South Asian Narrative* (Dhaka: BILIA and DUIR, 2016). https://www.researchgate.net/profile/Asm-Ashraf.

Dr. Niloy Ranjan Biswas is an Associate Professor of the Department of International Relations at the University of Dhaka. In 2016, he completed his Ph.D. in International Politics from City University of London. He was a recipient of the Fulbright Fellowship (2010–2012) to pursue a Master's degree in Security Policy Studies at The George Washington University, Washington DC. In September 2017, he successfully completed the United States Institute of Peace (USIP)-Resolve Fellowship to conduct an in-depth study on community policing and its challenges in preventing violent extremism. He has written extensively on refugees, law-enforcement agencies and preventing violent extremism, and South Asian contributions to United Nations peace support endeavors. He authored 'Myanmar's military and the garrison state: State-military relations in Myanmar and their influence in the [re]production of violence against minorities' in *Asian Journal of Comparative Politics*, 2020, Vol. 5(2). In 2019, he published 'Bangladesh Police in United Nations Peacekeeping Operations and Capacity Building: Striving for Perfection in an Imperfect World!' for *Policing: A Journal of Policy and Practice* He authored a book chapter on 'South Asian Regionalism and UN Peacekeeping Missions: A Case of "and Never the Twain Shall Meet"?' in Brendan Howe and Boris Kondoch (eds.) Peacekeeping and the Asia-Pacific (Lieden/Boston: Brill Nijhoff, 2016). In addition, he published an article in the special issue of The Round Table: The Commonwealth Journal of International Affairs, 106 (4), August 2017, titled: 'The Contribution of Commonwealth Armed Forces in UN Peacekeeping Missions: The Case of Bangladesh'. Besides, his most recent articles are published in National Security (VIF), Asian Journal of Comparative Politics, International Peacekeeping (Taylor & Francis), Journal of International Peacekeeping (Brill), and Bangladesh Institute of International and Strategic Studies Journal.

Prof. Dr. Md. Mamun Habib is a Professor at School of Business & Entrepreneurship (SBE), Independent University, Bangladesh (IUB). In addition, Dr. Habib is the Visiting Scientist of University of Texas—Arlington, USA. Prior to that, he was an Associate Professor at BRAC Business School, BRAC University, Bangladesh; Asia Graduate School of Business (AGSB), UNITAR International University, Malaysia; Department of Operations Research/Decision Sciences, Universiti Utara Malaysia (UUM), Malaysia and Dept. of Operations Management, American International University-Bangladesh (AIUB).

He has more than **19 years' experience** in the field of teaching as well as in training, workshops, consultancy, and research. At present, he is supervising some Ph.D. students locally and internationally. As a researcher, Dr. Habib published about 160+ research papers, including Conference Proceedings, Journal articles, and book chapters/books. He serves as the Editor-in-Chief/Lead Guest Editor/Editor/Editorial Board Member/Reviewer of more than 20 journals, particularly Elsevier

(Scopus) and Thomson Reuters (Web of Science) Indexed Journals. In addition, he delivers lecturesas a *Keynote Speaker* at 65+ international conferences around the globe.

His core research areas are supply chain management, production & operations management, operations research, research methodology. Finally, Dr. Habib is an active member of different professional organizations, including IEEE (Senior Member), IEOM (President, SCM Technical Division), IETI (Senior Member and Board of Director), IRED (Fellow), GRDS (Vice-President), IEB, AIMS, INFOMS, just to name a few. He is involved with QS World University Ranking and *Times Higher Education Ranking* as an academician.

Mr. Ikram Hasan works as a Research Assistant with Professor Dr. Md. Mamun Habib at the School of Business & Entrepreneurship, Independent University, Bangladesh. Earlier, he was a Teaching and Research Assistant at BRAC Business School at BRAC University. As an Intern and Junior Executive with Kuehne + Nagel Ltd. Chittagong office, Bangladesh, Mr. Ikram has also gained experience in the supply chain and logistics field. As an Executive of Conference Secretariat he was involved with the 2nd International Conference on Business and Management (ICBM, 2019), ISBN: 978-984-3443540, organized by Brac Business School, Brac University.

Mr. Ikram Hasan is a Doctoral (Ph.D.) Student at Universiti Tun Abdul Razak (UNIRAZAK), Malaysia. In addition, he holds a Master of Business Administration (MBA) and Bachelor of Business Administration (B.B.A.) with the highest distinction from BRAC University, Bangladesh.

As a researcher, Mr. Ikram has produced about 8 research papers, including Conference Proceedings, Journal articles, and book chapters. His core research areas are supply chain management, blockchain in supply chain management, finance, and marketing.

Delwar Hossain, Ph.D. is a Professor of International Relations, University of Dhaka, Bangladesh and concurrently the Director of the East Asia Center, University of Dhaka. Delwar was the Chair of the Department of International Relations, University of Dhaka during 2009–2012. Delwar earned his Bachelor's and Master's degrees in International Relations from the University of Dhaka, Bangladesh. He did his second Master's degree from International University of Japan (IUJ), Japan as an Asian Development Bank Scholar in 2001. Delwar earned his Ph.D. in global and intercultural studies from Ferris University in Yokohama, Japan as a Monbukagakusho scholar in 2007. Delwar recently published a book on *COVID-19 Global Pandemic and Aspects of Human Security in South Asia: Implications and Way Forward* (New Delhi, 2020) [co-author]; edited *Bangladesh-East Asia Relations: Changing Scenarios and Evolving Linkages* (The East Asia Study Center, University of Dhaka, 2019); He is also author of a book *Globalization and New Regionalism in South Asia: Issues and Dynamics* (Dhaka, 2010). Delwar has recently contributed a chapter titled 'The Dynamics of Bangladesh-India Relations: From a Paradigm Shift to a Challenging Era?', in Amit Ranjan (ed.), *India in South Asia: Challenges and Management*, Springer Nature, Singapore, 2019; and an article on 'Unfolding Bangladesh-India maritime connectivity in the Bay of Bengal region: A Bangladesh perspective', *Journal of the India Ocean Region*, Taylor and Francis, 2019.

Imtiaz A. Hussain As Head/Founder of Global Studies & Governance Program at Independent University, Bangladesh (2016–2022), Professor (Philadelphia University/Universidad Iberoamericana, 1990–2014), Imtiaz Hussain created/taught wide-ranging International Relations/Global Studies/Governance courses, evident in his 20-odd books. As samplers: *South Asia in Global Power Rivalry* (Springer, 2019), *Transatlantic Transactions* (Palgrave Macmillan, 2018); *North American Regionalism* (Palgrave 2015); *Evaluating NAFTA* (Palgrave, 2013); *Border Governance and the 'Unruly' South* (Palgrave, 2013), and *Afghanistan-Iraq and Post-conflict Governance* (Brill 2010); several scholarly articles in *Journal of International Relations (2020)*, *Encyclopedia of U.S.-Latin American Relations* (2012), *Handbook of Global Security and Intelligence* (2008), *South Asian Survey* (2008), *Politics & Policy* (2008), *Journal of the Asiatic Society of Bangladesh* (2006), & *Norteamérica* (2006); and even more articles on ongoing developments in Dhaka's *Daily Star* and *Financial Express* newspapers. He received several research fellowships (from Canadian, Indian, Mexican, & U.S. institutions); invitations for specialized conferences (Cambodia, Canada, France, Germany, India, Mexico, among others); and teaching awards (in University of Pennsylvania, 1985; *Universidad de las Americas*, Mexico City, several years, and Independent University, Bangladesh, 2020). His 1989 doctorate was in Political Science from Penn.

Dr. Md Abdul Awal Khan has been serving as an Associate Professor at the Department of Law, Independent University, Bangladesh (IUB). He obtained his Ph.D. at the School of Law, Western Sydney University,

Australia in 2015. His Ph.D. research area was on displacement, human rights, and climate change. After completing his Ph.D., Dr. Khan joined School of Law, Western Sydney University, Australia as a Research Fellow in 2015. He was the Country Lead Researcher of the project 'Protecting Persons Displaced in the Context of Disasters in Asia Pacific' funded by Raoul Wallenberg Institute (RWI), Sweden for the period 2017–2019. Currently, he has been serving as a researcher of the project 'Developing Modules for a Blended Learning Course on Displacement and human rights in the Context of Disaster and Climate Change' funded by RWI. Dr. Khan also served as a visiting researcher at the School of Global Studies, University of Gothenburg, Sweden and Department of Social Sciences, University of Rohampton, London, UK as an Erasmus Mundus Visiting Scholar in 2017.

Ziaur Rahman I have been actively engaged in teaching at private universities in Bangladesh. Currently, Adjunct Faculty at the Department of Business, Independent University, Bangladesh at the EMBA program teaching Strategic Management. I have also been guest faculty at Institute of Business Administration (IBA), University of Dhaka at the Executive M.B.A. program. I have taught at the Department of Business of various Universities in Bangladesh (Independent University, Bangladesh, University of Asia Pacific, East West University, Manarat International University) especially in the field of **Strategic Management, Marketing Management, Statistics, Financial Derivatives, Business Communication, International Business, etc. At the professional level, my focus is on Leadership Development and HR. Have taught at NSU at their change management initiative under the Post-Graduate Studies program for civil servants of Bangladesh (Senior Asst Secretaries, Deputy Secretaries) and have been invited as guest faculty to AIUB & BRAC University.** Also representing at various social forums focusing on awareness building on leadership & social development in Bangladesh. I have a strong orientation on field-level studies focusing on SMEs and market value chains.

Galia Rosemberg I have a very diverse curriculum. After graduating with a Bachelor's Degree in International Relations from the Universidad Iberoamericana in México City and 3 years working for the UN as a project manager, I completed my Master's Degree in Mass Media and Communications at the London School of Economics. A Diploma in Marketing Research from ITAM in Mexico (2009) complemented the theoretical aspect, but the practical learning never ends. My career path took me to marketing and advertising, where I discovered the world of qualitative market research more than 15 years ago. Since then, I have collaborated with various market research agencies, such as De la Riva Group, LDV Research Partners, GfK, Ipsos, and Kantar TNS.

Jessica Tartila Suma is a Senior Lecturer in Global Studies & Governance (GSG) Program at Independent University, Bangladesh (IUB). She completed her Master's in Political Science (United Nations and Global Policy Affairs) from Rutgers University, New Jersey, USA. Earlier she completed her Master's in Development Studies (MDS) in 2013 and BSS (Honors) in Media and Communication from Independent University, Bangladesh (IUB) in 2008. She is a core research member for establishing the Center for Social Science Research (CSSR), and served as Deputy Directory of the Center for Pedagogy (CP) at IUB. She takes interest in 'Humanitarian Assistance & Refugee' education, political communication, democratic transitions, and foreign policy analysis. Jessica's book chapter for *Rohingya Camp Narratives: Tales from the 'Lesser Roads' Traveled* has been accepted for publication (Palgrave Macmillan, 2021).

Hossain Ahmed Taufiq is currently a Ph.D. Student at the School of Public Policy at the Oregon State University, USA. He is also a lecturer (on study leave) at the Independent University, Bangladesh (IUB). He obtained his M.Sc. in Development Practice from Trinity College Dublin, Ireland and BSS in International Relations from the University of Dhaka, Bangladesh.

Lailufar Yasmin is a Professor at the Department of International Relations, University of Dhaka. She has undertaken her studies at the University of Dhaka, Bangladesh, Georgia State University, Atlanta, USA, and Macquarie University, Sydney, Australia. She has been a recipient of the US Fulbright, the British Chevening, and the Australian International Post-Graduate Research Scholarship (IPRS). She has done her fellowships on peace and conflict issues of South Asia in the University of Ulster, Northern Ireland, UK and in the Institute of World Economics and Politics (IWEP) of the Chinese Academy of Social Sciences (CASS), Beijing, China, as an Asia Fellow under the Ford Foundation Fellowship. Her latest fellowships were on Fellowships in Indo-Pacific Security Studies (FIPSS) at Daniel K. Inouye Asia-Pacific Center for Security Studies (APCSS), Hawaii, USA on Advanced Security Course (ASC 19-2) and the Fellowship on Women in Conflict 1325 Fellowship Programme, offered by Beyond Borders Scotland, under Scottish Government's initiative. Her areas of interest include Bangladesh's politics, economy and foreign policy, South Asian politics, maritime security and the Indo-Pacific Region, and Women's participation in the UN Peacekeeping, among others.

Rashed Uz Zaman has been teaching at the Department of International Relations, University of Dhaka since 1998. He holds a Bachelor's and a Master's degree in International Relations from the University of Dhaka. He has also obtained a Master's in Security Studies from the University of Hull, and a Ph.D. in Strategic Studies from the University of Reading, UK. In 2009–2011, Dr. Zaman was an Alexander von Humboldt postdoctoral research fellow at the University of Erfurt, Germany. He was a Fulbright Visiting Professor in the Department of Political Science at Vanderbilt University, USA, in 2012. Dr. Zaman works on strategic and international security issues and has spoken and written extensively on Bangladesh in UN peacekeeping missions. Among his publications are 'Bengal Terrorism and Ambiguity of the Bengali Muslims' in Jussi Hanhimaki and Bernhard Blumenau (eds.), An International History of Terrorism: Western and Non-Western Experiences (London and New York: Routledge, 2013). A book chapter titled 'South Asian Regionalism and UN Peacekeeping Missions: A Case of 'and Never the Twain Shall Meet'?' was published in Brendan Howe and Boris Kondoch (eds.) Peacekeeping and the Asia-Pacific (Lieden|Boston: Brill Nijhoff, 2016). A special issue on Commonwealth Armies and Peacekeeping carried his article, 'The Contribution of Commonwealth Armed Forces in UN Peacekeeping Missions: The Case of Bangladesh', The Round Table: The Commonwealth Journal of International Affairs, Volume 106, No. 4, August 2017. His essay 'Indian Political Realism' has been published in December 2018 in Edinburgh Companion to Political Realism edited by Robert Schuett and Miles Hollingworth and published by Edinburgh University Press. Dr. Rashed Uz Zaman is a regular speaker at National Defence College (NDC), Defense Services Command and Staff College (DSCSC), Bangladesh Institute of Peace Support Operation Training (BIPSOT), and Foreign Service Academy.

Abbreviations

ACSA	Acquisition & Cross Servicing Agency
ADB	Asian Development Bank
ADD	Anti-Dumping Duties
AIC	Advanced Industrial Countries
AL	*Awami League* (party in Bangladesh)
AMISOM	African Union Mission in Somalia
AOEI	ASEAN Our Eyes Initiative (Indonesian)
AQIS	*Al Qaeda in Indian Subcontinent*
ASEAN	Association of South East Asian Nations
ATU	Anti-Terrorism Unit
AU	African Union
BFIU	Bangladesh Financial Intelligence Unit
BIMSTEC	Bay of Bengal Initiative for Multi-sector Technological and Economic Cooperation
BNP	Bangladesh Nationalist Party
BREXIT	Britain's Exit (from the European Union)
BSB	Border Security Bureau
CDP	Climate-Displaced People
CGI	Coastal Guards Intelligence
CIC	Central Intelligence Cell
CIID	Customs Intelligence & Investigative Directorate
CISSA	Committee of Intelligence and Security Affairs of Africa
COVID	Corona Virus-19
CSO	Civil Society Organizations
CTED	Counter-Terrorism Committees Executive Director
CTIB	Counter-Terrorism Intelligence Board

CUFTA	Canada-U.S. Free Trade Agreement
CVD	Counter-Vailing Duties
DGIF	Directorate General of Forces Intelligence (Bangladesh)
DNA	Deoxyribonucleic Acid
ECC	Extraordinary Challenge Committee (part of NAFTA Chapter 19 creation)
ECE	Extraordinary Committee of Experts (part of NAFTA Chapter 19 stipulation)
ELG	Export-Led Growth
EMI	Enterprise for the Americas Initiative
ENIAC	Electronic Numeric Integrator and Computer
EU	European Union
FSU	Former Soviet Union
FTA	Free Trade Agreement
FTAA	Free Trade Agreement of the Americas
FVEY	Five Eyes (alternate name for UKUSA (Agreement Defense Pact)
GATT	General Agreement on Tariffs and Trade
GSOMIA	General Security of Military Information Agency
HUMINT	Human Intelligence
IB	Intelligence Bureau
ICSID	International Convention for the Settlement of Investment Disputes
ICT	Information & Communications Technology
IDC	International Donors Community
ILO	International Labor Organization
IMF	International Monetary Fund
INCB	International Narcotics Control Board
IR	International Relations (academic discipline)
ISI	Import-Substitute Industrialization
ISIS	Islamic State of Iraq and Syria
JISD	Joint Intelligence & Security Division (NATO body)
JMB	*Ja'ma'at ul Mujahideen Bangladesh*
LDC	Less Developed Country
LTRP	Land-Tenure Reform Program (Rwanda)
MERCOSUR	*Mercado del Sur* (Market of the South)
MNC	Multinational Corporation
MOHA	Ministry of Home Affairs (Bangladesh)
NAFTA	North American Free Trade Agreement
NATO	North Atlantic Treaty Organization
NBR	National Board of Revenue (Bangladesh)
NCIC	National Committee for Intelligence Coordination
NGO	Non-Governmental Organization

NSI	National Security Intelligence
OECD	Organization of Economic Cooperation and Development
PAN	*Partido Acción Nacional* (National Action Party, Mexico)
PRD	*Partido Revolucionario Democrático* (Democratic Revolutionary Party, Mexico)
PRI	*Partido Revolucionario Institucional* (originally *Partido Nacional Revolucionario*, Mexico)
RAB	Rapid Action Battalion (Bangladesh)
RAW	Research & Analysis Wing
RILP	Regional Intelligence Liaison Office
RMG	Ready-Made-Garment
SAARC	South Asian Association for Regional Cooperation
SAARCPOL	SAARC Police
SARPCCO	South African Regional Police Chiefs Cooperation Organization
SB	Special Branch
SCM	supply-chain management
SDOMD	SAARC Drug Offences Monitoring Desk
SIGINT	Signals Intelligence
STOMD	SAARC Terrorism Offenses Monitoring Desk
TCE	Transaction Cost Economics
UK	United Kingdom
ULFA	United Liberation Front of Assam
UN	United Nations
UNCITRAL	U.N. Conference on International Trade Law
UNDP	United Nations Development Program
UNESCO	United Nations Educational, Scientific, and Cultural Organization
UNFCCC	United Nations Framework Convention on Climate Change
UNODC	United Nations Office of Drugs & Crime
US	United States
WASP	White, Anglo-Saxon Protestant
WB	World Bank
WTO	World Trade Organization

List of Figures

Fig. 7.1	Registration fees paid (per parcel, in Rwandan Franc)	170
Fig. 7.2	Lease payment amount (in Rwandan Franc)	173
Fig. 8.1	RMG exports from Bangladesh (in $billion)	193
Fig. 8.2	Evolutionary timeline of supply chain management	196
Fig. 8.3	Monthly minimum wages in global garment industry	200

LIST OF TABLES

Table 1.1	Sources & aggregation levels of *fragmegrative* dynamics	8
Table 4.1	Five phases of U.N. peace missions	93
Table 7.1	Cross section with dummies for registration time: ordinary least squares test (to observe impact of LTRP on agricultural-based households)	177
Table 10.1	A brick in the wall: regional responses to Syrian refugee education access	235
Table 10.2	Underlying education conditions: impact factors and Syrian refugee response plan	246
Table 10.3	Underlying education conditions: impact factors and Rohingya refugee response plan	252
Table 10.4	Refugee access to education: comparative determinants	254
Table 10.5	Frieran critical pedagogy V. Rational actor theory: comparisons	258
Table 11.1	Political parties: television time allocation	277
Table 11.2	Presidential candidates: television time allocation	277
Table 11.3	Television time dedicated to primary election presidential candidate	278
Table 11.4	Radio time dedicated to primary election of presidential candidates 1999 (%)	278
Table 11.5	Time paid for televisa and channel 13 advertisement by primary election candidates	279
Table 11.6	Voting in presidential elections, 1934–1994	280
Table 11.7	NAFTA's dispute settlement mechanisms: institutional designs	286

Table 11.8	Process of NAFTA dispute settlement mechanisms	292
Table 11.9	Summary of NAFTA disputes	293
Table 12.1	Collapsing constructs and half-baked substitutes: post-cold war brinkmanship	314
Table 12.2	Fragmegration sources, aggregation levels, and a ten-chapter overview	315

LIST OF BOXES

Box 2.1	Two-way interacting processes of globalization and domestic governance	45
Box 2.2	Globalization induced institutional transformations in the developing countries	46
Box 2.3	Rules and norms of globalization	48
Box 7.1	Overall objectives of the Rwandan Land Tenure Regularization Programme	182
Box 7.2	Study areas	183

CHAPTER 1

Globalization, Localization, and Leaky Umbrellas: Problematic *Pot Pouri*?

Imtiaz A. Hussain

PUZZLE

Just as 9/11 severely dented globalizing forces at the start of the twenty-first century, so too is the Corona virus (COVID)-19 pandemic today, in mid-2021, similarly constraining diffusion. If we throw in the 2007–09 Great Recession mid-way through those defining moments and the increasing drifts in populist directions,[1] then the first-quarter of the twenty-first century leaves us all too much more introverted than the lifestyles we had gotten used to; and equally clueless as to the fate of the growing globalization-localization tussle. We have reached a threshold where technological advancements make their human innovators increasingly the very victims of their intellectual prowess. This is particularly true of artificial intelligence, which scrapes the boundaries of

---

I. A. Hussain (✉)
Global Studies & Governance Department, Independent University, Bangladesh (IUB), Dhaka, Bangladesh
e-mail: imtiaz.hussain@iub.edu.bd

© The Author(s), under exclusive license to Springer Nature Singapore Pte Ltd. 2022
I. A. Hussain (eds.), *Global-Local Tradeoffs, Order-Disorder Consequences*, Global Political Transitions,
https://doi.org/10.1007/978-981-16-9419-6_1

both human knowledge and inter-country relationships,[2] threatening to eliminate jobs and other human inputs. Restraining forces have also gathered momentum, through both anti-immigrant sentiments and anti-minority-group movements: corralling low-wage migrants, constraining commercial and investment flows show a more constipated and odorous atmosphere than the free-for-all face we once associated with a liberal order. "To be or not to be," a perennial Shakespearean dilemma,[3] stares today's civilizations as glaringly as ever, but with far sharper contours and claws.

To be sure, such a dilemma has always accompanied our existence, the degree of attention given varying. World War II gave us the United Nations (U.N.) as a step toward an ostensible global governance, opening sluice-gates for countries to join hands to contain the negative spillovers of economic, military, and political competitiveness; yet with the Security Council veto-power and the sudden surge of multiple new countries in the 1950s, 1960s, and 1970s, how U.N. interests have become localized and nationalized remains mind-boggling: even when we see or sense collective benefits to be a better choice, our tendency to go solo, or defect, trumps our own expectations. A similar predicament confronted World War I and the League of Nations on a far graver scale in the 1920s, and we paid the price: colonialism, one of history's most soft-spoken globalizing forces, was critically chopped to promote such localizing forces as self-determination, much as a later generation would see such extant ideological bubbles as capitalism, socialism, or communism, in their full globalizing form, challenge maturing nationalistic or state-centric variations when the scope for both to coexist simply did not exist. Still, no lessons were drawn for far too long.

In fact, the Great Depression of the 1930s produced one of the most enduring economic strategies, albeit locally structured: import-substitution industrialization (ISI). Though the first ISI foothold was in Central Europe (the *Volkswagen* automobile, meaning "people's car," was a conscious initiative sparked under Adolf Hitler in 1937, under the name *Gesellschaft zur Vorbereitung des Deutschen Volkswagens mbH*),[4] its more classical stay across Latin America,[5] not just to compensate for lost agricultural export income (the shift to mechanized farming in industrialized countries had a lot to do with that), but also to lay the foundations of the country's first industries. This "localizing" thrust contrasted the almost-simultaneously emerging export-led globalizing industries, part of it based on the "flying-geese" model of shifting declining industries abroad, by

Japan,[6] from the 1940s. Both the local and global patterns remain preferences even to this day, with China accenting the former, and Asia's Four Tigers the latter,[7] by and large.

As evident, the globalization-localization tug-of-war is neither new nor structured to yield a steady-state fulcrum for future policy-directions. Far more meaningful is to examine how these colliding forces can institutionalize, since that is a fair measure of their staying power, what secular stumbling forces they face, such as sudden technological outgrowths, and why we assume a constancy out of them when in many other arenas we invoke a revolving fate, as with the "rise" and "decline" of countries, or a "life-cycle" for products, that is, a "growth" phase followed by "mature" or most competitive phase, then a "diminishing" market-bite phase. In short, the heart of governance may be less in a "this" or "that" option/swing than in the "gray" zone between the "black" and "white" options: one day here, the next day there, and so forth, not across the board for policies, but selectively so given the nature of the setting (demand, supply, and competition, in turn, reflecting shifting tastes or population age-group dominance). Intuitively, this swaying exercise may be more amenable with policy fluctuations (given how governments began to alternate from authoritarian tendencies toward democratic, and vice versa, more frequently in the late twentieth century than ever before), than with institutions (especially those with across-the-board appeal, as security, peace, or development, or even mindsets/instincts, such as those rooted in racial or religious beliefs).

None of the arguments hitherto supplied offers any *raison d'etre* dismissing the globalization-localization contestation. On the contrary, they demand, to borrow from a different context, "eternal vigilance,"[8] if only to extract the maximum concurrent welfare of the most.

LITERARY ANTECEDENTS

If the twenty-first century, as appraised, is bedecked with localizing forces, so too was the Cold War, from 1947 to 1987. Just deciding whether to join the tightly pushed Soviet camp of socialism/communism or the looser-pitched liberal world of more democratic rights as the United States advocated. Or one could either play off the two sides or shift to an entirely different ballpark, say non-alignment. All of these involved far more local resources, commitments, and capabilities than global loyalties: joining collective military efforts, whether the North Atlantic Treaty

Organization (NATO) or the Warsaw Pact, and getting exposed to an externalizing, thus globalizing, thrust. Troop commitments and expenses were charged to the domestic cash-register, and losses had to be personally absorbed. Otherwise more lives would have been lost, or taxes raised to fight or defend. Against the Cold War, the 1990s decade stands out when globalizing forces outweighed the localizing habit, oftentimes by wide margins.

It was not just the 1989 fall of the Berlin Wall or the Soviet Union collapsing in 1991 that unleashed so many globalizing forces, whether through democratic yearnings or a relatively more liberalized economic setting. A final push toward full multilateral trade had begun, under the General Trade and Tariffs (GATT), at Punta del Este from September 1986[9]; and though it would take the longest time to reach an agreement, when the World Trade Organization was born in 1994,[10] the entire commercial world breathed a sigh of relief for the first time ever. It was not picture-perfect, but it opened more trade/investment windows/doors than ever before.

Similarly, the Third Industrial Revolution telescoped the world even farther and faster. Some of the seeds were sown primarily by mathematicians between the two world wars. One was the 1946 onset of a 30-ton 1800 square-footed room-sized computer (the Electronic Numerical Integrator and Computer, or ENIAC,[11] in University of Pennsylvania's Moore School of Electrical Engineering). By the 1980s, this had transformed into desk-top variations, thence the hand-held or pocket-sized contraption we routinely utilize today. With it, accessibility multiplied manifold, sowing a globalizing seed governments have been hard-pressed to control since it is in the very palm of more independent individuals than ever before. That seed could also be manipulated to breed the most distasteful localizing sentiments.

Subtle changes followed: as industrialized countries began shifting more attention to the service sector, as opposed to the assembly-lined manufacturing mainstay that helped them industrialize in the first place, production networks globalized, streaming low-waged work in one direction and high-waged in another. Not only did these take off from Japan's World War II flying-geese and the similarly structured (albeit with more geographically constrained space) Mexico-U.S. *maquiladora* modes of the 1960s.[12] Yet they also paved the way for free-trade agreements (FTAs) and deepened extant regional efforts. More multilateral FTA signatures were compiled during the 1990s (at least 10 were counted) than in any decade-long spell before or after[13]; and the European Community transitioned into the European Union, with its own currency speaking for about two-dozen countries today. Those speak profoundly of policies (instruments), institutions, and instincts at their very advanced levels. Localizing forces, like populism blatantly today also gathered momentum, but all too silently to be noticed: economic growth shifting into a declining mode, or one immigrant too many for local community comfort, or economic-resource-flows moving only in one direction for far longer than routinely fan the flames of restraints and resources.

Sure the twenty-first century setbacks had a lot to do with grinding these runaway forces to a halt, but endogenous forces also energized each arena. References have been made to the "rise and decline" and "life cycle" revolving dynamics: many of these developments also had their own internal restraints, such as instruments skewering economic distribution, institutions drifting in one-size-fits-all directions, more interest accumulation without building dispensation mechanisms, and personally making any generic trait too instinctual.

In the more euphoric 1990s, "Japan-bashing" cooled off in the U.S. public, though the start of Japan's longest recession fed this outcome. Accessing the massive Chinese market, in turn, opened more opportunities than any combination of constraints (albeit "China-bashing" really began in the twenty-first century).

When the Cold War collapse decimated long-held intellectual paradigms (for instance, *neo-realism* fitted the Cold War so well that it simply drowned in post-Soviet Union global dynamics[14]), authors/scholars began brewing their own counterparts. Globalization played a big part in the emergent literatures, eventually bringing the localizing counter-forces into the fray. It is this group of literary works at the cusp attracting most attention here, and supplying the platform for this volume's analytical works.

James N. Rosenau was not the first scholar to dig the globalization-localization mine.[15] Indeed, globalization was not the only entrance into studying this subject. References have already been made to "externalization," a process beginning with either an individual or an institution, like the state or non-state organization: it merely extends some compact to an outside partner, with globalization representing the upper limit of possible partners, that is, attaining the maximum space or members possible, with bilateralism highlighting the minimum, multilateralism the maximum.

From such a perspective, globalization is a phenomenon that can be traced back to, for example, the *Exodus* chapter of the Old Testament,[16] indeed the human-being first filtering out of the forests to begin cultivating land in Africa,[17] then migrating to other parts of the world. In terms of relevant literatures, it could easily be traced back to regionalization, a process like the foundation of the nation-state with a West European springboard, and particularly between the two world wars toward collective action. David Mitrany's *new world order* could be interpreted in this sense,[18] as it is widely seen as among the first stabs at interpreting West European integration. European integration in the post-BREXIT era sheds useful light on the fate and nature of globalization: the unit we are most attached to for various reasons, the state, exemplifies localizing forces at one end of the tussle, experiencing moments of both strengths and weaknesses[19]; and so too with globalization, at the other end, summoning restraints from a strong state more interested in elevating its own interests, or a weak one fearing vulnerability to globalizing forces.

How globalization over-flowed in the 1990s knew no boundaries.[20] Rosenau's analytical assessment propelled him to the apex. His penetration into the globalization-localization trade-off opens up the vocabulary commensurate to dealing with the ever-growing complexities today. For example, we see both contradictory forces, yet chaos and order have managed to coexist today. Rosenau juxtaposes both terms into *chaord*, as Dee W. Heck had done.[21] He likewise borrows *glocalization* (mixing globalization and localization) from Robert Robertson,[22] to propose *fragmegration*, mixing fragmentation and integration.[23] His *fragmegration* is presented as a worldview to compete with better-known counterparts: the state-centric *realism* family prioritizes military security and revolves around relative power; while the state/non-state-centric *liberalism* family seems a lot more concerned with economic interests and, thereby, absolute power, promotes power for collective benefits.

His *fragmegration*, thus, falls at the confluence of conflictive and cooperative orientations of both state and non-state organizations. As such, it goes beyond unilateralism (which is state-centric and conflict-minded), multilateralism (also state-centric but cooperative), transnational (involves non-state actors while remaining cooperative), and sub-groupism (brings in non-state actors, both within the state and outside of it, but with a conflictive tempo about it). A casual glance portrays how dense the dynamic and intricate the relationships are—clearly a picture the *neo-realist* Cold War era did not confront nor even anticipate. Even the load this entailed was too much for the sunny-sided *liberal* school whose partly pragmatic and partly *panglossian* disposition prevents it from supplying the most accurate assessment of topsy-turvy twenty-first-century global relations.

While these supply the prism or platform (or both) to interpret the various chapters in this volume for a more realistic (a term which has no automatic relationship with the *realist* school of thought), twenty-first-century appraisal, they also help project/cluster quite disparate global dynamics into more meaningful interpretive dimensions. Rosenau's nuances help again.[24] He first identifies a number of sources of *fragmegration*, then places them into conceptual levels of aggregation.

He identifies eight *fragmegrative* sources: skill revolution; authority crises; bifurcation of global structures; organizational explosion; mobility upheaval; microelectronic technology; weakening of territorialities, states, and sovereignty; and globalization of national economies. One can easily discern those prioritizing integrative outcomes (even though they could have *fragmegrative* consequences): skill revolution; organization explosion; microelectronic technological; and globalization of national economies. Fragmented sources can be similarly identified (which could foster *integrative* tendencies): authority crises; bifurcation of global structures; mobility upheaval; and weakening of territorialities, states, and sovereignty.

All of these disparate dynamics can then be assessed through four levels of aggregation. At the smallest is the individual (micro), and similarly at the maximum level of integration is what he calls *collectivities* (macro), which could be states or non-state. To these can be added interaction between *collectivities* (macro-macro), and those between individuals and collectivities (micro–macro). In plo tting these, Table 1.1 serves as the theoretical platform of the volume: dynamics from each chapter can be positioned into these boxes and any comparisons and overviews should be able to identify where at least a part of the twenty-first century may be headed.

Turning first to the aggregation-level sources, all eight already belong to our everyday vocabulary. For example, "skill revolution" and "authority crises" have partly shaped the dynamics of the entire twentieth century: the former was encapsulated in the 1930s Great Depression, itself the dividing line between an agriculture-driven economy and the

Table 1.1 Sources & aggregation levels of *fragmegrative* dynamics

Sources of fragmegration	Case-specific consequences (to look out for)
1. Skill revolution	Change of jobs/profession; shift from one location to another invites manual-automation trade-offs
2. Authority crises	Opposition (legitimacy challenged); obsolescence (technological challenge);
3. Bifurcation of global structures	Threat or decentralization, among others
4. Organizational explosion	Multiplicity of organizations, and with it, weakening of authorities/governance
5. Mobility upheaval	Human flows, typically: job-related, environmental crisis, or climate-change pressures
6. Micro-level technological dynamic	Farming/grassroots upgrade at expense of traditionally guaranteed manual labor
7. Weakening of territorialities, states, & sovereignty	Through flows of sorts (humans, products, transactions); questions of legitimacy; or conflicts (civil or conventional war); or more natural disasters than capacities to recover

Sources of fragmegration	Case-specific consequences (to look out for)
8. Globalization of national economies	Regional or multilateral allegiances growing more than allegiance to the state; greater dependence on foreign trade/investment than domestic
Aggregation levels of fragmegrative dynamics	***Actors & alliances***
1. Micro	Individual; grassroots levels
2. Micro-macro	Individual-state/individual-corporation/individual-organization/grassroots-state/grassroots-sorporation/grassroots-organization
3. Macro	State/corporation/organization
4. Macro-macro	State-state/corporation-corporation/organization-organization/state-corporation/state-organization/corporation-organization

Legend:
H: high impact
L: low impact
Mx: mixed impact
N: no impact
M: medium impact
O: opposite impact

emergent assembly-line-driven manufacturing society. Changing skills were as essential then as in the transition from the third Industrial Revolution to the Fourth today as it was in the form of government: many colonies turning into an independent country could not easily thwart militaristic tradition, given their authoritarian past, clearly not under Cold War global rivalries, with the result of dictatorships proliferating extensively. It is still a twenty-first-century predicament, this time from democracy exposing its own weak nesses, or in failing to sustain economic competitiveness, as in U.S. populism.

We have also seen how global structures have had to be bifurcated every now and then. During the Cold War, the U.N. Security Council was divided by Cold War allegiances (the "east–west" conflict), while the General Assembly divided over what was subsequently dubbed the "north–south" split over the attainment of development, measured linearly. Today's bifurcation similarly stems from membership proliferation, on the one hand, and the tendency to build groupings within international/multilateral settings, as the European Union exemplifies. Of course, this third *fragmegrative* source is also influenced by the fourth: the explosion of organizations, especially after the spike of free-trade agreements (FTAs) from the post-Cold War 1990s.

Growth and development have fueled human migration, the fifth *fragmegrative* source: the historical osmotic flows from areas of low-waged communities to high-wage continues for humans, as it also flows in reverse form for production networks. These, in turn, have shaken traditional structures, especially at the grassroots level, generating the sixth *fragmegrative* source, or capitalizing on it, in turn unleashing too many regulated and unregulated dynamics for any state to manage as firmly as before. As territorialities, states, and sovereign rights loosen up, emboldened national economies also seek a greater global stake. Just as the seventh and eighth *fragmegrative* sources intertwine freely and frequently, they too also mesh with the third, fourth, fifth, and sixth directly, and the first and second indirectly.

How do we keep tab of these flows? Rosenau's simple approach was to look at levels of decision-making beginning with the individual at the smallest level, which he called micro. It fitted an age of increasing (but not necessarily perfect) democracies, when more individuals gained more sovereign rights, exercised individually and independently in polling booths. How human beings interacted with each other, or in groups with each other, opened up macro-level decision-making. Ranging from grassroots groups and interest associations, they themselves needed a higher, law-making authority. The emergent of the state was the story of the twentieth century, their proliferations to 200-odd by today when a century ago there were barely 10% of that number.

It was not at all by chance that states began grouping, sometimes in large numbers (as with the United Nations), or in smaller more manageable factions (as the European Union). What we see in these are macro-macro relationships, sometimes micro–macro, like when Malala Yousafzai or Greta Thunberg set off on education or climate-change global crusades, using an international institution, such as the United Nations, as a vehicle. Mother Teresa or Mahatma Gandhi had done likewise many years before individually, alleviating poverty locally or liberating the human mind through autonomous actions, respectively.

TRANSITIONING

If the globalization-localization tussle had one underlying theme, that cannot but be transition: it has transited from the contending age-old *realism-liberalism* paradigmatic roots to open new windows to new dynamics; and we just noted how even within the globalization-localization context there can be many more catalytic springboards and levels of aggregation. Just the unpredictable nature of those transitions also opens a policy-making Pandora's Box of issues demanding immediate governance.

At its narrowest, politics is all about government and governance: how it functions, appraises, and prescribes. Yet, at the broadest level, every government policy falls under the rubric of politics with varying degrees: economic policies have to win legislative approval, environmental policies demand a sustainable monetary calculation to be efficient, even military outlays and allocations cannot be effectively pieced together without the collaboration of numerous inter-ministerial trade-offs. In other words, political transitions cover the gamut of what a community remembers, does, and aspires for, within this globalization-localization context at every level: from the community to the universal.

We will find in the various chapters the pervasive and multifaceted nature of transition, depicting peculiarities of sorts: even at an isolated individual's level (micro), we see the flavorings of globalization, for example, refugee-camp children being taught through a far broader, more universal curriculum; and contrariwise, at the global level (macro), traces of idiosyncratic lifestyles replete the picture, such as Chinese trademarks dotting the commercial landscape worldwide.

ORGANIZATION

All 10 substantive chapters draw the same conclusion in their different ways and to varying degrees. Since they interpret very distinctive episodes from a panoramic setting, Rosenau's *fragmegrative* worldview is resoundingly reaffirmed: though the sources do not exert the same level of force or influence, how they snugly nestle into the multiple levels of aggregation sets them apart from a pure *realist/neo-realist* or *liberal/neo-liberal* explanation. In other words, they show the cutting-edge of the *fragmegrative* view.

In Chapter 2, Delwar Hossain pitches the "international institutional" cause, yet too many localization elements seep in. He sees too many instances of new institutional forms in the global system after the Cold War collapsed. Though these have been "profoundly" impacted by "globalization and governance," he cannot but acknowledge the growth of "considerable economic reforms, political changes, and widespread NGO activities" pressuring "domestic governance patterns." It is upon such "domestic governance patterns" that he premises the post-Cold War global governance patterns; and although he does not dwell much upon micro-level dynamics, it is virtually impossible to consider of "economic reforms, political changes, and widespread NGO activities" without them. In other words, when the Cold War dissolved, curtains were also removed to let these forces loose.

Nowhere else in the volume have those festering forces under the lid received more scathing and scrupulous attention than in Lailufar Yasmin's successor chapter. She picks on one of the dominant movements of the day, populism. Though she makes sure the readers know this is not a single movement across the planet, how she distinguishes the current outbursts from previous counterparts (notably a century ago), informs us of the staying power of micro-level actors. How she transforms her subjects, subjected "little people," as they were dubbed before, into angry "populist publics" posing greater domestic and international threats. This suggests how anything global can be readily defused since their emergent group in many different parts of the world reject everything carrying a global context, like scientific knowledge and science. With the pandemic, that task becomes easier, she posits, as if reminding us to rein in our instincts against the rawness of the emerging threats.

From the Chapter 3 trenches, Chapter 4 takes us in another contrasting direction: peace operations. Rashed Uz Zaman and Niloy Ranjan Biswas go back to international institutions as Delwar Hossain had done, but this time probing the transformation from peacekeeping to peace enforcement. Acknowledging the growing complexities in peace operations, which tallies with not just the growing needs for peace-keepers but needs in increasingly murky circumstances, both cannot help but temper their hopes in one particular and relevant recommendation: to chop down these operations to the regional level. While this enhances macro-macro dynamics without extinguishing global platforms, the implicit attention-shift toward micro-level developments directly taps into the *fragmegrative* Rosenau reservoir.

In Chapter 5, A. S. M. Ali Ashraf takes us for a ride through a netherland: the realm of espionage, within a specific Bangladesh context. Even getting to Bangladesh with his argumentation (which is about how the *global South* can build clandestine partnerships), Ali Ashraf has to wade through multiple other cases, both regional and international. Given the sensitive nature of his subject, Ali Ashraf concludes, only through a *neo-realist* approach can its mission be properly cultivated and interpreted. What his observations suggest is the very fine-line separating *neo-realism* from *fragmegration* over cases like this: we get exposed to multiple macro-level actors externally, but with the growth of illegitimate violence and counter-terrorism, knocking on micro-level doors cannot be far behind or long ignored.

Shifting entirely to climate-change, Md. Abdul Awal Khan's Chapter 6 returns to the continued fascination with international institutions. Here the global platform cannot be monopolized only by *fragmegrated* interpretations: both *neo-realism* (as in the last chapter) and *neo-liberalism* (as in this) have a loud voice. What sets *fragmegration* apart is the growth of climate-change displaced persons. Not only is the micro-level thrust into that external macro domain, but how this is exacerbating local politics adds to the international/global-level rectification concerns. With the climate-change century barely opening up, the future may draw upon the practical observation and theoretical implications of studies such as Awal's.

On another planetary front, though, several globalization actions, beliefs, and mindsets have been trickling to the most micro of theaters. Land reforms represent one blatant example of how the increasing LDC desire to "keep up with the joneses" or "look like the flock" has been thrusting such a local force toward either global decision-making or global outlets. Hossain Ahmed Taufiq's Rwandan case-study in Chapter 7 highlights how returning exiles from abroad and soil erosion within have combined to load the gun of boosting export income and mobilizing funds, whether from within or abroad. Taufiq reiterates in no mild fashion why both sides have gotten too intertwined for any to retreat, a plight many countries of the world can share with Rwanda.

Just as the global coronavirus inflicted countless casualties measurable only where treatment facilities lie, that is, at the local level, so too did its economic impacts also rattle the global–local tandem. Md. Mamun Habib and Ikram Hasan walk us through, in Chapter 8, a global production network, the ready-made-garments (RMG) sector, as it reacted inside Bangladesh. As the country's largest export earner, RMG disruptions led to a number of stop-gap measures and policy overhauling, all of them underscoring the central *fragmegrative* feature: stabilizing earnings from abroad, even finding markets as shops and importers drew down their shutters, demands the capacity to make expeditious and frequent local changes, even restructuration. Although the study does not enter into automation as an alternative, it leaves the impression that plenty of mileage remains in manual RMG operations to resuscitate well-known global production networks.

Climate-change apart, another intermeshing global–local issue thrusting itself upon *fragmegrative* analysis has become democracy. In Chapter 9, Ziaur Rahman's brief survey of Bangladesh's rendezvous with democracy in the twenty-first century is laced with global (or external) lessons and learnings. He makes it rather clear how emergent democracies today cannot but require external validation to join the club; and that finding a suitable pathway is not only necessary, but also dependent on multiple macro–micro linkages. Clearly with Freedom House becoming some sort of a global watchdog, local initiatives, which can get into the nooks and corners of even micro-level communities/individuals, acquire a lion-sized external presence. Oftentimes a sea of tranquility, often a turbulent passage, here is one dynamic neither *neo-realism* nor *neo-liberalism* can explain as coherently as *fragmegration*.

So too with education, particularly if imparted to floating populations, like refugees. Jessica Tartila Suma compares two recent refugee flows in Chapter 10 (Rohingyas and Syrians), and how the huge children proportion have been catered to: what kind of education to be imparted depends upon the kind of curricula to be adopted, typically swinging from a U.N.-sponsored global version against the local variation depending murkily on a refugee-repatriation time-schedule. Politics permeate the mission, but how the very presence of educators stabilizes a punctured setting strengthens the local–global bonds, even if education goals do not always get filled. What sets this chapter apart is its comparative analysis: we get to see how the apple-orange difference extends to global–local comparisons, exposing how, though education can be easily internationalized, the proverbial pudding-proof has no choice but to be local.

This two-track approach underscores my own and last substantive chapter. As in Chapter 9, democracy is placed under the gun, this time mixed with *neo-liberalism*. Mexico becomes the test case. Having experienced both in the 1990s—a shift from a popularly believed "perfect dictatorship" and a stubborn import-substitution mindset shifting toward democracy and a market economy—Mexico's "liberal hour" informs us about transitions, how they happen, but also why, without adequate preparation for the most unpredictable developments that can only happen in open societies, long-term viability becomes a new concern.

Preview

Based on the above profiles, what can the volume say about both transitions and the post-Cold War worldview?

In reverse order, the post-Cold War worldview was itself premised upon transitions; and from the appraisals made in the various chapters, these transitions just happen to be (a) increasing in both intensity and extent; (b) plunging into a vacuous future with no ending in sight, or if a target is specified, how other dynamics derail progress in such a way as to alter somewhat the original goal; and (c) gasping for breath constantly, meaning the relevant dynamics were either too bottled-up previously as to desperately seek an outlet, or face too many options with every decision, often ending up experimenting more than one track to strengthen its evolving new structures and practices.

Against such a fluid setting, no worldview can go it alone across the board. If the dynamic is security-related, *neo-realism* cannot but lurk somewhere in the explanatory framework. Typically *neo-realism* faces so many more non-security dynamics that it begins to lose its cutting-edge explanatory power. If the dynamic is multifaceted, *neo-liberalism* helps where institutionalized behavior prevails, and since this entails organized behavior, it too gets overwhelmed when the planet's growing unorganized forms of behavior (cyber-related, for example) dominate the landscape: its optimistic orientation begins to shake at best, break down, at most. If it is *fragmegrative*, more dynamics can be captured than either of the above two, again, without any illusion of a coherent, clear explanation: democratization brings too many people into the fold, education opens too much more of the mind, *neo-liberalism* invites a free-for-all transactional arena, in short pure globalization falters, and the residual hotchpotch aligns better with the unstable *fragmegrative* framework than any other.

Notes

1. Bojan Bugaric, "The Two Faces of Populism: Between Authoritarian and Democratic Populism," *German Law Journal* 20, Special Issue 3 on *Populist Constitutionalism: Varieties, Complexities and Contradictions* (2019): 390–400; and Charles P. Kindleberger, *The World in Depression, 1929–1939* (Berkeley, CA: University of California Press, 1973).
2. Darrell M. West, "What is Artificial Intelligence?" *A Blueprint for the Future of AI* (2018–9), Brookings Institution, Report, October 4, 2018, from: https://www.brookings.edu/research/what-is-artificial-intelligence/, last accessed May 26, 2021.
3. Opening lines of William Shakespeare, *Hamlet*, Act 3, Scene 1.
4. Alfred O. Hirschman, *National Power and the Structure of Foreign Trade* (Berkeley, CA: University of California, 1945) discusses, in addition, the economic control of East European countries through this strengthened national economic power.
5. Fernando Henrique Cardoso and Enzo Faletto, *Dependency and Development in Latin America* (Berkeley, CA: University of California Press, 1969).
6. Coined in the 1930s by Kaname Akamatsu, "A Theory of Unbalanced Growth in the World Economy," *Weltwirtschaftliches Archiv*, no. 86 (1961): 196–217, in Hamburg. Also see his "A Historical Pattern of Economic Growth in Developing Countries," *The*

Developing Economies, Preliminary Issue, no. 1 (1962): 3–25, in Tokyo. Another original pre-World War analyst was Sabro Okita. See his "The Flying Geese Pattern of Development," Fourth Pacific Economic Cooperation Council Conference, Seoul, S. Korea, 1985. In addition, see Kiyoshi Kojima (2000): "The 'Flying Geese' Model of Asian Economic Development: Origin, Theoretical Extensions, and Regional Policy Implications," *Journal of Asian Economics* 11 (2000): 375–401; and Christian Schroeppel and Mariko Nakajima "The Changing Interpretation of the Flying Geese Model of Economic Development," *Japanstudien* 14 (2002), German Institute for Japanese Studies.

7. Shigehisa Kasahara, "The Flying Geese Paradigm: A Critical Study of Its Application to East Asian Regional Development," Discussion Paper, #169, April 2004, United Nations Conference on Trade and Development (Geneva, Switzerland: UNCTAD, 2004).
8. Lord Acton's famous late 19th Century quip: "eternal vigilance is the price of freedom".
9. Bernard M. Hoekman and Michael Kostecki, *The Political Economy of the World Trading System: From GATT to WTO* (Oxford, UK: Oxford University Press, 1995). Also see Francine McKenzie, *GATT and the Global Order in the Postwar Era* (Cambridge, UK: Cambridge University Press, 2020).
10. Craig VanGrassteck, *The History and Future of the World Trade Organization* (Berkeley, CA: University of California Press, 2017).
11. Gregory C. Farrington, "ENIAC, the Birth of the Information Age," *Popular Science* 248, no. 3 (March 1996): 74.
12. For *maquiladora* growth, see Mehrene Larudee, "Causes of Growth and Decline in Mexico's Maquiladora Apparel Sector," *International Review of Applied Economics* 21, no. 4 (2007): 539–59; Federal Reserve Bank of Dallas, "Maquiladora Industry: Past, Present, and Future," *El Paso Business Frontier*, no. 2 (2002); and William C. Gruben, and Sherry L. Kiser, "NAFTA and Maquiladoras: Is the Growth Connected?" *Federal Reserve Bank of Dallas* (June 2001): 22–24.
13. On FTA explosion, see Richard S. Belous and Rebecca Hartley, *The Growth of Regional Trading Blocs in the Global Economy* (Washington, DC: National Planning Association, 1990).
14. Kenneth N. Waltz, "Relations in a Multipolar World," Hearings, Senate Foreign Relations Committee, U.S. Congress, 102nd

Congress, 1st Session, November 26, 28, & 30 (Washington, D.C. Government Printing Office, 1991), 210; and "Structural Realism After the Cold War," *International Security* 25, no. 1 (Summer 2000): 5–41, esp. 18–20. Also see Robert O. Keohane and Joseph S. Nye, "The End of the Cold War in Europe," *After the Cold War: International Institutions and State Strategies in West Europe, 1989–91*, eds. Stanley Hoffmann, Keohane, and Nye (Cambridge, MA: Harvard University Press, 1993), 1–19; and John J. Mearsheimer, *The Tragedy of Great Power Politics* (New York, NY: Norton, 2001), esp. 394–395.
15. James N. Rosenau, *Turbulence in World Politics: A Theory of Change and Continuity* (Princeton, NJ: Princeton University Press, 1990).
16. Thomas B. Dozeman, Craig A. Evans, and Joel N. Lohr, *The Book of Exodus: Composition, Reception, Interpretation* (Leiden, The Netherlands: Brill, 2014).
17. Teresa Rito, Daniel Vieira, and Marina Silva, et al., "A Dispersal of *homo sapiens* from Southern to Eastern Africa Immediately Preceded the Out-of-Africa Migration," *Scientific Reports* 9, no. 4728 (2019), from: https://doi.org/10.1038/s41598-019-411 76-3, last accessed May 26, 2021.
18. David Mitrany, *A Working Peace System* (Chicago, IL: Quadrangle, 1966).
19. Peter Evans, "The Eclipse of the State? Reflections on Stateness in an Era of Globalization," *World Politics* 50, no. 1 (October 1997): 62–87.
20. Richard Baldwin, *The Great Convergence: Information Technology and the New Globalisation* (Cambridge, MA: Harvard University Press, 2016); and Adrian Wood, "How Globalization Affected Manufacturing Around the World," *Vox*, Center for Economic Policy Research, Washington, DC, March 17, 2018, from: https://voxeu.org/article/how-globalisation-affected-man ufacturing-around-world, last accessed May 26, 2021.
21. Dee W. Heck, *Bird of the Chaordic Age* (San Francisco, CA: Berritt-Koehler, 1999).
22. Robert Robertson, "Glocalization: Time–Space and Homogeneity-Heterogeneity," *Global Modernities*, eds., Mike Featherstone, Scott Lash, and Robertson (Thousand Oaks, CA: Sage, 1995), 25–44.

23. Rosenau, *Along the Domestic-Foreign Frontier: Exploring Governance in a Turbulent World* (Cambridge, UK: Cambridge University Press, 1997), ch. 3.
24. Rosenau, "The Governance of Fragmegration: Neither a World Republic nor a Global Interstate System," Paper, International Political Science Association, Annual Conference, Quebec City, August 1–5, 2000.

Bibliography

Akamatsu, Kaname. 1961. "A Theory of Unbalanced Growth in the World Economy." *Weltwirtschaftliches Archiv*, no. 86: 196–217.
———. 1962. "A Historical Pattern of Economic Growth in Developing Countries." *The Developing Economies*, Preliminary Issue, no. 1: 3–25.
Baldwin, Richard. 2016. *The Great Convergence: Information Technology and the New Globalisation*. Cambridge, MA: Harvard University Press.
Belous, Richard S., and Rebecca Hartley. 1990. *The Growth of Regional Trading Blocs in the Global Economy*. Washington, DC: National Planning Association.
Bugaric, Bojan. 2019. "The Two Faces of Populism: Between Authoritarian and Democratic Populism." *German Law Journal* 20, Special Issue 3 on *Populist Constitutionalism: Varieties, Complexities and Contradictions*: 390–400.
Cardoso, Fernando Henrique, and Enzo Faletto, 1969. *Dependency and Development in Latin America*. Berkeley, CA: University of California Press.
Dozeman, Thomas B. 2014. Craig A. Evans, and Joel N. Lohr. *The Book of Exodus: Composition, Reception, Interpretation*. Leiden, The Netherlands: Brill.
Evans, Peter. 1997. "The Eclipse of the State? Reflections on Stateness in an Era of Globalization." *World Politics* 50, no. 1 (October): 62–87.
Farrington, Gregory C. 1996. "ENIAC, the Birth of the Information Age." *Popular Science* 248, no. 3 (March): 74.
Federal Reserve Bank of Dallas. 2002. "Maquiladora Industry: Past, Present, and Future." *El Paso Business Frontier*, no. 2.
Gruben, William C., and Sherry L. Kiser. 2001. "NAFTA and Maquiladoras: Is the Growth Connected?" *Federal Reserve Bank of Dallas* (June 2001): 22–24.
Heck, Dee W. 1999. *Bird of the Chaordic Age*. San Francisco, CA: Berritt-Koehler.
Hirschman, Alfred C. 1945. *National Power and the Structure of Foreign Trade*. Berkeley, CA: University of California.

Hoekman, Bernard M., and Michael Kostecki. 1995. *The Political Economy of the World Trading System: From GATT to WTO*. Oxford, UK: Oxford University Press.

McKenzie, Francine. 2020. *GATT and the Global Order in the Postwar Era*. Cambridge, UK: Cambridge University Press.

Kindleberger, Charles P. 1973. *The World in Depression, 1929–1939*. Berkeley, CA: University of California Press.

Kasahara, Shigehisa. 2004. "The Flying Geese Paradigm: A Critical Study of Its Application to East Asian Regional Development." Discussion Paper, #169. United Nations Conference on Trade and Development. Geneva, Switzerland: UNCTAD.

Keohane, Robert O., and Nye, Joseph S. 1993. "The End of the Cold War in Europe." Stanley Hoffmann, Robert O. Keohane, and Joseph S. Nye, eds., *After the Cold War: International Institutions and State Strategies in West Europe, 1989–91*. Cambridge, MA: Harvard University Press, 1–19.

Kojima, Kiyoshi. 2000. "The 'Flying Geese' Model of Asian Economic Development: Origin, Theoretical Extensions, and Regional Policy Implications." *Journal of Asian Economics* 11: 375–401.

Larudee, Mehrene. 2007. "Causes of Growth and Decline in Mexico's Maquiladora Apparel Sector." *International Review of Applied Economics* 21, no. 4: 539–59.

Mitrany, David. 1966. *A Working Peace System*. Chicago, IL: Quadrangle.

Mearsheimer, John J. 2001. *The Tragedy of Great Power Politics*. New York, NY: Norton, 394–395.

Okita, Sabro. 2000. "The Flying Geese Pattern of Development." Fourth Pacific Economic Cooperation Council Conference, Seoul, S. Korea, 1985.

Rito, Teresa, Daniel Vieira, Marina Silva, et al., 2019. "A Dispersal of *homo sapiens* from Southern to Eastern Africa Immediately Preceded the Out-of-Africa Migration." *Scientific Reports* 9, no. 4728. From: https://doi.org/10.1038/s41598-019-41176-3. Last accessed May 26, 2021.

Robert Robertson, Robert. 1995. "Glocalization: Time-Space and Homogeneity-Heterogeneity." Mike Featherstone, Scott Lash, and Robertson, eds., *Global Modernities*. Thousand Oaks, CA: Sage, 25–44.

Rosenau, James N. 1990. *Turbulence in World Politics: A Theory of Change and Continuity*. Princeton, NJ: Princeton University Press.

———. 1997. *Along the Domestic-Foreign Frontier: Exploring Governance in a Turbulent World*. Cambridge, UK: Cambridge University Press.

———. 2000. "The Governance of Fragmegration: Neither a World Republic not a Global Interstate System." Paper, International Political Science Association, Annual Conference, Quebec City, August 1–5.

Schroeppel, Christian, and Mariko Nakajima. 2002. "The Changing Interpretation of the Flying Geese Model of Economic Development." *Japanstudien* 14.

VanGrassteck, Craig. 2017. *The History and Future of the World Trade Organization*. Berkeley, CA: University of California Press.

Waltz, Kenneth N. 1991. "Relations in a Multipolar World," Hearings, Senate Foreign Relations Committee, U.S. Congress, 102nd Congress, 1st Session, November 26, 28, & 30. Washington, D.C. Government Printing Office.

———. 2000. "Structural Realism after the Cold War." *International Security* 25, no. 1 (Summer): 5–41.

West, Darrell M. 2018. "What is Artificial Intelligence?" *A Blueprint for the Future of AI* (2018–9), Brookings Institution, Report, October 4. From: https://www.brookings.edu/research/what-is-artificial-intelligence/. Last accessed May 26, 2021.

Wood, Adrian. 2018. "How Globalization Affected Manufacturing around the World." *Vox*. Center for Economic Policy Research, Washington, DC. March 17. From: https://voxeu.org/article/how-globalisation-affected-manufacturing-around-world. Last accessed May 26, 2021.

CHAPTER 2

Globalization, Governance, and New Institutionalism: Exploring a New "Developing World" Framework

Delwar Hossain

INTRODUCTION

Both globalization and governance are contested terms with respect to their meanings, etiologies, and implications[1]; however, nobody denies their increasing relevance in the study of international relations (IR) and international political economy (IPE). As to globalization, the notion is "discussed so widely in scholarly and popular circles that it has become a 'buzzword', used by many to refer to some ill-defined phenomenon or tendency in the world, but hardly understood by any."[2] Today's overarching international system, which shapes every country's domestic politics and foreign relations, needs to be understood as such.[3]

Indeed, in scholarly deliberations, the debate on globalization refers to competing perspectives regarding its nature, as well as state impact

D. Hossain (✉)
International Relations Department, Dhaka University, Dhaka, Bangladesh

and power.[4] All kinds of globalization debates carry narrow disciplinary borderlines or major theoretical approaches, making the debate loci futile to find as there many branches of human knowledge. For example, on the one hand, the views from sociology, cultural studies, social geography, on the other, the perspectives of politics, economics, international relations (IR), international political economy (IPE), public policy studies, and so on are widely diverse that addressing contending theoretical approaches behind globalization sounds appropriate. Three approaches dominate: *liberal/neo-liberal* thread, *realist/neo-realist*, and *historical structuralism* (theories and themes henceforth in italics).

The chapter conceptualizes and re-conceptualizes new institutionalism and governance in the context of globalization-induced socio-political post-colonial changes. Scholarly works get reviewed through six sections, addressing: (a) contending views on globalization; (b) main aspects of contemporary globalization; (c) the meaning and scope of domestic governance; (d) traditional model of domestic governance; (e) theoretical investigations of the linkage between new institutionalism and domestic governance; and (f) a developmental framework linking globalization and domestic governance.

Before delving into the debate of globalization in a larger theoretical context, it is necessary to contextualize the process of globalization by stating briefly its background. It is argued that the notion itself is old. What's new is its speed and reflexivity considering its intricacy and the magnitude of implications for states and societies.[5] Although globalization did exist for centuries, it differs in the post-World War II era. Robert O. Keohane wrote, "Economic globalization took place between approximately 1850 and 1914 manifested in British imperialism and increased trade and capital flows between politically independent countries,"[6] but Charles Oman discerned three globalization waves in modern history. The first started fifty years prior to the World War I, while second and third waves took place in the 1950s and 1960s, then 1980s and 1990s, respectively.[7] Noam Chomsky traces contemporary globalization to the floating exchange rates and capital-flow limits of the mid-1970s.[8]

More importantly, the globalization intensification process was linked with the demise of the Cold War. Some posit the Cold War ending finally liberated the forces that can propagate new socio-political and economic movements within a state or beyond in the absence of obsessive superpower rivalry (meaning, the United States and the former Soviet Union).

Thus, the 1990s end of the Cold War dawns a new age of rapid and large-scale global change.[9] Robert Chambers argued economic power relations have polarized after the Cold War, with the North no longer inhibited by post-colonial guilt, and with the South weaker, the North more freely imposes its latest economic ideologies on Southern countries.[10] The political, economic, normative, and security implications of this change could be immense.

Economically, the fall of state socialism unfolded a new space for economic liberalism. It was estimated that in 1978 one-third of the world's workforce lived in centrally planned economies.[11] Following the radical political changes in East Europe and the subsequent demise of the Soviet Union, these economies integrated into world markets. Politically, the global spread of liberal democracies downplayed the relevance of alternative political ideologies. Although Fukuyama's proposition of "end of history" triggered off massive reactions from different parts of the world, including the United States itself, the changed global political context offered much awaited opportunities to the West to push forward the neo-liberal ideals all over the world. On the other hand, such issues as the widespread social movements, the shrinking of political and geographical distances by the new technological revolution, the growing global interdependencies promoted by environmental degradation, currency shocks, ethnic conflicts, drug trade, and women trafficking, have increasingly pressured public and private actors at national and global levels. New social relationship patterns made globalization notion a significant force behind human relations, from security to governance at domestic and international levels. Particularly, new institutionalism and governance demanded deeper theoretical engagements to understand changing realities in developing societies.

CONTESTING GLOBALIZATION

Globalization today is very often termed as the product of *neo-liberal* discourse in economic, social, and political thinking. It is manifested in close connection between international economic forces and the *neo-liberal* transformation of a large number of domestic economies in both the developed and developing countries since the early 1990s. *Neo-liberals*, the most ardent adherents of globalization identify this phenomenon through economic lenses: to them globalization and liberalization projects an express train to higher levels of development.[12] Theoretically, *neo-liberalism* is a political scheme predominantly concerned with promoting a market-led transition to a new economic system, with a focus on the individual as the explanatory factor, whether analyzing the market or economy. It relies on the dual principles of flexibility and supply-side innovation manifested by: (a) the liberalization of competitive market forces and (b) the abandonment of demand-side intervention in favor of supply-side policy measures and (c) the rejection of both social partnership and welfare dependence. International financial and economic organizations, such as the World Bank (WB), the International Monetary Fund (IMF) and the World Trade Organizations (WTO) both promoted and enforced neo-liberal policies throughout the capitalist world,[13] strengthening the *neo-liberalist* camp's claims of the world economy being globalized.[14]

The *liberal* view believes significant globalization erodes state control, marking the higher stage of *interdependence* through institutional lenses.[15] Globalization is seen as a process involving both the broadening and deepening of "*interdependence* among societies and states throughout the world."[16] Keohane and Joseph S. Nye attempt to see globalization as "contemporary globalism", warranting identifying it as the process of increasing globalism. Distinguishing "thin" and "thick" globalization, they posit today's globalism differs from the nineteenth century counterpart. Seen as a *process*, the degree of globalism thickening gives rise to three changes, not just in degree, but also in kind: increased density of networks, increased "institutional velocity," and increased transnational participation.[17] *Liberal* economists generally view any increase in capital flows as a favorable development because financial markets impose necessary discipline upon states, while global savings and resources move to their most productive locations.[18] They also believe that globalization is helping promote stable democratic governments throughout the world. For example, the spread of liberal democracies in southern Europe in the 1970s, in Africa, Asia, and Latin America in the 1980s, and across Eastern Europe and the Former Soviet Union (FSU) in the late-1980s and 1990s. A positive linkage is established between globalization and democracy as governments must open their societies both politically and economically. Thus, according to *neo-liberal* view, the globalization process promotes economic liberalization and liberal democracies amid diminishing state role in national development.

Although *neo-liberalism* is more conceptually acceptable in explaining the rationale behind the emergence of globalization, in reality, *neo-liberal* economic strategy has many flaws: market rationality does not function properly, leading to chaos, collusion, gangster behavior, and market-failure. Many argue that apart from social breakdown as a result of social polarization, social alienation, and the constant threat of macroeconomic crashes and crises, it exacerbates structural imbalances and deflation as states adopt *beggar-thy-neighbor* economic policies against global competition.[19] *Neo-liberalism* thus represents an institutional vacuum, and the search for an institutional fix becomes important in view of crises tendencies in the global economy today. *Neo-liberalism*, in its essence, blames everything that does not work on the works of the state and overwhelmingly depends on market forces. Ironically, the greatest inconsistency in this logic, that no matter how free it is, the market is an outcome of state action. "As pressures from the international economy intrude on domestic societies", in Suzanne Berger's words, "citizens turn even more urgently to their own governments for help".[20] *Neo-liberalism* "ignores the inequality and uneven development inherent within capitalist accumulation. Markets are unable to address these structural imbalances precisely because they are inherent in the free-market system."[21] Thus, it is largely unfounded in reality why the *neo-liberals* advocate the collapse of Westphalian state, achievements of market mechanism for economic development, and the inevitability of the convergence of *neo-liberal* institutions, both at domestic and global levels, so vigorously.

Realism/Neo-realism is another powerful theoretical approach to explain the phenomenon of globalization. Fathered by Thucydides,[22] *realism* experienced a strong revival in the post-War period by Hans J. Morgenthau,[23] and was successfully developed into a systemic theory of international relations by Kenneth N. Waltz. Incorporating the concepts of *structure* and *patterns* of international political behavior as the basic units of the global order, Waltz's "anarchy" notion became central to war and peace.[24] The core ideas of *realism/neo-realism* are based on power, security, distributional conflict, and national interests. As Barry Buzan argues, "no matter what the structure, or how differentiated the units, power politics, the logic of survival, and the dynamics of (in)security do seem to be universally relevant to international relations."[25] Emphasizing the continuing ascendancy of the state, the *realist* view often questions whether there is, in fact, a significant rise in globalization. More so, they argue that global *interdependence* occurs only with the consent or backing of the major powers, and these powers continue to decide the terms and limits of such transactions.[26] They believe that there will be long-term losers and winners from globalization. The most powerful states exert significant control over the process, speed, and directions of globalization, and they can use it "to reinforce their position and their relative power."[27] They reject the traditional notion of globalization, which emphasizes fundamental socio-economic changes by showing their strong inclination toward "national model of political economy" instead of "global economy model." For example, the predominant causes behind the economic policy changes of the developed countries like Germany, Japan, France, and Australia were more domestic than global. In this view, the process of globalization is seen as "northern transnationalization" or "internationalization" that has little, if not limited, impact on national economic policy changes. David Held,[28] an ardent supporter of globalization, argues that although national governments get sandwiched between global forces and local demands, globalization doesn't signal the death of state. As argued by Held and Anthony Mcgrew, "contemporary globalization is associated with a transformation of state power as the roles and functions of states are re-articulated, reconstituted and re-embedded at the intersection of globalizing and regionalizing networks and systems."[29] Rather it empowers the state with necessary readjustments with the changing realities. Even issues, such as human rights and migration, having global dimensions, are intricately related to realist position.[30]

Linda Weiss, in *The Myth of Powerless State*, indicated that globalization, has not been able to change the dominance of state in the artifacts of global and national power structure. Contrary to negative implications for states it may be argued that globalization has rather been an instrument for increasing the power of the nation-state, particularly powerful ones. The major powers are aptly poised to utilize integration of global markets, global financial openness, greater mobility of human resources, global spread of democratic impulse, and cross-cultural diffusion. Instead of challenging the traditional dominant power status of strong countries, globalization contributes to increasing relative gains under the global structure. Moreover, the *structural realists* argue that by direct extension, globalization goes to the heart of the analysis offered by *structural realism*, as globalization might be understood to mean simply a redefinition of the international structure.[31] Moreover, the proliferation of states and national cultures illustrate more divergence, in contrast, to convergence advocated by *neo-liberals*. Thus, according to the *realists*, globalization represents no threat to the Westphalian system, which "limits" of globalization through the "internationalization" of certain economic activities.

However, the *realist/neo-realist* arguments can be contested on several grounds. In the first place, the global changes for the last decade, particularly the demise of bipolarity, absence of internationally competitive economic and political systems and worldwide technological revolution have placed the realists at bay. The brighter prospects for cooperation in place of conflict, the devolution of power from the center to local, the ever-increasing role of the non-state actors, and the commercializing of human activities have brought fundamental changes in state authority, functions, and authority. This considerably justifies the globalization process, with enormous impact on state capacity to generate conflict and hegemony over society, in turn contradicting the traditional *realist* position based on the state centrality, ignoring society. Precisely, a decline of national power and sovereignty in an age of globalization is clearly understood in two key aspects: (a) the extent and pace of global economic exchanges have caused erosion of a nation's capabilities and (b) the cross-border expansion of market relations shrinks the attachment of citizens with the national authority that leads to a diminishing legitimacy of the central government.[32]

Historical structuralism also provides theoretical and methodological tools to examine the notion of globalization in a critical fashion. *Structuralists* emphasize the character of the global economic structure being an essentially uneven form of international *interdependence*. For example, Advanced Industrial Countries (AICs) export advanced goods and services to economies of all types, but predominantly to each other, generate very high living standards for their citizens, and exert a dominant influence upon the international political economy. Less Developed Countries (LDCs), by contrast, export primary commodities, or highly standardized manufactured goods, mainly to AIC blocs, generate low standards of living for their populations, and exert, with notable exceptions, negligible levels of positive influence upon the basic developments within the international economy. In addition, LDC imports get exchanged for advanced manufactured AIC goods and services.[33] So, a *historical structuralist* would argue that globalization has extremely negative consequences for the poorer states and classes in the global periphery. More importantly, the condition of *dependency* becomes an integral element of globalization. It demonstrates, as argued by Fuat Keyman,[34] how the globalization of capitalist development has produced world-scale unevenness and inequality, forming a system based on what Fernando Henrique Cardoso and Enzo Faletto call the "unity in diversity of capitalist-associated development".[35]

Another variant of the *structuralist* approach is the *Gramscian* concept of hegemony. Castigating the *realist* and *neo-liberalist* approaches as basically "statist", Stephen Gill and David Law argue the *Gramscian* concept of hegemony as a third way of explaining international order and governance. Hegemony brings structures (economic factors) and superstructures together in a dynamic interdependence through "consent". It pays enough attention to the existing power-domination relations, and focuses on the ideological dimension of power exercised by the dominant state within that order.[36] The concept of hegemony functions as the key to exploring the production and reproduction of "order". In its concrete manifestation, proponents of *Gramscian* view assert that globalization causes the development of a "trans-historical bloc" that consists of the major transnational corporation (TNCs), international financial institutions, and international business groups in the rich capitalist nations. A vital element of this transnational historic bloc is the capacity and mobility of global capital, putting domestic actors, such as employees' unions, on the defensive. In their view, "increased capital mobility" causes underdevelopment as the fear of "capital outflows" can drive political regimes to pursue policies badly affecting society's extreme poor and marginalized people.

Nederveen Pieterse argues how globalization is seen as another round of hegemony, reflecting the same sense of powerlessness and frustration that the people from the South experienced under imperialism, or as he claims, globalization referring to "a new distribution of power and comes in a new package together with informalization, informatization and flexibilization".[37] He makes an interesting analogy of globalization with imperialism although both have some differences, as shown in Box 2.1. Thus, according to *structuralists*, globalization is "simply another phase of exploitive capitalism, a pretext for socially regressive governmental policies, and the means by which both domestic and international inequalities are further entrenched."[38] It may be noted that despite condemning the global economic order or highlighting the nature of inequality and unevenness in economic development between AIC and LDC groupings, their overall approach remains reformist, in contrast to the rejectionist tendencies of many Marxist derivatives. The limitation with the *historical structuralist* approach lies with the arguments being abstractly fine and the issue well problematized, but in reality, failing to provide an appropriate exit. The idea of building a counter-hegemonic bloc, as *Gramscians* argue, in order to redress the ills of globalization is really implausible. However, they correctly identify the process of globalization aggravates global poverty, limits the LDC capacity in state management, and AIC-LDC inequalities persist.

As indicated above, the globalization literature demonstrates inadequate and a narrow understanding of reality. However, it is also true that these approaches make an important contribution in conceptualizing globalization. While the *realist/neo-realist* position basically sees it as an instrument of power politics, the *neo-liberals* emphasize economic dynamics for global change. On the other hand, *historical structuralists* focus on its impact on states and individuals. No single approach is able to answer a host of theoretical challenges posed by critics, emphasizing the importance of social and economic developments within the individual country or a LDC group. Hence, all the complexities of understanding the globalization process cannot be captured from a single perspective.[39]

In this context, it is better to dwell on a diverse range of competing ideas rather than following a narrow and a single philosophical perspective. Multiple theories help uncover their strengths and limitations and influence subsequent revisions while showing shortcomings in conventional wisdom. Globalization, thus, is an outcome of a mix of varied and complicated social realities generated by economic, political, and cultural contours as the key aspects of competing perspectives visibly demonstrate. Assumptions such as, centrality of state, anarchy, military power, and friend–foe rotation reveal a *realist* viewpoint that questions the process of globalization. Similarly, the *neo-liberal* perspective highlights market mechanisms, liberal democracy, and non-state actors, such as multinational corporations and civil society organizations (CSOs) in perceiving globalization as its major thrusts, implying the differences of values and identities, emphasized by the proponents of realism/neo-realism. The advocates of *structuralism* have also strongly argued of globalization seen from the "bottom": emerging as an inevitable outcome of economic systemic evolution, globalization would rather intensify structural changes at internal and global levels.

Key Components of Globalization

Having analyzed diverse theoretical ways and recognized globalization as an important variable, operationally defining and identifying procedural factors, Bhardwaj and Hossain observe, "globalization is best conceived as a multidimensional spatial phenomenon that emphasizes a continuing and steady expansion of interaction processes, forms of institutions, and forms of conflict and cooperation cutting across the internal and external boundaries."[40] They further argue that it encompasses a "set of economic, political, social and cultural developments across the whole world discernible through the growing role of market economy and democracy in the post-Cold War era."[41] It covers a broad range of tangible and intangible "aspects of production, distribution, management, finance, information and communications technologies, and capital accumulation."[42] In their view, "As a dynamic process it introduces transformational changes in a range of human activities generating a set of new conditions."[43] Perhaps, these shifting dynamics and trends drive the domestic arrangement of policies and actions to embrace the global system while, at the same time, they generate game-changing rules in domestic and international contexts.

From *Human Development Report 1999* we find four new rules and norms triggered by the globalization process: (a) market economic policies with greater privatization and liberalization; (b) adoption of democracy as the choice of political regime and human rights conventions; (c) conventions and agreements on the global environment—biodiversity, climate change, ozone layer; and (d) multilateral agreements on trade, services, and intellectual property, backed by strong enforcement mechanisms and more binding for national governments, reducing the scope for national policy.[44]

Over globalization, Benjamin Cashore and Steven Bernstein single out transnational entities and international organizations as major domestic causes behind the change. They specifically identified four different "paths of nondomestic influence on public policy such as use of the global market, international rules and regulations, changes in international normative discourse and infiltration of the domestic policy-making process."[45] This stands with strong relevance for the developing countries, because to them it is evolving as an irresistible phenomenon. Generally, these countries are more pressurized compared to those of industrialized to harmonize all kinds of external changes in their domestic governance structure in order to achieve the goal of development. Chambers posits, "[M]ore than ever before power is concentrated in the cores of the North, including power to determine national policies in the South."[46] In any case, globalization cannot be treated as the only path to development rather it signifies doing things in a particular fashion. Capturing its various dimensions, as analyzed earlier, globalization primarily appears as a dynamic ongoing process with strong pressure on societies and states for transnational integration and convergence in all kinds of capitalist human activities. With considerably high speed and wide reflexivity, enormous pressure is generated. The agency and scope of this process intricately intertwine with some crucial rule-changing factors and regulations at national and global levels: the growth of global finance, the expansion of global markets, the process of privatization, political transformation, innovation in information and communication technologies, and civil society organizations.

The Growth of Global Finance

There have been massive international financial flows across the globe. "As recently as 1855, the total value of cross-border financial claims was just 16 percent of one year of global economic output. By 1870, however, that figure had jumped to 94 percent. Today, it is over 400 percent."[47] The essential nature of present-day globalization is "ever expanding capital flows across the border caused by reforms in the financial sectors. World financial flows are so large that the numbers are overwhelming."[48] These flows are mainly fluid and are driven by temporary and instant benefits, and can disappear immediately once their purpose is achieved. Besides, trade-in currency, new financial instruments, such as floating rate bonds, mutual funds, junk bonds, and derivatives are widely used that have further contributed to financial liberalization and openness. The movement of capital is caused by the opening up of a financial arrangement of a nation that relies on some specific economic actions. *World Development Report 1989* suggests, "the major components of financial reform, specifically for developing countries, are (a) financing fiscal deficits, (b) interest rate policy, (c) directed credit and (d) institutional restructuring."[49] But practically, deregulation of the national economy from the public control genuinely opens up the financial sector. Another factor is that technology facilitates conditions of deregulation in many nations in the world. For instance, the invention of the cellular phone through lowering the cost brings many companies together to chop out the international market.[50] In addition, currency convertibility and devaluation and price reforms further contribute to the financial liberalization.

The Expansion of Markets

Technological revolution and deregulation process have contributed to build huge transnational networks in the areas of production, trade and finance facilitating unprecedented expansion of global markets. Many tend to call it the creation of the new "borderless" world. *Neo-liberals* maintain, "free international trade maximizes world income and welfare from a fixed quantity of available resources and technology.[51]" Analysts argue, "by contributing to a more efficient use of the world's resources, liberalization by any country contributes to the trade gains."[52] The opening of markets largely depends on the elimination of tariff and non-tariff barriers, which would contribute to liberalize both domestic and international trade regulations. For example, the widely practiced "export-led growth strategy", which leads to the remarkable economic progress in the East Asian countries largely benefitted from trade openness. Along with the domestic policy changes, international regimes based on the WTO rules promote an external condition to liberalize trade policies and practices in both developed and developing nations. Trade resultantly changes, linking domestic economies together deeper than in the past.

The Process of Privatization

Globalization and privatization are considered two sides of the same coin as they reinforce each other creating a new condition for bolstering economic activities. As a key aspect of globalization process, it promotes an economy where private individuals and organizations produce and distribute goods and services.[53] Bhardwaj and Hossain observe that as a fundamental component of privatization property rights relies on three interconnected factors, such as "the concept of property, exclusive rights to own, and transferability."[54] In the market economy, privatization almost exclusively depends on the development of private ownership of property through denationalization and the expansion of private entrepreneurship. In line with *neo-liberal viewpoint*, it is considered "an effective economic strategy to enhance efficiency and productivity in domestic economy, thereby increasing state wealth."[55] Practically, privatization creates profit-seeking and profit-making business groups who have limited contribution to national development. Contrary to the advanced nations, the privatization process has not necessarily played a major role in the national economic advancement of many developing and transitional economies. Yet, it continues to remain a critical ingredient of economic change in the globalization process.

The Political Transformation

The unprecedented spread of liberal political ideas in the post-Cold War era has caused political transformation in the developing world and post-Communist East European countries. Research on this subject demonstrates an intimate linkage between globalization and democratization. While globalization promotes growth that eventually fosters democracy, it leads to disparity in the society that "creates instability, lower growth, and a degradation of democratic institutions."[56] Ethan Kapstein asserts that the domestic political institutions, and more importantly, the nature and quality of capital market institutions determine the democratic process in a nation due to the predominance of endogenous factors.[57] It is strongly supported by the advocates of neoliberalism that democracy has a positive impact on peace and economic development in a society. Though one can contest whether globalization flourishes democratic values and norms, political globalization is widely perceived as contributing to the formation of the multiparty liberal democratic system. In this connection, democracy is viewed as a political order, which enables a polity to enjoy periodic constitutional opportunities for deciding the ruling regime. It is also widely believed that the process of democratization creates a conducive environment for market forces so that they could perform their role appropriately. Understandably, the political transformation took place in many developing countries toward building democratic polities after the demise of the Cold War. The core issue is that the degree of democratization captured a central feature in understanding how far a nation has experienced political globalization.

Innovation in Communication and Information Technologies

The use of international data has grown significantly in today's world. The hallmark of globalization is trade "technologization."[58] The creation, distribution, and exploitation of knowledge in today's world largely depend on information technologies that have become an important driver of globalization. The world has witnessed a new synergy of science, technology, and innovation in such a way that has major impact on the process of globalization. Alvin Toffler's *The Third Wave* envisaged the technological revolution which has revealed the difference between the two phases of globalizations—old and new. Economic growth profoundly depends on the use of ICT for both developed and developing countries. But it creates a new concern of divide among the people what the Organization for Economic Cooperation and Development (OECD), or more recently IC claims "as an enormous instrument to bridge the divide between the rich and poor, not just the digital divide, between those who have *Internet* access and those who do not."[59] Now the experts tend to call it ICT diffusion which has positive relations with the quality of governance.[60] Three components of ICT are generally found in its application. These include communications; computation; and internet-related communications and computing. It is widely shared that the expansion of *Internet* users in the world has altered the economic and political spheres of a state. "The emergence of virtual states, *e-governance, e-commerce,* and so on, has been changing the ways and operations of human activities."[61] Both the industrialized and developing countries welcome the advent of this new technological age. Thus, ICT contributions to current globalization have thickened.

Social Globalization

Nye Jr. and Welch talk about social globalization to signify the growing movements of people across the globe. In their words, "Social globalization is the spread of peoples, cultures, images, and ideas. Migration is a concrete example."[62] An ICT counterpart is the "emergence of civil society movements both in the domestic and international contexts, leading to the intensification of human interactions beyond the formal governmental process."[63] Social actors have been pushing globalization to the puzzling linkage of becoming both a cause and means for human actions. While its focus on market forces and devolution of power causes a larger role for civil society actors, an anti-globalization resistance network of local and grassroots organizations are being formed to voice new challenges created by the similar process of globalization. Social movements are generally ascribed to NGO and NPO (non-profit organization) emergence, and remarkable citizen and professional group growth in variety and number in the past 25 years.[64] The NGO list from sources, such as the OECD Directory of NGOs, the United Nations Development Program's (UNDP) *Human Development Report*, and research based on the *Yearbook of International Associations* indicate a significant degree of expansion of the NGO sector though the calculations of number may vary.[65] It can be safely assumed that tens of thousands of the worldwide NGO numbers impact "a multitude of concerns and working either at or across the local, national or international levels."[66]

Recent private actors sprawl across the global South profit from external forces substantially patronizing them. It is increasingly becoming a powerful trend that exerts significant pressure on the nation-states and global bodies to maintain interactions in a particular direction. Remarkably, though civil society actors staunchly oppose the globalization process in the contemporary world that is extensively visible in the areas of environment and labor, they turn into a significant globalization force.

The key components such as the growth of global finance, the expansion of markets, political transformation, the process of privatization, social globalization and innovation in information and communication technologies are largely associated with the framework of neo-liberal ideas and visions. During the Cold War era, the underlying purpose of maintaining and consolidating the liberal economic order against the menace of Soviet socialism always propelled the Western world to highlight these key issues in their external policies and actions in every corner of the world. However, the demise of the Cold War a more conducive environment for global dominance of *neo-liberal* ideologies, which made a major difference from the earlier phase. In the current era of globalization, ICT growth and burgeoning social movements are relatively new phenomena cutting across territorial boundaries, all creating new conditions of globalization.[67] The defining characteristics of globalization, as indicated above, have an enormous impact on society by facilitating or hindering domestic *governance*. More specifically, they influence *governance* by the way of transforming the old pattern into a new one. Concomitantly, globalization influences the capacity of domestic *governance* in harmonizing and organizing collective actions. Although it is too early to observe wholly transformed domestic *governance* structure, in many developing countries there has been emerged a phenomenon like "governance pattern in transition".

Meaning and Scope of Domestic Governance

The term *governance* originates from the Greek *kybernetes*, which means navigation or helmsmanship. Like many concepts, domestic governance is a term with multiple meanings. R.A.W. Rhodes refers to this term with the following six separate uses: "as the minimal state, as corporate governance, as the new public management, as "good governance", as a socio-cybernetic system, as self-organizing networks."[68] Some argue that governance is an instrumental process which influences the outcome of public policies,[69] while some even identify it as a "shared obligation".[70] Some emphasize political and administrative aspect of domestic governance as Rajesh Tandon suggests, "good governance implies: (a) universal protection of human rights; (b) laws that are enforced and implemented in a nondiscriminatory manner (c) an efficient, fair, and speedy judicial structure; (d) transparent public agencies and official decision making; (e) accountability for decisions made about public issues and resources by public officials; (f) devolution of resources and decision-making power to local levels and bodies in rural and urban areas and (g) participation and inclusion of all citizens in debating public policies and choices."[71] Thus, domestic *governance* is more than democratization and public sector reform or the structure of government or governability. It contains a complex mixture of sectors in which national governments, business firms, and civil society organizations all provide *governance* service in many different combinations. However, it may be noted that territorially, governance has three dimensions—domestic, regional, and global. Our concern is limited to investigate domestic *governance* in the context of the developing countries.

Scope of Domestic Governance

For the purpose of our research, *governance* at the domestic level refers to a harmonizing process to manage the diverse nature of human activities through establishing appropriate institutions with a view to achieving national development. It emphasizes the formal and informal inter-relationship between sub-national and national levels of government involving the state as the overarching policy networks. It is also intricately related to the capacity of governing actors to create an enabling environment for national activities. The underlying assumption behind our conceptualization is to look at the degree to which the institutional configuration of domestic *governance* delivers an acceptable degree of legitimacy and accountability. To make it more succinct, there are three key factors in conceptualizing the term domestic *governance*. First, it is basically a harmonizing and coordinating process of national activities. Second, it involves an institutional transformation within the country, as it is believed that institutions can adequately address the issues behind economic, political, and social failures. For instance, profit-making can be secured through general rules rather than in the pursuit of political favor, and monopolies that have been widely practiced in those countries. Similarly, social or political power can be secured through general rules and norms embodied in the constitutions and political and social organizations, not through money and terrorism. Third, the objective of domestic *governance* is to ensure both public and private goods.

The domestic *governance* scope encompasses a broad range of sectors from economic to migration and from the environment to human rights in different levels of society—sub-national/local to national. It involves the collective processes of rule making, monitoring, and implementation conducted by many intertwined social actors and institutions.[72] Three broad domestic *governance* domains prevail: economic, political, and societal. Each of these types of *governance* is interdependent, although they have distinct characteristics with regard to mechanisms and scope of activity. Economic *governance* embraces "the political and economic processes that coordinate activity among economic actors, occurred in different industries and industrial sectors."[73] It covers the policy, institutional and legal environment within which an economy operates. In this context, "macroeconomic, microeconomic and fiscal policies, government economic agencies, regulatory policies and bodies, company law and legal institutions all form part of economic governance."[74] Political governance is seen as a process that coordinates the activity of political actors in a country. The functions of the political institutions, such as the executive, the legislature, the judiciary, political parties, and the bureaucracy, are at the center of political governance. Political scientists often term political *governance* as democratic *governance* emphasizing the role of democracy and human rights. Finally, the question of societal governance comes to the fore in view of the fact that the forces of globalization had brought a situation where government alone cannot cope with today's increasingly complex socio-economic issues, leaving a growing CSO space. The diverse NGO, NPO, and "citizen group" civil society interest representation is the bedrock of societal *governance*.

A Conventional View of Domestic Governance

Traditionally, a hierarchy of institutions characterizes domestic governance with the state at the top.[75] Hence, the proliferation of literature on governance is heavily influenced by the rules and norms on administrative and market reforms in order to accommodate capitalist system. It is widely held that the World Bank as the leading organization for the International Donors Community (IDC) started to play around with the concept, identifying the African crisis as one of a crisis of governance. Subsequently, the UNDP, Asian Development Bank (ADB), and several other donor foundations and agencies have contributed to popularize this concept. In fact, the dismal failure of "structural adjustment programs" in Africa, Latin America, and Asia forced the IDC introduction of governance as a tool. Such as IDC view, of governance as synonymous with government consistently emphasizes "good governance," emphasizes the role of the government, arguing the notion of *governance* "refers to the competent provision of public services and the capacity to plan effectively and execute beneficial government policies."[76] Another influential multilateral donor agency, the UNDP (United Nations Development Program) emphasis on public sector management, for that matter, development management, helps define *governance* for developing countries.

It consists of: "(a) the form of political authority that exists in a country (parliament or presidential, civilian or military, autocratic or democratic); (b) the means through which authority is exercised in the management of economic and social resources; and (c) the ability of governments to discharge government functions effectively, efficiently and equitably."[77] The ADB states, in broad terms, "governance is about the institutional environment in which citizens interact among themselves and with government agencies/officials."[78] Thus, *governance*, according to the donors' perspective, comprises of five critical institutional components: "(a) the executive, (b) the bureaucracy, (c) the rule of law, (d) the character of the policy-making process, and (e) civil society."[79] In recent times, the IDC priority has been on civil society empowerment. Even many donor countries and agencies increasingly rely on NGOs delivery of foreign aid in the developing countries.

Despite a considerable degree of intellectual rigor and a reference to institutional aspect, the IDC view of *governance* from a narrow administrative context for all practical purposes, and hence, corruption and inefficiency of public sectors, became an all-important issue in the *governance* debate. It has become more parochial when it relentlessly emphasizes corruption as the overriding problem and thus seeking remedy only through administrative reform for ensuring "good governance" in the South. Interestingly, the IDC agenda in reforming the public administration is also aimed at not strengthening the government but expanding the role of the market and to reduce the role of the state in the society. So it could hardly hide the fact that the IDC continuity of its traditional policy of emphasizing neo-liberal market forces to resolve economic difficulties in the developing countries prefers organizing domestic *governance* to facilitate the role of the market in a society. This entirely misses the cultural idiosyncrasy and path dependence of institutions.

NEW INSTITUTIONALISM AND DOMESTIC GOVERNANCE

The traditional model of domestic *governance* has been challenged from different corners since the 1970s. The empirical findings in a number of developing countries and further theoretical sophistication by the development and political economists demonstrate that mere market forces and administrative reform cannot ensure domestic governance conducive for development. Even the World Bank's recent institutional emphasis remains highly market-oriented. Besides, there has been a linear understanding of the socio-economic and political backgrounds of the developing countries by the IDC and international financial and economic organizations. This rather impedes the development process in many of these countries.

Therefore, "new institutionalism" could better explain the pattern of governance in the South. "New institutionalism" emerges as the major critic of the market type governance structure. Markets, in this view, are regarded more as deliberate political constructs involving the conflict of contending interests than rational and technical, self-regulating mechanisms.[80] The central assertion of "new-institutionalism" is that institutions affect behavior by altering the incentives facing actors. Institutions are viewed as human artifacts that can be created, strengthened, diluted, or eliminated. Hence, *governance* must be viewed in relation to institutions. For example, in most of the developing countries technological backwardness, poverty, lack of social capital, corruption, over-centralization and internal conflicts are the major *governance* challenges, which are otherwise rooted in institutional failures.

Understanding institutions opens interdisciplinary doors. Arguably, "the study of institutions has been enriched by a growing body of work that combines "rational choice" theory, information economics, game theory, law and organizational theory."[81] Douglas North provides powerful insights toward understanding institutions. Institutions are "rules, enforcement characteristics of rules, and norms of behavior that structure repeated human interaction."[82] In the words of North, an institution "concerns the endless struggle of human beings to solve the problems of cooperation so that they may reap the advantages not only of technology but also of all the other facets of human endeavor that constitute civilization."[83] In that sense, institutions presumably would facilitate "development" and will enable people to get along with changes for the good. Institutions are "the humanly devised constraints that shape human interaction",[84] being either rules devised by human beings or conventions and codes of behavior. Robert Goodwin suggests, "institutions are organized patterns of socially constructed norms and roles, and socially prescribed behaviors expected of occupants of those roles, which are created and re-created."[85] Thus, institutions are understood to offer frameworks for all kinds of participation and flexibility to adjust to the evolving conditions, which may come over time.

"New institutionalism" gives less attention to the conventional issues, such as allocating resources, maintaining equilibrium, and problem of scarcity. Rather it emphasizes incentives, contracts, transactions costs, organization, information, process, rent-seeking, rules of choice, and asset specificity. In this context, Oliver Williamson's work drives governance to the analytical center stage. Set out and developed in his two best-known works, *Markets and Hierarchies* (1975) and *The Economic Institutions of Capitalism* (1985), the basic tenets of his transaction cost economics (TCE) posit, under certain conditions, hierarchical governance is less costly than market exchange.[86] His conceptualization is based on the key behavioral assumptions of bounded rationality and opportunism and on the analysis of the situations of market failure.[87]

However, the conceptual framework of Williamson is more relevant for the hierarchy type of domestic governance. Like the markets, the hierarchy literature ignores collective action and other non-market mechanisms. Mark Granovetter has put forward the network *embeddedness* idea of interpersonal relations. He argues that even under a market or a hierarchical economy networks could operate because economic life is embedded in social relations. Networks could develop their own capabilities to generate stable relations between planning and risk of uncertainty, to generate its own efficiency, and to reduce transactions. Besides, another dimension of new the *institutionalist* position defines governance as "organizing collective action".[88] According to David Lake, *governance* as organizing "collective action involves two analytically separate processes: bargaining and contracting. Bargaining divides the available costs and benefits between actors, while contracting enforces the bargains that have been reached."[89] Despite different variants of "new institutionalism", their overall thrust is on the creation of appropriate institutions to resolve all kinds of human problems.

However, the "new intuitionalist" view too has come under attack from different theoretical approaches. Apart from the *neo-liberalists* and *neo-realists*, the *structuralists* and *pluralists* argue that structural factors such as social groups, class relations, civil societies and political culture play the dominant role in the emergence of appropriate institutions. But, as indicated earlier, neither market nor structural factors could facilitate an effective *governance* pattern to accomplish the goal of national development under the condition of globalization.

Toward a General Framework of Analysis

Prior analysis elevates two components of understanding of relations between globalization and *governance* in the context of developing countries. First, it is important to explain the nature of the relationship between globalization and domestic governance. In light of the competing views regarding the conceptualization of globalization and domestic *governance* we have formulated operational definitions of these two notions considering the existing realities in the developing countries in general. Globalization is seen as a dynamic global process to bring about politico-economic and social changes at the domestic level, while *governance* provides a mechanism to achieve the goal of national development. It is increasingly recognized that the pursuit of development largely depends on *governance* structures. The relevance and importance of institutions for development are explicitly and implicitly linked with the degree to which a given country's *governance* characteristics can be changed over time. Globalization introduces a new pattern of governance with which the Western countries are more familiar than those in the South. What is more, some of the industrialized countries like Japan and Germany are also at odds, as they had been following different development strategies for decades. Box 2.1 shows that there is a two-way interacting process between globalization and domestic *governance*. Taking an analogy from Putnam's two-level games theorization,[90] it is convenient to decompose the process into two ways: (a) The nature and direction of domestic governance in the developing countries largely depends on a host of global factors caused by the process of globalization, leading to a causal relationship between the two phenomena; we may call that Way I. (b) The structure of domestic governance itself can determine the nature of transnational phenomena that are generating the process of globalization; we may call that Way II.

2 GLOBALIZATION, GOVERNANCE, AND NEW INSTITUTIONALISM ... 45

Box 2.1 Two-way interacting processes of globalization and domestic governance

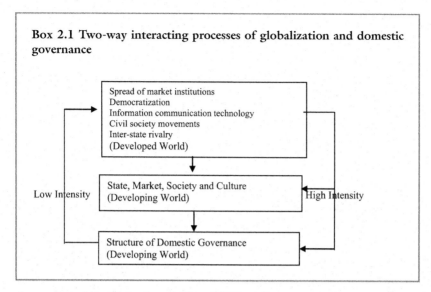

Source Based on Prakash and Hart 1997, p. 5

It is assumed that Way I is the most possible scenario in the case of developing countries, because these countries could exert a negligible positive influence upon the basic developments within the hierarchy of global economic and political orders. With some exceptions, they are extremely dependent on aid, trade, investment, and technology from the industrialized countries, showing a high level of subordination in their bilateral and multilateral relations.

Another component of our framework of analysis is to draw the dividing line between "pre-existing" or "old" and "present" governance structures in order to locate the issues of change and continuity in the basic tendencies of institutional arrangements and the end results in the socio-economic context. As the typical pattern of globalization emphasizes the elements of global practice, short-term gains and market, the present realities in the developing country demonstrate a significant degree of divergence in political, economic, and societal spheres.

As Box 2.2 demonstrates, many developing countries experience a number of new institutional configurations in their domestic life generating an institutional transformation. As a consequence, their existing *governance* structure differs to a great extent, from that of the past. This difference in old and present *governance* structures is rooted in the process of globalization. The changes in the present *governance* structure are seen at different sectors and levels of the state. The focus is observed mainly in political and economic spheres and there is a varying degree of the pace in the transformation process. On the other hand, a certain level of continuity is observed between the institutional features of "past" and "present" *governance* structures while compared with a broad range of rules and norms of globalization. For instance, lack of accountability and transparency, legal regime, technological backwardness, aid dependence and centralization of power continue to exist in a substantive way.

Box 2.2 Globalization induced institutional transformations in the developing countries

Old Institutional Features (1971-1990)		*Existing Institutional Features (1990-2015)*
• Political rigidity • Centralization of power • Public Ownership • Regulation • Bureaucratization • Trade Protectionism • Rent-seeking and corruption • Resistance to cross-border capital flows • Subsidies to domestic industries • Planning and control • Government intervention • Aid dependence • Technological Backwardness • Indigenous and colonial legal system	GLOBALIZATION PROCESS →	• Political openness • Privatization • Deregulation • Administrative reforms • Trade liberalization • Withdrawal of subsidies from domestic sectors • De-emphasizing planning and control • Declining government intervention • Lessening of aid dependence • Technological dependence • Limited legal reform • Rent-seeking and Corruption

Source Prepared by the author

While the *governance* structure based on the rules and norms of globalization is not new to the Western capitalist countries or it is not entirely new to the late industrialized countries of East Asia and Latin America, for many developing countries it is a novel experiment. Box 2.3 captures some of the arenas where enormous changes will take place (or have taken place). Ironically enough, this has been applied in those countries almost in a standardized way under strong IDC external pressures and their surrogate organizations, and under a somewhat hostile external economic environment. The countries who are relentlessly pleading for dwindling foreign aid, or repeatedly ask for global market access to sell their primary and standardized manufacturing commodities, or unsuccessfully allure cross-border capital, or grapple with old technologies are quite strange to this new phenomenon. As a result, we observe a considerable degree of contradiction between the "old" and "new" patterns of domestic *governance* while the developing countries are faced with the challenge of globalization.

These contradictions are caused by the contrasting scenarios as exemplified in developing countries where we observe a number of issues of incompatibility particularly in the following areas:

a. privatization and lack of entrepreneurship;
b. continuing trade deficit: the problem of market access;
c. deregulation, foreign direct investment, and financial volatility;
d. continuing aid dependence and the issues of aid utilization;
e. competition and competitiveness;
f. access to information and communication technology;
g. growing dependence on informal sector;
h. democratization, political instability and criminalization; and
i. continuing underdevelopment and poverty.

> **Box 2.3 Rules and norms of globalization**
>
> **Politico-legal Realm**
> Political openness
> Shrinking government intervention
> Devolution of power
> Accountability
> Transparency
> Liberal legal regime
>
> **Techno-economic Realm**
> Private property rights
> Deregulation
> Trade openness
> Competition
> Labor mobility
> Shrinking aid
> High dependence on ICT
>
> **Societal Realm**
> Individualism
> Consumerism
> Civil society empowerment
> Environmental awareness

Source Prepared by the author

Conclusion

The above-mentioned framework of analysis illustrates how the globalization forces transform domestic governance in the developing countries. Many developing societies are at a critical juncture in their search for political stability and socio-economic development. The economy inherited from colonial rule, was a relatively overregulated, based on import controls, foreign-exchange rationing, an overvalued exchange rate, subsidized food pricing as well as subsidized input and credit. The government carried out a policy of nationalization in its attempt to build a "socialist type" of economy.[91] Following the same pattern of economy throughout the 1970s, many countries embraced the agenda of liberal and market-oriented economic reforms in the mid-1980s under WB and IMF guidelines. But a substantive level of economic reforms started in the early 1990s and since then these countries continued to open up their different sectors of economy. On the other hand, developing countries witnessed political regimes of varied types, from democratic to military. In societal sector, there has been a transformation of civil society and

NGO activities in the developing world. NGO (and other organizational) socio-economic activities have made an important contribution to poverty alleviation, women empowerment, and mass literacy in the developing world. However, despite undertaking considerable economic reforms, introduction of political changes and widespread NGOs activities, many post-colonial countries have been struggling with governance mechanisms. Multifaceted process of globalization has added more challenges to the existing governance structure. In this context, a new framework based on critical role of institutions provides theoretical insights to policy makers to deal with globalization and domestic governance in the changing socio-political and economic milieu.

Notes

1. Aseem Prakash and Jeffrey A. Hart, "Globalization and Governance: An Introduction," *Globalization and Governance*, eds. Aseem Prakash and Hart (Routledge: London and New York, 1999), 1.
2. Victor D. Cha, "Globalization and the Study of International Security," *Journal of Peace Research* 37, no. 3 (2000): 391.
3. Thomas L. Friedman, *The Lexus and the Olive Tree: Understanding Globalization* (New York: Archer Books, 2000), xx.
4. Kevin Hewison, "Resisting Globalization: A Study of Localism in Thailand," *The Pacific Review* 13, no. 2 (2000): 280.
5. Arjun Bhardwaj and Delwar Hossain, "Globalization and Multinational Corporations in South Asia: Towards Building a Sustainable Partnership for Sustainable Development," *RCSS Policy Studies 20* (Colombo: Regional Centre for Strategic Studies, 2001), 9.
6. Cited in Ibid., 9. Robert O. Keohane and Joseph S. Nye, Jr., "Globalization: What's New? What's Not? (And so What?)," *Foreign Policy* (Spring 2000): 104–119.
7. Charles Oman, "Globalization, Regionalization, and Inequality," *Inequality, Globalization and World Politics*, eds. Andrew Hurrell and Nagaure Woods (New York, NY: Oxford University Press, 1999), 42.
8. "Marginalizing the Masses," *Journal of International Affairs* 53, no. 2 (Spring 2000), Noam Chomsky interviewed by Robert A. Schupp and Richard L. O. Hlemacher.

9. Some also argue that the Cold War ended in 1989 following the fall of socialist regimes in East Europe.
10. Robert Chambers, *Whose Reality Counts? Putting the First Last* (London: Intermediate Technology Publications, 1997), 4.
11. Suzanne Berger, "Globalization and Politics," *Annual Review of Political Science*, 3 (2000): 51–52.
12. Fantu Cheru, "Transforming Our Common Future: The Local Dimensions of Global Reform," *Review of International Political Economy* 7, no. 2 (Summer 2000): 354.
13. Henry Wai-Chung Yeung, "The Failure of the Weak States in Economic Liberalization: Liberalization, Democratization and the Financial Crisis in South Korea," *The Pacific Review* 13, no. 1 (2000): 137.
14. Ibid.
15. *Interdependence* raised a major theoretical debate in the 1970s between the neo-liberalists and neo-realists. Keohane and Nye extensively dealt with this issue. See, *Power and Interdependence: World Politics in Transition* (Boston, MA: Little, Brown 1977).
16. Theodore H. Cohn, *Global Political Economy: Theory and Practice* (Sydney: Longman, 2000), 356.
17. Keohane and Nye, op. cit., 104–119.
18. N. Yashiro, "Globalization and the Japanese Economy: The Challenge and the Prospect," *Japan Review of International Affairs* (Fall 1998): 178.
19. Henry Wai-Chung Yeung, "The Failure of the Weak States in Economic Liberalization: Liberalization, Democratization and the Financial Crisis in South Korea," *The Pacific Review* 13, no. 1 (2000): 137.
20. Berger, op. cit., 58.
21. Cohn, op. cit., 137–138.
22. Classical realism was developed by Thucydides; and his famous work *History of the Peloponnesian War* is still regarded as the bible of realism.
23. See, for details, Hans J. Morgenthau, revised by Kenneth W. Thomson, *Politics Among the Nations: The Struggle for Power and Peace* (Toronto: McGraw Hill, 1978).
24. Kenneth Waltz, *Man, the State and War* (Columbia University Press, 1983); and *Theory of International Politics* (London: Addison-Wesley Publishing Company, 1979).

25. See, for details, Barry Buzan, "The Timeless Wisdom of Realism?," *International Theory: Positivism and Beyond*, eds. Steve Smith, Ken Booth, and Marysia Zalewski (New York: Cambridge University Press, 1996), 60.
26. Cohn, op. cit., 356.
27. Ibid., 359.
28. David Held, et al., "Globalization," *Global Governance*, vol. 5 (1999): 483.
29. Held and Anthony McGrew, "Globalization and the End of the Old Order," *Review of International Studies*, vol. 24, Special Issue (December 1998): 237.
30. Although their approach seems to be altruistic as they examine the phenomena of international morality, cultural limits of international human rights and the question of national sovereignty, it reflects Kantian realism. See, for details, Jacobson and Lawson.
31. Ian Clark, *Globalization and International Relations Theory* (London: Oxford University Press, 1999), 4.
32. Berger, op. cit., 58.
33. R. J. Barry Jones, *Globalization and Interdependence in the International Political Economy: Rhetoric and Reality* (London: Pinter Publishers, 1995), 32.
34. Emin Fuat Keyman, *Globalization, State, Identity/Difference: Toward a Critical Theory of International Relations* (San Jose, CA: Humanity Press, 1997), 31.
35. Fernando Henrique Cardoso and Enzo Faletto, *Dependency and Development in Latin America* (Berkeley, CA: University of California Press, 1979), 2.
36. Stephen Gill and David Law, *The Global Political Economy* (London: Wheatsheaf, 1988), 77; quoted in Keyman, 113.
37. Nederveen Pieterse, "Globalization North and South: Representations of Uneven Development and Interaction of Modernities," *Theory, Culture and Society* 17, no. 1 (2000): 133–137.
38. Ian Clark, "Beyond the Great Divide: Globalization and the Theory of International Relations," *Review of International Studies*, Vol. 24, Issue 4, October 1998, 479–498.
39. Bhardwaj and Hossain, op. cit., 10.
40. Ibid., 11.
41. Ibid., 11.

42. See, for details, V. Birchfield, "Contesting the Hegemony of Market Ideology: Gramsci's 'Good Sense' and Polanyi's 'Double Movement'," *Review of International Political Economy* 6, no. 1 (Spring 1999): 30.
43. See, for details, R. J. Barry Jones, "Overview: Globalization and Change in the International Political Economy," *International Affairs* 75, no. 2 (1999): 357.
44. UNDP, *Human Development Report 1999: Globalization with Human Face* (New York: Oxford University Press, 1999), 30.
45. Benzamin Cashore and Steven Bernstein, "Globalization, Four-Paths of Internationalization and Domestic Policy Change: The Case of Ecoforestry in British Columbia, Canada," *Canadian Journal of Political Science* XXXIII, no. 1 (2000): 75.
46. Chambers, op. cit., 4.
47. Matthew C. Klein and Michael Pettis, *Trade Wars Are Class Wars* (New York: Yale University Press, 2020), 106.
48. For example, the volume and mobility of global finance capital has surprised many observers. In 1986, about $188 billion passed through the hands of currency traders in New York, London and Tokyo everyday. Presently $1.5 trillion is traded on the foreign exchange markets—as few traders seem to determine the economic fate of countries. See, for details, Held et al., op. cit., 493.
49. See, for details, World Bank, *The World Development Report 1989: Financial Systems and Development* (New York: Oxford University Press), 128–129. This report extensively discusses different dimensions of financial liberalization.
50. Bhardwaj and Hossain, op. cit., 12.
51. Bhardwaj and Hossain, op. cit., 12.
52. Beth V. Yarbrough and Robert M. Yarbrough, "Cooperation in the Liberalization of International Trade: After Hegemony, What?," *International Organization* 41, no. 1 (Winter 1987): 12–13.
53. Bhardwaj and Hossain, op. cit., 13.
54. Ibid., 13.
55. Bhardwaj and Hossain, op. cit., 13.
56. Ibid., 13.
57. Ethan Kapstein, "Globalization and Democratization: Friends or Foes?" May 5, 1999. Available Online: http://www.worldbank.org/poverty/inequal/themgrp/seminars/1999.htm#_Toc440 950986, February 14, 2001.

58. Prakash and Hart, "Introduction", op. cit., 17.
59. *The Daily Star* (Dhaka), January 19, 2001.
60. Darusalam, "The Influence of ICT Diffusion and Globalization on the Quality of Governance: A Study of Panel Data from ASEAN Countries", July 2021, https://journals.sagepub.com/doi/full/10.1177/02666669211026363, October 22, 2021.
61. Bhardwaj and Hossain, op. cit., 14.
62. Joseph S. Nye Jr. and David A. Welch, *Understanding Global Conflict and Cooperation: An Introduction to Theory and History*, (New York: Pearson, 2017), 301.
63. Bhardwaj and Hossain, op. cit., 14.
64. Ibid., 14.
65. The UNDP report of 1993 cites 50,000 NGOs worldwide. Between 1980 and 1990, the Organization for Economic Cooperation and Development (OECD) reported an increase from 1600 to 2500 organizations in its 24 member countries.
66. Peter Van Tuijl, "NGOs and Human Rights: Sources of Justice and Democracy," *Journal of International Affairs*, New York, March 1999. Vol. 52. No. 2, 494.
67. Bhardwaj and Hossain, op. cit., 14.
68. R. A. W. Rhodes, *Understanding Governance: Policy Networks, Governance, Reflexivity, and Accountability* (London: Open University Press, 1997); quoted in Yoichiro Usui, "Governance Legal Order, Social Integration: Reviewing New Governance Approaches in EU Studies," 23 pages, Online, http://www.nuis.ac.jp/~usui/Usui_2000_Journal_of_NUIS.htm, November 10, 2000.
69. Rehman Sobhan, *Reprioritizing South Asia's Development Agenda: The Role of Governance* (Dhaka: Center for Policy Dialogue, 1998), 1.
70. A. Madhavan, "Governance as a Shared Obligation," Paper Presented at a Seminar, "Cooperating for Good Governance in South Asia," Organized by Indian Council for South Asian Cooperation and India International Center at New Delhi, February 2000.
71. Rajesh Tandon, "What Is Good Governance?" *Foreign Policy* (Fall, 1999): 1 Special Advertising Section.

72. David Martin Jones, "The Politics of Economic Governance," *Governance in the Asia Pacific*, eds. Richard Maidment, et al. (London: Routledge, 1998), 1.
73. John L. Campbell, J. Rogers Holingsworth, and Leon N. Lindberg (eds.), *Governance of the American Economy* (Cambridge, UK: Cambridge University Press, 1991), 1.
74. "APEC Economic Governance Capacity Building Initiative," 3 pages, Online, http://www.apecsec.org.sg/ecotech/egcbi.html, January 12, 2001.
75. Prakash and Hart, op. cit., 25.
76. Dane Rowlands, "Domestic Governance and International Migration," *World Development* 27, no. 8 (1999): 1477.
77. Meghna Guhathakurta, "Donor Perceptions of Governance," Paper presented at the International Seminar on *Governance and Development: South Asia in the 21st Century*, organized by the Bangladesh Institute of International and Strategic Studies (BIISS), Dhaka, 21–23, December 1996.
78. Asian Development Bank, *Governance: Sound Development Management* (Manila: ADB, 1995), 1–2.
79. Nauro F. Campos and Jeffrey B. Nugent, "Development Performance and the Institutions of Governance: Evidence from East Asia and Latin America," *World Development* 27, no. 3 (1999): 439.
80. Garry Rodan, et al., *The Political Economy of South-East Asia: An Introduction* (Oxford, UK: Oxford University Press, 1997), 13.
81. The World Bank, *Reforming Public Institutions and Strengthening Governance: A World Bank Strategy*, November 2000, Public Sector Group, Poverty Reduction and Economic Management (PREM) Network (Washington, DC: The World Bank), 8.
82. Okada, Y. *Institutional Arrangements and the Japanese Competitive-Cum-Cooperative Business System* (Tokyo: Sophia University Press, 1995), December 27, 1.
83. Douglas North, *Institutions, Institutional Change and Economic Performance* (New York, NY: Cambridge University Press: 1990), 133.
84. Ibid., 3.
85. Robert Goodwin (ed.), *The Theory of Institutional Design* (Cambridge, UK: Cambridge University Press, 1996), 19.

86. Robert F. Freeland, *The Mechanisms of Governance*. (Review) by Oliver E. Williamson (New York, NY: Oxford University Press, 1996); *Administrative Science Quarterly*, Issue (March, 1999), vol. 44, nos. 1, 2.
87. Ibid.
88. Aseem and Hart, op. cit., 2.
89. David A. Lake, "Global Governance: A Relational Contracting Approach," op. cit., 33.
90. Robert D. Putnam, "Diplomacy and Domestic Politics: The Logic of Two-Level Game," *International Organization* 42, no. 3 (Summer 1988): 427–436.
91. Mustafizur Rahman, "A Brief Note on the Bangladesh Economy," *Governance and Electoral Process in Bangladesh*, ed. Jevan Thiagarajah (New Delhi: Vikash Publishing House, 1997), 14.

BIBLIOGRAPHY

"APEC Economic Governance Capacity Building Initiative," 3 pages, Online. http://www.apecsec.org.sg/ecotech/egcbi.html. January 12, 2001.
Asian Development Bank. 1995. *Governance: Sound Development Management*. Manila: ADB.
Berger, Suzanne. 2000. "Globalization and Politics." *Annual Review of Political Science* 3: 43–62.
Bhardwaj, Arjun, and Delwar Hossain. 2001. "Globalization and Multinational Corporations in South Asia: Towards Building a Sustainable Partnership for Sustainable Development." *RCSS Policy Studies 20*. Colombo: Regional Centre for Strategic Studies.
Birchfield, V. 1999. "Contesting the Hegemony of Market Ideology: Gramsci's 'Good Sense' and Polanyi's 'Double Movement'." *Review of International Political Economy* 6, no. 1 (Spring 1999).
Buzan, Barry. 1996. "The Timeless Wisdom of Realism?" Steve Smith, Ken Booth, and Marysia Zalewski, eds., *International Theory: Positivism and Beyond*. New York: Cambridge University Press.
Campbell, John L., J. Rogers Holingsworth, and Leon N. Lindberg, eds. 1991. *Governance of the American Economy*. Cambridge, UK: Cambridge University Press, 1.
Campos, Nauro F., and Jeffrey B. Nugent. 1999. "Development Performance and the Institutions of Governance: Evidence from East Asia and Latin America." *World Development* 27, no. 3: 439–452.

Cardoso, Fernando Henrique, and Enzo Faletto. 1979. *Dependency and Development in Latin America.* Berkeley, CA: University of California Press.

Cashore, Benzamin, and Steven Bernstein. 2000. "Globalization, Four-Paths of Internationalization and Domestic Policy Change: The Case of Ecoforestry in British Columbia, Canada." *Canadian Journal of Political Science* XXXIII, no. 1: 67–99.

Cha, Victor D. 2000. "Globalization and the Study of International Security." *Journal of Peace Research* 37, no. 3: 391–403.

Chambers, Robert. 1997. *Whose Reality Counts? Putting the First Last.* London: Intermediate Technology Publications.

Cheru, Fantu. 2000. "Transforming Our Common Future: The Local Dimensions of Global Reform." *Review of International Political Economy* 7, no. 2 (Summer 2000): 353–368.

Clark, Ian. 1998. "Beyond the Great Divide: Globalization and the Theory of International Relations." *Review of International Studies* 24, no. 4 (October 1998): 479–498.

———. 1999. *Globalization and International Relations Theory.* London: Oxford University Press.

Cohn, Theodore H. 2000. *Global Political Economy: Theory and Practice.* Sydney: Longman.

Darusalam. 2021. "The Influence of ICT Diffusion and Globalization on the Quality of Governance: A Study of Panel Data from ASEAN Countries." July 2021. https://journals.sagepub.com/doi/full/10.1177/02666669211026363. October 22, 2021.

Freeland, Robert F. 1996. *The Mechanisms of Governance.* (Review) by Oliver E. Williamson. New York, NY: Oxford University Press, 1996. *Administrative Science Quarterly,* Issue: (March, 1999), vol. 44.

Friedman, Thomas L. 2000. *The Lexus and the Olive Tree: Understanding Globalization.* New York: Archer Books.

Gill, Stephen, and David Law. 1988. *The Global Political Economy.* London: Wheatsheaf, 77; quoted in Keyman.

Goodwin, Robert, ed. 1996. *The Theory of Institutional Design.* Cambridge, UK: Cambridge University Press.

Guhathakurta, Meghna. 1996. "Donor Perceptions of Governance." Paper presented at the International Seminar on *Governance and Development: South Asia in the 21st Century,* organized by the Bangladesh Institute of International and Strategic Studies (BIISS), Dhaka, 21–23 December 1996.

Held, David, and Anthony McGrew. 1998. "Globalization and the End of the Old Order." *Review of International Studies,* vol. 24, Special Issue (December 1998).

Held, David, et al. 1999. "Globalization." *Global Governance,* vol. 5.

Hewison, Kevin. 2000. "Resisting Globalization: A Study of Localism in Thailand." *The Pacific Review* 13, no. 2: 279–296.
Jones, David Martin. 1998. "The Politics of Economic Governance." Richard Maidment, et al., eds., *Governance in the Asia Pacific*. London: Routledge.
Jones, R. J. Barry. 1995. *Globalization and Interdependence in the International Political Economy: Rhetoric and Reality*. London: Pinter Publishers.
———. 1999. "Overview: Globalization and Change in the International Political Economy." *International Affairs* 75, no. 2.
Kapstein, Ethan. 1999. "Globalization and Democratization: Friends or Foes?" May 5. Available Online: http://www.worldbank.org/poverty/inequal/the mgrp/seminars/1999.htm#_Toc440950986. February 14, 2001.
Keohane, Robert O., and Joseph S. Nye Jr. 1977. *Power and Interdependence: World Politics in Transition*. Boston, MA: Little, Brown.
———. 2000. "Globalization: What's New? What's Not? (And so What?)." *Foreign Policy* (Spring 2000).
Keyman, Emin Fuat. 1997. *Globalization, State, Identity/Difference: Toward a Critical Theory of International Relations*. San Jose, CA: Humanity Press.
Lake, David A. 1999. "Global Governance: A Relational Contracting Approach." Aseem Prakash & Hart, eds., *Globalization and Governance*. Routledge: London and New York.
Madhavan, A. 2000. "Governance as a Shared Obligation." Paper Presented at a Seminar, "Cooperating for Good Governance in South Asia," Organized by Indian Council for South Asian Cooperation and India International Center at New Delhi, February 2000.
Morganthau, Hans J., revised by Kenneth W. Thomson. 1978. *Politics Among the Nations: The Struggle for Power and Peace*. Toronto: McGraw Hill.
Noam Chomsky interviewed by Robert A. Schupp and Richard L. O. Hlemacher. 2000. "Marginalizing the Masses." *Journal of International Affairs* 53, no. 2 (Spring 2000).
North, Douglas. 1990. *Institutions, Institutional Change and Economic Performance*. New York, NY: Cambridge University Press.
Nye, Joseph S. Jr., and David A. Welch. 2017. *Understanding Global Conflict and Cooperation: An Introduction to Theory and History*. New York: Pearson.
Okada, Y. 1995. "*Institutional Arrangements and the Japanese Competitive-Cum-Cooperative Business System*." Tokyo: Sophia University Press, December 27.
Oman, Charles. 1999. "Globalization, Regionalization, and Inequality." Andrew Hurrell and Ngaire Woods, eds., *Inequality, Globalization and World Politics* (New York, NY: Oxford University Press, 1999).
Pieterse, Nederveen. 2000. "Globalization North and South: Representations of Uneven Development and Interaction of Modernities." *Theory, Culture and Society* 17, no. 1: 129–137.

Prakash, Aseem, and Jeffrey A. Hart. 1999. "Globalization and Governance: An Introduction." Aseem Prakash & Hart, eds., *Globalization and Governance*. Routledge: London and New York.
Putnam, Robert D. 1988. "Diplomacy and Domestic Politics: The Logic of Two-Level Game." *International Organization* 42, no. 3 (Summer 1988).
Rahman, Mustafizur. 1997. "A Brief Note on the Bangladesh Economy." Jevan Thiagarajah, ed., *Governance and Electoral Process in Bangladesh*. New Delhi: Vikash Publishing House.
Rhodes, R. A. W. 1997. *Understanding Governance: Policy Networks, Governance, Reflexivity, and Accountability*. London: Open University Press.
Rodan, Garry, et al. 1997. *The Political Economy of South-East Asia: An Introduction*. Oxford, UK: Oxford University Press.
Rowlands, Dane. 1999. "Domestic Governance and International Migration." *World Development* 27, no. 8: 1477–1491.
Sobhan, Rehman. 1998. *Reprioritizing South Asia's Development Agenda: The Role of Governance*. Dhaka: Center for Policy Dialogue.
Tandon, Rajesh. 1999. "What Is Good Governance?" *Foreign Policy* (Fall, 1999): 1 Special Advertising Section.
The Daily Star (Dhaka), January 19, 2001.
The World Bank. 2000. *Reforming Public Institutions and Strengthening Governance: A World Bank Strategy*, November 2000, Public Sector Group, Poverty Reduction and Economic Management (PREM) Network. Washington, DC: The World Bank.
Tuijl, Peter Van. 1999. "NGOs and Human Rights: Sources of Justice and Democracy." *Journal of International Affairs* 52, no. 2: 493–512 (New York, March 1999).
UNDP. 1999. *Human Development Report 1999: Globalization with Human Face*. New York: Oxford University Press.
Usui, Yoichiro. 2000. "Governance Legal Order, Social Integration: Reviewing New Governance Approaches in EU Studies," 23 page, Online. http://www.nuis.ac.jp/~usui/Usui_2000_Journal_of_NUIS.htm. November 10, 2000.
Yarbrough, Beth V., and Robert M. Yarbrough. 1987. "Cooperation in the Liberalization of International Trade: After Hegemony, What?" *International Organization* 41, no. 1 (Winter 1987): 1–26.
Yashiro, N. 1998. "Globalization and the Japanese Economy: The Challenge and the Prospect." *Japan Review of International Affairs* 12(Fall 1998): 178–197.
Yeung, Henry Wai-Chung. 2000. "The Failure of the Weak States in Economic Liberalization: Liberalization, Democratization and the Financial Crisis in South Korea." *The Pacific Review* 13, no. 1: 115–131.
Waltz, Kenneth. 1979. *Theory of International Politics*. London: Addison-Wesley Publishing Company.

———. 1983. *Man, the State and War*. Columbia University Press.
World Bank. 1990. *The World Development Report 1989: Financial Systems and Development*. New York: Oxford University Press.

CHAPTER 3

The Growth of Populism and Populist Publics: Globalization Under the Gun?

Lailufar Yasmin

INTRODUCTION: "LITTLE PEOPLE AND BIG EMOTIONS"

Unfolding seismic 2020 events—such as the novel Coronavirus pandemic[1]—has shifted our longstanding perspectives about what is "normal". Our regular life came to a halt, leading to revisiting extant patterns of how we connect with each other. Such changed perspectives did not limit themselves within state boundaries. Transcending local boundaries—natural in a pandemic—it led to questioning the patterns and practices of connecting beyond borders. For the first time since the European Union (EU) drew closest to reaching its dream of creating a borderless Europe, Europeans reaffirmed their greater faith in national governments than any European common platform. In other words, not only people turning to their governments for providing basic needs such as health

L. Yasmin (✉)
Department of International Relations, University of Dhaka, Dhaka, Bangladesh
e-mail: lyasmin@du.ac.bd

© The Author(s), under exclusive license to Springer Nature Singapore Pte Ltd. 2022
I. A. Hussain (eds.), *Global-Local Tradeoffs, Order-Disorder Consequences*, Global Political Transitions,
https://doi.org/10.1007/978-981-16-9419-6_3

security, but also finding how fewer connections means reducing imports of others' troubles. The fact that the novel Coronavirus originated in China before spreading across the rest of the world (primarily through air connectivity), led to the idea of decoupling with China, on the one hand, and strengthening one's own production-base to reduce dependence on China, on the other. This trend emanated in the words of populist leaders whose organized support-base through various communication media helped disseminate the blame-game. How incredibly the world is connected now—globalization no longer being a choice but a complex reality—might undermine this thrust.

Taking stock of the contemporary political trends, this chapter highlights the need to understand populism and how it is affecting globalization patterns. The central argument proposed here is how the rise of populism locally threatens twenty-first century globalization. In other words, while in many cases discussed later, the rise of populism is often attributed to an effect of globalization in the twentieth century, the latest forms of populism threaten the forces of globalization themselves. The nature of twenty-first century populism is an interesting area of research as it embraces not only challenging the elites and structures, but also, by challenging established knowledge and scientific data, empowers "little people" in a manner not noticed before. The rise of the "little people" has a different implication now: while internally populism challenges the political regimes and structures, externally it questions how states should engage with each other. The nature of "little people" has also changed: forming a category of the "populist public", they, without leaders, now rebel against not only the structure, but also against established knowledge and scientific truth. While the high politics of International Relations still remains largely unaffected by this, states have been prompted to reevaluate their strategic relations with each other.

Not discussed in this chapter are the effects of populism on strategic relations. Focusing on the patterns of local populism challenging globalization, the chapter finds such de-globalization and inclusionary state behavior as possible consequences. After this introduction, four substantive sections illustrate the argument of the chapter, followed by a discussion of the definitional ambiguity surrounding the concept of populism. Attention shifts to the localization-globalization debate next, focusing on de-globalization and anti-globalization, while the fourth section argues how twentieth century populism was different in nature than the emergent type by probing into cases across Europe, Latin America, and the

United States. In the next section, which addresses the central argument of this chapter—how the changing nature of contemporary populism threatens globalization—the concept of "populist public" (populism not always being driven to gain electoral benefits), is discussed. Emerging "populist public" as a new player in an old game that challenges established facts and knowledge, thus threatening globalization. Often, these "populist publics" find support from their populist leaders—but when they work on their own, a new dimension of populism enters the picture. Insights from the discussion close the chapter.

POPULISM—THE RISE OF THE "LITTLE PEOPLE"

Nationalism first brought people into the forefront of constructing their community's future with the 1789 French Revolution. The term *nation* originally referred to foreigners, and through a long historical journey acquired the meaning of revolving around elites.[2] While the French Revolution that infused the idea of transferring "inherited" power to the people in a "nation", various nationalistic forces centralized the idea of weaving community reflections into it—a blueprint to shape their future. No wonder nationalism and liberalism—putting people at the heart of a state's forward march—emerged as defining features of western civilization. Controversies galore exist on what liberalism is, and how scholars define and apply it.[3] A simple and plain way of covering the entire gamut of liberalism would be—"liberty, fraternity and equality". The development of the concept of liberalism, in reality, took so many varied paths that often scholars point out the banality of using the term "liberalism" and instead suggest its usage in a plural sense.[4] Whatever might be the divergent intra-school views, there has been much consensus, especially with the Soviet Union dissolution that liberalism emerged as the final destiny for humankind. In other words, it is rather the different branches of liberalism holding conversations against each other than contenders of *liberalism* itself.

Despite the liberal ascent today, challenging the basic assumptions behind it also emerged at a very early stage. While the radical democrats of the United Kingdom and France, for example, challenged some of the core mid-eighteenth century liberal beliefs demanding for more equal working hours and representation in the political system,[5] a new movement also originated, pointing out how hierarchy was being institutionalized under liberal systems by dwarfing the value and significance of those at the very crux of the ideology: people. Interestingly, this reaction institutionalizing hierarchy was demonstrated in ancient times too, when Senators, known as *populares* in the Roman Republic, would claim to speak for their people. Cicero and latter historians identified them as dangerous demagogues.[6]

In his analysis, James D. Ingram has shown that the rise of the plebs and "'plebeian politics' that extends from the strike of the Roman plebs to the Ciompi Revolt in 14th Century Florence, the French Revolution's *sansculottes*, the British Chartists, and the Paris Commune".[7] In modern times, the power of the people was identified and expressed by intellectuals in Russia in 1860s—the official beginning of populism. This populist—*narodnichestvo*—reaction to Russian liberalism idealized the peasantry and prepared them for a possible revolution against the Czarist Russia.[8] In fact, this idea of "going back to the people" also emerged in the United States (U.S.) around the same time—a central theme of populism.[9]

Despite an array of scholarship on the topic, scholars have divergent opinion on how to define populism. A string of movements claiming *thin similarities* with populism have often been brought under the populism rubric. The term is applied to explain quite varied contexts: anti-immigrant and xenophobic movements in Europe; protesting the *neoliberal* economic order, launching anti-immigration drives, and advocating "progressive" populism, as in the United States;[10] challenging established economic order and championing "the society's lower classes, or the *descamisados* (the shirtless ones)" in Latin America;[11] and "authoritarian-populism" in Malaysia's context;[12] to name a few. Such diversity makes it "an essentially contested concept", while also rationalizing why some authors reject using the term altogether for encompassing such variety.[13] A much-celebrated study of political scientists Ghita Ionescu and Ernest Gellner states:

> At present, there is no doubt about the importance of populism. But no one knows exactly what it is. As a doctrine or movement [it] is elusive and changeable. It springs from all sides, but in many contradictory formats.[14]

Despite this, two perspicuous trends in defining populism can be seen—using populism in political and ideational/ideological terms. A number of scholars identified the first school of thought while explaining the rise of McCarthyism in the United States during the Cold War era to the recent rise of Bernie Sanders and Donald Trump in the United States, Pauline Hanson and the One Nation in Australia, Nigel Farage and the Brexitin U.K. (United Kingdom) movement, Marine Le Pen in France—to name but a few who have raised scholarly interest to study populism. On the other hand, from an ideational point of view, Maudde and Kaltwasser propose populism as a "thin-centered ideology" containing a core of "the people, the elite and general will", defining it as:

> populism as *a thin-centered ideology that considers society to be ultimately separated into two homogeneous and antagonistic camps, "the pure people" versus "the corrupt elite," and which argues that politics should be an expression of the* volonté générale *(general will) of the people.*[15]

Populism, thus, can be identified, as a discursive ideology that clutches itself with other ideologies and, therefore, a contextual phenomenon. Thus, while it is difficult to come to a conclusive definition of populism, we find authors relying on two specific sets of propositions to define populism: that it is a thin-centered ideology; and the polar opposites represent the people and the elites. In defining populism, while we arrive at these minimum core, I argue in the fourth section that the role of "little people" has shifted and acquired a new perspective as to how it works now, especially in the twenty-first century. Along with the concept of "little people", I borrow from the analysis of Adele Webb and Nicole Curato, who introduced the idea of "populist publics" in the Filipino context.[16]

Webb and Curato contended how President Rodrigo Duterte created acceptance of people from all classes, and thus it "dispels the impression that only 'desperate' citizens find his populism appealing".[17] While the "little people" find agency with a political purpose to serve by political parties, the rise of populist publics in this century shows a worrisome independent streak. Populist publics mobilize quickly and often without the patronization of any political party, but their mobilization directly aids the political agenda of populist leaders as well. While both the "little people" and the "populist publics" concepts resist structures, the latter has limited understanding of anti-structuralism, a discussion of which follows in the fourth section. Beforehand, however, grasping the localization-globalization and de-globalization debates becomes crucial to understanding where the current forces of globalization may be headed.

From Localization and Globalization to De-globalization?

Since the invention of bricks and people establishing a place-based existence, some kind of *permanency* entered human civilization[18] driven by various needs, people, however, have moved from one place to the other. Intermingling people belonging to different cultures have often led to tensions, and even violence. By ensuring a formidable wall of separation among human beings for the first time, the state system ensured and cemented such differences in forming national identities. Irrespectively, with scientific and technological advances, as the world grew closer and smaller—into a *global village*—the degree of interdependence also increased since the 1970s, which caught the attention of policymakers and scholars alike. Interdependence was seen by early liberals, such as Adam Smith, acting as a deterrent to war. It was, however, proved that only free trade and economic interdependence may not be enough to stop wars when Germany and the United Kingdom crossed swords with the First World War despite a high level of economic interdependence. Edward Lorenz, a mathematician, redefined the pattern of interdependence in the modern world, arguing how it has evolved into creating a complex connection pattern among actors—states and human beings alike. His famous "butterfly effect" asks a metaphorical question[19]—"Does the Flap of a Butterfly's Wings in Brazil Set Off a Tornado in Texas?"[20] This complex interdependence in an age of globalization leaves us with few choices, in fact.

On the one hand, localizing forces—local trade, culture, and identity—even religion—emphasize indigenization of particularity. Thus, Japanese culinary nationalism is boosted with the UNESCO (United Nations Educational, Scientific, and Cultural Organization) recognition of *sushi* as an intangible heritage and a recognition of its distinct identity in the community of countries.[21] On the other hand, local cultures remain threatened as globalization and westernization are often seen as synonymous. Westernization is seen as reflected in similar patterns of urban downtowns and the sharing of similar consumer products and outlets, along with similar styles of dress and grooming that make one look "western".[22] True, global culture has also acquired localized dimensions in order to increase popularity to local audiences. That *McDonalds* does not sell beef in India is one of the prime examples of that.

Cultural localization and globalization went hand in hand in many parts of the world by highlighting differences and conceding accommodation. In the economic field however, globalizing forces have led to much resistance around the world. Originating from anti-capitalism drives, these have shaped into anti-globalization protests to highlight economic inequalities brought around by globalization. While the end of the Cold War was seen as championing a liberal and capitalist world order, soon, in the 1990s, anti-globalization protests opened the hollowness of such ideas. The Seattle protests against World Trade Organization (WTO) in 1999 heralded the beginning of such anti-globalization movements leading to other political and economic protests in different parts of the world. The crux of such movements is to work for "an alternative to corporate-dominated world system".[23] Walden Bello pointed out three particular phases of globalization crises in its latest wave of globalization—the 1997–8 Asian financial crisis; protests against financial institutions starting from the Seattle protests; and the end of the Clinton era financial boom.[24] While, on the one hand, anti-globalization movements were being carried out, on the other hand, a new perspective emerged to explain that the level of interdependence was in question and leading to de-globalization.

Bello, who coined the term "de-globalization" in 2009 in his *Focus on the Global South* column,[25] gradually expanded his research to propose a system in which national economies could connect with each other in a different manner than prevalent. This new engagement pattern would gradually strengthen national economies instead of weakening them, he believed. In other words, Bello's researches point out how the baleful impacts of neoliberal economic system have led to exploring alternatives to corporate-driven capitalism.[26] Since his work appeared as a response to the Asian economic crisis of 2007–08, this motivated an interesting audience to pay attention to the trends of addressing the pitfalls of globalization. On the one hand, anti-globalists point out the issue of rising inequality aided by corporate-driven globalization, yet on the other, de-globalists suggest both replacing corporate-driven globalization as well as redistribution of resources in order to provide global justice. Globalization, an irreversible process, needs better management. Turning to the changing dimension of twentieth century populism next, we get exposed to the brewing frustrations toward globalization.

Unfolding Populism

Putting "people" at the center has been at the heart of primarily liberal projects. The process of state- and nation-building brought forward the idea of popular emancipation unambiguously. Ensuring political enfranchisement and making people's voices heard was never given more priority in any other century than the twentieth. In *The Age of Extremes*, Eric Hobsbawm noted how the Century had seen unprecedented violence throughout the globe until geopolitical settlements were established.[27] We have seen a number of populist revolts during this period too—in North and South America, Asia, and Europe. The nature of populism, as this chapter argues, during the twentieth century revolved around challenging political authorities and elites. As discussed in the first section, the definition of populism—which stresses the rise of the "little people" and challenges the elites—generally challenged the political elites and political establishments. This was also directly related to challenging existing power in a given country. However, the idea of "leave it to the expert" became a generally recognized adage not typically challenged by populist leaders. However, this does not mean that scholars and experts went unchallenged previously.

Identifying the major characteristics of populism in the twentieth century, this particular discussion puts into perspective the changing local characteristics of twenty-first century populism, challenging globalization (discussed in the principal substantive next section). In other words, local troubles and inability to address crises prudently transformed the rise of the "little people" into the "populist publics" in a manner to increasingly promote xenophobic and inward-looking mindsets, instead of *only* challenging political structures. The unfolding of the COVID pandemic reality and states clamoring to create their own production houses and buying their own products, both elaborated later, demonstrate these de-globalization trends. In a rush to protect one's own economy, states tend to overlook the nature of tightly knitted chains of connections and globalization. In this process, they often misused or misinterpreted data and presented them as such to the masses in order to garner support. Although data misuse by political leaders is certainly not new—as the 2003 U.S. invasion of Iraq exemplified—however, it has become a part and parcel of twenty-first century populist leadership and "populist publics" to deny and misconstrue facts and data. This provides leaders their daily "bread and butter" to survive politically and to satisfy their fan-base. However, what we have not generally seen previously is the rise of the people who have taken up the lead to challenge the elites without the purposive motive of direct political shifts. Patterns of twentieth century populism and its strategies in Latin America, the United States and in Europe, in that order, help us understand the difference between "populist public" and populism.

Latin America has experienced three waves of populism since the 1920s, creating two separate yet formidable poles in stark contrast to each other—people versus the self-serving elites. The predominant nature of Latin American populism used to be directed toward "*desoligarquización*" (de-oligarchization).[28] Having its roots in the era of Great Depression,[29] Latin American populism later centered around challenging state-led industrialization, rising debt pressure, among others. While these have been significant characteristics of the first two waves of populism, the latest wave—often termed as *neo-populism*—draws significant attention to understand Latin American political contexts. However, some argue that terminological differences between "neo-populism" and "populism" may be arguably insignificant, with the former representing the more contemporary forms of emergent Latin populism emerged in Latin America since the decade of 1990s and populism to postwar trends.[30] On the contrary, the expression "neo-populism" became popular in the Latin American context as populism has been generally linked with popular dissatisfaction toward broader economic performances of governments, while the wave of "neo-populism" suggests popular leaders targeting the unorganized poor, who served as their base voters.[31] In other words, "neo-populism" has been anti-organizational in nature. This particular trait has been reinforced in the third wave when political leaders became successful in garnering mass support targeting neoliberal policies being the root of socio-economic distress of people.[32] Carlos de la Torre, for example, reminds us how Hugo Chavez perceived his role when he declared, "I demand absolute loyalty to me. I am not an individual, I am the people".[33] Populism in Latin America, thus held the usual characteristics of being anti-neoliberal, anti-establishment, offering expansionary economic policies and holding "a base of support centered on the underprivileged and poor".[34]

The comprehensive way of defining populism often catches the political appeal of populist leaders as well—when, in the U.S. context, Republican leaders learned how to "turn the language of working-class majoritarianism against liberalism"[35] in the late 1960s. However, the history of

U.S. populism began in the previous century with *The Know Nothings* (1849–1860), *The Greenback Party* (1874–1884), and *The Populist Party* (1892–1908).[36] In the twentieth century, a number of political figures found their legitimacy in populist appeals. U.S. historians have used different explanations to delve into the rise of populism in different parts of the country. John D. Hicks explained the origin of populism to downtrodden economic condition of the farmers in the Western and Southern provinces in the United States and termed it as a "frontier movement" in 1930s.[37] In another influential study, Richard Hofstadter provided a "revisionist historical perspective", in which both nostalgia for past-dominated political actions and reactions to U.S. capitalism made corruption and dishonesty key components.[38] Populism, thus, was identified as a "progressive reform movement".[39] Still, another school of thought identified populism as a regressive movement using racial and ethnic hostilities to create divide people. Political division played in Mississippi during the Depression-era illustrated this.[40]

It was not only the rightist politicians who were seen cuddling with populist appeal.[41] Scholars have argued that U.S. populism certainly always carried negativism—rather populism was used by a number of progressive politicians to further their cause. In fact, it has often been argued in this century that President Barack Obama rode a populist wave as well in 2008:

> The American Dream [sic] is slipping away…instead of enforcing rules of the road, Washington has turned a blind eye to abusive practices like fraudulent lending, and we've seen a symbol of the American Dream, the American home, turned into a source of insecurity for millions of families.[42]

While there are some debates on whether Obama was a populist leader or not, it is often argued that he turned into a "reluctant populist" since mid-2011 owing to a number of domestic compulsions.[43] For U.S. politics, one interesting shift seemed to have taken place in the second twenty-first century decade, when a survey revealed how more than half of white U.S. citizens believed that "whites have replaced blacks as the 'primary victims of discrimination'".[44] This shifted political choices and led to the rise of another round of populism in U.S. politics, represented primarily by Donald Trump. The nature of Trumpian populism is discussed below.

European populism has interesting twists and turns. For once, the origin of populism in its ancient and modern forms took place in Europe, as discussed earlier in this chapter. For another, when we talk about European politics, there is a general fallacy to explain it as an integrated geographic whole, disregarding diversity across the continent. Populism in Western Europe and Eastern Europe differs in many ways, often ignored in popular media by identifying, for example, the rise of the far right as "European" in nature. In other words, the general fallacy is to consider populism in the European context synonymously with right-wing populism.[45] In essence, as we shall see, different parts of Europe gave birth to different types of populism, which cannot be boxed within one type. As in the case of Latin America, Western Europe too experienced the wave of populism just after the First World War. It became easier for political leaders to work on the frustrations of people, which helped them to garner popular support easily and rally around fascism and Nazism. Radical right-wing nationalism in fact existed in France in the pre-First World era.[46] Disenchantment with the established political parties in Western Europe led to the rise of left-wing populism in the 1970s and 80s. The reasons for this are often contested—however, authors have argued how the loss of trust on established political parties led to exploring new possibilities by European voters, in turn promoting left-wing populism and green politics.[47]

Eastern Europe saw its fair share of populism as well. Here the Cold War politics and centralist system did not allow popular movements to flourish until after the fall of the Berlin Wall. Unbridled corruption and the failure to provide economic benefits of the post-Communist regimes diminished trust in established political parties in many East European countries.[48] Regional populist parties in this region have been both centrist and radical in nature, playing on their strengths and suiting the particular cases,[49] and have organized under the banners of "nationalism, an anti-immigration platform, and (soft) Euroscepticism to their agenda, thus creating a winning formula…" in the region.[50]

Having discussed three regions to identify the general characteristics of populism and identifying how patterns of populism vary in them, we notice how the fundamentals proposed by Maudde and Kaltwasser reverberated throughout the populist movements. African and Asian populism also remain essentially anti-establishment. In other words, no matter what the associated ideologies proposed by populists, discursive practices belie similar tactics—inciting popular anti-elite opinion. While populism often arose, particularly in latter decades of the past century as a reaction to globalization and *neo-liberalism*, populist parties and popular support did not directly attack globalization per se. Instead, the countries adjusted internally against globalizing *neoliberal* forces. This is what differentiates populism of the twentieth century and the populism of today, a discussion extended to the next section.

Populist De-globalization? A Fresh Analysis on How Populism Operates Today

Here the principal debates between localization and globalization, and the manners by which populists succeeded in different parts of the world demand attention. The previous discussions point out how globalization was seen as a threat to local culture and identity which populist leaders capitalized upon. The response to such factors of globalizations was met by enhancing national symbols and adjusting economic policies. However, it is widely understood how no option to closing the door on each other prevails—that is, globalization is here to stay. Countries must play to their strengths to provide better opportunities and protections to their people. The nature of contemporary populism differs because political parties manipulate the mass and technological globalization created a "populist public". The result: a different type of populist chaos. While Webb and Curato, who explain the rise of Filipino populism, first introduced this idea, the essence they emphasized most—debunking the myth populists generally ride upon to attract the poor, was not the case in the country.[51] This study finds the concept referring to not only Webb and Curato's descriptions, but also to refer to the power of social media and how it has strangely empowered a "regular" person to challenge established norms, principles as well as science. That is, while globalization has led to redefining and often also reawakening of a national identity, globalization has also created a "populist public" all around the world, especially in countries with greater digital access to create mass opinion on issues that may not have much validity in terms of scientific rigor. Local choices directly threatening globalization in primarily two cycles: globalization of technology enabling masses of people to get easy access to "information"; and in turn, empowering the masses and their leaders to present information in a manner that challenges globalization.

One might, in this context, refer to the popular "Arab Spring" in this century, a movement not relying upon on traditional political party-based supports or organization of the masses. It was pluralistic in nature,[52] against the power of one man to whom revolution throughout the Arab World and North-east Africa may be ascribed. It shook the elites and toppled one government after the other. It was the first time when the youth met with the masses, and it exposed the unprecedented power of social media. Often leaderless, the popular uprisings were able to change the course of history through the first massive populist uprising in this century. Perhaps this was populism, in the sense of the rise of the "little people"; but I argue how it was the first "populist public", or better categorized as "progressive populist publics". However, analysis on the power of the "populist public" has remained overlooked in understanding the new populism paradigm.

Modernity and the rise of people's power—or more precisely, the rise of individual human beings and their role in the making of a polity has been of much analysis. In fact, one byproduct of modernity, as predicted by scholars at the turn of twentieth century, was the rise of individualism and emancipation leading human beings to consider themselves free from structural bonding. In praise of the communist system in which *homo sapiens* would once again create their future together, Leon Trotsky, argued, "[T]he average human type will rise to the heights of an Aristotle, a Goethe, or a Marx. And above this ridge new peaks will rise".[53] While he argued this would be how a communist system would transform people, it is rather the technology and digital revolution to have turned an average human being into an Aristotle or a Goethe or a Marx. In other words, the rise of social media and easy access to *Internet* have reduced the knowledge-gap throughout the world. Information is easily available sitting either in Timbuktu or Rajshahi. Thus, a very significant dimension of the "populist public" can be seen in the rise of people's opinion on social media on issues beyond their pedigree affecting politics and the social fabric. The easy access to technology literally created this situation in which information is easily gathered—that provides a sense of emancipation for the populist public as know-it-all. Similarly, not only is it difficult to fact-check on information, but by the time this fact-checking is done, it also becomes viral. The general logic of "where there is a smoke, there must be a fire" is what gains currency in such a situation. Bangladesh has seen a number of riots which were incited by fabricated *Facebook* posts. These "populist publics" have emerged as a powerful medium of swaying public opinion against established truths and facts, most evident during the COVID pandemic when a number of false *Facebook* posts suggested unverified methods of getting cured from the virus or slowing down its effect, which proved to be false. However, from a scholarly point of view, there has been very little, if any, systematic study done on the rise and pattern of operation of "populist publics" in different countries. This is a new area of research that needs to be expanded to understand the strength, weaknesses, and the manners of operations of these populist public.

Not only via social media, but the "populist public" has taken to the streets to challenge scientific data-based instructions to follow during the COVID pandemic. In the United States, protests against lockdown began from mid-April 2020. Almost in half of all U.S. states, people protested against stay-at-home orders put forward by authorities. The logic provided by the protestors was that the number of cases were different in different states, which required not the same order throughout the United States.[54] Particularly in the state of Michigan, armed protesters entering the Capitol building were known as "the 'American Patriot Rally', and organized by *Michigan United for Liberty*".[55] These "populist publics" were chided by the President Donald Trump himself, who time to time provided unscientific and dangerous medical advice during his press briefings,[56] which he denied later,[57] and led authorities to issue warnings not to try.[58] In fact, since his unsolicited advice, reports surfaced on the number of cases in which people injected themselves using bleach.[59] It is significant in this context to understand the rise of Trump and both the populist public and Trump actively empower each other to sustain.

Trump's rise to power itself banked on the "collective anxieties"[60] of the white U.S. citizens on a number of issues. Scholars have pointed out that this also signifies a shift in U.S. core values—from WASP (White Anglo-Saxon Protestants) to *Whiteshift*.[61] The idea of *Whiteshift* is a result of a *gesalt psychology* in which whites perceive themselves as an integrated whole and respond to the declining number of whites in Western countries. Fareed Zakaria points out, "[I]mmigration is the final frontier of globalization"—which denotes the countries which have not been able to address emerging political and cultural questions due to increasing immigration, a byproduct of globalization—have experienced a rise in right-wing reactions.[62] He argues, Canada, in this respect has been successful. Thus, globalization is seen as one of the conspicuous elements causing worldwide restlessness among the whites,[63] who increasingly perceive themselves being threatened by immigrants—be that posing economic challenges (e.g., in the case of the United States) or cultural challenges (e.g., in the case of France)—although the examples of each category are not exhaustive in nature. It produced Trump in the United States with his *America First* policy, which he acknowledged in his inaugural January 20, 2017 speech:

> We, the citizens of America [sic], are now joined in a great national effort to rebuild our country and to restore its promise for all of our people...today we are not merely transferring power from one Administration to another, or from one party to another – but we are transferring power from Washington, D.C. and giving it back to you, the American People....[64]

A number of scholarly debates exist to explain the rise of Trump and unsettling the established order—whether this was an artful mastering of the media and the support of Rupert Murdoch (and consequently winning over the conservative *Fox* channel), or grievances against neoliberal economic order or the effect of globalization. On the other hand, rightist politics rose in Western Europe as well—in France, Hungary, the Netherlands, and Sweden, to name a few. The Hungarian Prime Minister's statement—"because Europe and European identity is rooted in Christianity"[65]—by securitizing both Muslims and migrants in the same box during the 2015 Syrian refugee crisis, once again unfolded the alt-right range in European political landscape.[66]

The rise of the right in Western Europe and in the United States is backed by the consolidation of democracy. In other words, it is the exercise of the democratic right of the "little people", as well as by the "populist public" who perceive their "identity" to be threatened by the influx of the "others" and their rights being denied by experts. In such a case, they chose the party or the person promising to take them back to the past—a past which seemed to have been the repository of "good", "unspoiled" and "authentic" version of "us". The ideology of populism thus promises to recreate the past—an illusion for which people will sacrifice the present, with democracy being the way to achieve this. Thus, Trump does not hesitate to chide in that he might stay on power indefinitely if "people" so want. He first hinted this sarcastically after China's President Xi Jinping consolidated his stay on power indefinitely, which earned him the title of "Dictator-Lover in Chief".[67] The 22nd Amendment of the U.S. Constitution puts a term limit for eight years per person to hold the highest office in the United States. Researchers show that Trump continued to promote this idea till date, which led to a concern in the United States regarding Trump's goodwill in transferring power and respecting democratic norms when it was required to do so.[68] Gradually, to feed into this populist publics, President Trump proclaimed several Executive Orders calling for employment of U.S. citizens, first by imposing bans on H-1B, L-1, H-2B, and J-1 entry beginning June 24, 2020.[69] Also, the president instructed to hiring federal workers on the basis of skills, not educational qualifications.[70] We can see a pattern forming here—"populist publics" feeding into the populist leader, who, in turn, takes measures to satisfy the former's appetite. Thus, a full circle is formed.

Bangladesh, a country not associated with popular uprisings in a populist manner, saw this interesting trend of "populist publics" as the COVID pandemic began. People, out of their own volition, formed their own opinions regarding dangers emanating from foreign returnees of Bangladesh origin as potential carriers of the virus. A gross stigmatization of foreign returnees as well as COVID-19 infected patients spread, some of whom were also attacked by mobs.[71] While one might argue if this can be cited as an example of "populist publics" working in tandem—but while we compare the patterns and trends of these cases, we can discern certain similarities. While mob violence is nothing new in Bangladesh, issue-specific organized and targeted violence at the same time in different parts of the country certainly indicates the rise of "populist publics". Once again, this is aided by the rising digital connectivity.

The concept of "populist publics" is yet to be fully developed and analyzed. We have only seen its rise so far in the United States, to some extent in other parts of the world. Despite that, it is quite evident that while populist leaders in the previous century exploited neoliberal economic system and globalization as a cause for "little people's" misery and banking on that, rode to power, they still found globalization to be beneficiary. Their economic policies would not mean to disengage with the rest of the world. In the changed circumstances of economic conditions already negatively impacted due to the virtual closure of economies around the world, these populist publics and their leaders rather launched attacks on globalization. While the world needs to formulate an improved strategy of connecting with each other in light of the COVID pandemic and the way it stalled national economies, this is perhaps the biggest threat to the degree and processes of globalization, where populist publics are playing a direct role. If the world's biggest economy plans to pursue reclusive policies, this will affect the global economy in a scale that has not been seen before.

Conclusion

In exploring development within populism, one stark conclusion is how populism is not a new concept in itself. It is often not considered a full-fledged ideology since it expresses itself by clutching to other ideologies. In other words, populism often means to achieve an end. The basic core of populism involves being anti-establishment and the rise of the "little people". In this piece, I pointed out that while these stand as the minimum core of populism, in the twenty-first century, we can see a new expression of populist power through the "populist publics", a group not necessarily poor and impoverished "little people" being exploited by populist leaders. Instead, they can belong to all walks of life, and who generally organize themselves taking advantage of globalization of technology and operating on social media platforms. Thus, they also feed into the plans of populist leaders and create an unseen relationship of give and take. While previously "little people" did not have direct agency, since the Arab Spring, we have seen that these group can create agencies of their own. Rather than being at the mercy of creating agenda; as before, they have the capacity to provide agenda for populist leaders. In other words, instead of "little people's" dependency on populist leaders to be organized, here "populist publics" emerge as equal rule-maker, challenging the establishment. The new kind of populism in the twenty-first century shows that populism now is a two-way traffic between the populist publics and their leaders instead of this being a hierarchical relationship between the populist leaders and the "little people". While German Chancellor Angela Merkel hopes that the pandemic shows populist leaders' fact-denying appeals would diminish,[72] due to the changing nature of populism, this may add a new dimension to populism. Interestingly, while globalization of culture and technology paves the way for the emergence of this new type of polity, the local groups of "populist publics" find globalization a threat to their survival. Thus, populist publics tend to threaten globalization by being inclusionary in nature.

Notes

1. This is interchangeably used as COVID-19 or COVID pandemic throughout the chapter.
2. Guido Zernatto, "Nation: The History of a Word," *The Review of Politics* 6, no. 3 (July 1944): 351–366.
3. Helena Rosenblatt, *The Lost History of Liberalism: From Ancient Rome to the Twenty-first Century* (Princeton, NJ: Princeton University Press, 2018).
4. Duncan Bell, "What Is Liberalism," *Political Theory* 42, no. 6 (2014): 682–715.
5. Roy C. Macridis and Mark Hulliung, *Contemporary Political Ideologies* (Pearson, 1997, 6th ed).
6. James D. Ingram, "Populism and Cosmopolitanism," *The Oxford Handbook of Populism*, eds. Cristóbal Rovira Kaltwasser, Paul Taggart, Paulina Ochoa Espejo, and Pierre Ostiguy (New York, NY: Oxford University Press, 2017).
7. Ibid.
8. Benjamin Moffitt, *The Global Rise of Populism: Performance, Political Style, and Representation* (Stanford, CA: Stanford University Press, 2016).
9. Jan-Werner Müller, *What Is Populism?* (College Park, PA: Pennsylvania University Press, 2016).
10. David McKnight, *Populism Now: The Case for Progressive Populism* (New South Wales: New South Publishing, 2018).
11. Robert R. Barr, *The Resurgence of Populism in Latin America* (Boulder, CO: Lynne Rienner Publishers, Inc, 2017).
12. Anne Munro-Kua, *Authoritarian Populism in Malaysia* (New York: MacMillan Press, LTD & St. Martin's Place, Inc., 1996).
13. Cas Mudde and Cristóbal Rovira Kaltwasser, *Populism: A Very Short Introduction* (New York: Oxford University Press, 2017).
14. Ghita Ionescu, and Ernest Gellner, *Populism: Its Meaning and National Characteristics* (Oakland, CA: University of California Press, 1969), 4.
15. Ibid., 6—emphasis original.
16. Adele Webb and Nicole Curato, "Populism in the Philippines," *Populism Around the World: A Comparative Perspective*, ed. Daniel Stockemer (Cham: Springer, 2019), 49–66.
17. Ibid., 60.

18. Martin van Creveld, *The Rise and Decline of the State* (Cambridge, UK: Cambridge University Press, 1999).
19. Peter Dizikes, "When the Butterfly Effect Took Flight," *MIT News Magazine*, February 22, 2011, https://www.technologyreview.com/2011/02/22/196987/when-the-butterfly-effect-took-flight/, accessed June 18, 2020.
20. Gen. Stanley McChrystal, Tantum Collins, David Silverman, and Chris Summell, *Team of Teams: New Rules of Engagement for a Complex World* (New York: Penguin, 2015), 49.
21. Voltaire Cang, "Policing *Washoku*: The Performance of Culinary Nationalism in Japan," *Food and Foodways* (2019), https://doi.org/10.1080/07409710.2019.1646473.
22. Peter N. Stearns, *Western Civilization in World History* (New York: Routledge, 2003), 128.
23. Adam Warner, "A Brief History of the Anti-Globalization Movement," *The University of Miami International and Comparative Law Review* 12, no. 237 (2005): 241, http://repository.law.miami.edu/umiclr/vol12/iss2/2, accessed April 19, 2016.
24. Walden Bello, *Deglobalization: Ideas for a New World Economy* (New York: Zed Books, 2009).
25. "The Economist Says Focus Coined 'Deglobalization'," *Focus in the News*, February 26, 2009, https://focusweb.org/the-economist-says-focus-coined-deglobalization/, accessed June 18, 2020.
26. Walden Bello, *Capitalism's Last Stand? Deglobalization in the Age of Austerity* (New York: ZED Books, 2013).
27. Eric J. Hobsbawm, *The Age of Extremes: The Short Twentieth Century, 1914–1991* (New York: Vintage, 1996).
28. Ignacio Walker, "The Three Lefts of Latin America," *Dissent* (Fall 2008), https://www.dissentmagazine.org/article/the-three-lefts-of-latin-america, accessed June 13, 2020.
29. Alan Knight, "Populism and Neo-Populism in Latin America, Especially Mexico," *Journal of Latin American Studies* 30, no. 2 (May 1998): 223–248.
30. Francisco Panizza, "Neopopulism and Its Limits in Collor's Brazil," *Bulletin of Latin American Research* 19, no. 2, Special Issue: Old and New Populism in Latin America (April 2000): 177–192.

31. Kurt Weyland, "Neopopulism and Neoliberalism in Latin America: How Much Affinity?" *Third World Quarterly* 24, no. 6 (December 2003): 1095–1115.
32. Robert R. Barr, *The Resurgence of Populism in Latin America* (Boulder, CO: Lynne Rienner, 2017), 15.
33. Carlos de la Torre, "Populism and Democracy: Lessons from Latin America," *Journal of Democracy* 2 (2018): 40.
34. Robert R. Barr, *The Resurgence of Populism in Latin America* (Boulder, CO: Lynne Rienner, 2017), 17.
35. Thomas Frank, "Forget Trump—Populism Is the Cure, Not the Disease," *The Guardian*, May 23, 2018, https://www.theguardian.com/books/2018/may/23/thomas-frank-trump-populism-books, accessed March 22, 2019.
36. *Populism in the United States: A Timeline* (2019), history.com, https://www.history.com/topics/us-politics/populism-united-states-timeline, accessed June 19, 2020.
37. James Turner, "Understanding the Populists," *The Journal of American History* 67, no. 2 (September 1980): 354–373.
38. J. F. Conway, "Populism in the United States, Russia, and Canada: Explaining the Roots of Canada's Third Parties," *Canadian Journal of Political Science / Revue canadienne de science politique* 11, no. 1 (March 1978): 99–124.
39. Ibid., 104.
40. Erik J. Engstrom and Robert Huckfeldt, *Race, Class, and Social Welfare: American Populism Since the New Deal* (Cambridge, UK: Cambridge University Press, 2020), 163.
41. Bart Bonikowski, "Three Lessons of Contemporary Populism in Europe and the United States," *Brown Journal of World Affairs* xxiii, no. i (Fall/Winter 2016): 9–24.
42. Michael Powell, "Obama, the Populist," *The New York Times*, April 1, 2008, https://thecaucus.blogs.nytimes.com/2008/04/01/obama-the-populist/, accessed March 22, 2019.
43. Glenn Thrush, "Obama the Reluctant Populist," *Politico*, January 25, 2012, https://www.politico.com/story/2012/01/obama-the-reluctant-populist-071933, accessed March 22, 2019.
44. Amy Chua, "Tribal World: Group Identity Is All," *Foreign Affairs* 97, no. 4 (July–August 2018): 30.
45. Yannis Stavrakakis, Giorgos Katsambekis, Nikos Nikisianis, Alexandros Kioupkiolis, and Thomas Siomos, "Extreme Right-Wing

Populism in Europe: Revisiting a Reified Association," *Critical Discourse Studies* (2017), https://doi.org/10.1080/17405904.2017.1309325.
46. John Abromeit, "Transformations of Procedurist Populism in Europe," *Transformations of Populism in Europe and the Americas: History and Recent Tendencies*, eds. John Abromeit, Bridget María Chesterton, Gary Marotta, and York Norman (London: Bloomsbury, 2017), 234.
47. Daniel Stockemer, "Introduction," *Populism Around the World: A Comparative Perspective*, ed. Daniel Stockemer (Cham: Springer, 2019), 5; Erik Jones, "Populism in Europe: What Scholarship Tells Us," *Survival: Global Politics and Strategy* 61, no. 4 (August–September 2019): 7–30, IISS, https://www.iiss.org/publicati ons/survival/2019/survival-global-politics-and-strategy-augustsep tember-2019/614-02-jones, accessed June 19, 2020.
48. Marko Mustapic, Ivan Balabanic, and Mateja Plenkovic, "Political News Coverage of the 2015 Election Campaign in Croatia: Populism and Media," *Mediated Campaigns, and Populism in Europe*, ed. Susana Salgado (Cham: Palgrave Macmillan, 2019); Yann Algan, Sergei Guriev, Elias Papaioannou, and Evgenia Passari, "The European Trust Crisis and the Tise of Populism," *Brookings Papers on Economic Activity* (Fall 2017), 309–382.
49. Ben Stanley, "Populism in Central and Eastern Europe," *The Oxford Handbook of Populism*, eds. Cristóbal Rovira Kaltwasser, Paul Taggart, Paulina Ochoa Espejo, and Pierre Ostiguy (New York: OUP, 2017).
50. Daniel Stockemer, "Introduction," *Populism Around the World: A Comparative Perspective*, ed. Daniel Stockemer (Cham: Springer, 2019), 4.
51. Webb and Curato (2019), op. cit.
52. Asef Bayat, "A New Arab Street in Post-Islamist Times," Foreignpolicy.com, January 26, 2011, http://foreignpolicy.com/2011/01/26/a-new-arab-street-in-post-islamist-times, accessed November 9, 2013.
53. Leon Trotsky, *Literature and Revolution* (London: Kindle Edition, 1924), 172. CITY OF PUBLICATION?
54. Zack Budryk, "Governors, Experts Await Results of Reopening States as Protests Continue," *The Hill*, May 3, 2020, https://thehill.com/homenews/sunday-talk-shows/495877-governors-

experts-await-results-of-reopening-states-as-protests, accessed June 21, 2020.
55. "Coronavirus: Armed Protesters Enter Michigan Statehouse," *BBC*, 2020, https://www.bbc.com/news/world-us-canada-524 96514, accessed June 21, 2020.
56. "Trump Suggests Injecting Disinfectant to Treat Coronavirus," *Al Jazeera*, 2020, https://www.aljazeera.com/programmes/new sfeed/2020/04/trump-suggests-injecting-disinfectant-treat-cor onavirus-200427124512820.html, accessed June 21, 2020.
57. "Coronavirus: Trump Says Disinfectant, Bleach and Ultra-Violet Light Comments Were 'Sarcastic'," *DW.com*, 2020, https://www.dw.com/en/coronavirus-trump-says-disinfectant-bleach-and-ultra-violet-light-comments-were-sarcastic/a-53227468, accessed June 21, 2020.
58. Kristen V. Brown and Justin Sink, "Trump's Comment on Disinfectant Prompts Experts to Warn Against Inhaling Bleach to Kill Coronavirus," *Time*, April 24, 2020, https://time.com/582 6882/coronavirus-trump-heat-bleach/, accessed June 21, 2020.
59. "New York City Sees Increase in Cases of People Ingesting Household Cleaners After Trump's Disinfectant Gaffe," *Strait Times*, April 26, 2020, https://www.straitstimes.com/world/united-sta tes/new-york-city-sees-increase-of-cases-people-ingesting-househ old-cleaners-after, accessed June 21, 2020.
60. Daniel Béland, "Donald Trump's Populism Preys Upon Collective Anxieties," *The Conversation*, November 29, 2018, https:// theconversation.com/donald-trumps-populism-preys-upon-collec tive-anxieties-107559, accessed March 22, 2019.
61. Eric Kaufmann, *Whiteshift: Populism, Immigration and the Future of White Majorities* (Allen Lane, 2018).
62. FareedZakaria, "Populism on the March: Why the West Is in Trouble," *Foreign Affairs* 95, no. 6 (November/December 2016): 9–16.
63. Michael Cox, "The Rise of Populism and the Crisis of Globalisation: Brexit, Trump and Beyond," *Irish Studies in International Affairs* 28 (2017): 9–17.
64. "The Inaugural Address," *The White House*, January 20, 2016, https://www.whitehouse.gov/briefings-statements/the-ina ugural-address/, accessed March 23, 2019. LIKELY JANUARY 20, 2017, NOT 2016.

65. Ian Traynor, "Migration Crisis: Hungary PM Says Europe in Grip of Madness," *The Guardian*, September 3, 2015, https://www.theguardian.com/world/2015/sep/03/migration-crisis-hungary-pm-victor-orban-europe-response-madness, accessed March 24, 2019.
66. "Hungarian PM: We Don't Want More Muslims," *Al Jazeera*, September 3, 2015, https://www.aljazeera.com/.../refugees-hungary-train-station-150903064140564.html, accessed March 24, 2019.
67. Chas Danner, "Trump Jokes About Staying in Power Indefinitely," *Intelligencer*, *New Yorker Magazine*, March 4, 2018, https://nymag.com/intelligencer/2018/03/trump-jokes-about-staying-in-power-indefinitely.html, accessed June 21, 2020.
68. Peter Nicholas, "Trump Could Still Break Democracy's Biggest Norm," *The Atlantic*, June 16, 2020, https://www.theatlantic.com/politics/archive/2020/06/when-does-trump-leave-whitehouse/613060/, accessed January 21, 2020; Barbara McQuade, "What Would Happen If Trump Refused to Leave Office?" *The Atlantic*, February 22, 2020, https://www.theatlantic.com/ideas/archive/2020/02/what-if-he-wont-go/606259/, accessed January 21, 2020.
69. "Proclamation Suspending Entry of Aliens Who Present a Risk to the U.S. Labor Market Following the Coronavirus Outbreak," *The White House*, June 22, 2020, https://www.whitehouse.gov/presidential-actions/proclamation-suspending-entry-aliens-present-risk-u-s-labor-market-following-coronavirus-outbreak/, accessed June 30, 2020.
70. Michael Collins, "Trump Signs Order Prioritizing Job Skills Over College Degree in Government Hiring," *USA TODAY*, June 26, 2020, https://www.usatoday.com/story/news/politics/2020/06/26/trump-executive-order-stresses-skill-over-college-degree-hiring/3263074001/, accessed June 30, 2020.
71. Zobaida Nasreen and Gopa Biswas Caesar, "Corona-Shaming Exposes the Fault Lines of Our Society," *The Daily Star*, April 3, 2020; "Unnecessary Panic Will Hinder Efforts to Prevent COVID-19, IEDCR Says," *The Financial Express*, February 22, 2020, https://thefinancialexpress.com.bd/national/unnecessary-panic-will-hinder-efforts-to-prevent-covid-19-1582374490, accessed June 30, 2020.

72. "Covid-19 Has Exposed the Limits of 'Fact-Denying Populism'," Merkel Tells European Parliament, July 8, 2020, https://www.france24.com/en/20200708-covid-19-has-exposed-the-limits-of-fact-denying-populism-merkel-tells-european-parliament, accessed July 13, 2020.

Bibliography

Abromeit, John. 2017. "Transformations of Procedurist Populism in Europe." John Abromeit, Bridget María Chesterton, Gary Marotta, and York Norman, eds., *Transformations of Populism in Europe and the Americas: History and Recent Tendencies*. London: Bloomsbury.
Algan, Yann, Sergei Guriev, Elias Papaioannou, and Evgenia Passari. 2017. "The European Trust Crisis and the Rise of Populism." *Brookings Papers on Economic Activity* (Fall).
Al Jazeera. 2015. "Hungarian PM: We Don't Want More Muslims." September 3. https://www.aljazeera.com/.../refugees-hungary-train-station-150903064140564.html. Accessed on March 24, 2019.
———. 2020. "Trump Suggests Injecting Disinfectant to Treat Coronavirus." https://www.aljazeera.com/programmes/newsfeed/2020/04/trump-suggests-injecting-disinfectant-treat-coronavirus-200427124512820.html. Accessed on June 21, 2020.
Barr, Robert R. 2017. *The Resurgence of Populism in Latin America*. Boulder, CO: Lynne Rienner Publishers, Inc.
Bayat, Asef. 2011. "A New Arab Street in Post-Islamist Times." *Foreign Policy*, January 26. http://foreignpolicy.com/2011/01/26/a-new-arab-street-in-post-islamist-times. Accessed on November 9, 2013.
BBC. 2020. "Coronavirus: Armed Protesters Enter Michigan Statehouse." https://www.bbc.com/news/world-us-canada-52496514. Accessed on June 21, 2020.
Béland, Daniel. 2018. "Donald Trump's Populism Preys Upon Collective Anxieties." *The Conversation*, November 29. https://theconversation.com/donald-trumps-populism-preys-upon-collective-anxieties-107559. Accessed on March 22, 2019.
Bell, Duncan. 2014. "What Is Liberalism?" *Political Theory* 42: 6.
Bello, Walden. 2009. *Deglobalization: Ideas for a New World Economy*. New York: Zed Books.
———. 2013. *Capitalism's Last Stand? Deglobalization in the Age of Austerity*. New York: ZED Books.

Bonikowski, Bart. 2016. "Three Lessons of Contemporary Populism in Europe and the United States." *Brown Journal of World Affairs* XXIII, no. 1 (Fall/Winter).

Brown, Kristen V., and Justin Sink. 2020. "Trump's Comment on Disinfectant Prompts Experts to Warn Against Inhaling Bleach to Kill Coronavirus." *Time*, April 24. https://time.com/5826882/coronavirus-trump-heat-bleach/. Accessed on June 21, 2020.

Budryk, Zack. 2020. "Governors, Experts Await Results of Reopening States as Protests Continue." *The Hill*, May 3. https://thehill.com/homenews/sunday-talk-shows/495877-governors-experts-await-results-of-reopening-states-as-protests. Accessed on June 21, 2020.

Cang, Voltaire. 2019. "Policing *Washoku*: The Performance of Culinary Nationalism in Japan." *Food and Foodways*. https://doi.org/10.1080/07409710.2019.1646473.

Chua, Amy. 2018. "Tribal World: Group Identity Is All." *Foreign Affairs* 97, no. 4 (July–August).

Collins, Michael. 2020. "Trump Signs Order Prioritizing Job Skills Over College Degree in Government Hiring." *USA TODAY*, June 26. https://www.usatoday.com/story/news/politics/2020/06/26/trump-executive-order-stresses-skill-over-college-degree-hiring/3263074001/. Accessed on June 30, 2020.

Conway, J. F. 1978. "Populism in the United States, Russia, and Canada: Explaining the Roots of Canada's Third Parties." *Canadian Journal of Political Science / Revue canadienne de science politique* 11, no. 1 (March).

Cox, Michael. 2017. "The Rise of Populism and the Crisis of Globalisation: Brexit, Trump and Beyond." *Irish Studies in International Affairs* 28: 9–17.

Creveld, Martin van. 1999. *The Rise and Decline of the State*. Cambridge, UK: Cambridge University Press.

Danner, Chas. 2018. "Trump Jokes About Staying in Power Indefinitely." *Intelligencer, New Yorker Magazine*, March 4. https://nymag.com/intelligencer/2018/03/trump-jokes-about-staying-in-power-indefinitely.html. Accessed on June 21, 2020.

Dizikes, Peter. 2011. "When the Butterfly Effect Took Flight." *MIT News Magazine*, February 22. https://www.technologyreview.com/2011/02/22/196987/when-the-butterfly-effect-took-flight/. Accessed on June 18, 2020.

DW.com. 2020. "Coronavirus: Trump Says Disinfectant, Bleach and Ultra-Violet Light Comments Were 'Sarcastic'." https://www.dw.com/en/coronavirus-trump-says-disinfectant-bleach-and-ultra-violet-light-comments-were-sarcastic/a-53227468. Accessed on June 21, 2020.

Engstrom, Erik J., and Robert Huckfeldt. 2020. *Race, Class, and Social Welfare: American Populism Since the New Deal*. Cambridge, UK: Cambridge University Press.

Focus in the News. 2009. "The Economist Says Focus Coined 'Deglobalization'." February 26. https://focusweb.org/the-economist-says-focus-coined-deglobalization/. Accessed on June 18, 2020.
France 24. 2020. "Covid-19 Has Exposed the Limits of 'Fact-Denying Populism'." Merkel Tells European Parliament, July 8. https://www.france24.com/en/20200708-covid-19-has-exposed-the-limits-of-fact-denying-populism-merkel-tells-european-parliament. Accessed on July 13, 2020.
Frank, Thomas. 2018. "Forget Trump—Populism Is the Cure, Not the Disease." *The Guardian*, May 23. https://www.theguardian.com/books/2018/may/23/thomas-frank-trump-populism-books. Accessed on March 22, 2019.
Hobsbawm, Eric J. 1996. *The Age of Extremes: The Short Twentieth Century, 1914-1991*. New York: Vintage.
Ingram, James D. 2017. "Populism and Cosmopolitanism." Cristóbal Rovira Kaltwasser, Paul Taggart, Paulina Ochoa Espejo, and Pierre Ostiguy, eds., *The Oxford Handbook of Populism*. New York, NY: Oxford University Press.
Ionescu, Ghita, and Ernest Gellner. 1969. *Populism: Its Meaning and National Characteristics*. Oakland, CA: University of California Press.
Jones, Erik. 2019. "Populism in Europe: What Scholarship Tells Us." *Survival: Global Politics and Strategy* 61, no. 4 (August–September). IISS. https://www.iiss.org/publications/survival/2019/survival-global-politics-and-strategy-augustseptember-2019/614-02-jones. Accessed on June 19, 2020.
Kaufmann, Eric. 2018. *Whiteshift: Populism, Immigration and the Future of White Majorities*. Allen Lane: UK.
Knight, Alan. 1998. "Populism and Neo-Populism in Latin America, Especially Mexico." *Journal of Latin American Studies* 30, no. 2 (May).
Macridis, Roy C., and Mark Hulliung. 1997. *Contemporary Political Ideologies*, 6th ed. Pearson.
McChrystal, Gen. Stanley, Tantum Collins, David Silverman, and Chris Summell. 2015. *Team of Teams: New Rules of Engagement for a Complex World*. New York: Penguin.
McKnight, David. 2018. *Populism Now: The Case for Progressive Populism*. New South Wales: New South Publishing.
McQuade, Barbara. 2020. "What Would Happen If Trump Refused to Leave Office?" *The Atlantic*, February 22. https://www.theatlantic.com/ideas/archive/2020/02/what-if-he-wont-go/606259/. Accessed on January 21, 2020.
Moffitt, Benjamin. 2016. *The Global Rise of Populism: Performance, Political Style, and Representation*. Stanford, CA: Stanford University Press.
Mudde, Cas, and Cristóbal Rovira Kaltwasser. 2017. *Populism: A Very Short Introduction*. New York: Oxford University Press.
Müller, Jan-Werner. 2016. *What Is Populism?* College Park, PA: Pennsylvania University Press.

Munro-Kua, Anne. 1996. *Authoritarian Populism in Malaysia*. New York: MacMillan Press, LTD & St. Martin's Place, Inc.

Mustapic, Marko, Ivan Balabanic, and Mateja Plenkovic. 2019. "Political News Coverage of the 2015 Election Campaign in Croatia: Populism and Media."

Susana Salgado, ed., *Mediated Campaigns, and Populism in Europe*. Cham: Palgrave Macmillan.

Nicholas, Peter. 2020. "Trump Could Still Break Democracy's Biggest Norm." *The Atlantic*, June 16. https://www.theatlantic.com/politics/archive/2020/06/when-does-trump-leave-white-house/613060/. Accessed on January 21, 2020.

Nasreen, Zobaida, and Gopa Biswas Caesar. 2020. "Corona-Shaming Exposes the Fault Lines of Our Society." *The Daily Star*, April 3.

Panizza, Francisco. 2000. "Neopopulism and Its Limits in Collor's Brazil." *Bulletin of Latin American Research* 19, no. 2, Special Issue: Old and New Populism in Latin America (April).

Populism in the United States: A Timeline. 2019. history.com. https://www.history.com/topics/us-politics/populism-united-states-timeline. Accessed on June 19, 2020.

Powell, Michael. 2008. "Obama, the Populist." *The New York Times*, April 1. https://thecaucus.blogs.nytimes.com/2008/04/01/obama-the-populist/. Accessed on March 22, 2019.

Rosenblatt, Helena. 2018. *The Lost History of Liberalism: From Ancient Rome to the Twenty-First Century*. Princeton, NJ: Princeton University Press.

Stanley, Ben. 2017. "Populism in Central and Eastern Europe." Cristóbal Rovira Kaltwasser, Paul Taggart, Paulina Ochoa Espejo, and Pierre Ostiguy, eds., *The Oxford Handbook of Populism*. New York: OUP.

Stavrakakis, Yannis, Giorgos Katsambekis, Nikos Nikisianis, Alexandros Kioupkiolis, and Thomas Siomos. 2017. "Extreme Right-Wing Populism in Europe: Revisiting a Reified Association." *Critical Discourse Studies*. https://doi.org/10.1080/17405904.2017.1309325.

Stearns, Peter N. 2003. *Western Civilization in World History*. New York: Routledge.

Stockemer, Daniel, ed. 2019. *Populism Around the World: A Comparative Perspective*. Cham: Springer.

Strait Times. 2020. "New York City Sees Increase in Cases of People Ingesting Household Cleaners After Trump's Disinfectant Gaffe." April 26. https://www.straitstimes.com/world/united-states/new-york-city-sees-increase-of-cases-people-ingesting-household-cleaners-after. Accessed on June 21, 2020.

The Financial Express. 2020. "Unnecessary Panic Will Hinder Efforts to Prevent COVID-19, IEDCR Says." February 22. https://thefinancialexpress.com.bd/national/unnecessary-panic-will-hinder-efforts-to-prevent-covid-19-1582374490. Accessed on June 30, 2020.

The White House. 2017. "The Inaugural Address." January 20. https://www.whitehouse.gov/briefings-statements/the-inaugural-address/. Accessed on March 23, 2019.

———. 2020. "Proclamation Suspending Entry of Aliens Who Present a Risk to the U.S. Labor Market Following the Coronavirus Outbreak." June 22. https://www.whitehouse.gov/presidential-actions/proclamation-suspending-entry-aliens-present-risk-u-s-labor-market-following-coronavirus-outbreak/. Accessed on June 30, 2020.

Thrush, Glenn. 2012. "Obama the Reluctant Populist." *Politico*, January 25. https://www.politico.com/story/2012/01/obama-the-reluctant-populist-071933. Accessed on March 22, 2019.

Torre, Carlos de la. 2018. "Populism and Democracy: Lessons from Latin America." *Journal of Democracy* 2.

Traynor, Ian. 2015. "Migration Crisis: Hungary PM Says Europe in Grip of Madness." *The Guardian*, September 3. https://www.theguardian.com/world/2015/sep/03/migration-crisis-hungary-pm-victor-orban-europe-response-madness. Accessed on March 24, 2019.

Trotsky, Leon. 1924. *Literature and Revolution*. London: Kindle Edition.

Turner, James. 1980. "Understanding the Populists." *The Journal of American History* 67, no. 2 (September).

Walker, Ignacio. 2008. "The Three Lefts of Latin America." *Dissent* (Fall). https://www.dissentmagazine.org/article/the-three-lefts-of-latin-america. Accessed on June 13, 2020.

Webb, Adele, and Nicole Curato. 2019. "Populism in the Philippines." Daniel Stockemer, ed., *Populism Around the World: A Comparative Perspective*. Cham: Springer.

Weyland, Kurt. 2003. "Neopopulism and Neoliberalism in Latin America: How Much Affinity?" *Third World Quarterly* 24, no. 6 (December).

Zakaria, Fareed. 2016. "Populism on the March: Why the West Is in Trouble." *Foreign Affairs* 95, no. 6 (November/December).

Zernatto, Guido. 1944. "Nation: The History of a Word." *The Review of Politics* 6, no. 3 (July).

CHAPTER 4

From Peacekeeping to Peace Enforcement Operations: What Next?

Rashed Uz Zaman and Niloy Ranjan Biswas

INTRODUCTION

Local peace support operations (both peacekeeping and peace enforcement) have become a major U.N. flagship venture.[1] After World War II, peace missions have been an essential tool to keep sustainable peace in post-conflict countries. Since the first U.N. peacekeeping deployment in 1948, international order and the understanding of [in]security have transformed: new conflicts have emerged, bringing with new actors and challenges to international security considerations, while the United Nations has itself redefined the scope of its mandates and resorted to different legal frameworks to conduct its peace support endeavors.

R. U. Zaman · N. R. Biswas (✉)
Department of International Relations, University of Dhaka, Dhaka, Bangladesh
e-mail: niloy@du.ac.bd

R. U. Zaman
e-mail: rashed@du.ac.bd

© The Author(s), under exclusive license to Springer Nature Singapore Pte Ltd. 2022
I. A. Hussain (eds.), *Global-Local Tradeoffs, Order-Disorder Consequences*, Global Political Transitions,
https://doi.org/10.1007/978-981-16-9419-6_4

Evidently, the United Nations uses Chapter VII's peace enforcement and mixed-mandated operations more often than Chapter VI's peaceful settlement of disputes.[2] Even the number of U.N. peacekeeping missions has significantly increased, indicating the growth of local threats undermining global stability. From 1948 to 1978, the United Nations deployed thirteen peacekeeping missions, but over the next ten years, not a single mission could be organized due to Cold War tensions. Once the Cold War ended, peacekeeping missions dramatically expanded with more U.N. missions between 1991 and 1994 than in the previous forty-five years combined.[3]

Enormous international peace and security challenges have emerged to contain local tensions amid these altered twenty-first century conflicts. Peace operations have undoubtedly faced many of these challenges. Local conflicts in Mali, Democratic Republic of Congo, and Central African Republic, for example, invite foreign state and non-state actors on this or that site, impacting peace operational efficacy. Resource constraints, ethical conundrum, and the lack of clarity of the political and strategic purposes of a mission may arguably have adversely implicated U.N. peacekeeper operations and missions.[4]

To understand the changing nature of U.N. peace support operations, and patterns of global challenges to ensure peace and security, we explore three major trends that demand attention: (a) technological development; (b) regional organization; and (c) the U.N. role in countering violent extremism (CVE). Our qualitative approach builds upon primary and secondary literatures, utilizing critical stakeholder discourses. Analysis follows in four more sections: appraising the historical backdrop of post-World War II peace missions; stocktaking contemporary trends of peace contribution; and interpreting the changing patterns of peace support activities; and estimating the challenges of contemporary peace missions, with special reference to enforcement activities. How future efforts require a context-driven approach flexibly formulating and operationalizing mandates seems to be the underlying study finding.

UN Peace Support Missions: Global Purpose, Historical Context

The United Nations—built on World War II ravages and World War I lessons—sought global governance with international peace and security from the outset. Though "peacekeeping" is not mentioned in the

U.N. Charter, it was invented to face immediate exigencies. Since its first mission in 1948, the United Nations generally has followed three cardinal principles—conflict prevention and peacemaking; peacekeeping; and peace-building.[5] Lester Pearson's 2 November 1956 initiative triggered the advent of modern peacekeeping, with the United Nations Emergency Force (UNEF) deploying armed, but neutral, troops between belligerent groups. It combined Chapter VI on the "Pacific Settlement of Disputes" and Chapter VII on "Action with Respect to Threats to the Peace, Breaches of the Peace and Acts of Aggression" of the U.N. Charter to produce three guiding principles of U.N. peacekeeping operations (UNPKOs): "consent of the parties to the conflict, impartiality, and the use of the force only in self-defense".[6]

Though the United Nations Security Council (UNSC) authorized a few limited "traditional peacekeeping" missions during the Cold War, thirteen were dispatched between 1948 and 1978, but none in the next decade. Only once did the U.N. authorize a Chapter VII peace enforcement mission, in 1950, for Korea (which, surprisingly, continues maintaining local peace two-thirds of a century later). On one other occasion (1960–1964), it allowed the peacekeeping mission in the Congo to turn into peace enforcement. The Congo mission, which allowed a third-party presence to monitor and verify peace agreement among the warring factions, was authorized to alert the United Nations in case of any breach of the agreement.[7] This Congo peacekeeping mission had set the framework of future post-Cold War operations.

Shifting from "peacekeeping" to "peace enforcement", U.N. peace operations gradually *naturalized* the use of force from self-defense to variegated usages of force. While the resort to force itself is prohibited in the Charter of the United Nations,[8] the changing internal, intra-state, and traditional nature of post-Cold War conflicts demanded re-hauling peacekeeping applications and mandates. Several U.N. documents, such as *An Agenda for Peace, Supplement to An Agenda for Peace* and the *Brahimi Report* testify to this.[9] They identified the ground realities creating unfamiliar terrains for peacekeeping missions, for example

> political patrons; arms vendors; buyers of illicit commodity exports; regional powers that send their own forces into the fray; and neighbouring states that host refugees who are sometimes systematically forced to flee their homes.[10]

Since conducting traditional peacekeeping missions proved unrealistic, newer challenges demanded newer provisions. One document, *An Agenda for Peace*, paved the way for such shifts. Its *Supplement to An Agenda for Peace* noted: "Nothing is more dangerous for a peacekeeping operation than to ask it to use force when its existing composition, armament, logistic support and deployment deny it the capacity to do so".[11] However, the same report particularly observed, since problems within a society had deep roots both political and the military, resolution was prohibitive. It nevertheless suggested the use of force with such cautionary notes as: "Peace-keeping and the use of force (other than in self-defence) should be seen as alternative techniques and not as adjacent points on a continuum, permitting easy transition...".[12] Emphasizing a political solution to conflicts, the 2015 *Jose Ramos-Horta* report identified four key U.N. priorities in its peacekeeping operations: primacy of politics, responsive operations which would be tailored to the context, stronger partnerships between international and regional actors, and field-focused and people-oriented.[13] With the use of force receiving U.N. validation, five distinct phases can be discerned. Table 4.1 illustrates them.[14]

Limited traditional peacekeeping operations have since given way to larger, more complex, and more ambitious peace operations, indicating the increasingly sophisticated expressions of local tensions (and perhaps why the need for global stewardship is but a palliative against idiosyncratic conflicts). A shift in warfare whereby "traditional" concepts such as "victory" and "defeat" have given way to "war amongst people", in which adversary dissuasion is targeted over destruction, and war-zone reconstruction and peace-building displaces military action. Likewise, trends in global politics—the increased prevalence of intra-state over inter-state warfare—exposed the peacekeeping flaws in a model largely evolving from a Cold War context, in which belligerents were usually state actors.

Today's peacekeepers have the challenging task of operating in civil conflicts which often have multiple actors. They perform a myriad of tasks—separating warring factions, disarmament, demobilization and reintegration (DDR), providing aid to refugees and internally displaced persons (IDPs), and supporting civilian administrators. UNSC (United Nations Security Council) mandates often change, without any reference to the size, force structure, and rules of mission engagement. Three "UNEF II" rules, for example, became UNPKO components from the aftermath of the Ramadan War (operating only with the consent of

Table 4.1 Five phases of U.N. peace missions

Phases of use of force	Missions	Mandates
Phase 1: Peace Observation Missions	United Nations Truce Supervision Organisation (UNTSO) and the United Nations Military Observer Group in India and Pakistan (UNMOGIP) in the late 1940s	Limited in terms of composition, less extensive mandates and armed only for self-defence
Phase 2: UNEF I	United Nations Emergency Force in the Suez (UNEF 1)	Larger in terms of composition and mandate; the changing nature of PKO is recognized for the first time; the three principles of UNPKO emerges with this PKO; self-defense of peacekeepers conceptualized by UN Secretary General Dag Hammarskjöld
Phase 3: Defense of Mandate Operations	U.N. Emergency Force in the Suez (UNEF II), in 1973	Peacekeepers were to take positive actions to defend their purposes; however, it was reluctantly used by peacekeepers considering the ground realities
Phase 4: Non-Forceful Peacekeeping Operations which Become Forceful when Confronted with Crisis (Mission Creep)	The U.N. peacekeeping operation established in the Congo in 1960 (ONUC), the U.N. operations in Somalia and the former Yugoslavia established in 1992 and the U.N. operations in East Timor established in 1999	Authorized for limited use of force; however, due to changing ground realities, U.N. Security Council authorized them to use offensive forces
Phase 5: The Brahimi Report and the Invocation of Chapter VII from the Outset	The current phase of peacekeeping missions	The difference with all the other phases lies in the UNSC invoking Chapter VII from the very outset of missions

the belligerents, using force only is self-defense, and being completely impartial). Yet, they do not apply to contemporary peacekeepers. Such changes often imperil peacekeepers, as epitomized by the grim fate of Chadian peacekeepers of the U.N. Multidimensional Integrated Stabilization Mission in Mali (MINUSMA): they were ambushed and killed by unidentified terrorists in January 2019.[15] One or more of the four war principles (objective specification, unity, mass, and surprise) often collides with peacekeeping itself.

From Peacekeeping to Peace Enforcement: Understanding Transformation Trends

Monitoring the peacekeeping-peace enforcement divide in U.N. peace doctrines, particularly against the mystifying chameleon-like transformation of the local conflict beast, opens its own trenches. Take, for example, peacekeeping, as it is framed in the U.N. Charter. Three core principles guide its behavior—consent, impartiality, and the minimum use of force.[16] First, actors in a conflict environment need to unanimously support U.N. assistance, either to formulate a ceasefire or a peace agreement among themselves, in spite of the attention shifting to local interests; and only a consensus at this local level can produce the ideal global requirement for support, validating a global–local U.N. role. However, since the post-Cold War era, the U.N. obligation to conduct peace support missions to protect civilians in "no cease-fire" or "no peace agreement" contexts actually reduces U.N. obligations to a "host country" consent.[17] Once again an implicit local veto dangles over global intervention, prompting a discussion of the impartiality principle. Although impartiality is an obligation, i.e., the United Nations must treat all parties in conflict equally, scholars observe a thin line of variation between impartiality and neutrality.[18] The United Nations must be impartial in its dealings with the local parties to any conflict, without necessarily being neutral in the execution of its mandates, which is fixed in consensus.[19]

Blue helmets can use the minimum force in peacekeeping to protect themselves, the mandate of the mission, and mission's ability to achieve any given mandate.[20] Scholars have skeptically measured the utility of peacekeeping operations in contemporary complex operational environments, based on U.N. Chapter VI.[21] One may wish to remember the

U.N. experiences in Bosnia, Rwanda, and Somalia to understand the loopholes in traditional peacekeeping operations. General Sir Michael Rose, Commander of the United Nations Protection Force (UNPROFOR) in former Yugoslavia, observed, "Rather than lose faith in the whole peace process, we need to analyze the changed operational circumstances and try to determine new doctrines for the future".[22] Once again, as the local interests threaten to steer collective responses, the globalized U.N. apparatus felt the significance of the independent use of force which would be dedicated to accomplishing the mandate of the mission.

Peace enforcement evolved as operations approved by the United Nations Security Council without a necessary consent from the belligerent parties or the conflict host-country.[23] It is based on Chapter VII of the U.N. Charter, which depicts Action with Respect to Threats to the Peace, Breaches of Peace, and Acts of Aggression; hence, it proposes the United Nations to take enforcement actions. As per another United Nations policy document, peace enforcement originally meant, "an aggressor(s) has(ve) been designated by the U.N. Security Council, and that the use of force has been authorized to impose the will of the Council on the aggressor(s)".[24] Unlike peacekeeping, which is considered to be a defensive posture to protect peace, peace enforcement offers an offensive standpoint in sustaining peace. Since 1999 with the U.N. Mission in Sierra Leone (UNAMSIL), the UNSC's invocation of Chapter VII authorized peacekeepers to use "all means necessary" to protect civilians has increased. At the same time, civilian protection and the authorization of "all means necessary" to that end have gradually become core aspects of U.N. peace operations and central to many of its new mandates, such as those for the Central African Republic (MINUSCA), Mali (MINUSMA), and South Sudan (UNMISS).[25] Moreover, Force Intervention Brigade (FIB) in the U.N. Stabilization Mission to the Democratic Republic of the Congo (MONUSCO) is a significant example of peace enforcement operation. This has come up with the mandate to neutralize the M23 and other rebel groups, forcing the U.N. decision to take side against a perpetrator.[26]

Special reports and panels have been critical of U.N. peacekeeping involvement. In 2000, the *Brahimi Report* recommended that the United Nations should not deploy peace operations where there is no peace to keep.[27] In 2015, after fifteen years, the *UN High Level Independent Panel on Peace Operations (HIPPO)* reaffirmed how the United Nations is not well suited to go beyond peacekeeping, recommending instead that the

U.N. Security Council turn to the African Union (AU) and others for peace enforcement.[28] However, the *HIPPO Report* also acknowledges the increased global demand for U.N. blue helmets has increased and the U.N. inability to deploy sufficient troops, police and civilian peacekeepers in accordance with its demand.[29] Moreover, a perceptible "robust turn" in U.N. peacekeeping presents a series of dilemmas and issues demanding attention to retain and enhance the long-term credibility of U.N. peace operations.

It is crucial to observe how changing peacekeeping mandates include new tasks, such as policing, counterinsurgency, and promoting national reconciliation. Moreover, the U.N. acknowledged how violence, asymmetric threats, and unclear political situations led to a greater number of "robust mandates", which already challenged the non-use of force, i.e., traditional peacekeeping missions.[30] Therefore, it becomes a reality that contemporary peace operations aim to enforce peace by using "all necessary means" to protect civilians, to prevent violent disruptions of the political process, and to assist authorities in maintaining law and order.

CHALLENGES OF PEACE ENFORCEMENT

Turning to the major challenges of transformation from peacekeeping to peace enforcement and robust mandates in peace support operations already alluded to, we find the challenges to be too manifold in nature. First, the peace enforcement operations with robust mandates in missions with aims to protect, stabilize, and sustain peace by the United Nations have increased stakeholder expectations. Scholars observe that U.N. peacekeepers cannot ensure peace in contexts where there is no peace to keep, lack of good governance, absence of human rights and antagonism between parties.[31]

Second, given the impartiality principle, it is important to observe *whether* and *how* diluting the consensus concept in contemporary peace operations affects the impartiality principles for the conflicting actors. Thierry Tardy projects the obviously provocative question: to what extent can robust peacekeepers be politically acceptable and operationally viable?[32] It is important to remember that there is a primacy of politics, as identified by the *HIPPO Report*, which indicating the obligation of U.N. peace support operations to acknowledge and support a political strategy to sustain peace-building efforts.[33] The political viability of peace enforcement is more complicated than ever in U.N. peace support history.

Third, one may confuse understanding the security and development nexus while resolving anxiety between robust peacekeeping and humanitarian principles. Undoubtedly, both these issues consider political support and sufficient resources. Yet it is a challenging task to successfully connect a bridge between peace enforcement and humanitarian activities. Though humanitarian agencies usually depend on the consent and cooperation of governments, communities and armed groups for any kinds of access,[34] in peace enforcement operations, lack of consent and insufficient political support might adversely influence the activities of humanitarian groups.

Fourth, funding and length of contribution could be a challenge for the donors and troop/police contributors, respectively. There is a strong possibility of reducing or drying-up U.N. peacekeeping missions, as President Donald Trump announced slashing U.S. contributions to U.N. peacekeeping by U.S. $2.2 billion annually.[35] As of September 2018, financial data shows that the United Nations owes 76 countries a total of U.S. $221 million for their troop contributions.[36] The reduction of funds will also influence the commitments of the troop contributors. As the peace enforcement missions require more time and resources with clear and achievable strategic plans, the reduced budget will drive this to an uncertain future.

Finally, peace enforcement operations with robust mandates face direct challenges from the perennial constraints, such as weak political support, scarcity of quality troops with required resources, and reservations of top troop contributors to embrace a robust approach.[37] To narrow discussions on challenges, only three most critical issues—technological advancement, the role of regional organizations, and the U.N.'s CVE role—have been chosen to highlight the potential set of effective responses to the previously identified challenges. This is not only required to ensure the success of current missions, but also offer a set of valued propositions to sustain U.N. efforts in peace support endeavors.

TECHNOLOGY AND U.N. PEACE SUPPORT OPERATIONS

Peace enforcement missions today will require more technological capabilities than ever, leading to a series of technological innovation and sophistication in peace support activities. The United Nations has already made a significant step forward in aerial reconnaissance by deploying Unmanned Aerial Vehicles (UAVs) in the Democratic Republic of Congo in 2013. In discussing the significance of technology in U.N. missions, Walter Dorn observed, "Remotely piloted or unmanned aerial vehicles (UAVs) provide new platforms for both cameras and (controversially) missiles. The revolution in artificial intelligence and robotics makes possible a new generation of devices for field operations".[38] However, a recent report on the *Expert Panel on Technology and Innovation in UN Peacekeeping* highlighted how the "missions frequently lack a wide range of the very capabilities now considered by most militaries, law enforcement agencies and international organizations to be minimally necessary to operate effectively".[39] It is important for both the troop contributing and host-states to sufficiently equip missions with necessary resources, when contemporary missions focus on protecting civilians. Therefore, the peace enforcement missions cannot overlook the need for technological sophistication.

Technological advances cover all areas of peace support operations, such as communication devices, weapons systems, surveillance, and so on. It is expected that there will be a joint effort to conduct innovation in this case which would benefit both donors and contributors. Yet a few critical factors block the pathways to technological innovation and its transfer among U.N. peace endeavoring members. First, cost is a prime issue for the delay in this case. The developing countries, apparently the major troops/police contributors of U.N. missions, often cannot afford up-to-date technologies and equipment. Second, sadly but truthfully, developed countries often hesitate to provide advanced technologies to developing countries since tech-transfers threaten monopolistic control over technological sophistication.[40] Finally, complex legal and ethical concerns about certain advanced equipment already in use in peace operations need re-consideration.

One may further question how would the United Nations prohibit itself from combat drone usage in the future? Should drone data collected about disasters be shared with humanitarian organizations? Could this data sharing now risk the future neutrality, impartiality, and independence of humanitarian work? Sophisticated training is further required to decode the data that are received from the drone. Therefore, another question arises—how do peace support missions acquire the means to properly analyze all the data gathered by drones? Finally, it is also very crucial to monitor whether and the extent to which surveillance drones construct a false sense of security among the people. Undoubtedly surveillance drones have brought a new dimension in peace support operations. However, one cannot deny that having drones covering an area can produce two contradictory effects: (a) recording human rights violations or armed attacks may be a deterrent to warring parties; and, (b) without the capacity to deploy personnel to stop the violence, it may severely harm the reputation of peacekeepers.[41]

REGIONAL ORGANIZATIONS & PEACE SUPPORT OPERATIONS

Regional organizations have become an integral part of peace support operations of the globally extended United Nations. They have proven their significance in peacekeeping, peace enforcement, and peace-building missions, and remain external to the local tension, reiterating not just the stubbornness of local conflicts against compromising gestures, but also the persistence behind globally-mandated conflict resolution steps. As a strong demand exists for coherence and interoperability between the contributing peace mission actors, it is expected that a strategic U.N.-regional partnership is necessary to improve the collective impact of such endeavors.[42] Chapter VIII of the U.N. Charter stipulates the aim of involving regional arrangements to be "to achieve pacific settlement of local disputes through such regional arrangements or by such regional agencies before referring them to the Security Council".[43]

Since 2004, the African Union has mandated nearly sixty-five thousand uniformed peacekeepers in Africa.[44] The Economic Community of West African States (ECOWAS) also conducts a minute un-mandated mission in Guinea Bissau.[45] It is important to remember that none of the Asian states has taken part either through a regional arrangement or to a regional peace mission with UNSC approval.[46] The Organization of American States (OAS) conducted small-scale civilian peacekeeping endeavors in the Americas.[47] Usually, these regional organizations have the potential to offer niche capabilities and respond rapidly to a conflict environment. Moreover, these organizations often enjoy a comparative advantage on two grounds: (a) possess a standing armed force as opposed to the United Nations, and (b) remain more familiar with socio-political contexts of the region. Therefore, the growing regional role has expanded U.N. options.

Regional organizational ambiguity is further deepened when defining regional organizations. The U.N. Charter, as argued by Angel Angelov, does not mention the term regional organizations, which instead refers to regional arrangements and agencies.[48] It, therefore, does not provide a clear definition of regional organization that would be able to contribute in peace support operations. Confusions may also arise from interpreting support exchanges between the United Nations and regional peace operations. It is not necessary that geographic proximity for countries to a conflict does automatically generate a consensus on how to respond in regional peacekeeping. Neighboring states have different views on how a local conflict should be resolved, which often made the deployment of peace operations complicated. Local hegemons have often used regional arrangements to legitimize their activities and self-interests in conflicts, as the Nigerian-led ECOWAS operations in Liberia (1990) and Sierra Leone (1997), the Russian-led CIS operations in Georgia (1994), and the Australian-led Pacific Islands Forum (PIF) operation in the Solomon Islands (2003) to understand the role of regional big powers in peace operations.[49] Starved of peace operation provisions, rather than resort to humanitarian interventions, the North Atlantic Treaty Organization (NATO) and PIF bodies lack adequate experiences in conducting peace operations. Questions arise, for instance, if franchising U.N. responsibilities to regional organizations will ensure international peace and security.

U.N. AND COUNTERING VIOLENT EXTREMISM (CVE)

Violent extremist or terrorist groups have increased their activities rapidly. The number of fatalities caused by terrorism has risen steadily. A U.N. report highlights that 195 personnel in U.N. missions have been killed by acts of violent extremism in 2013–2017, more than during any other 5-year period in history.[50]

The casualties were mostly reported in recent times, which happened due to the rise of the Islamic State, *Al Shabab*, *Boko Haram*, and the like. Peacekeepers also often find themselves thrust into the front line when armed groups target civilians. For example, on December 2017, fifteen U.N. peacekeepers were killed in a terrorist attack in the Democratic Republic of Congo (DRC), carried out by the militant Allied Democratic Forces. In addition to the U.N. peacekeepers, five members of the DRC armed forces were also killed and a further 53 people were injured in the attack.[51] Casualties, overshadowed by attention to the peace imperatives, also take a global face.

Mali is an important example to understand the CVE threats to the United Nations. The United Nations Multidimensional Integrated Stabilization Mission in Mali (MINUSMA) is one of the deadliest missions in U.N. peace support operations history, with ten peacekeepers killed in Northern Mali in January 2019.[52] Prior to that, from 1 July 2013 to 31 August 2016, Mali suffered 69 fatalities due to hostile acts.[53] In August 2017, terrorists attacked two neighboring U.N. camps in Douentza in the Mopti region of central Mali, killing a Malian soldier and a U.N. peacekeeper, and wounding another peacekeeper.[54] MINUSMA deployment was also the first multidimensional peacekeeping operation in parallel with on-going counter-terrorism operations, the French *Opération Serval* and *Opération Sabre*, later transitioned into the current *Opération Barkhane*. Al-Qaeda in the Islamic Mahgreb (AQIM), *Ansar Dine* and *al-Mourabitoun* (a branch of AQIM) are major terrorist actors in West Africa. Although the MINUSMA mandate "to stabilize the key population centers, especially in the north of Mali and, in this context, to deter threats and take active steps to prevent the return of armed elements to those areas" collides with the U.N. mandate to not counter terrorist groups, the blue helmets have often become the target of the terrorists for their support to the Malian government in this conflict.[55]

U.N. direct or indirect CVE engagements or counter-terrorist operations raise legitimate concerns. With the emergence of non-state actors and violent extremists exacerbating peacekeeper vulnerabilities, the safety and security of peacekeepers have become a matter of heightened concern in light of new and evolving threats.[56] It further raises two crucial but opposing questions. First, will it be possible for the United Nations to avoid an engagement in counter violent extremism operations? Second, will the direct U.N. engagement in CVE actions undermine U.N. legitimacy internationally and as an impartial conflict arbiter?

With the changing nature of conflicts and terrorism, and considering more unfolding cases, such as Syria and Yemen, in future there is no consensus on the role UN peace support operations should have in countering or/and preventing violent extremism and terrorism. In 2016, a high-level U.N. General Assembly debate on peace and security observed that there was a need "to further reflect on tools and means for the Organization and the Secretariat to respond in meaningful ways to the threat of terrorism and violent extremism in various contexts where the United Nations is confronted with this increasingly complex phenomenon, particularly where peace operations are deployed".[57]

The *HIPPO* Report notes the United Nations "lack[s] specific equipment, intelligence, logistics, capabilities and specialized military preparation". This needs to be reformed so the United Nations be given counterterrorism tasks too.[58] However, the policymakers must be cautious about the U.N. CVE role as this would be an enormous challenge for contributing states and may potentially tarnish the impartial image of the United Nations.

WHERE IS THE FUTURE: CONTEXT MATTERS?

This chapter primarily describes how the context and content of U.N. peace support operations have changed significantly in recent times. With the changing nature of conflicts, post-conflict mission environments and actors in the conflict experience transformations. These have become so diverse that rigid mission mandates fail to capture the changing nature of the context and jeopardizes lives of the peacekeepers. How the United Nations, in practice, has transformed its global mandates from peacekeeping to peace enforcement in accommodating the changing nature of regional and local conflicts is discussed, as to how the U.N. missions in Mali, Democratic Republic of Congo and Central African Republic have served to prove the statement's veracity. Yet, there is a need for careful consideration at academic and strategic levels as to how U.N. peace support missions will deal with these challenges.

How various challenges, with specific emphasis on technological development, growing trends of regionalism, and U.N. CVE roles become inevitable realities, pose existential future threats for U.N.-led peace support endeavors in future, needs the United Nations to reconsider investing in new technologies by collaborating with affluent member states. It should emphasize the transfer of technologies from developed to developing countries which contribute more troops and police on the ground, yet U.N. caution about the use of these technologies in peace support operations should not exacerbate any controversies with regard to the unethical use of technologies.

Regional and sub-regional organizations increasingly engage in peace missions under the U.N. mandate. There is an argument that competent regional peacekeepers should offer more roles in robust peace enforcement operations, whereas the United Nations could focus on situations where there is a peace to keep. This seems highly unlikely in practice for two reasons. First, it is very difficult to make a clear separation between peacekeeping and peace enforcement situations today; and second, U.N. engagements in multidimensional and robust peace operations, such as in Mali, Congo, and Central African Republic have been too deep to simply retreat or change guards. Bringing back the United Nations to its classical peacekeeping job and technological advancement to equip future U.N. missions are two contradictory policy options, which needs to be avoided. However, the United Nations must involve regional actors and individual contributing states in the formulation of mandates for peace operations.

Finally, in missions mandating countering/preventing violent extremism and counter-terrorism operations becomes a litmus test for the direct U.N. participation. Since U.N. missions have not considered counter-terrorism as one of its mandates, the global body could not save itself becoming a victim of a hybrid mission addressing counter-terrorism by other actors. Again, the U.N. experience with peace enforcement in hybrid missions suggests that one should not be utopian in drawing a clear separation between the United Nations and countering violent extremism. Particularly, this is unreal when other U.N. agencies (e.g., United Nations Development Program) deeply engage in CVE activities elsewhere. Ultimately, finding the future of peace operations too complex in nature, more cautious but optimistic stakeholder steps to accommodate changing patterns of peace operations could ease the plight. A context-driven approach with flexibility in mandates may address the complexities of future peace support endeavors.

Notes

1. An earlier version of this study was published in *Studia Politologiczne (Political Science Studies)*, Vol. 56, June 2020, pp. 299-318. Some analyses of this chapter are informed by the article with the due permission of the editor of the journal. The article itself uses the terms "peace operations" and "peace support operations" interchangeably to indicate *both peacekeeping, peace enforcement, and peace-building activities.*
2. Charles T. Hunt, "All Necessary Means To What Ends? The Unintended Consequences of the "Robust Turn" in UN Peace

Operations," *International Peacekeeping* 24, no. 1 (2017): 108–131.
3. Pierre Schori, "UN Peacekeeping," *The Oxford Handbook of Modern Diplomacy*, eds. Andrew F. Cooper, Jorge Heine, and Ramesh Thakur (Oxford, U.K.: Oxford University Press, 2013), 782.
4. Rashed Uz Zaman and Niloy Ranjan Biswas, "Bangladesh and United Nations Peacekeeping Missions: The Quest for a National Policy to Meet the Challenge of Uncertainty," *Journal of the Asiatic Society of Bangladesh (Hum.)* 62, no. 2 (2017): 155–181; and John Karlsrud, "The UN at War: Examining the Consequences of Peace-Enforcement Mandates for the UN Peacekeeping Operations in the CAR, the DRC and Mali," *Third World Quarterly* 36, no. 1 (2015): 40–54.
5. *Report of the Panel on United Nations Peace Operations* (2000), A/55/305, S/2000/809, 2.
6. Andrzej Sitkowski (2006), *UN Peacekeeping: Myth and Reality* (Westport, CT: Praeger), 2.
7. Salman Ahmed, Paul Keating, and Ugo Solinas, "Shaping the Future of UN Peace Operations: Is There a Doctrine in the House?," *Cambridge Review of International Affairs* 20, no. 1 (2007): 13.
8. See articles 2(4), 24(1), 39, 42, 48(1) and 51 of the Charter of the United Nations.
9. United Nations, *An Agenda for Peace*, Report of the Secretary-General, A/47/277, 17 June 1992; United Nations, *Supplement to An Agenda for Peace*, A/50/60, 3 January 1995; United Nations, *Report of the Panel on United Nations Peace Operations*, A/54/2000, 2000.
10. *Report of the Panel on United Nations Peace Operations*, 3.
11. *Supplement to An Agenda for Peace*, Paragraph 35.
12. Ibid., Paragraph 36.
13. Information note on High-Level Independent Panel on Peace Operations (2015), available at http://www.un.org/en/peacekeeping/documents/High-Level-Independent-Panel.pdf.
14. James Sloan, "The Evolution of the Use of Force in UN Peacekeeping," *Journal of Strategic Studies* 37, no. 5 (2014): 674–702.
15. Dakin Andone, "Ten UN Peacekeepers Killed in Attack in Mali," *CNN Online*, 21 January 2019, https://edition.cnn.com/2019/

01/20/africa/un-peacekeepers-killed-mali/index.html, accessed 25 January 2019.
16. Cedric de Coning, "Peace Enforcement in Africa: Doctrinal Distinctions between the African Union and United Nations," *Contemporary Security Policy* 38, no. 1 (2017): 145–160.
17. Ibid.
18. E. P. Rhoads, *Taking Sides in Peacekeeping: Impartiality and the Future of the United Nations* (Oxford, U.K.: Oxford University Press, 2016).
19. Ibid.
20. United Nations, *United Nations Peacekeeping Operations: Principles and Guidelines* (New York, NY: United Nations, 2008).
21. Ramesh Thakur, "From Peacekeeping to Peace Enforcement: The UN Operation in Somalia," *The Journal of Modern African Studies* 32, no. 3 (Sept., 1994): 387–410. Also, Karlsrud, *The UN at War* (2015), 40–54.
22. Tom Woodhouse and Oliver Ramsbotham, eds., *Peacekeeping and Conflict Resolution* (London: Frank Cass Publishers, 2000), 1.
23. Coning, *Peace Enforcement in Africa*.
24. United Nations, *United Nations Peacekeeping Operations*; cited from Coning, *Peace Enforcement in Africa*, 147.
25. Alex J. Bellamy and Charles T. Hunt, "Twenty-first Century UN Peace Operations: Protection, Force and the Changing Security Environment," *International Affairs Special Issue*: The United Nations at 70 91, no. 6 (2015): 1277–1298. https://doi.org/10.1111/1468-2346.12456.
26. M. Peter, "Between Doctrine and Practice: The UN Peacekeeping Dilemma," *Global Governance* 21: 351–370.
27. United Nations, *Report of the Panel on United Nations Peace Operations* (New York: UN, 2000).
28. United Nations, *Uniting our Strengths for Peace: Politics, Partnership and People: Report of the High-Level Independent Panel on United Nations Peace Operations* (New York, NY: United Nations, 2015).
29. Ibid.
30. Herve Ladsous, *New Challenges and Priorities for UN Peacekeeping* (Washington DC: The Brookings Institution, 17 June 2014).
31. Bellamy and Hunt, op. cit., 1283–1284.

32. Thierry Tardy, "A Critique of Robust Peacekeeping in Contemporary Peace Operations," *International Peacekeeping* 18, no. 2 (2011): 152–167.
33. United Nations, *Politics, Partnership and People*, op cit. Also, see: Jean-Marie Guéhenno, *The Fog of Peace: A Memoir of International Peacekeeping in the 21st Century* (Washington DC, Brookings Institution Press, 2015).
34. Bellamy and Hunt, op. cit.
35. Howard LaFranchi, "Trump Team Submits UN Peacekeeping to Scrutiny. Is it worth a bargain?," *The Christian Science Monitor*, 5 April 2017, available at http://www.csmonitor.com/USA/Foreign-Policy/2017/0405/Trump-team-submits-UN-peacekeeping-to-scrutiny.-Is-it-a-bargain, accessed 28 April 2017.
36. Charu Sudan Kasturi, "The UN Owes Millions to Ethiopia Because the US won't Pay Up," *The Daily Dose*, 27 November 2018, https://www.ozy.com/acumen/the-un-owes-millions-to-ethiopia-because-the-us-wont-pay-up/90588, accessed 25 January 2019.
37. Tardy, op. cit.
38. A. Walter Dorn, *Smart Peacekeeping: Toward Tech-Enabled UN Operations*, Providing for Peacekeeping No. 13 (New York, NY: International Peace Institute, 2016).
39. United Nations, *Final Report: Expert Panel on Technology and Innovation in UN Peacekeeping* (New York, NY: United Nations, 2014), 3.
40. Mark Piesing, "Why are UN Peacekeepers so Badly Equipped for Modern Conflict?" *The Independent*, 8 August 2011, http://www.independent.co.uk/news/world/politics/why-are-un-peacekeepers-so-badly-equipped-for-modern-conflict-2334052.html, accessed 12 January 2018.
41. Dorn, *Smart Peacekeeping: Toward Tech-Enabled UN Operations*, 2011.
42. Hervey Ladsous, *New Challenges and Priorities for UN Peacekeeping* (New York, NY: The Brookings Institution, 17 June 2014).
43. See Articles 52.2 and 53.1 of Chapter VIII: Regional Arrangements of The UN Charter, available at http://www.un.org/en/sections/un-charter/chapter-viii/index.html, accessed 6 January 2018.

44. Danielle Renwick, *Peace Operations in Africa*, cfr backgrounders, 15 May 2015, available at http://www.cfr.org/peacekeeping/peace-operations-africa/p9333, accessed 9 August 2015.
45. Ibid.
46. Mikael Eriksson, "Towards Selective Regionalization? The Intervention in Libya and the Emerging Global Order," *Regional Organizations and Peacemaking: Challengers to the UN?*, eds., Wallensteen and Bjurner, 217–232. Publisher information missing.
47. For details, see: OAS Peace Fund, *OAS Peace Missions*, available at http://www.oas.org/sap/peacefund/PeaceMissions/, accessed 9 August 2015.
48. Angel Angelov, "Regional Involvement in Peace Operations: An Analysis of the Debate within the UN Security Council," *Conflict, Security and Development* 10, no. 5 (November 2010): 599–623.
49. Alex J. Bellamy, Paul D. Williams with Stuart Griffin, "Regionalism," *Understanding Peacekeeping* (Cambridge, U.K.: Cambridge University Press, 2nd Edition, 2010), 312.
50. United Nations, *Improving Security of United Nations Peacekeepers: We need to change the way we are doing business* (New York, NY: United Nations, 19 December 2017), from https://peacekeeping.un.org/sites/default/files/improving_security_of_united_nations_peacekeepers_report.pdf, accessed 25 January 2019.
51. Aaron Brookes, "DRC: 15 UN Peacekeepers Killed in Terrorist Attack," *East Africa Monitor*, 10 December 2017, https://eastafricamonitor.com/drc-15-un-peacekeepers-killed-terrorist-attack/, accessed 9 January 2018.
52. TRT World, *Are the UN Peacekeepers in Africa Sitting Ducks to Terror Groups?*, 23 January 2019, https://www.trtworld.com/africa/are-the-un-peacekeepers-in-africa-sitting-ducks-to-terror-groups-23527?utm_source=other&utm_medium=rss, accessed 25 January 2019.
53. John Karlsrud, "Towards UN Counter-terrorism Operations?" *Third World Quarterly* 38, no. 6 (2017): 1215.
54. Edith M. Lederer, "'Terror Attack' on UN Peacekeeping Headquarters in Mali kills 7," *Global News*, available at https://globalnews.ca/news/3669909/un-peacekeeping-headquarters-terror-attack/, accessed 9 January 2018.

55. Karlsrud, op. cit. (2017), 1215.
56. Bellamy and Hunt, op. cit.
57. U.N. General Assembly, "Conclusions and Observations by the President of the Seventieth Session of the UN General Assembly," from A. Boutellis and N. C. Fink, *Waging Peace: UN Peace Operations Confronting Terrorism and Violent Extremism* (New York, NY: International Peace Institute, 2016).
58. Karlsrud, op. cit. (2017), 1221.

References

Ahmed, Salman, Paul Keating, and Ugo Solinas. 2017. "Shaping the Future of UN Peace Operations: Is There a Doctrine in the House?" *Cambridge Review of International Affairs* 20, no. 1: 13.

Andone, Dakin. 2019. "Ten UN Peacekeepers Killed in Attack in Mali." *CNN Online*, January 21. From: https://edition.cnn.com/2019/01/20/africa/un-peacekeepers-killed-mali/index.html. Last consulted January 25, 2019.

Angelov, Angel. 2010. "Regional Involvement in Peace Operations: An Analysis of the Debate within the UN Security Council." *Conflict, Security and Development* 10, no. 5 (November): 599–623.

Bellamy, Alex J., and Charles T. Hunt. 2015. "Twenty-First Century UN Peace Operations: Protection, Force and the Changing Security Environment." *International Affairs Special Issue: The United Nations at 70 November* 91, no. 6: 1277–1298.

Bellamy, Alex J., Paul D. Williams, and Stuart Griffin. 2010. *Regionalism, Understanding Peacekeeping* (2nd ed.). Cambridge, UK: Cambridge University Press.

Boutellis, Arthur, and Naureen C. Fink. 2016. *Waging Peace: UN Peace Operations Confronting Terrorism and Violent Extremism*. New York, NY: International Peace Institute.

Brookes, Aaron. 2017. "DRC: 15 UN Peacekeepers Killed in Terrorist Attack." *East Africa Monitor*, December 10. From: https://eastafricamonitor.com/drc-15-un-peacekeepers-killed-terrorist-attack/. Last consulted January 9, 2018.

Coning, Cedric de. 2017. "Peace Enforcement in Africa: Doctrinal Distinctions between the African Union and United Nations." *Contemporary Security Policy* 38, no. 1: 145–160.

Dorn, Walter A. 2016. *Smart Peacekeeping: Toward Tech-Enabled UN Operations, Providing for Peacekeeping No. 13*. New York, NY: International Peace Institute.

Eriksson, Mikael. 2015. "Towards Selective Regionalization? The Intervention in Libya and the Emerging Global Order." Peter Wallensteen and Anders Bjurner, eds., *Regional Organizations and Peacemaking: Challengers to the UN?* Oxon: Routledge.

Franchi, Howard La. 2017. "Trump Team Submits UN Peacekeeping to Scrutiny. Is it Worth a Bargain?" *The Christian Science Monitor*, April 5. From: http://www.csmonitor.com/USA/Foreign-Policy/2017/0405/Trump-team-submits-UN-peacekeeping-to-scrutiny.-Is-it-a-bargain. Last consulted April 28, 2017.

Guéhenno, Jean-Marie. 2015. *The Fog of Peace: A Memoir of International Peacekeeping in the 21st Century*. Washington, DC: Brookings Institution Press.

Hunt, Charles T. 2017. "All Necessary Means To What Ends? The Unintended Consequences of the 'Robust Turn' in UN Peace Operations." *International Peacekeeping* 24, no. 1: 108–131.

Karlsrud, John. 2015. "The UN at War: Examining the Consequences of Peace-Enforcement Mandates for the UN Peacekeeping Operations in the CAR, the DRC and Mali." *Third World Quarterly* 36, no. 1: 40–54.

Kasturi, Charu Sudan. 2018. "The UN Owes Millions to Ethiopia Because the US Won't Pay Up." *The Daily Dose*, November 27. From: https://www.ozy.com/acumen/the-un-owes-millions-to-ethiopia-because-the-us-wont-pay-up/90588. Last consulted January 25, 2019.

Ladsous, Herve. 2014. *New Challenges and Priorities for UN Peacekeeping*. Washington, DC: The Brookings Institution.

Lederer, Edith M. 2017. "Terror Attack' on UN Peacekeeping Headquarters in Mali kills 7." *Global News*, August 14. From: https://globalnews.ca/news/3669909/un-peacekeeping-headquarters-terror-attack/. Last consulted January 9, 2018.

OAS Peace Fund. *OAS Peace Missions*. From: http://www.oas.org/sap/peacefund/PeaceMissions/. Last consulted August 9, 2018.

Peter, Mateja. "Between Doctrine and Practice: The UN Peacekeeping Dilemma." *Global Governance* 21: 351–370.

Piesing, Mark. 2011. "Why are UN Peacekeepers so Badly Equipped for Modern Conflict?" *The Independent*, August 8. From: http://www.independent.co.uk/news/world/politics/why-are-un-peacekeepers-so-badly-equipped-for-modern-conflict-2334052.html. Last consulted January 12, 2018.

Renwick, Danielle. 2015. "Peace Operations in Africa." *Cfr backgrounders*, May 15. From; http://www.cfr.org/peacekeeping/peace-operations-africa/p9333. Last consulted August 9, 2018.

Rhoads, E. P. 2016. *Taking Sides in Peacekeeping: Impartiality and the Future of the United Nations*. Oxford, UK: Oxford University Press.

Schori, Pierre. 2013. "UN Peacekeeping." Andrew F. Cooper, Jorge Heine and Ramesh Thakur, eds., *The Oxford Handbook of Modern Diplomacy*. Oxford, UK: Oxford University Press.
Sitkowski, Andrzej. 2006. *UN Peacekeeping: Myth and Reality*. Westport, CT: Praeger.
Sloan, James. 2014. "The Evolution of the Use of Force in UN Peacekeeping." *Journal of Strategic Studies* 37, no. 5: 674–702.
Tardy, Thierry. 2011. "A Critique of Robust Peacekeeping in Contemporary Peace Operations." *International Peacekeeping* 18, no. 2: 152–167.
Thakur, Ramesh. 1994. "From Peacekeeping to Peace Enforcement: The UN Operation in Somalia." *The Journal of Modern African Studies* 32, no. 3 (September): 387–410.
TRT World. 2019. "Are the UN Peacekeepers in Africa Sitting Ducks to Terror Groups?" *TRT World*, January 23. From: https://www.trtworld.com/africa/are-the-un-peacekeepers-in-africa-sitting-ducks-to-terror-groups-23527?utm_source=other&utm_medium=rss. Last consulted January 25, 2019.
United Nations. 1945. *Charter of the United Nations*. From https://www.un.org/en/about-us/un-charter/full-text. Last consulted January 29, 2019.
———. 1992. *An Agenda for Peace, Report of the Secretary-General*, A/47/277, June.
———. 1995. *Supplement to an Agenda for Peace*, A/50/60, January.
———. 2000. *Report of the Panel on United Nations Peace Operations*, A/54/2000/809.
———. 2008. *United Nations Peacekeeping Operations: Principles and Guidelines*. New York, NY: United Nations.
———. 2014. *Final Report: Expert Panel on Technology and Innovation in UN Peacekeeping*. New York, NY: United Nations.
———. 2015a. *Information Note on High-Level Independent Panel on Peace Operations*. From: http://www.un.org/en/peacekeeping/documents/High-Level-Independent-Panel.pdf. Last consulted January 29, 2019.
———. 2015b. *Uniting Our Strengths for Peace: Politics, Partnership and People: Report of the High-Level Independent Panel on United Nations Peace Operations*. New York, NY: United Nations.
———. 2017. Improving Security of United Nations Peacekeepers: We Need to Change the Way We Are Doing Business. *United Nations*, December 19. From: https://peacekeeping.un.org/sites/default/files/improving_security_of_united_nations_peacekeepers_report.pdf. Last consulted January 25, 2019.
Woodhouse, Tom, and Oliver Ramsbotham, eds. 2000. *Peacekeeping and Conflict Resolution*. London: Frank Cass Publishers.
Zaman, Rashed Uz, and Niloy Ranjan Biswas. (2017). "Bangladesh and United Nations Peacekeeping Missions: The Quest for a National Policy to Meet the Challenge of Uncertainty." *Journal of the Asiatic Society of Bangladesh (Hum.)* 62, no. 2: 155–181.

CHAPTER 5

Spying and Hidden Partnerships in the *Global South*: Bangladesh's Case

A. S. M. Ali Ashraf

INTRODUCTION

Spying is one of the oldest professions, and "hidden partnership" of spy agencies is a longstanding practice in international politics.[1] Yet, such cooperation constitutes a "paradox of public criticism and private partnership," and hence kept "hidden" from the mass people.[2] The intelligence studies literature has long focused on cooperation among Anglosphere spy agencies, only recently scoping beyond.[3] As that intelligence field grows, there is a new approach to looking at the *global South* that involves the postcolonial states of Africa, Asia, and Latin America.[4] From a methodological point, such exercise has involved both single-country case studies,[5] and comparative case studies,[6] leveraging mostly the use of historical and qualitative data.[7]

A. S. M. A. Ashraf (✉)
Department of International Relations, Dhaka University, Dhaka, Bangladesh
e-mail: aliashraf@du.ac.bd

© The Author(s), under exclusive license to Springer Nature Singapore Pte Ltd. 2022
I. A. Hussain (eds.), *Global-Local Tradeoffs, Order-Disorder Consequences*, Global Political Transitions,
https://doi.org/10.1007/978-981-16-9419-6_5

Such an appraisal feeds the globalization-localization theoretical discourse. Since strategic intelligence has no fixed boundaries, it generically qualifies as a globalizing force and as a globally conducted phenomenon. How it is narrowed to suit a particular country's case introduces the local theater, which can be narrowed even farther from the macro state-level to micro-level individuals. Spying fits this architecture: not only can the individual serve, as in espionage, but also double-cross, thus elevating the local-level punch. Since the spying game is about what "others" may be doing, its global DNA trademark is not just central, but also the means to cooperate with (or defect from) other countries, groups of countries, collaborative rules and norms, in essence, silent institutional properties and practices, if not robustly spelled out.

For students of International Relations (IR), two key questions arise: How do states in the *global South* develop hidden partnerships of spy agencies? Which IR theory can best explain such partnerships? Bangladesh, a former British colony and site for geopolitical competition between regional and global powers, is placed under this study's microscope. There are compelling reasons for choosing Bangladesh as a case to study intelligence partnership in the context of the *global South*. Although Bangladesh rarely draws global media attention, a deadly terrorist attack in 2016 and the influx of more than 750,000 Myanmar-origin Rohingya refugees from August 2017 thrust the country into international limelight.[8] On top of that, the geo-strategic location of Bangladesh as a littoral in the Indian Ocean has brought it closer to the world's major naval powers in search of maritime connectivity, security, and trade.[9] An in-depth case study, therefore, allows us to rethink various security concerns, especially the effects of terrorist and extremist threats on shaping the hidden partnerships between Bangladesh's spy agencies with other states in South Asia and the wider world.

Knowledge of the political and strategic Bangladesh culture helps here. As a small and densely populated country approaching a 170 million population mark within 148,460 sq km area, of every 8 out of every 10 persons in the country being Muslims, with Hindus, Buddhists, and Christians constituting the rest, in that order of size. Since independence in 1971, three major political parties have governed the state: the *Awami League* (AL), the Bangladesh Nationalist Party (BNP), and the *Jatiya Party* (JP), representing a wide range of political ideologies, with their varying foreign and security policies, altering the directions and tasking of the intelligence agencies and their foreign partnerships. The center-left AL has historically maintained a "special relationship" with India for better trade and connectivity, whereas the center-right BNP and JP priorities include "strategic partnership" with China, primarily to benefit from the latter's defense supplies on favorable terms.[10] Over the years, successive governments across the political aisle have also developed partnerships with the United States, the European Union (EU), and other major powers and international institutions in search of economic prosperity and national security.[11]

Like many states in the *global South*, a salient feature of Bangladesh's political culture concerns the role of the military in domestic politics. In fact, the BNP and JP founders were army chiefs who took the helm of government for a considerable period of time (1975–1990).[12] A military-backed interim caretaker government also ruled the state for two years (2007–2009), before transferring power to an elected AL government.[13] Due to their longstanding involvement in domestic politics, military forces and their intelligence agencies in Bangladesh maintain an active role in the internal and external affairs.

Four sections explain the analytical framework, Bangladesh's intelligence community, intelligence sharing practices between Bangladesh and other global and regional actors, and how *neo-realism* provides the best theoretical lens to analyze Bangladesh's intelligence partnerships.

Analytical Framework

The term "hidden partnership" is borrowed from Richard Aldrich, a guru of intelligence studies, to refer to "intelligence cooperation."[14] It is used synonymously with intelligence alliance, intelligence exchange, intelligence liaison, and intelligence sharing. Employing an analytical framework accenting the levels of analysis, scopes, and theories of intelligence cooperation, this chapter reaffirms the globalization-localization interplay at stake.

Levels of Analysis

Lefebvre and Rudner specify three levels of intelligence partnership analysis, each with its own distinct cooperation characteristics: bilateral, regional, and multilateral.[15] Bilateral cooperation, which occurs between two states and their intelligence services, is the most preferred intelligence sharing channel. This is evidenced from historical intelligence sharing practices between the former Soviet Union and East Germany, Israel and Jordan, as well as the United Kingdom and the United States. Drawing evidence from the *global North*,[16] Rudner notes that some bilateral arrangements are more active than others. For instance, the United States has active intelligence sharing arrangements with more than 100 states,[17] and although Canada also has bilateral liaisons with an equal number of states, many such Canadian partnerships remain inactive. He also observes the robustness of Canada–U.S. and U.K.–U.S. intelligence cooperation practices in the domains of border control, counterterrorism, cyber security, and nonproliferation, not necessarily because of these being catalyzers, but for other historical convergences and overlaps.

Second, regional institutions facilitate intelligence cooperation to deal with a wide variety of threats, and at multiple levels of externalization (defined as the antonym of localization), like hemispheric, regional, and other smaller membership compacts. The European Union (EU) offers the best example. The Intelligence and Situation Center (IntCen) of the External Action Service and the Intelligence Directorate of the Military Staff represent the EU's civilian and military intelligence hubs, respectively.[18] They draw on the collective efforts of the national intelligence services to co-produce strategic assessment for senior decision-makers and the member-states through the Single Intelligence Analysis Capacity.[19] In the EU law enforcement domain, the Europol and its Counter Terrorism Task Force act as a surveillance hub of the member-states.[20] Another European inter-governmental initiatives, the Club of Berne and its constituent Counter Terrorism Group, have a link with the IntCen to provide terrorist threats assessment to EU decision-makers as well as Norway and Switzerland.[21]

Beyond Europe, members of the Association of Southeast Asian Nations (ASEAN) have also developed strong security partnerships. For instance, the trilateral Our Eyes Initiative (OEI) of Indonesia, Malaysia, and the Philippines has evolved into ASEAN Our Eyes Initiative (AOEI).[22] The AEOI envisions utilizing the ASEAN Direct Communications Infrastructure as a secure communication system for the regional defense ministers.

African and Latin American intelligence sharing arrangements remain nascent. Three notable African initiatives include the African Union (AU) Mission in Somalia (AMISOM), the Committee of Intelligence and Security Services of Africa (CISSA), and the South African Regional Police Chiefs Cooperation Organization (SARPCCO).[23] Each has a distinct priority, the AMISOM providing inputs to military operations against *Al Shabab* and other extremist groups,[24] the CISSA complements AU policymaking by offering a backdoor channel during crisis,[25] and the SARPCCO facilitating intelligence exchange on transnational crimes including money laundering and the smuggling of arms, diamond, and endangered species.[26] In Latin America, the Union of South American Nations created the South American Council to develop concerted action against the drug-trafficking problem.[27] The Central American Integration System provides another platform not only to promote economic cooperation but also to deal with the threats of illicit trafficking, organized crime, and terrorism.[28] Internal feuds have weakened these regional intelligence sharing arrangements in Africa and Latin America, impeding any emulation of the ASEAN and EU intelligence partnership counterparts.[29]

Third, multilateral intelligence sharing represents two models: civilian and military. As civilian entities, the Egmont Group, Interpol, and the International Narcotics Control Board (INCB) carry sharply different mandates. Whereas the Egmont Group unites 167 financial intelligence units around the world to stimulate the exchange of confidential data on money laundering and terrorist financing,[30] the Interpol and INCB role is vital in the fight against drugs smuggling, human trafficking, and money laundering.[31] In the military domain, the UKUSA Agreement and the North Atlantic Treaty Organization (NATO) have a longstanding record of promoting intelligence liaison.[32] The UKUSA Agreement, also known as the Five Eyes (FVEY) Defence Pact, is a full-fledged intelligence liaison system comprising Australia, Canada, New Zealand, United Kingdom, and United States.[33] On the other hand, the Joint Intelligence and Security Division of NATO works closely with the North Atlantic Council, the Military Committee, and senior NATO leaders to provide strategic assessment of complex and diverse security threats including an assertive Russia, cyber-attacks, environmental challenges, refugee influx, and the spread of weapons of mass destruction.[34]

Scope of Intelligence Cooperation

Westerfield provides a five-fold typology on the scope of intelligence cooperation. Writing within a U.S. context, he argues that the scope of intelligence partnership takes five distinct forms including full-fledged liaison, limited and episodic cooperation, operations sharing, intelligence support, and crypto diplomacy.[35] His typology needs to be modified: a new mode of cooperation must be added to analyze the challenges of intelligence liaison in the *global South*. This sixth proposed form of cooperation can be called limited and conceptual intelligence sharing.

The first, full-fledged liaison, requires a formal agreement and long-standing practices specifying "an agreed system of classification and codewords and procedures for the protection of exchanged intelligence information" and "exchange of specially designated liaison officers [posted] to the embassies and High Commissions in the capitals of the cooperating countries."[36] Such cooperation enjoys the benefits of "formal contacts and close personal relationships among the countries' services at the senior level."[37] The UK–USA signals intelligence (SIGINT) partnership, known as the "cousins" relationship, is the best known case of full-fledged liaison.

Second, limited and episodic cooperation occurs when intelligence services trade information for information, information for operational access, and information in anticipation of other benefits. Hundreds of defense installations around the world lend the United States an opportunity to receive limited and episodic but cost-effective intelligence. U.S. relations with the Shah of Iran and his secret SAVAK intelligence fell into the category of information for information and information for access deal.[38]

Third, operations sharing can take several forms: parallel, allocated, and joint operations. Parallel operations refer to simultaneous involvement of intelligence operatives pursuing a common threat, while allocated operations involve a clear division of responsibility for various tasks of a large operation. By contrast, joint operations refer to team building by intelligence services of cooperating countries. For instance, during the Falklands War, the Anglo-American SIGINT agencies jointly attacked Argentinian communications.[39]

Fourth, intelligence support is usually a one-directional phenomenon in which a state with longer experience, better expertise, and requisite resources provide advising and training to a partner state's intelligence services. A prime example is the U.K. support to the U.S. intelligence agencies in the 1940s to build up the latter's human intelligence (HUMINT) capacity for counterespionage, cryptography, and agent recruitment.[40]

Fifth, crypto-diplomacy refers to back-channel intelligence exchange that occurs in the absence of traditional open diplomacy. Israel's long-standing cooperation with Jordanian intelligence agencies and U.S.-Pakistan cooperation to drive out Soviet forces from Afghanistan glaringly exemplified crypto-diplomacy.[41]

Sixth, limited and conceptual cooperation occurs mostly between the governments and their intelligence services in the *global South*, where ambitious plans are often taken but cannot be implemented due to a lack of trust or political will among the participating states. The South Asian Association for Regional Cooperation (SAARC) member-states might have explored the idea of creating a South Asian Police (SAARCPOL) to facilitate intelligence sharing among the national law enforcement agencies, but the idea of SAARCPOL has progressed only at the conceptual level, and failing to evolve into a functional entity largely due to India-Pakistan rivalry.[42]

Theories of Intelligence Cooperation

Munton has rightly observed how under-theorized intelligence studies and intelligence cooperation have been.[43] He argues how three dominant IR theories—*realism*, *liberalism*, and *constructivism*—provide useful analytical frameworks for understanding why countries choose to cooperate with each other in the domain of espionage and surveillance. Munton and Svendsen posit each theory carries a comparative advantage of defining one particular aspect of intelligence sharing.[44] Interestingly a *fragmegrative* worldview combines traits from all three paradigms: *fragmegrative* sinews from *realism*, integrative from *liberalism*, and a mixture of both from *constructivism* for a more uneven *fragmegrative* perspective.

Realists see intelligence cooperation as a strategy for states to maximize their power *vis-à-vis* rival states and hostile actors. Writing in the U.K. context, Lander notes how intelligence sharing gives a state "comparative political and strategic advantage over a political adversary."[45] Svendsen adds that *realists* define intelligence liaison as "business like relationships, where intelligence is the product that is 'bartered' and traded over, or marketed, in a similar manner to any other product or commodity over which deals are negotiated."[46] Taking cues from the *neo-realist* hegemonic stability theory, Svendsen goes further:

The major intelligence alliances of the last century have been demonstrably hegemonic. This appears to hold true for the substantial systems of intelligence exchange developed in the early twentieth century by the European colonial empires as much as for the Soviet and American dominated intelligence alliances witnessed after 1945.[47]

Liberals do not consider intelligence sharing to be a zero-sum game but rule-based cooperation among states pursuing mutual interests. Rudner refers to the U.S.-led global war on terrorism in developing a complex structure of intelligence coalition based on "comparative advantages of the participating intelligence agencies," which enhance the "overall capabilities" of the coalition.[48] Drawing on the Cold War era historical precedence, Aldrich uses the term "clandestine kinship" to refer to intelligence liaisons among secret services pursuing national interests.[49] When foreign policies and national interests diverge, even among military alliance members, their "hidden partnerships" fray. This is precisely what happened during the 1973 Yom Kippur War, when the United Kingdom cut down the flow of SIGINT data to the United States, and in the 1980s, when the United States did the same to New Zealand after the latter's anti-nuclear policy denied U.S. nuclear warships access to New Zealand waters.[50] But these were more like temporary hiccups rather than deep cracks in their alliance relationships. Aldrich continues how the theory of *liberal internationalism* can best explain secret intelligence cooperation:

> Perhaps clandestine agencies and their intelligence alliances should be viewed less as exponents of realism and more as the smooth and experienced exemplars of liberal institutionalism ... This complex web of unseen agreements and networks arguably raises expectations about co-operation and regulates some rather awkward practices by radiating established norms and conventions.[51]

Unlike *realists* and *liberals*, which consider states to be strategic actors either seeking to maximize national interests or pursuing rule-based cooperation for mutual benefits, *constructivists* define states as sociological actors whose identities and interests are mutually constructed through a process of interactions. Therefore, *constructivist* intelligence scholars argue that a state may not accrue net gain from trading a specific intelligence information with a partner, yet continue to share intelligence for ideational reasons.[52] In such a case, one needs to observe how interactions among intelligence partners develop a distinct identity facilitating intelligence cooperation. Svendsen notes that:

> [I]nternational intelligence liaison is formalized to the extent to which it has its own history, culture and 'mythology', can be cited as helping to contribute towards the development of more of a structural manifestation of shared values.[53]

My argument is simply how *liberal* and *constructivist* assumptions of comparative advantage and shared identity become more relevant for states in the *global North* which can dictate the terms of trade and can enjoy relative freedoms in foreign and security policy choices. By contrast, the *realist* theory, to be more precise, its *neo-realist* variant, provides a better explanation for analyzing the intelligence partnerships of states in the *global South*. This is due to the fact that most of the postcolonial states have weak economic and military power, and hence the dominant states in the regional and the global systems would structure their choices for intelligence partnerships. The last section of the chapter elaborates on this, but how the *fragmegrative* counterpart may be gaining ground must first be acknowledged. It is not that the *global North* is attenuating as intra-camp fissures grow, such as the European Union sparring even more with the United States over trade relations or interpreting Iran's nuclear concessions. The dramatic rise of China is also helping the *global North* splinter since a new player with new intelligence rules joins the party. Such intra-camp splintering may be even more pronounced in the non-*global North*, given how China's Belt and Road Initiative (BRI) has been loosening many multilateral practices in favor of new counterparts.

In summary, intelligence agencies can cooperate at the bilateral, regional, and multilateral levels. However, the scope of such cooperation may vary from full-fledged intelligence partnership to limited and conceptual development in intelligence exchange. Among the dominant IR theories, *neo-realism* provides the best possible explanation for analyzing intelligence partnerships in the *global South* presently since the *global South* intelligence institutions remain intact in spite of the see-saw changes caused by a leaderless international system and China's gate-crashing the intelligence club.

The Bangladesh Intelligence Community

The Bangladesh intelligence community comprises more than a dozen agencies and their constituent entities which report to various ministries. The three largest agencies are the Directorate General of Forces Intelligence (DGFI), the National Security Intelligence (NSI), and the Special Branch (SB) of Police. Among them, the DGFI and the NSI lead strategic intelligence producers, and as major players in international security cooperation, they report to the prime minister. On the other hand, the SB focuses on internal political surveillance and reports to the Ministry of Home Affairs (MOHA). These agencies operate with administrative orders and historical precedence, rather than any formalized roles specification and an overarching legal framework.

The DGFI defense intelligence agency is supposed to be all-source, dedicated to the protection of sovereignty and territorial integrity, whereas the NSI all-source civilian intelligence agency was established with both internal and external security mandates. The British Raj SB legacy was established primarily for watching political party leaders, student leaders, and trade union activists. Security analysts see a convergence of these three agencies' role in spying over political dissidents who pose a direct threat to the incumbent regime's political authority.

In the post-9/11 era, the MOHA counterterrorism (CT) agencies for intelligence and operational purposes have maintained international cooperation. Three newly formed intelligence-led law enforcement agencies include the Anti Terrorism Unit (ATU), the Counter Terrorism and Transnational Crime (CTTC) Unit, and the Rapid Action Battalion (RAB). These CT agencies vary in terms of composition and size. Established in 2004, RAB is the largest elite police unit in Bangladesh with 10,000 personnel, nearly half of whom are drawn from the armed forces and the rest from civilian police. By contrast, the CTTC formation in 2016 recruited 600 personnel, while the ATU formation in 2018 another 600 recruited personnel.[54] The older DGFI and NSI intelligence agencies have also developed their CT capacities by forming new entities, the DGFI's Counter Terrorism Intelligence Bureau (CTIB) and the NSI's Counter Terrorism Wing being two examples.

At least five domestic macro-level agencies work closely with their external counterparts to combat cross-border and transnational crimes, each having some levels of DGFI and NSI coordination. Among them, the Border Security Bureau (BSB) and the Coast Guard Intelligence (CGI) directly contribute to the operations of the Border Guard Bangladesh and the Bangladesh Coast Guard, respectively. Operating under the MOHA jurisdiction, the BSB and CGI tasks include collection, analysis, and dissemination of intelligence pertaining to cross-border crimes, with arms-and-drug-smuggling and maritime piracy, in the list. Two other agencies—the Customs Intelligence and Investigation Directorate (CIID) and the Central Intelligence Cell (CIC)—operate under the National Board of Revenue (NBR) to detecting, analyzing, and seizing perpetrators of customs fraud and tax-evasion. The fifth agency, Bangladesh Financial Intelligence Unit (BFIU), leads analysis and dissemination of intelligence pertaining to money laundering and terrorist financing. The latter three agencies—BFIU, CIC, and CIID—report to the Ministry of Finance.

Several intelligence agencies are tasked with classified matters operating under the Ministry of Defense, which goes beyond the scope of this study. For instance, the three defense services—Army, Navy, and Air Force—have their own intelligence directorates working on defense services personnel, operations, training, weapons acquisition, and interagency coordination. In addition, the Armed Forces Division, which acts as a national command and control authority for the Prime Minister, also has a small intelligence directorate for maintaining and internal and external liaison on intelligence matters.

There is an institutional arrangement for coordination among the intelligence agencies. Chaired by the Prime Minister and coordinated by the Defense and Security Adviser to the Prime Minister, the National Committee for Intelligence Coordination (NCIC) was established in 2009. As key NCIC members, the heads of DGFI, NSI, Special Security Force, and Bangladesh Police meet on a need-to-know basis, with their intelligence-direction, -tasking, and -sharing agenda remaining classified.

INTELLIGENCE SHARING PRACTICES OF BANGLADESH

This section has four parts. The first three describe Bangladesh's intelligence cooperation at the bilateral, regional, and multilateral levels, the fourth analyzes the scope of intelligence partnership between Bangladesh and other actors.

Bilateral Cooperation

Distinct trends in bilateral intelligence cooperation practices prevail between Bangladesh and other partners around the world. A brief cooperation analysis is made here with India, China, and Saudi Arabia in the *global South*, and the United States and its allies in the *global North*.

Bilateral intelligence liaison between Bangladesh and India dates back to 1971 when the latter's external intelligence agency, Research and Analysis Wing (RAW), provided active support in organizing and training the Bangladeshi freedom fighters against the then West Pakistani forces and their Inter-Services Intelligence (ISI) Directorate.[55] India also extended SIGINT support by allowing its radio and transmission network to be used by *Swadhin Bangla Betar Kendra [Independent Bangla Radio Center]* having its first office in Calcutta Radio Station of India's West Bengal provincial state.[56]

Cooperation between the intelligence services of Bangladesh and India has grown over the years, and played out largely at local or micro levels. For instance, the crucial RAW role of withdrawing support for the Bangladesh-focused ethnic insurgent group *Shanti Bahini* helped the latter to surrender arms following the 1997 Chittagong Hill Tracts Peace Accord. Bangladeshi security agencies reciprocated by denying the Indian rebel group, United Liberation Front of Assam (ULFA), sanctuary in the country.[57]

Counterterrorism cooperation has emerged as a new dimension in Bangladesh–India security partnership. This is often illustrated by exchange visits of intelligence officials from both countries. For instance, investigations into the accidental bomb explosion in India's Burdwan district of West Bengal state in October 2014 revealed the presence of Bangladeshi militant group *Jama'at ul Mujahideen Bangladesh* (JMB) in three Indian states: West Bengal, Assam, and Jharkhand. The Burdwan explosion drew India's federal crime investigation unit, National Investigation Agency (NIA), closer to Bangladesh's CTIB, CTTC, and RAB agencies to develop a common JMB threat assessment.[58]

As Bangladesh Navy is now equipped with two Chinese made Ming-class submarines, with Chinese companies heavily investing in the construction of a deep-sea port in Bangladesh's southern district of Patuakhali,[59] Delhi has sought to counterbalance Beijing's growing influence by developing closer maritime ties with Dhaka. Against this backdrop, on

October 5, 2019 both countries signed a memorandum of understanding to set up the first coastal surveillance radar system in Bangladesh.[60] If Bangladesh builds up the coastal surveillance system with Indian radars, it would create the possibility of some SIGINT exchange between Dhaka and Delhi on the movement of vessels in the surface water.[61] For skeptics in Bangladesh, despite pre-existing bilateral cooperation on border security and counterterrorism, large-scale SIGINT exchange with India is unlikely to materialize given the profound level of distrust between the strategic communities in both countries.[62]

After India, Bangladesh has prioritized intelligence liaison with the United States and its major allies. In mid-October 2019, Bangladesh and U.S. delegates discussed the prospect of signing two deals—General Security of Military Information Agreement (GSOMIA) and Acquisition and Cross Servicing Agreement (ACSA).[63] If signed, these deals will pave the opportunities for defense technology transfer, intelligence sharing, and military cooperation between the two countries.[64] The United States has a GSOMIA deal with 76 countries and an ACSA counterpart with more than a hundred countries around the world.

Counterterrorism cooperation between Bangladesh and the United States has grown in the post-9/11 era. This includes sharing threat assessment through strategic dialogues and providing capacity building support to the security practitioners in Bangladesh. In August 2016, during his Dhaka visit, the U.S. Secretary of State John Kerry observed how the Islamic State of Iraq and Syria (*ISIS*) had contacts with Bangladeshi militants.[65] Kerry's observation did not alter the official stance of Bangladesh Government, which rejects the possibility of any ties between ISIS and homegrown neo-JMB group. But privately, Bangladeshi and U.S. intelligence officials hold identical views regarding the evolving threats of *Al Qaeda* and *ISIS* in the South Asian region.[66]

Bangladesh and the United Kingdom have also developed counterterrorism partnerships. For instance, cooperation between the Bangladeshi agencies DGFI and RAB and the U.K. MI5 and MI6 agencies have been well-documented in the media. In 2011, *The Guardian* reported about an extensive Bangladesh and U.K. level of intelligence sharing regarding the interrogation of dual citizens in a secret Task Force for Interrogation cell.[67] In March 2017, Bangladesh and the United Kingdom launched a strategic dialogue to boost up their economic and security cooperation. At the third Bangladesh-U.K. strategic dialogue, held in March 2019, senior officials from the two countries emphasized "countering terrorism and violent extremism to safeguard their citizens and global humanity."[68]

Bangladesh has also pursued bilateral intelligence cooperation with Australia and Canada. In 2008 and 2015, Bangladesh and Australia signed two memoranda of understanding to facilitate cooperation on counterterrorism and transnational crime, with the law enforcement agencies of the two states conducting joint counterterrorism exercises.[69] Since 2016, Canadian security and intelligence agency officials have also shown an interest in developing partnership with Dhaka to address the threats of ISIS foreign fighters. This came in response to growing concerns over radicalization of a Bangladeshi-origin Canadian, Tamim Chowdhury, who masterminded the Holey Artisan Bakery attack in Dhaka in 2016.[70]

The preceding discussion focused on two trends in bilateral intelligence cooperation practices of Bangladesh: with India, and the United States and its allies. A third and new trend emerges in which intelligence sharing is identified as a sub-set of security cooperation between Bangladesh and China, and Bangladesh and Saudi Arabia. In October 2018, at the first home minister-level meeting, Bangladesh and China signed an agreement on intelligence sharing to address the threats of terrorism and transnational crime.[71] In April 2019, at the second home minister-level meeting, Bangladesh and China highlighted the need for police cooperation and intelligence sharing for combating terrorism and cyber-crime.[72] Earlier, in 2015, Bangladesh joined the *ISIS*-combatting Saudi-led international coalition.[73] The two countries have recently explored cooperation in military construction, border surveillance, mine clearing, and training.[74] In 2018, Bangladeshi military forces participated in a joint military exercise in Saudi Arabia. Next year Bangladesh and Saudi Arabia signed a memorandum of understanding to facilitate military cooperation and intelligence sharing, to expedite the deployment of 1800 troops to Saudi Arabia to clear the mines along the Saudi-Yemen borders.

Regional Cooperation

Bangladesh has taken an active interest in regional intelligence cooperation through the Bay of Bengal Initiative for Multi-Sectoral Technical and Economic Cooperation (BIMSTEC) and the SAARC. In 2017, the national security chiefs of BIMSTEC countries met in New Delhi to discuss a wide range of threats including cyber-crime, violent extremism, and maritime piracy. In the first meeting of the national security chiefs, a resolution was made to establish a Track 1.5 Security Dialogue Forum bringing in the perspectives of both government officials and civil society experts to assess a wide range of both traditional and non-traditional security threats. The second meeting of the Track 1.5 BIMSTEC Security Dialogue Forum was held in Dhaka that resolved to promote intelligence sharing for regional peace and stability.

Efforts to boost SAARC-level security cooperation have a much longer history. Bangladesh is a contracting party to various conventions, protocols, and ministerial declarations, which have created a normative basis for intelligence sharing among the SAARC members. Such instruments include: *SAARC Regional Convention on Suppression of Terrorism 1987*, *Additional Protocol to the SAARC Regional Convention on Suppression of Terrorism 2004*, *SAARC Ministerial Declaration on Cooperation in Combatting Terrorism 2009*, and *SAARC Ministerial Statement on Cooperation against Terrorism 2010*. Although a hostage to India–Pakistan geopolitical rivalry, the SAARC role through the adoption of these normative instruments is a clear indication of member-states' emphasis on intelligence sharing.

Bangladesh has also supported the establishment of institutional bodies for SAARC-level regional intelligence sharing. Two such institutional platforms, SAARC Drug Offenses Monitoring Desk (SDOMD) and SAARC Terrorism Offenses Monitoring Desk (STOMD) have existed since the early 1990s, and a third one, SAARC Cyber Crime Offenses Monitoring Desk, was established in 2014. As stated before, a further initiative to establish SAARCPOL for law enforcement cooperation among South Asian police agencies failed. Yet, for more than half a decade, Bangladesh Police, an advocate of regional police cooperation, has been organizing an annual week-long training program on transnational crime under the banner of SAARCPOL.[75] The purpose of the training program is to promote a professional network of South Asian law enforcement and intelligence agencies.

Multilateral Cooperation

At the multilateral level, Bangladesh works with the United Nations (U.N.) Counter Terrorism Committee Executive Directorate (CTED) to promote compliance with the U.N. Security Council Resolution (UNSCR) 1373 (2001) that criminalizes terrorism, and calls for punitive actions against terrorist financing. In 2009, Bangladesh organized a three-day workshop on counterterrorism that featured the UNSCR 1373 very highly. The workshop was attended by police and prosecutors from the SAARC member-states.[76] The U.N. High Commissioner for Human Rights was represented in the workshop to disseminate the knowledge that counterterrorism actions of UN members must comply with the rule of law.

In 2018, Bangladesh joined an initiative of the United Nations Office on Drugs and Crime (UNODC) to establish the South Asian Regional Intelligence Coordination Center (SARICC). Under UNODC and SARICC auspices, SAARC member-states wish to develop a criminal intelligence sharing database to combat transnational crime.[77]

Bangladesh has been an Interpol member since 1976. It regularly cooperates with global police agencies using the Interpol's intelligence sharing platform. Such cooperation has produced tangible benefits in the fight against drug smuggling, human trafficking, and transnational terrorism,[78] all key threats within a globalized domain, but obviously with each threat having significant localized claims. Since 1976, Bangladesh has issued Interpol red alerts against 80 individuals who absconded after committing a serious crime in the country.[79]

Bangladesh has also been part of the global initiatives for financial intelligence sharing. As an Egmont Group member since 2013, the BFIU agency has accessed the global financial intelligence hub to take effective measures against transnational organized crime and terrorism.[80] Its customs intelligence, CIID entity, works with the World Customs Organization's Regional Intelligence Liaison Office (RILO) to share intelligence on smuggling of goods and communities.[81]

In summary, the foregoing discussion has shown increasing bilateral, regional, and global partnerships between the intelligence agencies of Bangladesh and other agencies around the world.

Scope of Cooperation

The relevance of the six-fold typology regarding the scope of intelligence sharing is tested here. First, full-fledged cooperation can be observed in the context of Bangladesh's bilateral cooperation with India and multilateral cooperation at the United Nations. Indo-Bangladesh security partnership is backed by bilateral agreements on cooperation in criminal matters and extradition of criminal and terrorist suspects. Such partnership is often widely circulated in the media. In 2010, the Bangladesh

High Commissioner to India claimed there was a "real-time intelligence sharing" between the security agencies of the two countries.[82] He was referring to various channels of intelligence sharing. In meetings at the "home minister" and "home secretary" levels, the two states have agreed to share intelligence on various types of terrorist and insurgent groups, cattle smuggling, and currency counterfeiting. Senior officials from the Bangladesh ministries of Home and Foreign Affairs and the chiefs of Border Guard Bangladesh, Customs, and Police attend such bilateral discussions to develop the modus operandi for intelligence sharing.[83]

At the multilateral level, Bangladesh's counterterrorism cooperation through the UNCTED also falls into the category of full-fledged cooperation. This is due to Bangladesh fully complying with the UNSCR 1373 (2001) regarding proscription of terrorist actors and freezing their assets.

Second, limited and episodic cooperation can be observed at the bilateral, regional, and multilateral levels. Bilateral cooperation between Bangladesh and China, and Bangladesh and Saudi Arabia appear to be limited and episodic. The first is aimed at sharing intelligence to protect the huge Chinese investment in Bangladesh, whereas the second is designed to support the demining activities in Saudi areas bordering Yemen.

Limited and episodic intelligence sharing has also occurred between Bangladesh and several states in the *global North* including Australia, Canada, the United Kingdom, and the United States.[84] In four such cases, with varying levels of outcomes, concerned foreign intelligence agencies either sought or exchanged information regarding the background of Bangladeshi-origin terrorist suspects. In the first case, in 2009 a Bangladeshi–U.S. immigrant, Ehsanul Islam Sadequee, was convicted and sentenced to 17 years in Georgia state on charges of supporting a radicalized terrorist network.[85] In the second case, a Bangladeshi-origin British citizen, Saimun Rahman, was jailed in Bangladesh for more than two years and, after his release in April 2017, he was arrested by Delhi Police in September 2017.[86] Saimun, a suspect in terrorist financing and recruitment, became a subject of interest for Bangladeshi, Indian, and U.K. intelligence agencies. Thirdly, a Bangladeshi non-immigrant student in Australia, Momena Shoma, was sentenced to 42 years in Melbourne for stabbing her homestay landlord in February 2018.[87] In the fourth case, a Bangladeshi–Canadian immigrant, Tamim Chowdhury, who masterminded the Holey Artisan attack in Dhaka, was killed in a major CT operation in Bangladesh.[88]

Bangladesh's BIMSTEC and SAARC cooperation on security and intelligence matters is also very limited. Although, the BIMSTEC members have initiated a forum of the national security chiefs and have introduced a Track 1.5 security dialogue, it still operates conceptually, rather than developing any formal and institutionalized intelligence sharing mechanism. On the other hand, the SAARCPOL idea has failed to evolve into an intelligence sharing hub, and the process has forestalled largely due to India-Pakistan conflict. At the multilateral level, Bangladesh's cooperation with Egmont Group of FIUs and WCO are mostly demand-driven, limited, and episodic. Such cooperation often concentrates on sharing best practices.

Third, operations sharing has also occurred between Bangladeshi agencies and their bilateral partners. Westerfield's concept of three categories of operations support comprising parallel, allocated, and joint operations is very relevant here.

In recent years, Bangladesh has shared operational intelligence with India for parallel investigation into terrorist incidents, for instance, the Indian NIA investigation into the terrorist explosion in West Bengal's Burdwan district. While Bangladesh conducted a parallel CTTC investigation into a possible JMB nexus with its Indian operatives, after the devastating Holey Artisan terrorist attack in Dhaka, Indian intelligence agencies also conducted parallel, rather than a joint, investigation to explore the extent to which the Bangladeshi terror operatives secured funds and weapons from India. Although investigations into the Burdwan blast and Holey Artisan attack required meetings of mid- and senior-level intelligence officials from both Bangladesh and India, there was no evidence of joint operations or investigations. This was clearly due to the fact that national intelligence agencies often consider the presence of foreign agencies in their operational areas as an "intrusion" or "interference" that may cause more harm rather than benefits.[89]

Allocated operational cooperation is also evident between Bangladeshi and Indian agencies. In response to the emergence of *Al Qaeda in Indian Sub-Continent* (AQIS) as a potent threat in South Asia, Bangladeshi and Indian intelligence agencies have kept an eye on groups either AQIS affiliated or AQIS sympathizers. The threat of the global *ISIS* terrorist network and its South Asian JMB affiliate has also drawn attention from the intelligence agencies of Bangladesh and India. In this context of allocated operational cooperation, the Intelligence Bureau (IB) of India issued a warning in May 2019, referring a potential *ISIS* attack (or its affiliate JMB in India's West Bengal state or the neighboring Bangladesh territory).[90] The IB warning not only prompted strong security measures in both Bangladesh and India, but also led to a JMB ban as a proscribed terrorist organization by the Indian Ministry of Home Affairs.[91]

Joint operations also occurred, albeit rarely. In one such instance, the Indian NIA and Bangladeshi RAB agencies jointly acted to arrest and interrogate suspects behind a terrorist explosion in Delhi High Court in 2011. Following NIA probes in India, the RAB arrest of two Kashmiri medical students and two Kashmiri intern doctors, led to NIA interrogation.[92] Both the arrest and the interrogation occurred in the eastern city Sylhet, where the medical students and intern doctors were affiliated with a private medical college hospital. Although the four were later released, the nature of the arrest and the interrogation reveal the practice of joint operations by Bangladeshi and Indian law enforcement and intelligence agencies.

Fourth, Bangladesh has received support from both India and the United States for capacity-building of the counterterrorism analysts, practitioners, and judicial officials. Such partnerships come in the form of technology transfer and training at home and abroad. According to the *U.S. Country Report on Terrorism 2018*:

> Bangladesh continued to participate in the Department of State's Antiterrorism Assistance program and received counterterrorism training on building unit capacity in crisis response, evidence collection, crime scene investigation, infrastructure protection, instructional development and sustainment, as well as enhancing cyber and digital investigation capabilities.[93]

In 2019, the U.S. Ambassador to Bangladesh emphasized a joint initiative of U.S. Department of State and the Department of Justice's Office of Prosecutorial Development, Assistance and Training in providing training for investigation into money laundering and terrorist financing for Bangladeshi officials.[94]

India has also provided similar training to Bangladeshi officials. Media reports suggest that nearly 80 percent of fake Indian currency enter India through Bangladesh territory. Indian officials claim that Pakistan's ISI secret service injects tens of billions of dollars to India as part of a strategy of economic warfare.[95] Hence, a NIA project trains Bangladeshi law enforcers and intelligence personnel to detect fake currency and support India against economic warfare threats.

Fifth, both India and Bangladesh followed a crypto-diplomacy model in exchanging information on ethnic rebel groups hostile to each other. This came in the form of India withdrawing large-scale support for the *Shanti Bahini* rebels and Bangladesh handing over top ULFA leaders to Indian authorities. Such cooperation has been more an outcome of favorable political regimes on both sides of the Bangladesh–India border rather than any formal agreement between two countries.

Sixth, Bangladesh's limited bilateral cooperation with India and the United States on some sensitive defense intelligence deals may simply be conceptual at best. Despite all the doubts and skepticisms, if the Bangladesh–India coastal surveillance cooperation is materialized, and the proposed Bangladesh–U.S. GSOMIA and ACSA deals get signed, they may create the context for episodic, rather than, full-fledged intelligence cooperation for the exchange of HUMINT and SIGINT data. Given the fact that Bangladesh pursues a peaceful stance in its foreign policy posture, the coastal surveillance and arms trade deals may contribute more to Bangladesh's military modernization for defensive purposes.

Two key findings over Bangladesh's intelligence sharing practices emerge: First, evidence validates the longstanding assumption of how bilateral intelligence sharing is more widely practiced than regional and multilateral sharing. Second, widening scope of intelligence cooperation in the domain of counterterrorism remains limited in sensitive defense matters.

A Neo-realist Explanation

Foregoing discussions over Bangladesh's intelligence cooperation with other states and institutions at the bilateral, regional, and global levels clearly indicate the relevance of *neo-realist* theory. *Neo-realists* contend how power distribution has an effect on shaping the foreign and security policy of a state. In the intelligence studies literature, the *neo-realist* concept of "hegemony" can explain how the dominant states in the international system shape the formation and outcome of intelligence exchange.

A *neo-realist* understanding of intelligence cooperation would require us to first recognize that for a state like Bangladesh, India and the United States constitute the regional and global hegemons, respectively. Hence, intelligence cooperation with them becomes part of a geopolitical "great game" behind the façade of a mutually beneficial project.[96]

This is precisely why India's proposed coastal surveillance system is not merely aimed at capacity building of both Bangladesh Navy and Coast Guard. If implemented, it would also allow India to monitor the IOR movements of Chinese warships. While the proposed coastal surveillance system would develop an enhanced capacity for both countries to fight maritime piracy, transnational criminals, and terrorists operating in the IOR sea lanes, it would give the Indian Navy an upper hand by making sure the radar system is consistent with Indian maritime security.

Neo-realists argue how powerful states in the international system pursue intelligence cooperation to promote their foreign policy and to project military power. Such an assumption is also validated by the most recent bilateral security cooperation between Bangladesh and the United States. Since 2012, Dhaka and Washington have been organizing partnership dialogues focusing on cooperation in the areas of defense, trade, and disaster management. In 2016, Bangladesh was enlisted in the U.S. Counter Terrorism Partnership Fund to promote cooperation in addressing the threats of radicalization, improving civilian law enforcement-led counterterrorism, and training in producing counter-narratives of terrorist discourse.[97] In recent years, the United States has given Bangladesh an estimated US $43 million of counterterrorism aid to strengthen the law enforcement and judicial capacity of Bangladesh to combat terrorists and to bring them under a free and fair trial system.[98]

For *realist* South Asia watchers, U.S. geopolitical and geo-economic interests dictate the U.S.–Bangladesh security dialogues and U.S. counterterrorism support to Bangladesh. By developing security partnerships with Bangladesh and other IOR states, the United States wishes to see reduced Chinese influence in the region and to develop an international coalition against transnational terrorists.[99] Here Lander's concept of "comparative political or strategic advantage" captures the value that Bangladeshi intelligence agencies can add to the U.S. global counterterrorism strategy. Although the United States has its own HUMINT and SIGINT resources, none of them can create a nuanced threat assessment in the absence of intelligence sharing with partner states like Bangladesh. This is precisely why Munton observes:

> [A]lmost all states, and particularly great powers, conduct intelligence as a critical element of maintaining and expanding their power. International intelligence cooperation can augment that power – if one can pursue it so as not to weaken oneself in the process.[100]

Returning to the rise of intelligence liaison among BIMSTEC countries and the fall of cooperation among the SAARC members, the relative SAARC decline and the corresponding BIMSTEC growth clearly indicate India's preference to promote the BIMSTEC agency not only to undermine SAARC but also to counterbalance the influence of China's BRI project. In essence, security and intelligence cooperation through the BIMSTEC channel would allow India to pursue economic interests and create a network of allies including Bangladesh that would contain China's BRI project and keep Pakistan at bay.[101]

In explaining multilateral intelligence cooperation through the United Nations, the Egmont Group, and the RILO agency, one may also find the utility of the *neo-realist* theory. A key question concerns whether these multilateral institutions can function independently or represent great power interest. For Mearsheimer, a prominent *neo-realist* scholar, international institutions have historically served the interests of United States and its allies.[102] It is thus not surprising that in the post-9/11 era, the United States has steered the paths in creating an international security regime through interlocking agreements and institutions. For Bangladesh and other states in the *global South*, the risk of non-compliance with the U.S.-led security regime would be enormous: it would make it a pariah state and increase the cost of doing business.[103] A logical consequence is compliance with the global regime for combating terrorism and transnational crime.

Conclusion

Two questions regarding hidden partnerships of spy agencies beyond "Anglosphere" were addressed in this chapter. The first questioned how states in the *global South* develop intelligence partnerships, and the second inquired which IR theory best explains such partnerships. It employed an analytical framework with the levels of analysis, scopes, and theories of intelligence cooperation as components in the Bangladesh context. Three key findings emerge. First, Bangladesh has developed a complex dynamics of intelligence partnerships at the bilateral, regional, and multilateral levels in pursuit of national security and foreign policy. Second, the scope of cooperation in the domain of counterterrorism has increased with states both in the *global North* and *global South*. Third, the *neo-realist* IR theory can best explain Bangladesh's intelligence partnerships. The data and analysis presented in this chapter show that regional and global hegemons have largely influenced the intelligence sharing practices of Bangladesh. This is a scenario that reflects traditional power politics in the international system.

The findings remain tentative, and their reliability and validity need to be tested with further studies. As the Bangladesh case study suggests, scholars researching intelligence partnership in the *global South* will need to confront the challenge of limited archival documents, and overcome this challenge with expert interviews and open source data.

Notes

1. Richard Aldrich, "Dangerous Liaisons: Post-September 11 Intelligence Alliances," *Harvard International Review* 24, no. 3 (September 2002): 49–54.
2. Richard Aldrich, "US–European Intelligence Co-operation on Counter-Terrorism: Low Politics and Compulsion," *British Journal of Politics and International Relations* 11 (2009): 122–139.
3. P. H. J. Davis and K. C. Gustafson, eds., *Intelligence Elsewhere: Spies and Espionage Outside the Anglosphere* (London: Georgetown University Press, 2013); A. S. M. Ali Ashraf, *Intelligence, National Security, and Foreign Policy: A South Asian Narrative* (Dhaka: Bangladesh Institute of Law and International Affairs and Department of International Relations, University of Dhaka, 2016); and Bob de Graaff, ed., *Intelligence Communities and Cultures in Asia and the Middle East: A Comprehensive Reference* (Boulder, CO: Lynne Rienner, 2020).
4. Zakia Shiraz and Aldrich note that "in IR, political science, and development studies, the North–South dichotomy incorporates the history of colonialism, neo-colonialism, geopolitical relations, and differences in social, political, and economic processes." For area studies scholars, 'global South' refers to "a region of distinctive intellectual production" See: Shiraz and Aldrich, "Secrecy, Spies and Global South: Intelligence Studies Beyond the 'Five Eyes' Alliance," *International Affairs* 96, no. 6 (2019): 3.
5. Davis and Gustafson, op. cit.
6. Marco Cepikand Gustavo Möller, "National Intelligence Systems as Networks: Power Distribution and Organizational Risk in

Brazil, Russia, India, China, and South Africa," *Brazilian Political Science Review* 11, no. 1 (2017): 1–26.
7. Shiraz and Aldrich, op. cit.; Patrick F. Walsh, "Improving Strategic Intelligence Analytical Practice Through Qualitative Social Research," *Intelligence and National Security* 32, no. 5 (2017): 548–562; and Erik J. Dahl, "Getting Beyond Analysis by Anecdote: Improving Intelligence Analysis through the Use of Case Studies," *Intelligence and National Security* 32, no. 5 (2017): 563–578.
8. Julfikar Ali Manik, Geeta Anand, and Ellen Berry, "Bangladesh Attack Is New Evidence That ISIS Has Shifted Its Focus Beyond Mideast," *New York Times*, July 3, 2016; Inter Sector Coordination Group, *Joint Response Plan for Rohingya Humanitarian Crisis*, January–December 2019 (Dhaka: Strategic Executive Group of UN Resident Coordinator, UNHCR Bangladesh and IOM Bangladesh, 2019), 10.
9. Anu Anwar, "How Bangladesh Is Benefiting from the China–India Rivalry," *The Diplomat*, July 12, 2019; Delwar Hossain and Shariful Islam, "Unfolding Bangladesh–India Maritime Connectivity in the Bay of Bengal Region: A Bangladesh Perspective," *Journal of the Indian Ocean Region* 15, no. 3 (2019): 346–355.
10. Bhumitra Chakma, "Sheikh Hasina Government's India Policy: A Three-Level Game?" *Journal of Asian Security and International Affairs* 2, no. 1 (2015): 27–51; Md. Abdul Mannan, "Bangladesh–China Relations: Mapping Geopolitical and Security Interests," *Monograph 2* (Dhaka: East Asia Study Centre, University of Dhaka, 2018).
11. Iftekhar Ahmed Chowdhury, "Foundations of Bangladesh's Foreign Policy Interactions," *ISAS Insights*, no. 120 (March 23, 2011), Singapore: Institute of South Asian Studies; Lailufar Yasmin, "Bangladesh and the Great Powers," *Routledge Handbook of Contemporary Bangladesh* (Abingdon: Routledge, 2016), 389–401.
12. S. M. Shamsul Alam, "Democratic Politics and the Fall of the Military Regime in Bangladesh," *Bulletin of Concerned Asian Scholars* 27, no. 3 (1995): 28–42.
13. Nizam Ahmed, "Party Politics Under a Non-Party Caretaker Government in Bangladesh: The Fakhruddin Interregnum

(2007–09)," *Commonwealth & Comparative Politics* 48, no. 1 (2010): 23–47.
14. Aldrich, "Dangerous Liaisons," 51.
15. Stephane Lefebvre, "The Difficulties and Dilemmas of International Intelligence Cooperation," *International Journal of Intelligence and Counterintelligence* 16, no. 4 (2003): 527–542; Martin Rudner, "Hunters and Gatherers: The Intelligence Coalition Against Islamic Terrorism," *International Journal of Intelligence and Counterintelligence* 17, no. 4 (2004): 193–230.
16. Global North refers to advanced industrialized and developed countries in the Northern Hemisphere, with the exception of Australia and New Zealand. See: Royal Geographic Society, "The Global North/South Divide," https://www.rgs.org/CMS Pages/GetFile.aspx?nodeguid=9c1ce781-9117-4741-af0a-a6a 8b75f32b4&lang=en-GB, accessed June 19, 2020.
17. Rudner, ibid.
18. Rubén Arcos and José-Miguel Palacios, "EU INTCEN: A Transnational European Culture of Intelligence Analysis?" *Intelligence and National Security* 35, no. 1 (2020): 72–94.
19. "EU INTCEN Fact Sheet 05/02/2015," https://statewatch.org/news/2016/may/eu-intcen-factsheet.pdf, accessed June 18, 2020.
20. Aldrich, "US–European Intelligence Co-operation on Counter-Terrorism," 127.
21. Bjorn Fagersten, "For EU Eyes Only? Intelligence and European Security," *Issue Brief* 8 (2016). Paris: European Union Institute for Security Studies, 2.
22. Angaindrankumar Gnanasagaran, "'Our Eyes' to Combat Terrorism," *The ASEAN Post*, October 22, 2018.
23. Peter Clottey, "African Union Urges Global Intelligence-Sharing Against Terrorism," *Voice of America*, May 12, 2014.
24. "Somali, AU Forces Seek to Step Up Intelligence Sharing to Flush Out Terrorists," *Xinhua*, March 27, 2019.
25. "African Union Inaugurates New HQ of Intelligence and Security Services," *The North Africa Post*, February 12, 2020.
26. Wilfried Scharf, "African Security Via Police, Justice, and Intelligence Reform," *Providing Security for People: Enhancing Security Through Police, Justice, and Intelligence Reform in Africa*, eds.

Chris Ferguson and Jeffry O. Isima (Shrivenham, UK: Global Facilitation Network for Security Sector Reform), 64.
27. Ernesto Vivares, ed., *Exploring the New South American Regionalism* (NSAR) (London and New York: Routledge, 2016), 177.
28. United Nations Office on Drugs and Crime, *Promoting the Rule of Law and Human Security in Central America: Regional Programme 2009–2012* (UNODC, 2010).
29. Ann Hammerstad, "Domestic Threats, Regional Solutions? The Challenge of Security Integration in Southern Africa," *Review of International Studies* 31, no. 1 (2005): 69–87; Zakia Shiraz, "Drugs and Dirty Wars: Intelligence Cooperation in the Global South," *Third World Quarterly* 34, no. 10 (2013): 1749–1766.
30. Egmont Group, "About," https://egmontgroup.org/content/about, accessed June 18, 2020.
31. Mathieu Deflem, "International Police Cooperation Against Terrorism: Interpol and Europol in Comparison," *Understanding and Responding to Terrorism*, ed. H. Durmaz, B. Sevinc, A. S. Yayla, and S. Ekici (Amsterdam: IOS Press, 2007), 17–25.
32. Lefebvre, "The Difficulties and Dilemmas."
33. Rudner, "Hunters and Gatherers"; Aldrich, "US–European Intelligence Co-operation"; and Fagersten, "For EU Eyes Only?"
34. Arndt Freytag von Loringhoven, "A New Era for NATO Intelligence," *NATO Review*, October 29, 2019.
35. H. Bradford Westerfield, "America and the World of Intelligence Liaison," *Intelligence and National Security* 11, no. 3 (1996): 523–560.
36. Ibid., 529.
37. Ibid.
38. Ibid., 530.
39. Ibid., 531; Christopher Andrew, *For the President's Eyes Only: Secret Intelligence and the American Presidency from Washington to Bush* (NY: HarperCollins, 1995), note 5, 467–468.
40. Ibid., 535.
41. Ibid., 538; Aharon Klieman, *Statecraft in the Dark: Israel's Practice of Quiet Diplomacy* (Boulder, CO: Westview, 1988), 111.
42. A. S. M. Ali Ashraf, "Regional Police Cooperation in South Asia: Progresses and Challenges," *Intelligence, National Security and Foreign Policy: A South Asian Narrative*, ed. A. S. M. Ali Ashraf (Dhaka: Bangladesh Institute of Law and International Affairs

and Department of International Relations, University of Dhaka, 2016), 215–236.
43. Don Munton, "Intelligence Cooperation Meets International Studies Theory: Explaining Canadian Operations in Castro's Cuba," *Intelligence and National Security* 24, no. 1 (2009): 119–138.
44. Munton, "Intelligence Cooperation"; D. Svendsen, "Connecting Intelligence and Theory: Intelligence Liaison and International Relations," *Intelligence and National Security* 24, no. 5 (2009): 700–729.
45. Stephen Lander, "International Intelligence Cooperation: An Inside Perspective," *Cambridge Review of International Affairs* 17, no. 3 (2004): 481.
46. Svendsen, "Connecting Intelligence," 717.
47. Ibid., 719.
48. Rudner, "Hunters and Gatherers," 215–216.
49. Aldrich, "Dangerous Liaisons," 52.
50. Ibid., 51.
51. Ibid., 54.
52. Douglas Ford, "Strategic Culture, Intelligence Assessment, and the Conduct of the Pacific War: The British–Indian and Imperial Japanese Armies in Comparison, 1941–1945," *War in History* 14, no. 1 (2007): 63–95; J. M. Bonthous, "Understanding Intelligence Across Cultures," *International Journal of Intelligence and Counter Intelligence* 7 (1994): 7–34; Ralf G. V. Lillbacka, "Realism, Constructivism, and Intelligence Analysis," *International Journal of Intelligence and Counter Intelligence* 26, no. 2 (2013): 304–331.
53. Svendsen, "Connecting Intelligence," 721–722.
54. The CTTC is a unit of the Dhaka Metropolitan Police but enjoys a mandate to operate as a national CT force. Since its inception in 2016, it has conducted several high profile raids against terrorist dens leading to the arrest and killing of top terrorists. On the other hand, ATU is a national CT force that collaborates with CTTC and other police entities.
55. Imtiaz Ahmed, *State and Foreign Policy: India's Role in South Asia* (Delhi: Vikas, 1991), 254.
56. Ibid., 245.

57. A. S. M. Ali Ashraf and Md. Sohel Rana, "External Influence, Domestic Politics, and Bangladesh Government's Northeast India Policy," *Bangladesh's Neighbours in the Indian Northeast: Exploring Opportunities and Mutual Interest*, ed. Akmal Hussain (Dhaka: Asiatic Society of Bangladesh, 2017), 26–27.
58. Kamal Hossain Talukder, "Bangladesh Intelligence Team to Go to India," *bdnews24.com*, November 27, 2014.
59. Sayed Mahmud Ali, "South Asia in Strategic Competition: Tracing Chinese, Indian, and U.S. Footprints," *South Asia in Global Power Rivalry*, ed. Imtiaz Hussain (London: Palgrave, 2019), 248.
60. Such radars usually have a capacity to detect smaller boats of 20 m from a 50 km range, and can perform in all weather conditions. India has set up similar radars in Mauritius, Seychelles, and Maldives, and has a plan to setup one in Myanmar. See: Kamran Reza Chowdhury, "Bangladesh Gives India Greenlight to Install Surveillance Radar System," *BenarNews*, July 10, 2019.
61. From an Indian perspective, coastal intelligence will enable Delhi to monitor Chinese military activities in the Indian Ocean. See: Dipanjan Roy Chaudhury, "India, Bangladesh Sign MoU for Coastal Surveillance System Radar in Bangladesh," *The Economic Times*, October 7, 2019.
62. Interviews with anonymous defense analysts in Dhaka and Delhi, June 2020.
63. Nurul Islam Hasib, "Bangladesh, US in Talks to Sign Two Defence Deals," *bdnews24.com*, October 17, 2019; Diplomatic Correspondent, "US Wants 2 Defence Deals with Bangladesh," *The Daily Star*, October 18, 2019.
64. Although U.S. officials in Bangladesh claim no GSOMIA requirement to share information, for East Asia watchers this is hardly the case, since the South Korea–Japan GSOMIA basis has long facilitated sensitive information sharing on North Korean missiles and nuclear weapons program. Similarly, ACSA does not commit a U.S. partner to a joint military action, rather it aims to simplify the procurement and payment of logistic support, supplies and services between U.S. and partner forces. See: Kyodo, "Tokyo Ready to Share Info on North Korea Missile with Seoul Despite Row," *Japan Times*, October 4, 2019.

65. Steve Herman, "Bangladesh US Agree to Enhance Cooperation to Fight Terrorism," *Voice of America*, August 29, 2016.
66. Interviews with intelligence practitioners in Bangladesh, February 2020.
67. Ian Cobain and Fariha Karim, "UK Linked to Notorious Bangladesh Torture Centre," *The Guardian*, January 17, 2011.
68. British High Commission Dhaka, "UK and Bangladesh Hold Third Strategic Dialogue," https://www.gov.uk/government/news/third-bangladesh-uk-strategic-dialogue, accessed June 9, 2020.
69. Australia Department of Foreign Affairs and Trade, "Bangladesh Country Brief," Canberra: Australian Government.
70. Staff Correspondent, "Tamim Chy: An Evil Mind," *The Daily Star*, August 9, 2016; Associate Press, "Bangladesh Police Kill Canadian Suspect in Restaurant Attack," *CBC*, August 27, 2016.
71. "Dhaka, Beijing Sign Agreements on Intelligence Sharing, Counterterrorism," *Dhaka Tribune*, October 26, 2018.
72. "Bangladesh–China 2nd Home Minister-Level Meeting Held," *Bangladesh Sangbad Sangstha*, April 16, 2019.
73. "Bangladesh in 34-State Islamic Military Alliance," *The Daily Star*, December 15, 2015.
74. Golam Moshi and S. M. Anisul Haque, "Bangladesh Prime Minister's Visit to Saudi Arabia: Quest for Enhanced Friendship," *Saudi Gazette*, December 9, 2018.
75. Bangladesh Police, "Police Activities," accessed June 14, 2020; A. S. M. Ali Ashraf, "Counterterrorism Cooperation in South Asia," *bdnews24.com*, February 25, 2016.
76. "Press Conference by Chief, Counter-Terrorism Committee Executive Directorate," November 13, 2009, https://www.un.org/press/en/2009/091113_CTED.doc.htm, accessed June 12, 2020.
77. UNODC, "India: South Asian Officials and Experts Extend Support to UNODC's Regional Intelligence Sharing Initiative," https://www.unodc.org/southasia//frontpage/2018/April/india_-south-asian-officials-and-experts-extend-support-to-unodcs-regional-intelligence-sharing-initiative.html, accessed February 22, 2019.
78. Arifur Rahman Rabbi, "Interpol Chief Pledges Support Against Militancy in BD," *Dhaka Tribune*, March 12, 2017.

79. Rabbi, "Interpol Warrant Out for 22 Bangladeshis," *Dhaka Tribune*, August 22, 2017.
80. Staff Correspondent, "Bangladesh in Egmont Group," *bdnews24.com*, July 4, 2013.
81. Jamal Uddin, "Customs Intelligence Alarmed at Arms Trade, Dealers Disagree," *Dhaka Tribune*, July 13, 2017.
82. PTI, "India, Bangladesh Have Real-Time Intelligence Sharing on Terror: Karim," *Hindustan Times*, January 22, 2010.
83. PTI, "India Bangladesh Agree to Intelligence Sharing on Terrorism, Insurgency," *NDTV*, November 17, 2015.
84. Interviews with senior officials from security and intelligence agencies in Bangladesh; visiting officials from several western countries.
85. In 2006 a second generation Bangladeshi–American Ehsanul Islam Sadequee was arrested in Dhaka and handed over to the Federal Bureau of Investigation for prosecution in Georgia state. For details, see: "U.S. Department of Justice, Terrorism Defendants Sentenced in Atlanta," *Justice News*, December 14, 2009; "Atlanta College Student Faces Terror Charge," *CNN*, April 21, 2006. https://edition.cnn.com/2006/US/04/20/bangladesh. arrests/index.html, accessed June 9, 2020; Staff Correspondent, "US Citizen of Bangladesh Origin Handed Over to FBI," *The Daily Star*, April 22, 2006.
86. Concerned Bangladeshi and UK agencies shared information about Saimun Rahman, a Bangladeshi immigrant to UK, who was arrested in Bangladesh in September 2014 on charges of involvement in terrorist financing and terrorist recruitment.See: Rajshekhar Jha, "Al-Qaida Man on Mission to 'Recruit Rohingya Youth' Held in Delhi," *Times of India*, September 19, 2017; Tribune Desk, "Bangladesh Seeks Details of Suspect Militant from India," *Dhaka Tribune*, October 3, 2017.
87. Australian Federal Police and Bangladeshi CTTC Unit exchanged information about Momena Shoma, a Bangladeshi female student in Australia, who was inspired by ISIS ideology to stab her homestay landlord in February 2018. See: James Oaten, "Bangladeshi Student Momena Shoma Sentenced to 42 Years for Terror Attack on Homestay Landlord," *ABC News*, June 5, 2019; Staff Correspondent, "Melbourne Student Had Contact with Nibras: Police," *Prothom Alo English*, March

29, 2018, https://en.prothomalo.com/bangladesh/Melbourne-student-had-contact-with-Nibras-Police, accessed June 9, 2020.
88. In July 2016 after media reports unveiled that Tamim was the mastermind behind the Holey Artisan attack, the Bangladeshi and Canadian intelligence agencies exchanged information about Tamim's background and terrorist connections. See: "Bangladesh Police Kill Canadian Suspect in Restaurant Attack," *CBC News*, August 27, 2016; "Tamim chy, an Evil Mind," *The Daily Star*, August 9, 2016.
89. Author's interviews with Bangladeshi and Indian officials, 2018, 2019.
90. Kamran Reza Chowdhury, "Bangladesh, India Share Intelligence on Potential Militant Attacks," *Benar News*, May 20, 2019; Staff Correspondent, "Targeting Buddha Purnima: Indian Intel Agency Warns of Terrorist Attacks in WB, BD," *Daily Observer*, May 12, 2019.
91. Counter Terrorism and Counter Radicalization Division, "Banned Organizations: Terrorist Organizations Listed in the First Schedule of the Unlawful Activities (Prevention) Act, 1967," New Delhi: Ministry of Home Affairs, https://mha.gov.in/node/91173, accessed November 23, 2019.
92. "Delhi Blast: NIA Team in Bangladesh Quiz Students," *The Hindu*, October 9, 2011; "Sylhet Students Interrogated by NIA," *bdnews24.com*, October 9, 2011.
93. United States Department of State, *Country Reports on Terrorism 2017—Bangladesh*, September 19, 2018.
94. UNB, Dhaka, "US to Continue Supporting Bangladesh in Tackling Money Laundering, Terrorism Financing: Miller," *The Daily Star*, September 19, 2019.
95. India Correspondent, "NIA to Train Bangladesh Police to Detect Fake Currency," *bdnews24.com*, October 24, 2016.
96. Imtiaz Hussain, ed., *South Asia in Global Power Rivalry: Inside-Out Appraisals from Bangladesh* (Singapore: Springer, 2019).
97. U.S. Embassy Dhaka, "Joint Statement of the Fifth U.S.-Bangladesh Partnership Dialogue," June 24, 2016.
98. Interview with a U.S. Embassy official in Dhaka, November 17, 2019.

99. Kaewkamol Pitakdumrongkit, "The Impact of Trump Administration's Indo-Pacific Strategy on Regional Economic Governance," *Policy Studies* 79 (Honolulu: East West Center, 2019), 3–7.
100. Munton, "Intelligence Cooperation," 127.
101. "BIMSTEC Invite Indicates India Shaping Alternative Regional Platform: Former Indian Diplomat," *The Economic Times*, May 30, 2019; Sudha Ramachandran, "India's BIMSTEC Gambit," *The Diplomat*, May 31, 2019; and Harsh V. Pant, "To Strengthen BIMSTEC Is to Reimagine India's Strategic Geography in the Bay of Bengal," *Observer Research Foundation Commentaries*, August 30, 2018.
102. John Mearsheimer, "The False Promise of International Institutions," *International Security* 19, no. 3 (1994–1995): 5–49.
103. Both financial intelligence analysts and foreign policy practitioners in Bangladesh interviewed by the author in July 2018 confirmed that pressures from the U.S. State Department and the U.S. Treasury played a key role in improving Bangladesh's compliance with the international financial regime for combating money laundering and terrorist financing.

Bibliography

Ahmed, I. 1991. *State and Foreign Policy: India's Role in South Asia*. Delhi: Vikas.

Ahmed, N. 2010. Party Politics Under a Non-Party Caretaker Government in Bangladesh: The Fakhruddin Interregnum (2007–09). *Commonwealth & Comparative Politics* 48, no. 1: 23–47.

Alam, S. M. S. 1995. "Democratic Politics and the Fall of the Military Regime in Bangladesh." *Bulletin of Concerned Asian Scholars* 27, no. 3: 28–42.

Aldrich, R. 2002. Dangerous Liaisons: Post-September 11 Intelligence Alliances. *Harvard International Review* 24, no. 3: 49–54.

———. 2009. US–European Intelligence Co-operation on Counter-Terrorism: Low Politics and Compulsion. *British Journal of Politics and International Relations* 11: 122–139.

Ali, S. M. 2019. "South Asia in Strategic Competition: Tracing Chinese, Indian, and U.S. Footprints." I. Hussain, ed., *South Asia in Global Power Rivalry*. London: Palgrave, 248.

Andrew, C. 1995. *For the President's Eyes Only: Secret Intelligence and the American Presidency from Washington to Bush.* New York: HarperCollins.
Anwar, A. 2019. "How Bangladesh Is Benefiting from the China–India Rivalry." *The Diplomat*, July 12.
Arcos, R., and J. M. Palacios. 2020. "EU INTCEN: A Transnational European Culture of Intelligence Analysis?" *Intelligence and National Security* 35, no. 1: 72–94.
Ashraf, A. A. 2016. "Counterterrorism Cooperation in South Asia." *bdnews24.com*, February 25.
———, ed. 2016. *Intelligence, National Security, and Foreign Policy: A South Asian Narrative.* Dhaka: Bangladesh Institute of Law and International Affairs and Department of International Relations, University of Dhaka.
———. 2016. "Regional Police Cooperation in South Asia: Progresses and Challenges." A. A. Ashraf, ed., *Intelligence, National Security and Foreign Policy: A South Asian Narrative.* Dhaka: Bangladesh Institute of Law and International Affairs and Department of International Relations, University of Dhaka, 215–236.
Ashraf, A. A., and M. S. Rana. 2017. "External Influence, Domestic Politics, and Bangladesh Government's Northeast India Policy." A. Hussain, ed., *Bangladesh's Neighbours in the Indian Northeast: Exploring Opportunities and Mutual Interest.* Dhaka: Asiatic Society of Bangladesh, 26–27.
Australia Department of Foreign Affairs and Trade. 2021. Bangladesh Country Brief. https://www.dfat.gov.au/geo/bangladesh/Pages/bangladesh-country-brief. Accessed on June 9, 2020.
Bangladesh Police. Police Activities. https://www.police.gov.bd/en/activities. Accessed on June 14, 2020.
Bdnews24.com. 2011. "Sylhet Students Interrogated by NIA." *bdnews24.com*, October 9.
Bonthous, J. M. 1994. "Understanding Intelligence Across Cultures." *International Journal of Intelligence and Counter Intelligence* 7: 7–34.
British High Commission Dhaka. 2019. UK and Bangladesh Hold Third Strategic Dialogue. https://www.gov.uk/government/news/third-bangladesh-uk-strategic-dialogue. Accessed on June 9, 2020.
BSS. 2019. "Bangladesh–China 2nd Home Minister-Level Meeting Held." *Bangladesh Sangbad Sangstha*, April 16.
Cepik, M., & G. Möller. 2017. "National Intelligence Systems as Networks: Power Distribution and Organizational Risk in Brazil, Russia, India, China, and South Africa." *Brazilian Political Science Review* 11, no. 1: 1–26.
Chakma, B. 2015. "Sheikh Hasina Government's India Policy: A Three-Level Game?" *Journal of Asian Security and International Affairs* 2, no. 1: 27–51.
Chaudhury, D. R. 2019. "India, Bangladesh Sign MoU for Coastal Surveillance System Radar in Bangladesh." *The Economic Times*, October 7.

Chowdhury, I. A. 2011. "Foundations of Bangladesh's Foreign Policy Interactions." *ISAS Insights*, 120.

Chowdhury, K. R. 2019. "Bangladesh Gives India Greenlight to Install Surveillance Radar System." *BenarNews*, July 10.

———. 2019. "Bangladesh, India Share Intelligence on Potential Militant Attack." *Benar News*, May 20.

Clottey, P. 2014. "African Union Urges Global Intelligence-Sharing Against Terrorism." *Voice of America*, May 12.

CNN. 2006. Atlanta College Student Faces Terror Charge. https://edition.cnn.com/2006/US/04/20/bangladesh.arrests/index.html. Accessed on June 9, 2020.

Cobain, I., and F. Karim. 2011. "UK Linked to Notorious Bangladesh Torture Centre." *The Guardian*, January 17.

Counter Terrorism and Counter Radicalization Division, Ministry of Home Affairs, India. Banned Organizations: Terrorist Organizations Listed in the First Schedule of the Unlawful Activities (Prevention) Act. 1967. https://mha.gov.in/node/91173. Accessed on November 23, 2019.

Dahl, E. J. 2017. "Getting Beyond Analysis by Anecdote: Improving Intelligence Analysis Through the Use of Case Studies." *Intelligence and National Security* 32, no. 5: 563–578.

Davis, P. H. J., and K. C. Gustafson. 2013. *Intelligence Elsewhere: Spies and Espionage Outside the Anglosphere*. London: Georgetown University Press.

Deflem, M. 2007. "International Police Cooperation Against Terrorism: Interpol and Europol in Comparison." H. Durmaz, B. Sevinc, A. S. Yayla, and S. Ekici, eds., *Understanding and Responding to Terrorism*. Amsterdam: IOS Press, 17–25.

Diplomatic Correspondent. 2019. "US Wants 2 Defence Deals with Bangladesh." *The Daily Star*, October 18.

Egmont Group. About. https://egmontgroup.org/content/about. Accessed on June 18, 2020.

European Union Intelligence and Situation Centre. 2015. EU INTCEN Fact Sheet. https://statewatch.org/news/2016/may/eu-intcen-factsheet.pdf. Accessed on June 18, 2020.

Fagersten, B. 2016. "For EU Eyes Only? Intelligence and European Security." *Issue Brief* 8: 2. Paris: European Union Institute for Security Studies.

Ford, D. 2007. "Strategic Culture, Intelligence Assessment, and the Conduct of the Pacific War: The British–Indian and Imperial Japanese Armies in Comparison, 1941–1945." *War in History* 14, no. 1: 63–95.

Gnanasagaran, A. 2018. "Our Eyes' to Combat Terrorism." *The ASEAN Post*, October 22.

Graaff, B. 2020. *Intelligence Communities and Cultures in Asia and the Middle East: A Comprehensive Reference*. Boulder, CO: Lynne Rienner.

Hammerstad, A. 2005. "Domestic Threats, Regional Solutions? The Challenge of Security Integration in Southern Africa." *Review of International Studies* 31, no. 1: 69–87.
Hasib, N. I. 2019. "Bangladesh, US in Talks to Sign Two Defence Deals." *bdnews24.com*, October 17.
Herman, S. 2016. "Bangladesh US Agree to Enhance Cooperation to Fight Terrorism." *Voice of America*, August 29.
Hossain, D., and S. Islam. 2019. "Unfolding Bangladesh–India Maritime Connectivity in the Bay of Bengal Region: A Bangladesh Perspective." *Journal of the Indian Ocean Region* 15, no. 3: 346–355.
Hussain, I. 2019. *South Asia in Global Power Rivalry: Inside-Out Appraisals from Bangladesh*. Singapore: Springer.
India Correspondent. 2016. "NIA to Train Bangladesh Police to Detect Fake Currency." *bdnews24.com*, October 24.
Japan Times. 2019. Tokyo Ready to Share Info on North Korea Missile with Seoul Despite Row, October 4.
Jha, R. 2017. "Al-Qaida Man on Mission to 'Recruit Rohingya Youth' Held in Delhi." *Times of India*, September 19.
Klieman, A. 1988. *Statecraft in the Dark: Israel's Practice of Quiet Diplomacy*. Boulder, CO: Westview.
Lander, S. 2004. "International Intelligence Cooperation: An Inside Perspective." *Cambridge Review of International Affairs* 17, no. 3: 481.
Lefebvre, S. 2003. "The Difficulties and Dilemmas of International Intelligence Cooperation." *International Journal of Intelligence and Counterintelligence* 16, no. 4: 527–542.
Lillbacka, R. G. V. 2013. "Realism, Constructivism, and Intelligence Analysis." *International Journal of Intelligence and Counter Intelligence* 26, no. 2: 304–331.
Manik, J. A., G. Anand, and E. Berry. 2016. "Bangladesh Attack Is New Evidence That ISIS Has Shifted Its Focus Beyond Mideast." *New York Times*, July 3.
Mannan, M. A. 2018. "Bangladesh–China Relations: Mapping Geopolitical and Security Interests." *The East Asia Study Centre Monograph* Volume 2. Dhaka: East Asia Study Centre, University of Dhaka.
Mearsheimer, J. 1994–1995. "The False Promise of International Institutions." *International Security* 19, no. 3: 5–49.
Moshi, G., and S. A. Haque. 2018. "Bangladesh Prime Minister's Visit to Saudi Arabia: Quest for Enhanced Friendship." *Saudi Gazette*, December 9.
Munton, D. 2009. "Intelligence Cooperation Meets International Studies Theory: Explaining Canadian Operations in Castro's Cuba." *Intelligence and National Security* 24, no. 1: 119–138.

Oaten, J. 2019. "Bangladeshi Student Momena Shoma Sentenced to 42 Years for Terror Attack on Homestay Landlord." *ABC News*, June 5.
Pant, H. V. 2018. "To Strengthen BIMSTEC Is to Reimagine India's Strategic Geography in the Bay of Bengal." *Observer Research Foundation Commentaries*, August 30.
Pitakdumrongkit, K. 2019. "The Impact of Trump Administration's Indo-Pacific Strategy on Regional Economic Governance." *Policy Studies* 79: 3–7.
PTI. 2010. "India, Bangladesh Have Real-Time Intelligence Sharing on Terror: Karim." *Hindustan Times*, January 22.
———. 2011. "Delhi Blast: NIA Team in Bangladesh Quiz Students." *The Hindu*, October 9.
———. 2015. "India Bangladesh Agree to Intelligence Sharing on Terrorism, Insurgency." *NDTV*, November 17.
Rabbi, A. R. 2017. "Interpol Chief Pledges Support Against Militancy in BD." *Dhaka Tribune*, March 12.
———. 2017. "Interpol Warrant Out for 22 Bangladeshis." *Dhaka Tribune*, August 22.
Ramachandran, S. 2019. "India's BIMSTEC Gambit." *The Diplomat*, May 31.
Reuters. 2015. "Bangladesh in 34-State Islamic Military Alliance." *The Daily Star*, December 15.
Royal Geographic Society. Global North South Divide. https://www.rgs.org/CMSPages/GetFile.aspx?nodeguid=9c1ce781-9117-4741-af0a-a6a8b75f32b4&lang=en-GB. Accessed on June 19, 2020.
Rudner, M. 2004. "Hunters and Gatherers: The Intelligence Coalition Against Islamic Terrorism." *International Journal of Intelligence and Counterintelligence* 17, no. 4: 193–230.
Scharf, W. 2004. "African Security Via Police, Justice, and Intelligence Reform." C. Ferguson and J. O. Isima, eds., *Providing Security for People: Enhancing Security Through Police, Justice, and Intelligence Reform in Africa*. Shrivenham, UK: Global Facilitation Network for Security Sector Reform, 64.
Shiraz, Z. 2013. "Drugs and Dirty Wars: Intelligence Cooperation in the Global South." *Third World Quarterly* 34, no. 10: 1749–1766.
Shiraz, Z., and R. J. Aldrich. 2019. "Secrecy, Spies and Global South: Intelligence Studies Beyond the 'Five Eyes' Alliance." *International Affairs* 96, no. 6: 3.
Staff Correspondent. 2006. "US Citizen of Bangladesh Origin Handed Over to FBI." *The Daily Star*, April 22.
———. 2013. "Bangladesh in Egmont Group." *bdnews24.com*, July 4.
———. 2016. "Tami Chy: An Evil Mind." *The Daily Star*, August 9.
———. 2018. "Melbourne Student Had Contact with Nibras: Police." *Prothom Alo English*, March 29. https://en.prothomalo.com/bangladesh/Melbourne-student-had-contact-with-Nibras-Police. Accessed on June 9, 2020.

———. 2019. "Targeting Buddha Purnima: Indian Intel Agency Warns of Terrorist Attacks in WB, BD." *Daily Observer*, May 12.
Strategic Executive Group of UN Resident Coordinator, UNHCR Bangladesh and IOM Bangladesh. 2019. 2019 Joint Response Plan for Rohingya Humanitarian Crisis, January–December. https://reporting.unhcr.org/sites/default/files/2019%20JRP%20for%20Rohingya%20Humanitarian%20Crisis%20%28February%202019%29.comp_.pdf. Accessed on May 5, 2020.
Svendsen, D. 2009. "Connecting Intelligence and Theory: Intelligence Liaison and International Relations." *Intelligence and National Security* 24, no. 5: 700–729.
Talukder, K. H. 2014. "Bangladesh Intelligence Team to Go to India." *bdnews24.com*, November 27.
The Associated Press. 2016. "Bangladesh Police Kill Canadian Suspect in Restaurant Attack." *CBC News*, August 27.
The Economic Times. 2019. BIMSTEC Invite Indicates India Shaping Alternative Regional Platform: Former Indian Diplomat, May 30.
The North Africa Post. 2020. African Union Inaugurates New HQ of Intelligence and Security Services, February 12.
Tribune Desk. 2017. "Bangladesh Seeks Details of Suspect Militant from India." *Dhaka Tribune*, October 3.
———. 2018. "Dhaka, Beijing Sign Agreements on Intelligence Sharing, Counterterrorism." *Dhaka Tribune*, October 26.
Uddin, J. 2017. "Customs Intelligence Alarmed at Arms Trade, Dealers Disagree." *Dhaka Tribune*, July 13.
UNB. 2019. "US to Continue Supporting Bangladesh in Tackling Money Laundering, Terrorism Financing: Miller." *The Daily Star*, September 19.
United Nations. 2009. Press Conference by Chief, Counter-Terrorism Committee Executive Directorate. https://www.un.org/press/en/2009/091113_CTED.doc.htm. Accessed on June 12, 2020.
United Nations Office on Drugs and Crime. 2010. Promoting the Rule of Law and Human Security in Central America: Regional Programme 2009–2012. https://www.unodc.org/documents/commissions/FINGOV/Background_Documentation2009-2011/Agenda_Item_2-Regional-Programmes/Promoting-the-Rule-of-Law-and-Human-Security_Central-America.pdf. Accessed on May 5, 2020.
United States Department of State. 2018. Country Reports on Terrorism 2017—Bangladesh. https://www.state.gov/reports/country-reports-on-terrorism-2017/. Accessed on May 5, 2020.
UNODC. 2018. India: South Asian Officials and Experts Extend Support to UNODC's Regional Intelligence Sharing Initiative. https://www.unodc.org/southasia//frontpage/2018/April/india_-south-asian-officials-and-exp

erts-extend-support-to-unodcs-regional-intelligence-sharing-initiative.html. Accessed on February 22, 2019.

U.S. Department of Justice. 2009. "Terrorism Defendants Sentenced in Atlanta." *Justice News*, December 14.

U.S. Embassy Dhaka. 2016. Joint Statement of the Fifth U.S.–Bangladesh Partnership Dialogue. https://bd.usembassy.gov/joint-statement-fifth-u-s-bangladesh-partnership-dialogue/. Accessed on May 5, 2020.

Vivares, E. 2016. *Exploring the New South American Regionalism (NSAR)*. London and New York: Routledge.

von Loringhoven, A. F. 2019. "A New Era for NATO Intelligence." *NATO Review*, October 29.

Walsh, P. F. 2017. "Improving Strategic Intelligence Analytical Practice Through Qualitative Social Research." *Intelligence and National Security* 32, no. 5: 548–562.

Westerfield, H. B. 1996. "America and the World of Intelligence Liaison." *Intelligence and National Security* 11, no. 3: 523–560.

Xinhua. 2019. "Somali, AU Forces Seek to Step Up Intelligence Sharing to Flush Out Terrorists." *Xinhua*, March 27.

Yasmin, L. 2016. "Bangladesh and the Great Powers." A. Riaz and M. S. Rahman, eds., *Routledge Handbook of Contemporary Bangladesh*. Abingdon: Routledge, 389–401.

CHAPTER 6

Climate Change-Induced Displacement and the United Nations

Md Abdul Awal Khan

INTRODUCTION

Climate Change-Induced Displacement (CCID) (both internal and cross border) not only profoundly affects the human rights of displaced people, but also injures national and international peace and security. Therefore, a relevant United Nations (UN) role is crucial in assessing law and policy measures for climate change displaced people (CDP). UN responsibility to protect such people, so as to ensure UN purposes and principles,[1] has not produced an appropriate regime to address CDP human rights.

This book chapter is extracted from my Ph.D. thesis, which is available online on the university library website. http://researchdirect.uws.edu.au/islandora/object/uws%3A32643/datastream/PDF/download/citation.pdf.

M. A. A. Khan (✉)
Department of Law, Independent University, Bangladesh, Dhaka, Bangladesh
e-mail: awalkhanlaw@iub.edu.bd

© The Author(s), under exclusive license to Springer Nature Singapore Pte Ltd. 2022
I. A. Hussain (eds.), *Global-Local Tradeoffs, Order-Disorder Consequences*, Global Political Transitions,
https://doi.org/10.1007/978-981-16-9419-6_6

Since comprehensive international legal and policy initiatives are required to protect CDP rights effectively, a fresh impetus accompanies the very formation of the UNFCCC climate change regime, even though no specific UNFCCC CDP provisions get UNFCCC acknowledgement.

Since a new protection regime could be developed on the basis of the UNFCCC principles, the framework for local–global networking grows: any institutional interest on the subject at the global level representing a macro-level platform, confronts population shifts at the local level. The key emergent question becomes: whether the increasing/diminishing gap between the two represents a direct offshoot of tackling the puzzle.

UNFCCC Principles and CDP Context

The principles of the UNFCCC Article 3 reflect the convention objectives and how to implement its provisions by parties.[2] These principles are not precisely related to CDP cases, but they have CDP implications and significance. No single institution is responsible for CDP-related matters,[3] and no international legal instruments clearly describe the CDP notion, including cross-border movement. Proposals, conventions, models or legal instruments find this UNFCCC link because it is the sole climate change international convention.[4]

Principle of Common but Differentiated Responsibilities (CBDR)

UNFCCC engagements rank among the largest feasible cooperation and participation by all states through an active and appropriate international response in line with the CBDR (Common but Differentiated Responsibilities) principles, capabilities and social and economic conditions.[5] It pits the 'global' against the local views under such a CBDR framework, UNFCCC commitments on developed countries, compel them to consider the particular demands and unique conditions of developing countries.[6] The CBDR principle establishes that the common responsibility of all states protects the global environment, exposing a case of local-level macro interest, as with the state, and a global-level macro unit, as through an international organisation. With industrialised countries bearing primary responsibility of creating environmental problems,[7] local–global interplay intensifies symmetrically across the playground. The UNFCCC obligation for developed countries to support under developed countries adopts the CBDR-focused recognition that the unfolding global climate change imposes greater mitigation costs and needs more technological support against every incremental expense.[8] CBDR principles fundamentally distinguish, through UNFCCC Article 3,[9] between developed and developing countries, on the basis of vulnerabilities, national capabilities and historical responsibilities.[10] This CBDR concept allows commitments to be fixed for DC obligations to achieve specified emissions reductions. Less developing countries (LDCs) can voluntarily partake in commitments to limit emissions, but not as a requirement.[11] There is an argument on the nature of the commitment, as per CBDR principle, and the contention to take CDP liability under the CBDR principle of creating extra DC tasks beyond emissions reduction. However, it is clear that UNFCCC and *Kyoto Protocol* ratification obliges states to comply with the CBDR principles.[12] Climate change, for which industrialised countries bear more responsibilities, leave a CDP residue. CBDR principles open this UN role to claim DC assistance to relocate and manage CDP victims as permanent migrants.[13] Though, there is little sign to date that these principles are being satisfied, or that they are still sufficient to translate ethical priorities into legal obligations. We observe how greater pressure is exerted upon global intentions from local springboards.[14]

Principle of International Cooperation

International cooperation or 'Good-neighbourliness' principle is in the UN Charter in relation to economic, social and commercial matters,[15] and 'has been translated into the development and application of rules promoting international environmental co-operation'.[16] As an example, the provision 'the global nature of climate change calls for the widest possible cooperation by all countries and their participation in an effective and appropriate international response' stipulation, exposes this UNFCCC principle.[17] Other UNFCCC highlights include international cooperation of state parties in the growth and transfer of technology[18]; maintenance and development of GHG sinks[19]; research[20]; exchange of information[21]; and education, training and public consciousness.[22] Being reliant on international support, and having significant financial and technological assistance from the international community on climate change, any plight shows how local dynamics can be pressured by global dynamics. In fact, this flow is stronger than the reverse flow of local concerns seeking palliative global intervention. Any climate change affected country could call for certain and greater international CDP cooperation, a principle also applicable if such countries need to form a domestic framework for the protection and promotion of CDP human rights. However, in order to control the movement of a huge number of CDP flows and not violate CDP environmental legal principles and human rights, CDP cooperation must be further developed.[23]

INTERNATIONAL NORMATIVE DEVELOPMENT AND INTERNAL DISPLACEMENT GAPS

The UN *Guiding Principles on Internal Displacement* (GPID) (a non-binding international instrument) describes CDP protection within specified territories.[24] These guiding principles do not have a major legal impact on implementation actions due to their non-binding nature. The UNFCCC Conference of the Parties (COP) has released hundreds of decisions already relating to climate change, yet many of them remain too common, with CDP rights and CDP statuses clarified. Moreover, for the binding decisions that empower the global against the local in the equation, only the UNFCCC ratifying states can reaffirm the strength of local resistance.

As Climate Change Displacement usually happens within the area of an affected state,[25] the main responsibility is required upon that state to handle its internal displacement and protect internally displaced people, as stated in the UN's document.[26] CDIP purposes and scopes apply to individuals and groups 'who have not crossed an internationally recognized State border'.[27] The main GPID objective is to control human rights violations of internally displaced people.[28] Internal entitlements to have universal human rights protection as citizens of the affected state also prevail for displaced people.[29] GPID details state responsibilities to avoid displacement, respond to the demands of those who have been displaced, and to provide for durable solutions for their displacement.[30] In spite of its legally non-binding character as a soft-law instrument, GPID support among states and international organisations is significant.[31] Presently, the GPID provision is internationally accepted as a crucial document for protecting ICDP, with the principles emerging popular among the United Nations, regional organisations, governments, non-government organisations (NGOs) and other actors involved with internal displacement.[32] GPID principles suggest assistance for countries facing internal movement, and protection in a human rights-based ICDP structure.[33]

Although the cross-border displacement issues are not included by the GPID clause, it is recognised as an incremental process of accumulating and adapting the broad range of present legal and normative frameworks to protect displaced people, as well as those left behind.[34]

The UNHCR *Summary of Deliberations of Climate Change and Displacement* (SDCD) gave both external and internal climate displaced people legal personalities.[35] Although this instrument does not have any legal enforceability, states could use the guidelines in their domestic jurisdiction.

The SDCD document states how a GPID provision reflects current international law and applies to the context of internal displacement triggered by climate change-related displacement. No need exists for a new set of principles relating to internal displacement in the context of climate change.[36] Most importantly, the SDCD document suggests how the number of GPID principles could be used to external displacement (although the SDCD document did not refer to explicitly which principles could be used).[37]

Although the above normative framework is useful to indicate a way for states to develop suitable responses to CDP human rights through their national legislation, policies and institution; these norms offer sufficient CDP protection internationally because they are scattered, fragmented and disorganised. Effective CDP assistance requires integrated and comprehensive normative approaches. Beyond normative development, a UN institutional approach is necessary to protect CDP human rights. How the United Nations Human Rights Council could play a crucial role in this regard indicates the ideally superior global role over the local in climate change dynamics, while also exposing macro-macro global-level interaction over a single issue.

MANDATE OF THE OFFICE OF THE HIGH COMMISSIONER FOR HUMAN RIGHTS (OHCHR) AND UNITED NATIONS HUMAN RIGHTS COUNCIL (UNHRC) FOR CDP

UNHRC is responsible for maintaining the promotion and protection of human rights around the world, as an intergovernmental body under the United Nations.[38] Since it also addresses and makes advisory recommendations about human rights violations,[39] the UNHCR presence is instrumental to global–local mediation. This body can provide protective measures under the UN platform for CDP victims. Adopting UNHRC resolutions in the United Nations General Assembly (UNGA), authorises UNHRC values and political effects upon UNGA member states over human rights matters. For example, since Bangladesh and India are UN and UNGA members, any human rights violations between them also involves UNHRC purview. UNHRC involvement introduces reliable political impact on the issue. The UNHRC collaboration with UN Special Procedures, 'made up of special rapporteurs, special representatives, independent experts and working groups that monitor, examine, advise and publicly report on thematic issues or human rights situations in specific countries',[40] involves CDP human rights protection cases. Yet, since UNHRC adequacy to uphold CDP human rights remains questionable owing to its non-binding resolutions, advantage again slips to the local.

Direct and indirect impacts of climate change on human rights, particularly on the most vulnerable and poor regions of the world, have allowed UNHRC direction for affected states regarding protecting CDP human rights,[41] though without specific direction how CDP movement should be properly managed.[42] It further provides an impression of the legal obligations of states towards climate change victims, both within and outside their country and jurisdiction.[43] It also refers to the GPID provisions for ICDP victims, and reports how ICDP victims are eligible to the full range of human rights secured by the given states. However, it does not give any legal identity to climate displaced people, or detailed direction to a receiving state regarding voluntary and forced population movements and the ECDP treatment. Such UNHRC mandates that, if a person cannot be reasonably returned to the land from which he or she was displaced due to inadequate assistance and protection from the country of origin, he or she should be considered a victim of forced displacement and granted at least a short-term stay,[44] thus promoting global rights over the local.

As per international human rights law, individuals rely first and primarily on their own states for the protection of their human rights. Thus, it is doubtful, against climate change, for the above-mentioned reasons, that an individual can hold a particular state responsible for climate change harm. Human rights law provides more active protection regarding measures taken by states to address climate change and their impact on human rights.[45]

Should individuals transfer from a high-risk UNHCR zone, the state must make sure sufficient protections and actions to avoid forced evictions.[46] However, this UNHRC direction is too general, and forced eviction due to climate change has become a normal scenario. Another UNHRC resolution notes how human rights obligations, standards and principles have the potential to inform and strengthen international and national policymaking in any climate change area, thus promoting legitimacy, sustainable outcomes and policy coherence.[47]

In 2012, the United Nations Human Rights Council, discussed the specific human rights of internally displaced people, with an ambitious set of creeping concerns displaced by climate change[48]: about these, the UNHCR role as a political body with no power to implement the provision of human rights law, how to hold states responsible for human rights violations, and the resolutions it must adopt deprive a legal binding for any state.[49] Though these automatically run into limitations, it should be realised by states that the quasi-judicial functions of UNHRC type international human rights bodies remain the key to strengthening the capacity of international legal order to protect human beings (such as CDP victims) against the adverse effects of climate change.[50]

Since there are no other recognised UN institutions to deal with human rights issues, the CDP susceptibilities could be taken to the United Nations Human Rights Council by individuals, groups and NGOs for human rights violations claims,[51] until and unless CDP protection by a new international institution with a specific mandate is adopted. The UNHCR resolution, *Institution-Building of the United Nations Human Rights Council*,[52] created a new complaint system to address gross and reliably attested violations of all human rights happening in any part of the world.[53] Although compliance with human rights obligations is largely dependent on the states, a 'contextual assessment of the state's factual control in respect of facts and events that apparently constitute a violation of a human right' is progressively improving in the international field,[54] indicating how much forward movement local dynamics have been making towards a global admixture.

FORWARD PATH FOR CDP PROTECTION

Treating climate displaced people as refugees by expanding the definition of the *Refugee Convention*, is not incorporated here. Instead, a subject matter of the domestic legal system with the help of the international law and community (the United Nations) is advocated so that climate displaced people can be provided better support, and displacement-related challenges can be addressed more effectively. Moreover, it is unlikely that the international community will agree to amend the *Refugee Convention* to develop and include CDP because this procedure might be very uncertain, politically impracticable and does not provide an actual solution to resolve the emerging climate displacement crisis effectively.[55] Moreover, including internal climate displaced people in the *Refugee Convention*'s definition would degrade the position of the country's citizens because such rights already are subordination to existing citizens.[56] Climate displaced people may choose effective assistance and resilience from their own country, rather than being treated as passive victims waiting for help from developed countries.[57] An expanded definition would be superfluous,[58] if not potentially dangerous because it could provide a pretext for states to refuse the human rights of the victims of environmental events.[59] Moreover, it would burden any UNHCR mandate to manage a large number of refugees, and could undermine relevant assistance and protection activities.[60] A new UN convention could be made for the unique CDP migrant category as their vulnerabilities and number can only increase in magnitude.

It would not be an ambitious proposal, if the existing prediction over the CDP number is correct, that approximately one person in every 14 will be displaced worldwide due to climate change by 2050.[61] But the problem lies in the CDP identity definition because no international mechanism can clearly identify any specific CDP case. Although two regional mechanisms—the Organisation of African Unity (OAU),[62] and the *Cartagena Declaration on Refugees*[63]—have a wider definition of 'refugee' than that of the UN *Refugee Convention*.[64] These definitions may encompass CDP identity; though, neither definition says the environment or climate change particularly.[65] Therefore, a unique CDP definition might be required if any new convention is put into effect.

There are evident problems between developed and developing countries that may generate deadlocks in important CDP decision-making procedures. UNFCCC and Kyoto Protocol enforcement mechanisms should be developed to facilitate an effective climate legal regime and useful decision-making procedure. UNFCCC commitments and agreements must be respected by the state parties, or they will lose their value. Governments of climate-affected countries should consider the major environmental principles (as discussed earlier), while creating CDP plans and policies. In addition, based on those principles, the international community should create binding CDP protection though. The UNHRC mandate should be enhanced to include human rights. Developed countries should take responsibility for keeping international connections among developing countries so that developing countries could actively fight the adverse impact of climate change. Arguably the current climate change system needs strengthening to provide better legal and human rights CDP protection.

The very absence of any remedy under the *Refugee Convention*, UNFCCC limitations, UNHRC shortcomings and international legal and political barriers preventing CDP protection, combine to strongly favour a unique CDP protocol for CDP.

Conclusions

Improving international policies and laws is vital to managing and protecting climate displaced people because no country can face climate change challenges alone. Therefore, the role of the United Nations and its relevant organisations are important if any country launches any CDP legal instrument. Despite substantial improvements at an international stage about climate change, CDP attention is inadequate. CDP protection aims, from the United Nations adopting an effective international legal regime with a comprehensive international approach to overcoming shortcomings in understanding the displacement, decrease numbers of CDP and implement legal mechanism. Since the United Nations can improve coordination, understanding and cooperation over climate displaced people for prearranged relocation at international and regional levels, international climate change law and policy require more focus with the United Nations playing a driving role because both climate change affected countries and developed countries enjoy UN membership. A connection between international and national responsibilities with respect to climate displaced people is crucial, and the United Nations can play a role to establish the link. International dialogues and negotiations between the less vulnerable, least vulnerable, non-vulnerable and vulnerable countries due to climate change are vital to protect climate displaced people worldwide.

NOTES

1. See Preamble, Art 1 of the Charter of the United Nations.
2. *UNFCCC*, Art 3.
3. United Nations High Commissioner for Refugees, *The State of the World's Refugees: In Search of Solidarity* (Geneva: UNHCR, 2012), 12.
4. David Hodgkinson and Lucy Young, "In the Face of Looming Catastrophe: A Convention for Climate Change Displaced Persons," *Threatened Island Nations Legal Implications of Rising Seas and a Changing Climate*, eds. Michael B. Gerrard and Gregory E. Wannier (Cambridge: Cambridge University Press, 2013), 299–300.
5. Ibid.; *UNFCCC*, preamble.
6. *UNFCCC*, Art 3, para. 2.
7. Siobhán McInerney-Lankford, Mac Darrow, and Lavanya Rajamani, *Human Rights and Climate Change: A Review of the International Legal Dimensions* (Washington, DC: World Bank, 2011), 52.
8. Lavanya Rajamani, *Differential Treatment in International Environmental Law* (Oxford: Oxford University Press, 2006), 108–109; International Council for Human Rights Policy, *Climate Change and Human Rights: A Rough Guide* (Switzerland: ATAR Roto Press SA, 2008), 62.
9. *UNFCCC*, Art 24; *Kyoto Protocol to the UNFCCC*, Art 3 (1) (2).
10. Siobhán McInerney-Lankford, Mac Darrow, and Lavanya Rajamani, *Human Rights and Climate Change: A Review of the International Legal Dimensions* (Washington, DC: World Bank, 2011), 49.
11. Lal Kurukulasuriya and Nicholas A. Robinson, *Training Manual on International Environmental Law* (UNEP, 2006), 112. See *UNFCCC*, Art 24; *Kyoto Protocol to the UNFCCC*, Art 4. See Annex I of the Convention to view the list of developed countries.
12. McInerney-Lankford, Darrow and Rajamani, op. cit., 53.
13. Frank Biermann and Ingrid Boas, "Protecting Climate Refugees: The Case for a Global Protocol," *Environment* 1 (November–December 2008): 3.
14. International Council for Human Rights Policy, op. cit., 60.
15. *Charter of the United Nations*, Art 74.

16. Philippe Sands, *Principles of International Environmental Law* (Cambridge: Cambridge University Press, 2nd ed., 2004), 249.
17. *UNFCCC*, preamble.
18. Ibid., Art 4(1)(c).
19. Ibid., Art 4(1)(d).
20. Ibid., Art 4(1)(g).
21. Ibid., Art 4(1)(h).
22. Ibid., Art 4(1)(i).
23. Laura Horn and Steven Freeland, "More Than Hot Air: Reflections on the Relationship Between Climate Change and Human Rights," *University of Western Sydney Law Review* 13 (2009): 124.
24. Guiding Principles on Internal Displacement, annex, 54th sess, Agenda Item 9(d) UN Doc E/CN.4/1998/53/Add.2 (11 February 1998) principle 1, para. 1, and principle 6, para. 1.
25. Walter Kälin and Nina Schrepfer, *Protecting People Crossing Borders in the Context of Climate Change Normative Gaps and Possible Approaches* (Bern: UNHCR, 2012), 30.
26. Guiding Principles on Internal Displacement, Annex, 54th sess, Agenda Item 9(d) UN Doc E/CN.4/1998/53/Add.2, February 11, 1998.
27. Ibid., Introduction: Scope and Purpose, para. 2.
28. Walter Kalin, *Protection of Internally Displaced Persons in Situations of Natural Disaster* (Geneva: OHCHR, 2005).
29. Kälin and Nina Schrepfer, op. cit., 25, 30.
30. Ibid.
31. Walter Kalin, "The Future of the Guiding Principles on Internal Displacement," (Special Issue), *Forced Migration Review* (2006): 5.
32. Ibid.
33. Jane McAdam, *Climate Change Displacement and International Law: Complementary Protection Standards* (UNHCR Division of International Protection, 2011).
34. C. Boano, R. Zetter, and T. Morris, *Environmentally Displaced People: Understanding the Linkages Between Environmental Change, Livelihoods and Forced Migration* (Oxford: Policy Briefing Series Refugee Studies Centre, University of Oxford, 2008), 1.
35. UNHCR, "Summary of Deliberations on Climate Change and Displacement," *International Journal of Refugee Law* 23, no. 3 (2011): 561, 574.

36. Ibid.
37. Ibid.
38. The UNGA created the council on 15 March 2006, and replaced the former UN Commission on Human Rights. See UNGA, *Resolution Adopted by the General Assembly*, 60th sess, Agenda Items 46 and 120, Un Doc A/RES/60/251, April 3, 2006, para. 1.
39. United Nations Human Rights Office of the High Commissioner for Human Rights, United Nations Human Rights Council, *Background Information on the Human Rights Council, About the Council*, November 26, 2013, http://www.ohchr.org/EN/HRBodies/HRC/Pages/AboutCouncil.aspx, last accessed April 11, 2019.
40. United Nations Human Rights Office of the High Commissioner for Human Rights, United Nations Human Rights Council, *Welcome to the Human Rights Council*, February 10, 2014, http://www.ohchr.org/EN/HRBodies/HRC/Pages/AboutCouncil.aspx, last accessed April 11, 2019.
41. United Nations Human Rights Council, *Report of the Human Rights Council on Its Seventh Session*, GA Res 7/23, 7th sess, Agenda Item 1, UN Doc A/HRC/7/78, July 14, 2008; *Annual Report of the United Nations High Commissioner for Human Rights and Reports of the Office of the High Commissioner and the Secretary General—Report of the Office of the United Nations High Commissioner for Human Rights on the Relationship Between Climate Change and Human Rights*, 10th sess, Agenda Item 2 Un Doc GA Res A/HRC/10/61 HRC, January 15, 2009.
42. United Nations Human Rights Council, *Report of the Human Rights Council on Its Seventh Session*, GA Res 7/23, 7th sess, Agenda Item 1, UN Doc A/HRC/7/78, July 14, 2008.
43. Margaretha Wewerinke, *Climate Change, Human Rights and the International Legal Order: The Role of the UN Human Rights Council* (Cambridge: Cambridge Centre for Climate Change Mitigation Research, 2013).
44. Representative of the Secretary-General on Human Rights of Internally Displaced Persons, *Displacement Caused by the Effects of Climate Change: Who Will Be Affected and What Are the Gaps in the Normative Framework for their Protection?* Background Paper, 2008, http://www2.ohchr.org/english/issues/climatechange/submissions.htm, last accessed April 11, 2019.

45. Ibid.
46. Ibid.
47. United Nations Human Rights Council, *Report of the Human Rights Council on Its Seventh Session*, GA Res 7/23, 7th Sess, Agenda Item 1, UN Doc A/HRC/7/78, July 14, 2008.
48. General Assembly, Human Rights Council, *Promotion and Protection of All Human Rights, Civil, Political, Economic, Social and Cultural Rights, Including the Right to Development Human Rights of Internally Displaced Persons*, 20th session, Agenda Item 3, UN Doc A/HRC/20/L.14, June 29, 2012.
49. Wewerinke, op. cit., 2.
50. Ibid., 12–13.
51. United Nations Human Rights Office of the High Commissioner for Human Rights, *Human Rights Council Complaint Procedure*, February 17, 2014, http://www.ohchr.org/EN/HRBodies/HRC/ComplaintProcedure/Pages/HRCComplaintProcedure Index.aspx, last accessed April 11, 2019.
52. UN Human Rights Council, *Institution-Building of the United Nations Human Rights Council*, 9th meeting, UN Doc A/HRC/RES/5/1, June 18, 2007, part IV.
53. Ibid.
54. UN Office of the High Commissioner for Human Rights, *Human Rights Indicators: A Guide to Measurement and Implementation* (HR/Pub/12/5, 2012).
55. Frank Biermann and Ingrid Boas, "Protecting Climate Refugees: The Case for a Global Protocol," *Environment* (November–December 2008): 1.
56. James C. Hathaway, *The Rights of Refugees Under International Law* (Cambridge: Cambridge University Press, 2005).
57. McAdam, op at, 12.
58. Michael Barutciski, "Tensions Between the Refugee Concept and the IDP Debate," *Forced Migration Review* 3 (1998): 12.
59. Kalin,Walter, *Guiding Principles on Internal Displacement Annotation* (Washington, DC: The American Society of International Law, 2008), 8.
60. Ibid.
61. Two hundred million people may be displaced due to climate change by 2050. Norman Myers, *Environmental Refugees: An*

Emergent Security Issue (Viena: Organisation for Security and Cooperation in Europe, 13th Economic Forum, 2005), 1–2.
62. Organization of African Unity (OAU), *Convention Governing the Specific Aspects of Refugee Problems in Africa (OAU Convention)*, opened for signature September 10, 1969, 1001 UNTS 45 (entered into force June 20, 1974).
63. *Cartagena Declaration on Refugees, Colloquium on the International Protection of Refugees in Central America, Mexico and Panama*, opened for signature November 22, 1984.
64. McAdam, op. cit., 44.
65. Koko Warner et al., "Climate Change, Environmental Degradation and Migration," *Natural Hazards* 55 (2010): 694.

References

Annual Report of the United Nations High Commissioner for Human Rights and Reports of the Office of the High Commissioner and the Secretary General—Report of the Office of the United Nations High Commissioner for Human Rights on the Relationship Between Climate Change and Human Rights. 2009. 10th sess, Agenda Item 2 Un Doc GA Res A/HRC/10/61 HRC.

Barutciski, Michael. 1998. "Tensions Between the Refugee Concept and the IDP Debate." *Forced Migration Review* 3: 12.

Biermann, Frank, and Ingrid Boas. 2008. "Protecting Climate Refugees: The Case for a Global Protocol." *Environment* 1: 3.

Boano, C., R. Zetter, and T. Morris. 2008. *Environmentally Displaced People: Understanding the Linkages Between Environmental Change, Livelihoods and Forced Migration*. Oxford: Policy Briefing Series Refugee Studies Centre, University of Oxford.

Cartagena Declaration on Refugees. 1984. *Colloquium on the International Protection of Refugees in Central America, Mexico and Panama.*

General Assembly. 2012. Human Rights Council, *Promotion and Protection of All Human Rights, Civil, Political, Economic, Social and Cultural Rights, Including the Right to Development Human Rights of Internally Displaced Persons*, 20th session, Agenda Item 3, UN Doc A/HRC/20/L.14.

Guiding Principles on Internal Displacement. 1998. Annex, 54th sess, Agenda Item 9(d) UN Doc E/CN.4/1998/53/Add.2.

Hathaway, James C. 2005. *The Rights of Refugees Under International Law*. Cambridge: Cambridge University Press.

Hodgkinson, David, and Lucy Young. 2013. "In the Face of Looming Catastrophe: A Convention for Climate Change Displaced Persons." Michael B. Gerrard and Gregory E. Wannier, eds., *Threatened Island Nations Legal Implications of Rising Seas and a Changing Climate.* Cambridge: Cambridge University Press, 299–300.
Horn, Laura, and Steven Freeland. 2009. "More Than Hot Air: Reflections on the Relationship Between Climate Change and Human Rights." *University of Western Sydney Law Review* 13: 124.
International Council for Human Rights Policy. 2008. *Climate Change and Human Rights: A Rough Guide.* Switzerland: ATAR Roto Press SA.
Kalin, Walter. 2005. *Protection of Internally Displaced Persons in Situations of Natural Disaster.* Geneva: OHCHR.
———. 2006. "The Future of the Guiding Principles on Internal Displacement." *Forced Migration Review* 24: 5.
———. 2008. *Guiding Principles on Internal Displacement Annotation.* Washington, DC: The American Society of International Law.
Kälin, Walter, and Nina Schrepfer. 2012. *Protecting People Crossing Borders in the Context of Climate Change Normative Gaps and Possible Approaches.* Bern: UNHCR.
Kurukulasuriya, Lal, and Nicholas A. Robinson. 2006. *Training Manual on International Environmental Law.* UNEP.
McAdam, Jane. 2011. *Climate Change Displacement and International Law: Complementary Protection Standards.* UNHCR Division of International Protection.
McInerney-Lankford, Siobhán, Mac Darrow, and Lavanya Rajamani. 2011. *Human Rights and Climate Change: A Review of the International Legal Dimensions.* Washington, DC: World Bank.
Myers, Norman. 2005. *Environmental Refugees: An Emergent Security Issue.* Viena: Organisation for Security and Cooperation in Europe, 13th Economic Forum.
Organization of African Unity (OAU). 1974. *Convention Governing the Specific Aspects of Refugee Problems in Africa (OAU Convention).*
Rajamani, Lavanya. 2006. *Differential Treatment in International Environmental Law.* Oxford: Oxford University Press.
Representative of the Secretary-General on Human Rights of Internally Displaced Persons. 2008. *Displacement Caused by the Effects of Climate Change: Who Will Be Affected and What Are the Gaps in the Normative Framework for Their Protection?* Background Paper. Retrieved 11 April 2019 from http://www2.ohchr.org/english/issues/climatechange/submissions.htm.
Sands, Philippe. 2004. *Principles of International Environmental Law.* Cambridge: Cambridge University Press.

The Kyoto Protocol to the United Nations Framework Convention on Climate Change, opened for signature 11 December 1997, 37 ILM 22 (1998) (Entered into Force 16 February 2005).
UN Human Rights Council. 2007. *Institution-Building of the United Nations Human Rights Council*, 9th meeting, UN Doc A/HRC/RES/5/1, June 18.
UN Office of the High Commissioner for Human Rights. 2012. *Human Rights Indicators: A Guide to Measurement and Implementation* (HR/Pub/12/5, 2012).
UNGA. 2006. *Resolution Adopted by the General Assembly*, 60th sess, Agenda Items 46 and 120, Un Doc A/RES/60/25.
UNHCR. 2011. "Summary of Deliberations on Climate Change and Displacement." *International Journal of Refugee Law* 23, no. 3: 561, 574.
UN General Assembly, United Nations Framework Convention on Climate Change: Resolution/Adopted by the General Assembly, 20 January 1994, A/RES/48/189.
United Nations. Charter of the United Nations, 24 October 1945, 1 UNTS XVI.
United Nations High Commissioner for Refugees. 2012. *The State of the World's Refugees: In Search of Solidarity*. Geneva: UNHCR.
United Nations Human Rights Council. 2008. *Report of the Human Rights Council on Its Seventh Session*, GA Res 7/23, 7th sess, Agenda Item 1, UN Doc A/HRC/7/78.
United Nations Human Rights Office of the High Commissioner for Human Rights. 2013. United Nations Human Rights Council, *Background Information on the Human Rights Council, About the Council*. Retrieved 11 April 2019 from http://www.ohchr.org/EN/HRBodies/HRC/Pages/AboutCouncil.aspx.
———. 2014. *Human Rights Council Complaint Procedure*. Retrieved 11 April 2019 from http://www.ohchr.org/EN/HRBodies/HRC/ComplaintProcedure/Pages/HRCComplaintProcedureIndex.aspx.
———. 2014. United Nations Human Rights Council. 2014. *Welcome to the Human Rights Council*, February 10. Retrieved 11 April 2019 from http://www.ohchr.org/EN/HRBodies/HRC/Pages/AboutCouncil.aspx.
Warner, K., M. Hamza, A. Oliver-Smith, F. Renaud, and A. Julca. 2010. "Climate Change, Environmental Degradation and Migration." *Natural Hazards* 55: 694.
Wewerinke, Margaretha. 2013. *Climate Change, Human Rights and the International Legal Order: The Role of the UN Human Rights Council*. Cambridge: Cambridge Centre for Climate Change Mitigation Research.

CHAPTER 7

Rwandan Land-Tenure Reforms: Local Socio-Economic Impacts and External Inputs

Hossain Ahmed Taufiq

INTRODUCTION

Land is a part of common heritage of all Rwandans: past, present, and future generations.[1]

As one of the most populous countries in Sub-Saharan Africa,[2] Rwanda has experienced significant political and social upheavals since emerging from a genocide that killed almost 800,000 people and exiled two million more in the space of three months.[3] Most of these crises were directly or indirectly related to the accommodation of competing claimants' land

H. A. Taufiq (✉)
Public Policy Analysis, Oregon State University, Corvallis, OR, USA
e-mail: taufiqh@oregonstate.edu; taufiqh@tcd.ie

Global Studies and Governance Program, Independent University, Bangladesh (IUB), Dhaka, Bangladesh rights in the midst of veritable land shortage,[4] In turn correlating land-ownership and poverty,[5] which earlier land laws struggled to address. Staggering post-genocide population growth enormously pressures the small land area of the country, resulting in extreme land fragmentation, reduced agricultural production, and swelling land holdings conflicts.[6] Returning exiles and other expatriates, as well as severe soil erosion (due to low yields and over-cultivation), further exacerbated the situation, in a country where 80% of all households depend on subsistence agriculture.[7]

To address these issues, the Rwandan Government drafted a new Land Reform Policy in 2004, formulated through a wide-ranging consultative process with the FAO (Food and Agricultural Organization) and The World Bank,[8] and was followed the next year by the Organic Land Law (OLL). Land-related narratives have converged upon the Organic Land Law (OLL), highlighting the need for land entitlement reform, which led to large-scale land registration and lease programme—known as the "Land Tenure Regularization Programme" (LTRP).[9] The LTRP pilot phase started in 2008, and in 2009 it was launched at the national level.[10] Without a local–global confluence, such an outcome would not have been possible. Broadly, LDC (less developed countries) growth/modernization, which drives the local–global nexus, institutionalizes over time.

Land reform is a Rwandan Government political priority. Rwanda's Economic Development and Poverty Reduction Strategy has put clear priorities on improving the land institutions related to land issues, land-registration mechanisms, and land-use planning,[11] unlocking a fair and future sustainable economic growth.[12]

Ample arguments for and against land-tenure regularization prevail, but whose impacts can hardly be measured precisely without a robust scholarly investigation, it is hard to measure the impacts. Executing such a systematic research on different types of land-tenure programme in different countries is needed, distinguishing urban and peri-urban contexts cannot but draw analogous conclusions and pertinent recommendations for unalike realities.[13] A cross-sectional investigation of the Rwandan Land Tenure Regularization Programme below takes one step in that direction, and prominent in its conclusion is the very local–global discourse alluded to.

Land Tenure Regularization: Concepts and Debates

Land productivity (whether agricultural or urban or commercial) is reliant on multiple complementary investments, which could be upgrading a dwelling or facilitating adequate drainage, structural improvement, irrigation for cultivation, or any other improvements. Investor investment to improve land-productivity could be challenged by disputes over ownership, forced eviction, or expropriation by the government, under a "tenure insecurity" clause.[14] Tenure insecurity can distort prices for land and basic services and reinforces social exclusion and poverty.[15] Also, insecure tenure can adversely impact taxation, economic and property-based activities, thus hindering government policy-making.[16]

Formal land titling and registration systems often emerge as the best institutional arrangements to reduce such tenure insecurity,[17] and most commonly known as Land Tenure Regularization initiatives/channels by the government. According to FAO sources, the programme also promotes a cadastral system (tax and lease), consisting of a systematic registration and legal title deeds distribution.[18] Payne, et al., defines land titling as the genuine allocation of property rights to a land, opposable to a third-party, and can be inherited, transferred, and mortgaged.[19]

According to Hernando de Soto's renowned book, *The Mystery of Capital (2000)*, holding assets in "defective forms" prevent poor people from converting those assets into useful means. He argues the lack of property titling, which they could invest in business effectively, renders their assets as "dead" capital, and indeed, so far, the net estimated value of the "dead" capital amounts to a whopping US$ 9.3 trillion.[20] Valid property ownership enables the poor to access much-needed formal credits and capital to transform the dead capital into useful means.[21]

Formal land titling is a precondition for developing a vibrant land market,[22] since it facilitates low-cost land transfer through rent/sales and establishes an active property market.[23]

When it comes to agriculture, land-tenure regularization exerts considerable influence.[24] Several LTRP studies show that, with legal title, farmers are able to use their land as collateral to obtain credit lines, thus facilitating their access to liquidity, and hence developing the agrarians' investment.[25] Moreover, many economists and social scientists agree that without title deed, land tenancy leads to inefficient farm resource allocation.[26] Indeed, land rights formalization has been well-grounded in the literature.

Research Questions

Given the nature of the Rwandan LTRP, and the successes of similar land reforms discussed in the literature review section, this study seeks for answers to the following question: "What are the socio-economic impacts of land-tenure regularization on poor land holders in urban and peri-urban Rwanda?" A series of secondary questions follow:

1. What kind of cadastral arrangements have been introduced through LTRP in urban and peri-urban areas?
2. How does the land market operate in Rwanda and to what extent have land transactions been formalized through LTRP?
3. To what extent do cadastral arrangements and market formalizations impact the different wealth groups? How much does the impact differ between those who are well off in relation to more disadvantaged groups?
4. To what extent are household's agricultural investments linked and affected by the land-tenure regularization?

Any casual glimpse would show our analytical and scholarly attention turning so much to local and national levels that the global connection gets obscured out of consideration. It is precisely how we can coax so much more out of even parochial assessments that this local–global perspective permits: development/modernization, no matter how "nationalistic" its purposes and preferences, cannot arguably prevail without a global context.

Data and Methodology

Considering the nature of the research problem, a sequential exploratory mixed methodology has been chosen. As such mixed methodology consists of both quantitative and qualitative methods, it widens the scope of receiving better insights and results.[27]

Study Methodology

The study was conducted in three stages. Firstly, an extensive literature review was conducted. Secondly, based on this literature review, two separate semi-structured questionnaires were prepared for second stage of the study which was qualitative. One questionnaire was used to interview land officials and the other one to interview landowners.[28] Finally, the third stage consisted of a separate structured questionnaire developed based on the comments from the questionnaires in the second stage.[29]

Study Geographical Area

The research was conducted in three districts. Gasabo was selected from Kigali Province and Nyamagabe and Kamonyi from Southern Province. From each of those districts one urban sector and one rural sector were selected. The reason for selecting these districts (for details please see Box 7.2 in Appendix).

FINDINGS

Given its 2009–2010 start, government officials claim that the LTRP mission is now almost 99% complete. For each plot registration, authorities ask for documents like a leasing contract, deed plan, title deed, and cadastral plan from the households. Based on the same documents, government calculates the tax and lease fees. Officials use "*UBUDEHE*", a wealth classification system, during all calculations. *UBUDEHE* categorizes Rwandese households into five different wealth groups—the *extreme poor (Abakenebikabije)*, the *poor (Abakene)*, the *progressive poor (Abakenebifashije)*, the *wealthy (Abakungu)*, and *the rich (Abakire)*.

Data confirms the registration fee claim. A statistical analysis has been performed from the sample to check how much actual registration fee has been paid against the registration by the landholders. It infers that the average Registration Fee amounts to RWF 2936 ($4.55); 92% of respondents paid up to 5000 RWF ($7.75) in registration fees. However, 78.4% of respondents possess up to 3 plots indicating that several households incurred over 1000 RWF in fees per plot, caused by the fact that 16% of total plots were located in Gatsata, an urban area.[30] On the other hand, 28.8% of respondents paid only 1000 RWF, whereas 36.8% of respondents only possess a single plot. Therefore, this observation suggests that a few households are overpaying registration fees related to their plots (till research date).

To better understand the reason behind such a gap between a number of plots possessed and the amount of registration fee paid, a scatter plot test has been conducted, as in Fig. 7.1.

The scatter plot shows a reasonably strong relationship between the registration fees paid and the number of plots registered. It shows some high registration fee payments. This can be explained by the fact that landholders from Gatsata sector (considered as urban) of Gasabo district from Kigali Province paid 5000 RWF for registering each land plot.

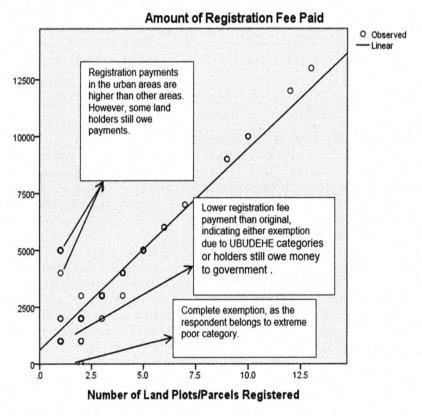

Fig. 7.1 Registration fees paid (per parcel, in Rwandan Franc)

On the other hand, landholders from other sectors in the Southern Province as well as the Rutungo sector (considered as peri-urban), in Kigali province, paid only 1000 RWF for each plot registration. It thus appears that some landholders paid lower or no registration fees, either because the household did not pay registration fees for all their plots, or because the government decided to exempt extremely poor households from paying the registration fee until they have ample funds.

Systematic Registration and Formalized Land Market

The 2005 Rwandan Organic Land Law proclaims that "all land belongs to public entities: the state, the Cities and the Districts".[31] The GoR considers two types of lands:

- **Public land**: reserved for environmental cause or public use.
- **Private land**: public owners allocate the land to natural or legal persons, transforming it into "individual land". Public owner can lease the land for up to 99 years, in exchange for an annual lease fee. By paying a 10 years of lease fee at once and by building infrastructure on the land, the lessee can obtain an ownership certificate.[32] Through sale, inheritance, and donation, the land rights can be transmitted. The new law allows the landholder to register the individual lands customarily owned before 2005.[33]

The systematic land registration includes the registration of *titre proprietre*, *contrats de cession gratuite*, *acte de notoriété*, and *paysannat land*.[34]

Two types of certificates are provided under the registration: the Certificate of Registration of Full Title and the Certificate of Registration of Emphyteutic Lease.[35]

Formalized Land Market

An active land market is present everywhere in Rwanda. However, before the LTRP, most land transactions were informal, where all land records were only held by the buyers and sellers.[36] LTRP targets formalizing all kinds of land transactions. Buyers and sellers during land transactions now must visit authorities such as the Village Chief, the Land Committee Council at Cell (Sub-sector) level, and Sector Land Officials.

To resolve land-related conflicts, systematic registration provides written proof of ownership documents. According to the interviewed landholders and government officials (July 2013), both buyers and sellers are obliged to provide such documents to the authority to formalize the transfer of land, with both obliged to pay 30,000 RWF ($46.51). Formalization process takes place at the district cell level.[37] However, in Kigali, an individual transfer (sell or purchase) of the land and the formalization process differ between emphyteutic lease (a form of real estate contract for 99 years) and full ownership titles.

New Cadastral Arrangements

As previously mentioned, the GoR introduced a new cadastral (land lease and tax programme) system through the LTRP. The implementation of the cadastral system is ongoing and will take several years. As a significant part of the Rwandan population is below the poverty level, the government has promised to consider the household's income situation during the imposition of taxes and fees.

The *Abakenebikabijes* are exempted from registration fees, lease fees, and taxes until their income level improves, and they amass enough funds to pay; The *Abakenes* are exempted from leases and taxes until their income level improves; The *Abakenebifashije* have to pay the lease fees; The *Abakungu* and the *Abakire* are subject to both land lease and taxes for properties, and government charges lease fees and taxes based on their comparatively high level of income and value of property.

Lease Fee

Although, the announcement of lease and tax payments has been officially made; leases and taxes are yet to be fully imposed in many sectors but will be fully imposed in most areas in the coming years. Initial annual lease fee payment was 1000 RWF for each land plot. However, the government is now preparing a different scale.

Although not every eligible household (till July 2013) has started to pay lease fees for their plots, a statistical analysis has been carried out for the households that already started paying lease fees, to understand the variation between different wealth categories (Fig. 7.2).

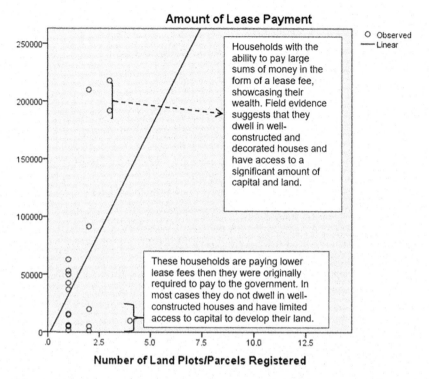

Fig. 7.2 Lease payment amount (in Rwandan Franc)

The scatter plat indicates that some households are paying relatively high lease fees (up to 21, 8000 RWF). This is because some of *the wealthy (Abakungu), and the rich (Abakire)* households in urban and relatively developed peri-urban sectors have started to pay lease fees, and the government is charging the lease fees based on their income and the value of their property. In particular, these households are from Gatsata, Runda, Musambira, and Gasaka sectors which are urban and relatively well-developed peri-urban sectors.

On the other hand, the result shows that some households paid comparatively lower lease fees against the number of plots they possess. These are mostly from the *progressive poor (Abakenebifashije)* households; they have paid lease fees for some of their plots and not all of them. Although such households are observed in Gatsata, Runda, Musambira, and Gasaka sectors, most of such households are based in comparatively rural and poor sectors of Tare and Rutungo. Nevertheless, many households admitted that they have to start paying lease fees in the coming years.

Tax

Tax payments are issued on buildings/properties or any activities that generate income within the land. Like the lease fee payment, land-related property tax also differs from urban to rural areas.[38] The property taxes are implemented in two categories: 1st base—Occupied houses; and 2nd base—Registered land yet not developed.

The highest concentration of tax payment is at Gatsata sector of Gasabo district (50% respondents from Gatsata, and 8% of total respondents),[39] while other taxpayers are from Runda sector of Kamonyi District (4% respondents from Runda, and 1% of the total respondents). (The tax payment ranges from 2500 to 33,500 RWF = $3.87–51.93.) Although number of taxpayers in Runda tends to be lower than Gatsata sector, many respondents admit that they must start paying tax from the next year. Gatsata is a part of the capital city Kigali, and Runda is close to the capital (only 16 kms). Also, field observation suggests that these taxpayers are comparatively richer than other residents.

Eligible respondents from other sectors have not yet started paying tax. Respondents from Musambira and Rutungo which fall under the above criteria were informed by local government institutions that they will be required to pay taxes in the upcoming years.

Transformation in Agricultural Rental Activities

The survey indicates that observable transformation took place regarding agricultural contractual arrangements since the registration process started.

- Among the respondents, 42% acknowledged that their involvement in agricultural rental activities has been increased since they registered their plots.
- Contractual rental agreements between the landlords and leaseholders over the past 24 months that took place for owner cultivation, sharecropping, fixed rent, and wage cultivation were, respectively, 73, 8, 2, and 17%.

- Changes in rental activities have been observed by 46%. Also, 12% responded that they observed rental rate reduction, 69% observed land redistribution, 5% observed a reduction in sharecropping, 10% observed rental term decrease, while 4% said other changes.
- Among all the survey respondents, 91% feel that due to title registration their bargaining capacity during contractual rental agreements has been improved.

Access to Formal Credit

During Focus Group Discussions, respondents answered that they seek for formal credits from cooperatives, banks, NGOs, and moneylenders. The most popular among farmers are *SACCO* (Savings and Credits Cooperative Society), *TUZAMURANE, DUTABARANE, DUTERANINKUNGA, TURWANYE MALARIYA* cooperatives. Land is most commonly used as collateral for obtaining formal credit for agricultural investment in rural areas.

Survey result further shows that

- 41 respondents obtained loans in the last 24 months and among them 46% used land as collateral for obtaining institutional credit;
- 83% respondents agreed that registered land title used as collateral made it easier to access to official line of credits.

Impact on Household Income

Although the provision of universal property ownership with clear title rights is considered as a powerful instrument to improve a household's income level,[40] and the GoR envisions the LTRP as a similar instrument, it is difficult to predict to what extent the Rwandan LTRP has positively contributed to improve households income since it began.

Indeed, according to the study results there are some indications of income level improvement since registration (9%), however the majority of households (63%) responded that they did not observe any change in their income level since registration. Although a number of households agreed their income level improved in the past 24 months, however a large number of households (48%) observed their income level decreased in the last 24 months.

However, it is not certain whether tenure regularization is responsible for this increase, decrease or stagnation. In fact, a large number of respondents, the majority of whom are dependent on agriculture—responded that their primary source of income which is staple crop production was hit hard by natural calamities like droughts and floods in the last couple of years (until the finalization of the data collection for this dissertation). Furthermore, lack of inputs and lands could also be responsible for the decrease or stagnation (see Appendix 7.1).

The OLS test of "LTRP among agricultural based households" shows that lack of land is significantly correlated with the change in income over the past 24 months. No other variables showed any significance (Table 7.1).

Discussions

From the result, it is clear that since the registration process started access to formal credit and investments has been significantly improved; land market has been formalized, as well as the efficiency in the land rental market has been improved. However, the programme still needs to take certain issues under consideration regarding poverty alleviation, tax and lease payment, and tenure security.

Formalization of the Land Market

Despite the presence of a highly organized informal land market; swelling land fragmentation, decreasing productivity, and increasing need for capital investment in land have led to noteworthy support for Government-backed registration and formalization. The majority of the respondents acknowledged that government-backed tenure formalization is a better guarantor for tenure security than the customary laws. According to a respondent from Musambira (respondent no. 19, 2013), "I am satisfied with the land formalization program, and I believe that a formal title deed will solve all misunderstandings among neighboring landholders, which is crucial to prevent any further land-based conflicts".

Respondents also witnessed changes in the value of land since the registration process started, as one respondent (Runda, respondent number 54, 2013) states, "The registration process was acceptable, the value of my land has been increasedand now everyone has a strong legitimate right to land. The legal title also made it easier for me to obtain loan".

Table 7.1 Cross section with dummies for registration time: ordinary least squares test (to observe impact of LTRP on agricultural-based households)

Change in income level in last 24 months (from study date 2013)	Coefficient	Standard error	T	p > |t|	[95% confidence interval]
Registration in 2009	−0.7570867	1.082111	−0.70	0.486	−2.911845 1.397672
Registration in 2010	−1.23268	1.031762	−1.19	0.236	−3.287181 0.8218208
Registration in 2011	−1.133742	0.988992	−1.15	0.255	−3.103077 0.8355925
Registration in 2012	−0.7223586	1.122477	−0.64	0.522	−2.957495 1.512778
Lack of Lands	−0.6943999	0.2324254	−2.99	0.004	−1.157218 −0.2315818
Floods	−0.0900552	0.2148559	−0.42	0.676	−0.5178879 0.3377775
Droughts	−0.2530363	0.2956614	−0.86	0.395	−0.8417734 0.3357008
Lack of Inputs	0.1195309	0.2779565	0.43	0.668	−0.4439511 0.6730129
Lack of Finance	0.3703227	0.2656948	1.39	0.167	−0.1587433 0.8993886
Lack of Technical Assistance	−0.2604406	0.3632328	−0.72	0.476	−0.9837294 0.4628483
Monoculture	0.5052852	0.5199972	0.97	0.334	−0.5301615 1.540732
Lack of Labour	0.8465708	0.5319603	1.59	0.116	−0.2126974 1.905839
Pest/Diseases	0.0582175	0.2358079	0.25	0.806	−0.411336 0.5277709
No Market	0.7953752	0.8090958	0.98	0.329	−0.8157403 2.406491
Consolidation Policy	0.5145821	0.7965911	0.65	0.520	−1.071633 2.100798
Frequent Illness	0.3865803	0.5189514	0.74	0.459	−0.6467839 1.419945
Other	0.3701406	0.3952057	0.94	0.352	−0.4168145 1.157096
N\A	−0.9156925	0.6578434	−1.39	0.168	−2.225626 0.3942411
_Cons	3.912307	1.014633	3.86	0.000	1.891914 5.9327

Note Registration 2013 omitted because of collinearity (also no respondents)

One of the LTRP objectives is to abolish gender discrimination in land inheritance and in other forms of land transfers. The title deed is now shared among legally married couples in 50-50 ownership. Despite such GoR efforts, field evidence suggests that women often inherit lands which have a low productivity and do not possess the necessary means to develop them. As one respondent (Runda, respondent number 29, 2013) describes the situation, "Land registration has brought me luck. Before the title formalization, I was a victim of family discrimination, landwas only divided among male heirs of my family andIwas deprived of land. Now I have received land. However, I am yet to receive fair share of the inherited capital which is still held by my brothers. Since my husband died, I do not have enough savings to develop the received land".

Cadastral Arrangements Need: Further Alignment with Household Income

The implementation of the cadastral system raises questions about the types of impacts on income it has on low-income groups both in the short and long term. Indeed, the GoR maintains a categorised UBUDEHE programme exempts extremely poor and poor people from paying tax and lease, until they become financially capable. However, doubts remain regarding the future efficiency and transparency of this cadastral arrangement. According to a UNDP report, a large segment of the population in Rwanda lives below the income poverty line with average purchasing power parity (PPP) of $1.25 per day.[41] This large proportion of the population falls under the two poorest UBUDEHE categories, and they would, therefore, be unable to pay the tax and lease fees. Thus, it is not clear how the government is going to generate the necessary revenues to fund future development projects if they have to exempt such a large proportion of the population.

Landholder Confusion and Cadastre Measurement: Sensitization and Support Need

The tenure formalization programme still needs massive sensitization. Despite significant GoR expenditure on the campaign and advertisement of the LTRP, landholders are still unclear at what measurement taxes will be imposed on them. A respondent from Runda (respondent number 41, 2013) states that, "local authority declines to take any responsibility for citizens whom are not able to pay tax that is starting soon, and the government did not provide information about how much square metre at what rate will be taxed". Furthermore, there are consternations among landholders with the tax and lease giving a process for each single parcel rather than paying in total. In particular, claims have been made from the title-holders side that they are yet to receive any justification of such process. According to one respondent from Musambira (respondent number 21, 2013), "We are concerned with the tax and lease fee payment process; the cadastral process of paying for each parcel is confusing. Despite possessing different size of lands and the combined size is lesser than 1 hectare, I am entitled to pay more than those who have one single piece of land measuring 1 hectare". Similar concerns have been raised from the Gatsata sector as one respondent (respondent number 106, 2013) states, "He is not satisfied with the mode of tax payments on his own land which is not used for business and governing income and even estimation on tax per square meter is not clearly understood".

Agricultural Output and Food Security: Obstacles Remain

It is clear from the result that, efficiency in the rental market has been improved. Both landowners and tenants can now negotiate better with legal titles during subleasing.[42] As the majority of landholders belong to agriculture-based households, such land tenancies primarily take place for cultivation purposes. When it comes to increasing staple crop production, lack of land is a major obstacle. The survey result found that among the respondents 82% have less than 0.75 ha. Food and Agricultural Organization insists that land below 0.90 hectare is nutritionally not viable.[43] The FGD results indicate that farmers, especially in the southern district of Nyamagabe, are struggling to raise their income from cash-cropping. The district agronomist is of the opinion that the anticipated economic output has not been achieved so far due to a recent fall in the market price of these cash crops. As a result, many farmers are now rolling back to auto-subsistence agriculture.

However, to generate income from auto-subsistence agriculture, a significant amount of agricultural investment is necessary. Most of the people in this region are poor and do not have the necessary means to invest for the next year. As a result, people have to rely again on formal credit sources for their agricultural investment. Although the systematic registration made it easier for the people to access to formal credit sources, the culture of continuous borrowing of institutional credits and subsequent repayment leaves most of the farmers with inadequate savings.

Registration fee imposed by the government is quite low, as average household possesses five plots of land,[44] the average cost of registration is no more than (5 × 1000=) 5000 RWF (US$7.51). However, the cost significantly increases in the urban areas, in the Gatsata sector where the registration fee for each plot is 5000 RWF. Also, paying for several plots together is hard for most landholders (for instance, those who have more than 10 plots).

However, exclusion of the poorest households (if they do not receive the title documents before payment) is dangerously leaving them exposed to multiple tenure insecurities such as forced eviction, land grab by powerful neighbours, and government expropriation.

CONCLUSIONS

Today, land registration and tenure regularization is a global issue. Land titling can refer to the allocating real property rights, as opposed to a third party; and it can be transferred, inherited, and mortgaged. de Soto argues how holding assets in "defective forms" prevent poor people from converting those assets into a useful means. And, title deed is the best way forward according to him, as he argues that tenure regularization can unlock the "dead" capital globally, amounting to a whopping US$ 9.3 trillion. In light of such arguments, the paper investigated the Rwandan land-tenure regularization as the country faced many problems before due to the absence of such formalization. The outcomes of the tenure regularization in this paper can be used to conduct further investigations in other countries on similar projects.

The legal title deed improved access to formal credit. It has shown potentials to generate revenue and stimulate investment at various levels. The LTRP also aimed to enhance tenure security and agricultural production. However, challenges remain at the ground level regarding tenure security and agriculture.

The study shows that since the inauguration of land-registration process Rwandan landowners are being benefited from the programme. Though the informal land market is still fully operational, landowners have recognized that government-backed tenure formalization is a better guarantor for tenure security than the customary laws as it provides better protection from future land-based conflicts. Moreover, the registered landowners also experienced an increase in their land prices and the legal title helped them obtain loan with less aggravation. The formalization of title also reduced gender discrimination as the title is now shared to legally married couples.

A large portion of Rwandan population lives below poverty line who are not able to pay necessary taxes and lease fees to the government for necessary developments. How government deals with such complexity remains to be seen. Furthermore, there remains confusion regarding the taxes and lease fees payment.

The formalization of the deed title increased the effectiveness of the rental market for all the parties involved. But as the majority of the lands are used for agricultural purposes, the main obstacle is the lack of lands and fall in the market prices of the cash-crop. It forces the farmers to look for investments. Though the formal credit sources are now made it easier to obtain such funding the need to borrow continuously and inability to repay in time leave the farmers with meagre savings. As a result, in spite of the benefits of deed formalization the farmers are not able to improve their income level.

A national-scale research on social and economic impacts of the LTRP is required to have a comprehensive understanding of the benefits and challenges of the programme.

The following initiatives can also help achieve the Rwandan authority more success:

- To measure the actual impacts of land titling over household income level.
- To measure to what extent agricultural investment has been stimulated.
- To consider the comparative efficiency and resource allocation in agricultural rental arrangements. Land titling can be used as a robust policy instrument to ensure proper allocation of resource and enhance agricultural income generation.
- To align the agricultural reform policies (monoculture and land consolidation policy) with poor households' income level and ensuring that these policies are benefiting the poor households, both socially and economically.

- To promulgate an expropriation law that ensures households are receiving fair value of the expropriated land and ensuring that the law is implemented in a transparent way as well as providing protection against any unfair land grab.
- To measure the impacts of modest or rapid increases in property values after titling.

One major limitation encountered during field work was that respondents appeared concerned. Perhaps this is because most of them have experienced land-related problems for a long time without effective solutions. For some, interviews were boring as they learnt that the aim of the research was not to provide solutions or alternatives to the issues.

Another gate-keeping problem was experienced during the field work. Enumerators were complaining that some people kept information to themselves and refused to reveal them. Thus, some respondents interviewed did not appear comfortable giving the appropriate information and, in some cases, skipped answers for unknown reasons. Most of the respondents failed to provide approximated volume of their harvest and the earning from agricultural products.

APPENDIX 7.1: OBJECTIVES, STUDY AREAS

See Boxes 7.1 and 7.2.

Box 7.1 Overall objectives of the Rwandan Land Tenure Regularization Programme

- Land titles will be accepted as collateral for loans, will build confidence for investments in economic development and combat land degradation
- Regularization will bring efficiency to the land market; allow its true value to be realized and other Government of Rwanda policies on agricultural reform and industrialisation, encourage its optimum use
- Overall Land Tenure Regularization programme will lead to the following impact: *contribute to poverty reduction, increased productive investment, optimisation of land use, gender equality and social harmony, throughout Rwanda* by 2015

Box 7.2 Study areas

Province	District	Sector	Sector characteristics
Kigali Province	Gasabo	1. Gatsata	Urban
		2. Rutungo	Rural
Southern Province	Kamonyi	1. Runda	Urban
		2. Musambira	Peri-Urban/Rural
	Nyamagabe	1. Gasaka	Urban
		2. Tare	Rural

NOTES

1. Jamie Crook, "Promoting Peace and Economic Security in Rwanda Through Fair and Equitable Land Rights," *California Law Review*, no. 94 (2006): 1487.
2. UNICEF, "Rwanda," The United Nations Children's Fund, https://www.unicef.org/appeals/rwanda.html#:~:text=Rwanda%20is%20one%20of%20the,rapid%20spread%20of%20Ebola%20infection.
3. Johan Pottier, "Land Reform for Peace? Rwanda's 2005 Land Law in Context," *Journal of Agrarian Change* 6, no. 4 (2006): 509–537; Crook, "Promoting Peace and Economic Security in Rwanda," 1487.
4. Crook, "Promoting Peace and Economic Security in Rwanda," 1487.
5. Herman Musahara, "Improving Tenure Security for The Rural Poor," *Rwanda—Country Case Study Improving Tenure Security for the Rural Poor* (FAO: Nakuru, Kenya, 2006), 19.
6. Herman Musahara and Chris Huggins, "Land Reform, Land Scarcity and Post-Conflict Reconstruction: A Case Study of Rwanda," *From the Ground Up: Land Rights, Conflict and Peace in Sub-Saharan Africa* (Pretoria and Cape Town: Institute of Security Studies, 2005), 16; Pottier, "Land Reform for Peace?" 509–537.
7. Musahara, "Improving Tenure Security," 19.
8. Musahara and Huggins, "Land Reform, Land Scarcity," 16; Pottier, "Land Reform for Peace?" 509–537.
9. Binda E. Mbembe, J. Daale, and A. Kairaba, "The Impact of Land Lease Fee on Landowners: Rwanda Case Study," *Land Lease Fees Rwanda* (2012).

10. Ibid.
11. Richard Baldwin, "Annual Review: Support for Land Tenure Regularisation Programme in Rwanda (Including Comments)," DFID (2015), http://iati.dfid.gov.uk/iati_documents/3673459.docx.
12. Ibid.
13. Nora Clichevsky, *Pobreza y acceso al suelo urbano. Algunas interrogantes sobre las políticas de regularización en América Latina* (Cepal, 2003).
14. Gershon Feder and Akihiko Nishio, "The Benefits of Land Registration and Titling: Economic and Social Perspectives," *Land Use Policy* 15, no. 1 (1998): 25–43.
15. Pietro Garau and Elliott Sclar, "Interim Report of the Task Force 8 on Improving the Lives of Slum Dwellers," *Millennium Project, United Nations Development Programme* (2004).
16. E. D. Sclar and P. Garau, "Interim Report of the Task Force 8 on Improving the Lives of Slum Dwellers," *Millennium Project* (2003), 57.
17. Fedar and Nishio, "The Benefits of Land Registration and Titling," 25–43; Hernando De Soto, *The Mystery of Capital: Why Capitalism Triumphs in the West and Fails Everywhere Else* (Civitas Books, 2000); D. Bromley, *The Empty Promises of Formal Titles: Creating Potemkin Villages in the Tropics* (Madison, Wisconsin: University of Wisconsin, 2005); and Thomas E. Schweigert, "Land Title, Tenure Security, Investment and Farm Output: Evidence from Guatemala," *The Journal of Developing Areas* (2006): 115–126.
18. Gérard Ciparisse, ed. *Multilingual Thesaurus on Land Tenure* (Food & Agriculture Organization, 2003 [2009]).
19. Geoffrey Payne, Alain Durand-Lasserve, Carole Rakodi, Colin Marx, Margot Rubin, and Selle Ndiaye, *Social and Economic Impacts of Land Titling Programmes in Urban and Peri-Urban Areas: International Experience and Case Studies of Senegal and South Africa* (Swedish International Development Authority, 2008), 5.
20. de Soto, *The Mystery of Capital*.
21. Ibid.

22. Julian Quan, "Reflections on the Development Policy Environment for Land and Property Rights, 1997–2003 (Draft)," *Background Paper for International Workshop on Fundamental Rights in the Balance: New Ideas on the Rights to Land, Housing & Property* (IDS, University of Sussex, 2003), 16–18.
23. Klaus W. Deininger, *Land Policies for Growth and Poverty Reduction* (World Bank Publications, 2003).
24. Frank Place, "Land Tenure and Agricultural Productivity in Africa: A Comparative Analysis of the Economics Literature and Recent Policy Strategies and Reforms," *World Development* 37, no. 8 (2009): 1326–1336; Lorenzo Cotula, Camilla Toulmin, and Ced Hesse, *Land Tenure and Administration in Africa: Lessons of Experience and Emerging Issues* (London: International Institute for Environment and Development, 2004); and Timothy Besley and Robin Burgess, "Land Reform, Poverty Reduction, and Growth: Evidence from India," *The Quarterly Journal of Economics* 115, no. 2 (2000): 389–430.
25. Mitchell A. Seligson, "Agrarian Reform in Costa Rica: The Impact of the Title Security Program," *Inter-American Economic Affairs* 35, no. 4 (1982): 31–56; Peter Dorner and Bonnie Saliba, "Interventions in Land Markets to Benefit The Rural Poor," *Land Tenure and Economic Development* (St. Lucia 1981); Gershon Feder, Tongroj Onchan, and Tejaswi Raparla, *Land Ownership Security and Access to Credit in Rural Thailand*, No. ARU53 (The World Bank, 1986); and Sarah Gavian and Marcel Fafchamps, "Land Tenure and Allocative Efficiency in Niger," *American Journal of Agricultural Economics* 78, no. 2 (1996): 460–471.
26. Dale W. Adams and Norman Rask, "Economics of Cost-Share Leases in Less-Developed Countries," *American Journal of Agricultural Economics* 50, no. 4 (1968): 935–942; Pranab K. Bardhan and T. N. Srinivasan, "Cropsharing Tenancy in Agriculture: A Theoretical and Empirical Analysis," *The American Economic Review* (1971): 48–64; Nicholas Georgescu-Roegen, "Economic Theory and Agrarian Economics," *Oxford Economic Papers* 12, no. 1 (1960): 1–40; Earl O. Heady, "Economics of Farm Leasing Systems," *Journal of Farm Economics* 29, no. 3 (1947): 659–678; Charles Issawi, "Farm Output Under Fixed Rents and Share Tenancy," *Land Economics* 33, no. 1 (1957): 74–77; and Rainer

Schickele, "Effect of Tenure Systems on Agricultural Efficiency," *Journal of Farm Economics* 23, no. 1 (1941): 185–207.

27. Alan Bryman, *Social Research Methods* (Oxford University Press, 2016); John W. Creswell, "Mapping the Developing Landscape of Mixed Methods Research," *SAGE Handbook of Mixed Methods in Social & Behavioral Research*, eds. Abbas Tashakkori and Charles Teddlie (Sage, 2010), 45–68; Donna M. Mertens, *Transformative Research and Evaluation* (Guilford Press, 2008); and David L. Morgan, "Paradigms Lost and Pragmatism Regained: Methodological Implications of Combining Qualitative and Quantitative Methods," *Journal of Mixed Methods Research* 1, no. 1 (2007): 48–76.

28. Two separate interviews were conducted with the Deputy Director General from Department of Lands and Mappings, and Deputy Director General from Ministry of Agriculture and Animal Resources. In addition to these high official interviews, individual interviews with field level land officials and agricultural officers were organized. A pre-prepared semi-structured questionnaire was used for the land officials. Also interviewed were two District Land Officers, two Sector Land Executive Secretaries, one Land Surveyor and one Agronomist from Nyamagabe, Kamonyi and Gasabo districts were interviewed. For the Agronomist, questionnaire was slightly modified and some additional randomly picked unstructured questions were asked.

Two separate focus group discussions among landholders were organized. Each time five men and five women from different wealth categories were invited. A pre-tested semi-structured guideline was used for the focus group discussions. The land-tenure issues regarding agricultural productivity and poverty situation were raised, discussed, and recorded on tape.

29. Information from formal interviews and focus group discussions formed the basis of the structured questionnaire. This questionnaire was piloted among farmers in Rutungo Sector of Gasabo District. After piloting the questionnaire, a total of 125 surveys was conducted in Gatsata, Rutungo (Gasabo); Runda, Musambira (Kamonyi); Gasaka, Tare (Nyamagabe) sectors. Two research assistants were hired and trained as Enumerators to conduct the surveys.

30. Registration fee in the urban Kigali sectors for each plot is 5000 RWF.
31. "rwanda.eRegulatins.org," RDB, http://rwanda.eregulations.org/menu/37?l=en.
32. Ibid.
33. Ibid.
34. Government of Rwanda, "Organic Law Establishing the Land Tenure System in Rwanda" (2005); Government of Rwanda, "Land Lease Order 2007c" (Kigali: GOR, 2007); Government of Rwanda (2008), "Land Registration Order 2008d" (Kigali, 2005); *Titre Proprietre*, a certificate equivalent to freehold title and available after land is developed in accordance with a contract of location, *Contrats de Cession Gratuite*, granted to NGO, Churches, and other non-profit associations for donated or sanctioned land with no limit on duration, *Acte de Notoriété* is an occupancy permit with no fixed term which widely held in urban areas. However, an annual rent with 6% tax on value of the land must be paid to the Government on registration, and *Paysannat Land* is given by the Rwandan Government under a condition such as using for tea plantation.
35. RDB, "rwanda.eRegulatins.org."
36. MINIRENA, *Strategic Road Map for Land Tenure Reform* (Kigali: Ministry of Natural Resources, 2009).
37. RDB, "rwanda.eRegulatins.org."
38. Rwanda Revenue Authority 2013.
39. The number of respondents paying tax was small, result could differ in a larger sample.
40. de Soto, "The Mystery of Capital"; D. Bromley, *The Empty Promises of Formal Titles: Creating Potemkin Villages in the Tropics* (Madison: University of Wisconsin: Madison, 2005).
41. UNDP, *HDR, Human Development Report 2013—The Rise of the South: Human Progress in a Diverse World* (New York: United Nations Development Programme, 2013).
42. Landowners often rent out their land for a specified time which most often attached with various form of conditions, vice versa a tenant rent in the land for specific purpose such as for agricultural purpose by agreeing such conditions.

43. Jason Mosley, "Land Policy in Rwanda: Issues for UK Policy," *All Party Parliamentary Group on the Great Lakes Region and Genocide Prevention, Working Paper* 3 (2004).
44. Musahara and Huggins, "Land Reform, Land Scarcity," 1.

BIBLIOGRAPHY
=============

Adams, Dale W., and Norman Rask. 1968. "Economics of Cost-Share Leases in Less-Developed Countries." *American Journal of Agricultural Economics* 50, no. 4: 935–942.
Baldwin, Richard. 2015. "Annual Review: Support for Land Tenure Regularisation Programme in Rwanda (Including Comments)." DFID. http://iati.dfid.gov.uk/iati_documents/3673459.docx.
Bardhan, Pranab K., and T. N. Srinivasan. 1971. "Cropsharing Tenancy in Agriculture: A Theoretical and Empirical Analysis." *The American Economic Review*.
Besley, Timothy, and Robin Burgess. 2000. "Land Reform, Poverty Reduction, and Growth: Evidence from India." *The Quarterly Journal of Economics* 115, no. 2: 389–430.
Binda, E. Mbembe, J. Daale, and A. Kairaba. 2012. "The Impact of Land Lease Fee on Landowners: Rwanda Case Study." *Land Lease Fees Rwanda*.
Bromley, D. 2005. *The Empty Promises of Formal Titles: Creating Potemkin Villages in the Tropics*. Madison: University of Wisconsin.
Bryman, Alan. 2016. *Social Research Methods*. Oxford University Press.
Ciparisse, Gérard, ed. 2003 (2009). *Multilingual Thesaurus on Land Tenure*. Food & Agriculture Organization.
Clichevsky, Nora. 2003. *Pobreza y acceso al suelo urbano. Algunas interrogantes sobre las políticas de regularización en América Latina*. Cepal.
Cotula, Lorenzo, Camilla Toulmin, and Ced Hesse. *Land Tenure and Administration in Africa: Lessons of Experience and Emerging Issues*. London: International Institute for Environment and Development.
Crook, Jamie. 2006. "Promoting Peace and Economic Security in Rwanda Through Fair and Equitable Land Rights." *California Law Review* 94: 1487.
De Soto, Hernando. 2000. *The Mystery of Capital: Why Capitalism Triumphs in the West and Fails Everywhere Else*. Civitas Books.
Deininger, Klaus W. 2003. *Land Policies for Growth and Poverty Reduction*. World Bank Publications.
Dorner, Peter, and Bonnie Saliba. 1981. "Interventions in Land Markets to Benefit the Rural Poor." *Land Tenure and Economic Development*. St. Lucia.

Feder, Gershon, Tongroj Onchan, and Tejaswi Raparla. 1986. *Land Ownership Security and Access to Credit in Rural Thailand*, No. ARU53. The World Bank.

Feder, Gershon, and Akihiko Nishio. 1998. "The Benefits of Land Registration and Titling: Economic and Social Perspectives." *Land Use Policy* 15, no. 1: 25–43.

Garau, Pietro, and Elliott Sclar. 2004. "Interim Report of the Task Force 8 on Improving the Lives of Slum Dwellers." *Millennium Project, United Nations Development Programme.*

Gavian, Sarah, and Marcel Fafchamps. 1996. "Land Tenure and Allocative Efficiency in Niger." *American Journal of Agricultural Economics* 78, no. 2: 460–471.

Georgescu-Roegen, Nicholas. 1960. "Economic Theory and Agrarian Economics." *Oxford Economic Papers* 12, no. 1: 1–40.

Government of Rwanda. 2005. "Organic Law Establishing the Land Tenure System in Rwanda."

———. 2007. *Land Lease Order 2007c.* Kigali: GOR.

———. 2008. *Land Registration Order 2008d.* Kigali.

Heady, Earl O. 1947. "Economics of Farm Leasing Systems." *Journal of Farm Economics* 29, no. 3: 659–678.

Issawi, Charles. 1957. "Farm Output Under Fixed Rents and Share Tenancy." *Land Economics* 33, no. 1: 74–77.

Mertens, Donna M. 2008. *Transformative Research and Evaluation.* New York: Guilford Press.

Morgan, David L. 2007 "Paradigms Lost and Pragmatism Regained: Methodological Implications of Combining Qualitative and Quantitative Methods." *Journal of Mixed Methods Research* 1, no. 1: 48–76.

Mosley, Jason. 2004. "Land Policy in Rwanda: Issues for UK Policy." All Party Parliamentary Group on the Great Lakes Region and Genocide Prevention, Working Paper 3.

Musahara, Herman, and Chris Huggins. 2005. "Land Reform, Land Scarcity and Post-Conflict Reconstruction: A Case Study of Rwanda." *From the Ground Up: Land Rights, Conflict and Peace in Sub-Saharan Africa.* Pretoria and Cape Town: Institute of Security Studies.

Musahara, Herman. 2006. "Improving Tenure Security for the Rural Poor." *Rwanda—Country Case Study Improving Tenure Security for the Rural Poor.* Nakuru, Kenya: FAO.

Payne, Geoffrey, Alain Durand-Lasserve, Carole Rakodi, Colin Marx, Margot Rubin, and Selle Ndiaye. 2008. *Social and Economic Impacts of Land Titling Programmes in Urban and Peri-Urban Areas: International Experience and Case Studies of Senegal and South Africa.* Swedish International Development Authority.

Place, Frank. 2009. "Land Tenure and Agricultural Productivity in Africa: A Comparative Analysis of the Economics Literature and Recent Policy Strategies and Reforms." *World Development* 37, no. 8: 1326–1336.

Pottier, Johan. 2006. "Land Reform for Peace? Rwanda's 2005 Land Law in Context." *Journal of Agrarian Change* 6, no. 4: 509–537.

Quan, Julian. 2003. "Reflections on the Development Policy Environment for Land and Property Rights, 1997–2003 (Draft)." *Background Paper for International Workshop on Fundamental Rights in the Balance: New Ideas on the Rights to Land, Housing & Property*. IDS, University of Sussex.

"rwanda.eRegulatins.org." RDB. http://rwanda.eregulations.org/menu/37?l=en.

Schickele, Rainer. 1941. "Effect of Tenure Systems on Agricultural Efficiency." *Journal of Farm Economics* 23, no. 1: 185–207.

Schweigert, Thomas E. 2006. "Land Title, Tenure Security, Investment and Farm Output: Evidence from Guatemala." *The Journal of Developing Areas*, 115–126.

Sclar, E. D., and P. Garau. 2003. "Interim Report of the Task Force 8 on Improving the Lives of Slum Dwellers." *Millennium Project*.

Seligson, Mitchell A. 1982. "Agrarian Reform in Costa Rica: The Impact of the Title Security Program." *Inter-American Economic Affairs* 35, no. 4: 31–56.

UNDP, HDR. 2013. *Human Development Report 2013—The Rise of the South: Human Progress in a Diverse World*. New York: United Nations Development Programme.

UNICEF. "Rwanda." The United Nations Children's Fund. https://www.unicef.org/appeals/rwanda.html#:~:text=Rwanda%20is%20one%20of%20the,rapid%20spread%20of%20Ebola%20infection.

CHAPTER 8

Ready-Made-Garments: Supply-Chain Management & COVID-19 Impacts

Md. Mamun Habib and Ikram Hasan

INTRODUCTION

Academics began to focus on ways to increase the value of the supply chain while simultaneously shortening reaction times and decreasing costs for various stakeholders as supply chain management (SCM) concerns became increasingly relevant to profit-making firms in past decades. Only a few studies looked at nonprofit organizations, i.e., corporations that finance them, and even fewer looked into academic SCM interest.[1] At stake is a local–global tradeoff of growing interests given the COVID-19 pandemic: here we have a viral outbreak instigating community lockdowns the world over, including manufacturing hubs, and thereby

Md. M. Habib (✉)
School of Business & Entrepreneurship, Independent University, Bangladesh, Dhaka, Bangladesh
e-mail: mamunhabib@iub.edu.bd

I. Hasan
Graduate School of Business, Universiti Tun Abdul Razak, Lumpur, Malaysia

© The Author(s), under exclusive license to Springer Nature Singapore Pte Ltd. 2022
I. A. Hussain (eds.), *Global-Local Tradeoffs, Order-Disorder Consequences*, Global Political Transitions,
https://doi.org/10.1007/978-981-16-9419-6_8

disrupting not only production and shipping but also threatening an automation replacement for raw human labor. Local frontiers and production take the hit, but global supply networks also get drawn in. Nowhere can the "local" be better depicted globally and, likewise, the "global" counterpart be locally illustrated better than with the RMG production network.

Nonprofit pursue a variety of objectives, including overall quality of life for all people and increasing literacy rates, as well as ensuring equal opportunity for men and women from all walks of life. For-profit businesses, on the other hand, are driven only by financial gain.[2] One notices how literary, life quality and gender considerations also cast global networks which leave "local" parties like countries or companies no choice but to take a stand. While a nonprofit organization's income usually covers its costs, running a successful profit business varies significantly from running a nonprofit organization owing to conflicting objectives.[3] SCM relevance as a method for guaranteeing an organization's performance has lately been highlighted in a rising number of studies.

SCM linkages assist the corporate structure in competing in the rapidly expanding global market. Academia, which is a type of nonprofit organization, may be related to the SCM objective of integrating activities from across and inside companies to deliver customer value. We strive to create the best students and research outputs possible in order to serve society. Because it involves all stakeholders in the process, communication and data exchange are key components of an integrated educational supply chain. Because of modern technology that makes information flow easier, it is now feasible to create a coordinated supply chain to help educational institutions achieve their operational objectives, strategies, and plans. As a result, it's critical to establish strong, mutually beneficial relationships both inside and beyond the company.[4]

SCM linkages are required for a variety of reasons, increasing profitability, including improving operations, customer satisfaction, and outsourcing, as well as dealing with competitive difficulties, delivering top-notch outcomes, and increasing supply chain complexity. For example, supply chains in the industrial sector are straightforward to describe since each member of the chain gets input signals from a group of suppliers and then processes and distributes the signals to a different group of clients. Customers are an important source of information for the support operations of educational institutions. Customers contribute to the processes by bringing their things, thoughts, bodies, and knowledge to bear on the proceedings.[5]

Bangladesh is presently one of the world's major exporters of ready-made garments (RMGs). From the late 1970s through the early 1990s, this industry grew rapidly in Bangladesh, with most of the growth taking place during that decade and the next decade. The industry's rapid growth was made possible by the use of advanced technology and low-cost labor. Figure 8.1 depicts that RMG export tapestry as a proportion of total comparative Bangladeshi exports, broadly exposing the enormous potential within international commerce to smash "local"-"global" barriers.

Companies can reduce inventory, save money, shorten order cycles, and increase output while also responding more rapidly to the market by implementing supply chain management methods. Aside from these benefits, effective supply chain management systems allow the clothing industry to respond swiftly. The concept of rapid reaction, which involves suppliers, manufacturers, and vendors working and exchanging information to respond swiftly to customer needs, is an essential instance of the local–global connection.[6]

For the sake of job creation, tourist attraction, as well as women's empowerment, Bangladesh's economy is primarily based on the ready-to-wear industry. Approximately 11.2% of the country's gross domestic

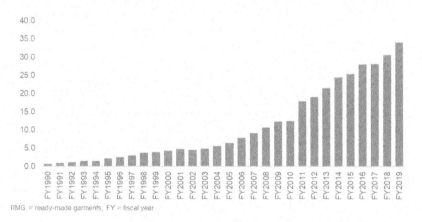

Fig. 8.1 RMG exports from Bangladesh (in $billion)

product is derived from the industry.[7] Approximately 36% of the country's manufacturing services business is represented by more than 4600 RMG enterprises, which employ a total of 4.1 million people.[8] This indutry is run largely by dedicated women workers following strict guidelines. For example, women's empowerment and gender parity have played an important role in the RMG industry, which employs 61% of the total number of the country's female employees.[9]

In international RMG trade, Bangladesh has had a 6.5% market share since the 1970s, and it has been China's second largest exporter for many decades.[10] Exports to Canada, the European Union countries, and the United States account for 62% of all of Bangladesh's exports. While exports have grown at an average annual pace of 14.8% during the previous three decades, they reached $34.2 billion in FY2019, accounting for 84.2% of total country exports at the time.[11] As seen in Figure 8.1, the RMG company has fared admirably in the face of natural calamities on a local and global scale since 1990. As a result of the ramifications of COVID-19, the organization is currently in a perilous financial position.

COVID-19 raises the issue of what is wrong with our supply chain. Rigidity, just-in-time manufacturing, and centralized production might all be to blame. Coronavirus-related disruptions show how vulnerable the RMG business is to a worldwide pandemic. Take a look at the top ten *Apple* service providers: More than two-thirds of the business's plants are in Asia, placing the company in danger of closure due to COVID. The formal term for this sort of concentrated manufacturing is centralized production, which basically implies that companies all over the world (and not only *Apple*) diversify their portfolio and avoid gambling everything in one basket.

The COVID-19 coronavirus outbreak has demonstrated an increase in the number of wildlife invasions affecting public health throughout the world for the second time this century. While not the same as SARS CoV-1, which was responsible for the 2002 SARS outbreak, SARS CoV-2, which was responsible for the COVID-19 pandemic, is separate from, yet closely resembles SARS CoV-1 in many ways.[12] Since the RMG sector significantly contributes to the Bangladesh market, this study exemplifies how COVID-19 affects the Bangladesh RMG sector, as a preview of possible future pandemic outbreaks. This supply chain chapter utilizes short-term and mid-to-long-term action considerations to combat this kind of unprecedented disruptive situation.

Literature Review

This review comes in three segments: distinguishing the SCM evolution, management, and COVID intrusion.

Supply Chain Management's Evolutionary Timeline

For the first time in history, the military utilized logistics in the 1950s. It is in charge of the acquisition, maintenance, and shipment of heavy weaponry, supplies, and personnel across the world. During the 1960s and 1970s, there was a resurgence of practical and theoretical attention in physical logistics and distribution.[13]

Prior to the 1950s, logistics was not a tactical issue, and as a result, it was a dormant field of endeavor. Around the 1950s, a series of events happened that may be considered the beginning of a "transformation." During the early 1980s, when physical supply management was elevated to the level of an organizational function in industrial firms, experts in logistics came up with the notion of supply chain management (SCM). The importance of logistics has substantially risen as a result.[14] As a result, they said that senior executives must make strategic decisions in order to cope with the chain efficiently at its early stages. This is a point of view that both logisticians and marketing channel theorists agree on.[15]

The SCM concept has risen in popularity among corporate executives since its introduction in the early 1980s.[16] SSCM studies or SCM-related subjects have appeared in a variety of journals in marketing, distribution, manufacturing, client management, integration, transportation, and other fields. SCM has evolved throughout time as a result of increased global competition in the 1990s.[17]

When it became obvious that human businesses could no longer compete on their own, the paradigm in management literature altered. This has ushered in a new era of inter-network competitiveness, with a firm's greatest success now resting on its senior executives' ability to integrate the organization's intricate network of commercial ties.[18]

National Health Service SCM spawned the first paper from the service industry.[19] Customer service provider *Duality* from S.E. Sampson's (2000) service associations applied to ceremonial industry SCM techniques.[20] An investigation on the support industry's distribution chain program was carried out by Kathawala and Abdou (2003).[21] A study by R. Kenneth and E. M. O'Brien found that tertiary education

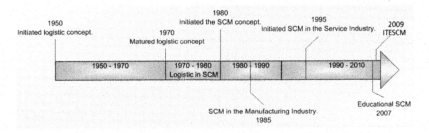

Fig. 8.2 Evolutionary timeline of supply chain management

institutions may use an educational supply chain in their strategic planning. The researchers polled both employers and students as part of the investigation.[22]

Students and businesses might have been encouraged to collaborate more closely, according to the survey's findings. Cozzi, R. Cigolini, and M. Perona (2004) used the car, grocery, machinery, book publishing, and other service sectors to build a framework for SCM.[23] Using City University of Hong Kong as a case study, A. K. W. Lau (2007) discovered two distinct supply chains: the "Student" and the "Research" networks.[24]

Researchers employed an educational SCM platform to evaluate the university's input and output signals as part of the first large-scale empirical investigation.[25] The ITESCM (Integrated Tertiary Educational Supply Chain Management) model was utilized as a guide in this study, which looked at supply chains for teaching, study, and educational direction. Several studies from leading tertiary educational institutions across the world have confirmed and supported its usefulness. Earlier 2012, the ITESCM Model was modified to make it easier to use for mass people.[26] Figure 8.2 shows an evolution and development of SCM as a timeline.

RMG Industry Supply Chain Management

Bangladesh's SCM textile and apparel analysis owes a lot to M. S. Islam. evaluating Bangladesh's textile and garment supply networks to determine the country's benefits and drawbacks.[27] According to him, Bangladesh's manufacturing and retail sectors are both unaware of the SCM concept and industrial benchmark. Bangladesh's competitive edge in the global clothing industry was examined by A. H. Nuruzzaman and A. Azad (2010) in order to develop a more productive Bangladeshi RMG supply network and investigate the links between the participants in the supply chain of the supply chain.[28]

Developing Bangladesh's garment business must learn to decrease the amount of distribution necessary to satisfy orders placed by international enterprises since the garment supply chain is concentrated on raw materials, production processes, logistics, and new orders linked to completed items. In order to satisfy orders from international companies, Bangladesh's garment industry has to learn how to decrease the quantity of distribution needed.[29] In order to minimize delivery time, M.S. Islam's results support the use of modern, quick, and efficient technology.

The garment sector in Bangladesh takes distribution chain management extremely seriously, and this strategy attempts to bring everything together.[30] Because of the features of the worldwide supply chain, the "distribution chain direction" for RMG is more difficult (SC). Crossing borders presents a host of unique problems for transcontinental firms in the global supply chain, including tariffs, non-tariff barriers, switchover rates, and variations in product needs. Borders are a common source of transportation service barriers in Bangladesh's RMG industry. The RMG market is decentralized as a result of this. The various supply chain stages' aims and objectives are at variance with one another.

An opportunity lies within an integrated supply chain to give the Bangladesh RMG sector a competitive advantage.[31] The major supply chain facilitators, outcomes, and inhibitors in the RMG business are identified using a dynamic systems approach in this study. As end users become more time-sensitive, a shorter lead time, as well as quality and pricing criteria, are necessary to win over more consumers in the clothing fashion sector.

BACKGROUND OF COVID-19

After seeing many patients with symptoms comparable to severe acute respiratory syndrome in Wuhan, Wuhan physician Li Wenliang notified the WHO Country Office on December 31. Wuhan is a large city in China's Hubei province.[32] After Chinese scientists released the virus' genome on January 12, WHO entrusted a Berlin-based team with creating a diagnostic test to detect active disease. Four weeks after the test was developed, it was made public. The World Health Organization (WHO) proclaimed a Public Health Emergency of International Concern on January 30, 2020 (PHEIC). According to the latest available information, the first verified incidence of Ebola transmission from person to person in the United States occurred in mid-February 2020. The World Health Organization designated COVID-19 a pandemic on March 11th, and it has since spread around the world.

METHODOLOGY

Secondary sources of information, such as digital libraries, online databases, journals, books, and conference papers, are employed in research projects. These are all common sources. The bulk of academic and practitioner SCM research papers came from prominent international journal hubs, including *IEEE, PROQUEST, JSTOR, EMERALD, Science Direct, EBSCO, ACM*, and others. Evolutionary deadlines and future trends were created based on a literature review. The author categorizes SCM disparities in the manufacturing and service sectors based on their industry uniqueness.

DISCUSSIONS

The latest coronavirus epidemic demonstrated how shaky today's supply networks are. According to current data, the crisis has had a devastating financial impact on China, the United States, and European countries, with weekly trade in each country half. As a result, more diversification in sourcing and digitalization will be necessary in order to develop stronger, more intelligent distribution networks and assure a long-term recovery (the process of transforming information into an electronic version).

The worldwide economic effect of the COVID-19 epidemic on investment and commerce has been tremendous, according to the World Bank. As more countries adopted the rule of law, multinational corporations were subjected to supply and demand fluctuations. Governments, corporations, and even individuals have found themselves unable to get vital items and resources, forcing them to address the brittleness of today's supply chain in order to continue their operations. Another important lesson learned from this tragedy is the urgent need to provide stronger, better, and more diverse supply networks. This is one of the most critical lessons learned from this disaster.

RMG Industry Impact of COVID-19

This industry, more than any other, is on the verge of a moral and financial catastrophe unlike any other. To limit the spread of the coronavirus, authorities proclaimed national vacations around April 25, 2020, and all industrial and business activity were halted save for emergency services. Global customers canceled or delayed shipments of $3.16 billion on April 18, 2020, hurting 1,142 companies employing a combined 2.26 million people, according to the Bangladesh Garment Manufacturers and Exporters Association (BGMEA).[33] Due to a drop in global demand for clothes, thousands of workers have been let off as fresh orders have dried up. As a result of the government shutdown, one million people have either lost their jobs or been placed on leave.[34] One-fourth of RMG employees said they had not received their pay, according to a study conducted by BRAC University, and one-third said they were unclear about their present employment situation.[35] Thousands of RMG employees defied authorities' orders to stay indoors and marched to the streets around the country. They were suing for unpaid wages.[36]

According to the Stern Center for Business and Human Rights at New York University, although Bangladesh's garment exports have increased significantly in recent years, the sector has largely remained stagnant beyond cutting and sewing basic products with little added value and low profit margins, according to the Stern Center. Bangladesh's garment sector has provided more independence to rural young women in Bangladesh while also supporting the country's weak market. Nonetheless, in terms of job quality, value added to exports, and actual wage increases for employees, it hasn't had as much success as it could have.[37]

Given its status as one of the lowest-paid firms in the global textile supply chain, the sector requires at least $470 million each month in order to pay salaries to its employees at the statutory minimum of Tk 8,000 ($95). Mr. BGMEA President appealed with overseas consumers to assume ownership of the created items and to reimburse the BGMEA just for the salary of employees who were still working in the production cycle (Figure 8.3) [30]. Beyond the obvious humanitarian and economic consequences, a decrease of foreign exchange flows has also been noticed, creating external business risks. Employees needed urgent cash support for subsistence livelihood, but businesses required medium-term liquidity support for subsequent revival.

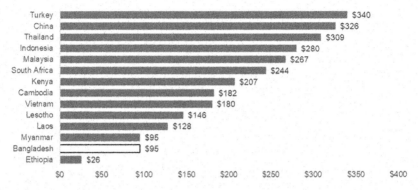

Fig. 8.3 Monthly minimum wages in global garment industry

THE IMPACT OF COVID-19 ON RMG'S SUPPLY CHAIN

Other businesses, customers, and service providers may be impacted by the RMG industry's repercussions, which might have far-reaching consequences. With the emergence of backward-linkage companies, the value added by the RMG industry has gradually grown to 63.2%.[38] A massive, capital-intensive textile market was developed in order to supply yarn and textile to the export-oriented RMG sector, which was valued at BDT 6 billion.[39] With 1,461 businesses in the textile value chain, 425 manufacture yarns and fabrics, 796 make cloth, and 240 offer dyes, printing inks, and other finishing agents for the completed items, there are currently 1,461 firms in the textile value chain. Buttons, accessories, threads, zippers, and other SMEs are among the various accessory suppliers.

In addition to banking, real estate, packaging, and insurance, the RMG business has a substantial influence on a wide range of other industries as well. An investigation conducted by the World Bank discovered that commercial banks provide finance to 98% of RMG firms. All equipment and plants are covered by insurance firms, and 87% of importers and 15% of exporters have insurance policies covering their imports and exports, respectively. Port usage fees received from RMG firms contribute for 40% of the authority's annual revenue on average.[40] There is a considerable demand for low-cost consumer items such as clothing and cosmetics, as a result of the industry's 4.1 million employees. The imminent tragedy of RMG would have a cascade impact on the entire economy, thus rescuing it will assist other industries as well.

The Effects of COVID-19 on RMG Employees

Bangladesh's Rural Advancement Committee (BRAC) conducted a study of 2,675 persons from low-income households when the COVID-19 epidemic hit the country, and discovered that 14% of those questioned had no food reserves at home, and 29% had just enough food for 1-3 days' supply of life.[41] The weak and destitute may face starvation as a result of COVID-19's food shortages and lockdown situations. P. Anthem prophesied an appetite pandemic following the COVID-19 breakout, which may be the biggest humanitarian tragedy since World War II. He was right.[42] They would starve to death before they are infected with coronavirus, said an RMG employee in Bangladesh. As the COVID-19 epidemic spreads around the world, some countries are able to give assistance to their vast populations; yet Bangladesh and many other countries are unable to do so. That implies that the lowest earners who are made to leave their homes as a result of the closure of COVID-19 and the ensuing recession run the danger of catching diseases that might be harmful to them and their loved ones. As of April 25, 2020, an RMG employee claimed that he was compelled to sell vegetables at a market to assist provide for his family's nutritional needs.

On March 25, 2020, Bangladeshi Prime Minister Sheikh Hasina announced the beginning of a $587,925,000 stimulus package for the country's export-oriented economy as part of the country's efforts to battle the COVID-19 outbreak.[43] That the mill owners utilize this money to pay their employees' wages was her advice, and she supported this recommendation. As a result, manufacturing business owners were unable to pay their employees their full salary in March and April of 2020. Because they were unable to make good on unpaid pay, hundreds of employees came to the streets to demand that they be paid in full for their efforts.[44] Exports of RMG products totaled $30.61 billion in the 2017–2018 fiscal year, which went to the plant owners.[45] To make matters worse, when they needed to be together, the manufacturing owners stayed split. Not being paid for two months or more displaced some employees, while other concerns were more muted.

On the other hand, with death rates and infection, Bangladesh has moved to the top of the list. As of July 7, 2020, 155 individuals had died as a result of pollution and COVID-19-related illnesses.[46] BGMEA's declaration of the reopening of garment factories on April 26, 2020, despite the growing sickness and mortality rates associated with COVID-19, got the blessing of the authorities, allowing for the completion of already ordered apparel imports.[47] The management of the RMG factory has reportedly called and threatened its employees, telling them that if they did not return to work, they would forfeit their jobs as well as any income that they were entitled to. People who lived in rural regions but needed to go into the industrial sector for work found it impossible to get there during the lockdown since public transportation was unavailable and no substitute transportation was provided. Workers had to arrange their own transportation, which included packed trucks and cramped vehicles, making it more susceptible to virus transmission than other modes of transportation were available to them.

When the workers got COVID-19, no one warned them if they would be able to keep a social distance from one another at work or whether they would have access to medical treatment if they contracted the virus. According to earlier assessments, social space in industries is not properly preserved, and employees are not appropriately safeguarded.[48] The inability of RMG employees to gain access to clinics and healthcare institutions increases the likelihood of COVID-19 infections spreading across the population, throwing the lives of millions of people in danger.[49] Following the reopening of the RMG sector, new illnesses and fatalities among RMG employees have been documented. The Bangladesh Garment Shramik Sanghati performed research on COVID-19 illnesses among RMG personnel and concluded that 96 RMG employees were infected between April 9 and May 6, 2020, with COVID-19.[50] A number of RMG employees have died as a result of undetected fever and respiratory problems.[51]

Upon returning to the workplace, RMG employees worried about illnesses linked to COVID-19 due to an increase in new infections and fatalities published across the country's print and electronic media. People's psychological well-being, as well as their ability to work during a pandemic, is impacted when the infection is seen as severe.[52,53] RMG employees' mental health may be impacted if they are afraid of catching or dying from the COVID-19 pandemic.[54] It's also crucial to remember that RMG employees are suffering psychologically as a result of the uncertainty surrounding their future possibilities. The unexpected discovery of rape and suicide complaints during the COVID-19 pandemic phase may put women working in the RMG industry at risk for psychological health problems in the future. A rape instance and a suicide death of a female RMG employee were publicized in national newspapers during the COVID-19 epidemic period, which likely heightened strain and worry among female RMG personnel.[55]

Response of the Government

In order to counter COVID-19's emerging consequences and revitalize the market, the government plans to spend Tk956 billion ($11.2 billion), or 3.3% of GDP, on a stimulus program that will bolster the social safety net, export sectors, small and medium-sized enterprises (SMEs), and other high priority industries. Together, RMG and other export-oriented businesses would have access to Tk50 billion in additional funds for paying wages and allowances for their personnel. The Export Development Fund's volume has been expanded from $3.5 billion to $5.0 billion in order to provide short-term import capabilities for export-oriented firms, according to the White House. RMG and other export-oriented companies will get a $600 million pre-shipment loan refinancing program from the central bank as part of the package. This much-needed package, although welcome, will only cover a small fraction of the company's enormous needs, which total at least $470 million each month in salaries. More aid is required for the country's workers' basic sustenance as well as for the survival of the company.[56]

CONSIDERATIONS FOR SHORT-TERM AND MID-TO-LONG-TERM ACTION

Action concerns for the short-term and the medium to long-term necessitate that the supply chain be operated in a pandemic condition[57]:

Short-Term Action:

- Analyze the financial and operational consequences of various scenarios. Wal-Mart and Tesco are two examples of big box retailers.
- Concentrate on achieving a balance between supply and demand, as well as on building a buffer stock if this is essential to ensure supply–demand balance.

- For the purpose of determining the potential impact on your supply chain, examine the financial status of your primary suppliers, such as *Tata Corporation*.

Mid-to-Long-Term Action:

- Micro-supply chains, which are finite, decentralized, and agile "mini-operating models," can help increase the agility and speed of any supply chain by establishing flexible supplier contracts and links with manufacturers close to the point of purchase. With the help of these strategies, one can learn how to "purchase where one produces, and manufacture where one sells."
- Analyze potential prospects for expanding the company's supplier pool. Make a list of suppliers from different parts of the country to have on board in case of an emergency. Critical components should have at least two sources of supply considered.
- In supply chains, shift away from a short-term confrontational mentality and toward a long-term value-creation approach to achieve success. Test and update one's plans on a regular basis to account for the development of your company and changes in the environment.

CHANGING THE COURSE OF HISTORY

According to Jesse Lin and Christian Lanng, the COVID-19 conference has brought to light the flaws in complicated global supply chains that are based on lean manufacturing ideas (2020).[58] When it comes to medical equipment, for example, the competition for personal protective equipment (PPE) has brought to light the inherent risks of inventory management and single-sourcing models that are exclusively motivated by cost savings. The issue with contemporary supply chains has been brought to light by China's economic clampdown and the country's dominance in major manufacturing locations. A lack of supplier pliability exacerbated the difficulty of pivoting when Chinese manufacturing collapsed. To avoid becoming completely dependent on China in the future, multinational corporations may choose to diversify their supply networks. That shift will most likely benefit countries with large manufacturing sectors, such as Mexico, Vietnam, and India.

Decentralization of manufacturing capabilities will also be seen, with companies seeking to bring generation in-house. Small batch production and automation have both gained in popularity in recent years, and as a result, components of the supply chain are now being relocated back to their original locations. Decision-makers may be compelled to consider whether particular items can be produced elsewhere or if they must be produced within the United States. Supply networks will be caught off guard by the rapid and widespread digitalization of documentation that enables global trade to be communicated.[59]

Conclusions

In this article, the temporal development of SCM is discussed for the manufacturing and service industries, respectively. It also demonstrates how COVID-19 has impacted the existing RMG supply chain management system. Therefore, the author clearly shows how this pandemic disrupts the supply chain. This paper also will help to understand how coronavirus catastrophe is reshaping the future supply chain.

COVID-19's impacts have only just begun to surface, but they're expected to grow rapidly. The full ramifications won't be apparent for several months or perhaps years. If one wants to avoid a financial and social meltdown, one needs to remain on top of the situation and have emergency and post-crisis support on hand in various forms. In order to increase the efficacy and long-term viability of ADB's autonomous and non-sovereign activities, it may be essential to arrange them in a risk-measured fashion. Other financial industries will be affected by COVID-19 in addition to the RMG business. In addition to reducing urban poverty, aiding the RMG business may benefit other industries throughout the supply chain and assist to stabilize the market much more quickly.

Worker and general health, as well as the well-being of people in other countries, must be protected during the COVID-19 pandemic by the international health community, the Bangladesh RMG industry, international brands/retailers, the International Labour Organization (ILO) and the Government of Bangladesh (GoB). The global supply-chain and the RMG trade must be maintained in order for Bangladesh to preserve its long-term financial stability. There should be no clothing manufacturing during the COVID-19 pandemic without an immediate system overview and a strategy to ensure worker health and safety. As a last point of clarity, the United Nations Development Program has begun an urgent evaluation of the need for foreign trades to perform human rights due diligence in relation to the COVID-19 epidemic as soon as possible.[60] The government of Bangladesh and the RMG industry in Bangladesh ought to take notice of this warning.

Despite significant advancements in technology, most business transactions still take place over paper. Building strong supply chains requires digitizing the buyer-supplier relationship, and doing so will save time in the recruitment and identification of new suppliers. The Internet of Things (IoT) and artificial intelligence (AI) are enabling supply chains to quickly switch to other suppliers if their usual ones have problems. Because of the current financial crisis, it's a great time to overhaul an outdated system. Building business-driven supply networks that are both smart and flexible will be critical in building a trade and capital system that can withstand storms.

Notes

1. M. Habib, and I. Hasan, "Supply Chain Management (SCM)—Is it Value addition Towards Academia?" *IOP Conference Series: Materials Science and Engineering* 528 (2019): 012090.

   M. Habib (eds), "Supply Chain Management (SCM): Theory and Evolution," *Supply Chain Management–Applications and Simulations* (2011).

   M. Habib, "Supply Chain Management: Theory and Its Future Perspectives," *Int. J. of Business, Management and Social Sciences (IJBMSS)* 1, no. 1 (2010).
2. M. Habib, 2011.
3. M. Habib, 2010.
4. M. Habib, and I. Hasan, 2019.

   M. Habib, "An Integrated Educational Supply Chain Management (ITESCM)," Ph.D. Dissertation (Graduate School of Information Technology, Assumption University of Thailand, 2009).
5. *Op cit.*; and B. B. Pathik, and M. Habib, "Redesigned ITESCM Model: An Academic SCM for the Universities," *Int. J. of Supply Chain Management* (UK: ExcelingTech Publisher) 1, no. 1 (2012).
6. M. S. Islam, "Supply Chain Management on Apparel Order Process: A Case Study in Bangladesh Garment Industry," *Asian*

Journal of Business and Management Sciences 2, no. 8 (2012): 62–72.
7. M. Akter, "Review and Outlook, 2020 Bangladesh Garments and Textile Industry," *Textile Focus*, February 22, 2020. http://textilefocus.com/review-outlook-2020-bangladesh-garments-textile-industry/, accessed November 26, 2020.
8. Quarterly Labor Force Survey Bangladesh, 2015–2016.
9. *Centre for Policy Dialogue*, "Dialogue on Ongoing Upgradation in RMG Enterprise: Results from a Survey," Dhaka (2018).
10. Asian Development Bank, "COVID-19 and the Ready-Made Garments Industry in Bangladesh" (n.d.), https://www.adb.org/sites/default/files/linked-documents/54180-001-sd-04.pdf.
11. Export Promotion Bureau, "Export Data 2018–19" (n.d.), http://epb.gov.bd/site/view/epb_export_data/2018-2019/July-June, accessed November 26, 2020.
12. Miriam N. Lango, "How Did We Get Here? A Short History of COVID-19 and Other Coronavirus-related Epidemics" (2020), https://doi.org/10.22541/au.158888276.61023550.
13. M. Habib, and I. Hasan, 2019.
    M. Habib (eds), 2011.
    M. Habib, 2010.
    M. Habib, 2009.
14. *Op cit.*
15. *Op cit.*
16. M. Habib (eds), 2011.
17. M. Habib, 2010.
18. M. Habib, 2009.
19. M. Habib, 2011.
20. S. E. Sampson, "Customer–Supplier Duality and Bidirectional Supply Chains in Service Organization," *Int. J. of Service Industry Management* 11, no. 4 (2000): 348–364.
21. Y. Kathawala, and K. Abdou, "Supply Chain Evaluation in the Service Industry: A Framework Development Compared to Manufacturing," *Managerial Auditing J.* 18, no. 2 (2003): 140–149.
22. E. M. O'Brien, and R. Kenneth, "Educational Supply Chain: A Tool for Strategic Planning in Tertiary Education?" *Marketing Intelligence & Planning* 14, no. 2 (1996): 33–40.
23. Cozzi R. Cigolini, and M. Perona, "A New Framework for Supply Chain Management," *Int. J. of Operations & Production Management* 24, no. 1 (2004): 7–41.

24. A. K. W. Lau, "Educational Supply Chain Management: A Case Study," *On the Horizon* 15 (2007): 15–27.
25. M. Habib (eds), 2011.
26. M. Habib, and I. Hasan, 2019; B. B. Pathik, and M. Habib, 2012; and B. B. Pathik et al. "Descriptive Study on Supply Chain Management Model for the Academia," *The 6th IEEE Conf. of Management of Innovation and Tech* (Indonesia, 2012mA).
27. M. S. Islam, 2012.
28. A. Haque Nuruzzaman and R. Azad, "Is Bangladeshi RMG Sector Fit in the Global Apparel Business? Analyses in the Supply Chain Management," *The South East Asian Journal of Management* IV, no. 1 (2010).
29. M. S. Islam, 2012.
30. S. I. Tanvir, and N. Muqaddim, "Supply Chain Management Offering the New Paradigm for Bangladesh Garment Industry," *Journal of Economics and Sustainable Development* 4, no. 20 (2013).
31. B. Asgari, and M. A. Hoque, "A System Dynamics Approach to Supply Chain Performance Analysis of the Ready-Made-Garment Industry in Bangladesh," *Ritsumeikan Journal of Asia Pacific Studies* 32 (2013).
32. Cozzi R. Cigolini, and M. Perona, 2004.
33. BGMEA, 2020.
34. L. Frayer, "1 Million Bangladeshi Garment Workers Lose Jobs Amid COVID-19 Economic Fallout," NPR (2020), https://www.npr.org/sections/coronavirus-live-updates/2020/04/03/826617334/1-million-bangladeshi-garment-workers-lose-jobs-amid-covid-19-economic-fallout, accessed November 26, 2020.
35. *The Daily Star*, "Brac Rapid Survey: 47pc Garment Workers Yet to Be Paid," April 19, 2020, https://www.thedailystar.net/frontpage/news/brac-rapid-survey-47pc-garment-workers-yet-be-paid-1894444, accessed November 26, 2020.
36. A. Alif, A. R. Rabbia, and Ibrahim Hossain, "RMG Workers Take to Streets in Dhaka, Gazipur, Chittagong for Salaries," April 15, 2020, https://www.dhakatribune.com/business/2020/04/15/rmg-workers-take-to-streets-in-dhaka-gazipur-chittagong-for-salaries, accessed November 26, 2020.
37. Paul M. Barrett, and Dorothee Baumann-Pauly, "Made in Ethiopia: Challenges in the Garment Industry's New Frontier,"

New York University Stern Center for Business and Human Rights (New York, 2019).
38. R. Ralph, "COVID-19 (Coronavirus): ADB's Response," *Asian Development Bank* (2020), https://www.adb.org/what-we-do/covid19-coronavirus, accessed November 26, 2020.
39. *Ibid.*
40. K. M. Faridul Hasan et al. "Role of Textile and Clothing Industries in the Growth and Development of Trade & Business Strategies of Bangladesh in the Global Economy," *International Journal of Textile Science* 5, no. 3 (2016): 39–48, 10.5923/j.textile.20160503.01.
41. Tim Zanni, "Technology Supply Chain Disruption," *KPMG Blog*, April 21, 2020, https://home.kpmg/xx/en/blogs/home/posts/2020/04/technology-supply-chain-disruption.html, accessed November 15, 2020.
42. P. Anthem, "Risk of Hunger Pandemic as COVID-19 Set to Almost Double Acute Hunger by End of 2020," *World Food Program Insight* (2020), https://insight.wfp.org/covid-19-will-almost-double-people-in-acute-hunger-by-end-of-2020-59df0c4a8072?gi=efb9121, accessed November 2020.
43. United News of Bangladesh, "Tk 5,000cr for Workers' Pay," *The Daily Star*, March 26, 2020, https://www.thedailystar.net/frontpage/news/tk-5000cr-workers-pay-1885891, accessed on November 26, 2020.
44. Fair Wear, "Covid-19 Impact and Responses: Bangladesh," *Fair Wear*, May 4, 2020, https://www.fairwear.org/covid-19-dossier/covid-19-guidance-for-production-countries/covid-19-impact-and-responses-bangladesh/, accessed November 26, 2020; *The Daily Star*, "RMG Workers Agitate for Full April Salary," May 10, 2020, https://www.thedailystar.net/frontpage/news/rmg-workers-demonstrate-demanding-full-wages-1901209, accessed on November 26, 2020.
45. Bangladesh Garment Manufacturers and Exporters Association (BGMEA), "About Garment Industry of Bangladesh," (2020), https://www.bgmea.com.bd/home/about/AboutGarmentsIndustry, accessed November 26, 2020.
46. Health Bulletin, Directorate General of Health Services, Ministry of Health and Family Welfare, Bangladesh, July 6, https://corona.

gov.bd/storage/press-releases/July2020/KDEsHotTIYV0QG3 rxOpY.pdf, accessed November 26, 2020.
47. *The Daily Star*, "Some RMG Factories Reopen on a Limited Scale," April 27, https://www.thedailystar.net/frontpage/news/some-rmg-factories-reopen-limited-scale-1897177, accessed November 26, 2020.
   The Daily Prothom Alo, "The Closed Garment and Textile Factory Has Reopened," April 26, 2020, https://www.protho malo.com/economy/article/1653215/, accessed November 26, 2020.
48. *The Daily Star*, "Factories Open in Port City with Lax Health and Safety Measures," *The Daily Star*, May 4, 2020, https://www.the dailystar.net/business/news/factories-open-port-city-lax-health-and-safety-measures-1899259, accessed November 26, 2020; and *The Daily Prothom Alo*, "Physical Distance Is Not Being Observed in Most of the Garment Factories," *The Daily Prothom Alo*, May 9, 2020, https://www.prothomalo.com/economy/article/165 5466/, accessed November 27, 2020.
49. L. O. Gostin, E. A. Friedman, and S. A. Wetter, "Responding to COVID-19: How to Navigate a Public Health Emergency Legally and Ethically," *Hastings Cent Rep* 50, no. 2 (2020): 8–12.
50. *The Daily Star*, "RMG Worker with Fever and Respiratory Problem Dies in Lalmonirhat," *The Daily Star*, May 8, 2020, https://www.thedailystar.net/country/news/rmg-worker-fever-and-respiratory-problem-dies-lalmonirhat-1900720, accessed November 27, 2020; *The Daily Prothom Alo*, "96 Garment Workers are Affected By Corona," *The Daily Prothom Alo*, May 7, 2020, https://www.prothomalo.com/economy/article/1655181/, accessed November 22, 2020.
51. Banglanews24.com, "The Hanging Body of a Woman Garment Worker Was Recovered in Mirpur," *Banglanews24.Com*, May 3, 2020, https://www.banglanews24.com/national/news/bd/786 462.details, accessed November 23, 2020.
   Bangla News 24.com, "The Death of a Garment Worker with Corona Symptoms in Nalchiti," *Banglanews24.com*, May 17, 2020, https://www.banglanews24.com/national/news/bd/789134.det ails, accessed November 23, 2020; *The Daily Star*, "Infected RMG Workers: Half Tested Positive After Factories Reopened," *The Daily Star*, May 8, 2020, https://www.thedailystar.net/bac

kpage/news/infected-rmg-workers-half-tested-positive-after-factories-reopened-1900540, accessed November 24, 2020.
52. Jian-Bin Le et al., "Self-Control Moderates the Association Between Perceived Severity of Coronavirus Disease 2019 (COVID-19) and Mental Health Problems Among the Chinese Public," *Int Journal of Environment Research and Public Health* 17, no. 13 (July 4, 2020): 4820, https://pubmed.ncbi.nlm.nih.gov/32635495/, accessed November 28, 2020.
53. M. F. Chersich et al., "COVID-19 in Africa: Care and Protection for Frontline Healthcare Workers," *Global Health* 16, no. 46 (2020): 1–6.
54. R. C. W. Hall, and M. J. Chapman, "The 1995 Kikwit Ebola Outbreak: Lessons Hospitals and Physicians Can Apply to Future Viral Epidemics," *Gen Hosp Psychiatry* 30, no. 5 (2008): 446–452.
55. Banglanews24.com May 3, 2020; and Banglanews24.com, May 17, 2020.
56. R. Ralph, 2020.
57. Tim Zanni, 2020.
58. Jesse Lin, and Christian Lanng, "Here's How Global Supply Chains Will Change After COVID-19," *World Economic Forum* (May 6, 2020), https://www.weforum.org/agenda/2020/05/this-is-what-global-supply-chains-will-look-like-after-covid-19/, accessed November 15, 2020.
59. *Ibid.*
60. United Nations Development Program (UNDP, "Human Rights Due Diligence and COVID-19: Rapid Self-Assessment for Business" (April 10, 2020), https://www.undp.org/content/undp/en/home/librarypage/democratic-governance/human-rights-due-diligence-and-covid-19-rapid-self-assessment-for-business.html, accessed 28 November 2020.

Bibliography

Akter, M. 2020. " Review and Outlook, 2020 Bangladesh Garments and Textile Industry." *Textile Focus*, February 22. http://textilefocus.com/review-outlook-2020-bangladesh-garments-textile-industry/. Accessed November 26, 2020.

Alif, A., A. R. Rabbia, and Ibrahim Hossain. 2020. "RMG Workers Take to Streets in Dhaka, Gazipur, Chittagong for Salaries." *Dhaka Tribune*, April 15. https://www.dhakatribune.com/business/2020/04/15/rmg-workers-take-to-streets-in-dhaka-gazipur-chittagong-for-salaries. Accessed November 26, 2020.

Asgari, B., and M. A. Hoque. 2013. "A System Dynamics Approach to Supply Chain Performance Analysis of the Ready-Made-Garment Industry in Bangladesh." *Ritsumeikan Journal of Asia Pacific Studies* 32.

Asian Development Bank. n.d. "COVID-19 and the Ready-Made Garments Industry in Bangladesh." Covid-19 Active Response and Expenditure Support (CARES) Programs.

———. 2020. "COVID-19 (Coronavirus): ADB's Response." *Asian Development Bank*, November 23. https://www.adb.org/what-we-do/covid19-coronavirus. Accessed November 26, 2020.

Bangladesh Garment Manufacturers and Exporters Association(BGMEA). 2020. "About Garment Industry of Bangladesh." *BGMEA*. https://www.bgmea.com.bd/home/about/AboutGarmentsIndustry. Accessed November 26, 2020.

Banglanews24.com. 2020. "The Death of a Garment Worker with Corona Symptoms in Nalchiti." *Banglanews24.com*, May 17. https://www.banglanews24.com/national/news/bd/789134.details. Accessed November 23, 2020.

———. 2020. *The Hanging Body of a Woman Garment Worker was Recovered in Mirpur* [online]. Available at: https://www.banglanews24.com/national/news/bd/786462.details. Accessed November 23, 2020.

Barrett, Paul M., and Dorothee Baumann-Pauly. 2019. *Made in Ethiopia: Challenges in the Garment Industry's New Frontier*. New York: New York University Stern Center for Business and Human Rights.

BGMEA. n.d. Accessed November 26, 2020.

Center for Policy Dialogue. 2018. "Dialogue on Ongoing Upgradation in RMG Enterprise: Results from a Survey." Dhaka.

Chapman, R. C. W., and M. J. Hall. 2008. "The 1995 Kikwit Ebola Outbreak: Lessons Hospitals and Physicians Can Apply to Future Viral Epidemics." *Gen Hosp Psychiatry* 30, no. 5: 446–452.

Chersich, M. F., et al. 2020. "COVID-19 in Africa: Care and Protection for Frontline Healthcare Workers." *Global Health* 16, no. 46: 1–6.

Cigolini, Cozzi R., and M. Perona. 2004. "A New Framework for Supply Chain Management." *Int. J. of Operations & Production Management* 24, no. 1: 7–41.

Export Promotion Bureau. n.d. "Export Data 2018–19." http://epb.gov.bd/site/view/epb_export_data/2018-2019/July-June. Accessed November 26, 2020.

Fair Wear. n.d. "Fair Wear, 2020, Covid-19 Impact and Responses: Bangladesh." *Fair Wear*, May 4. https://www.fairwear.org/covid-19-dossier/covid-19-guidance-for-production-countries/covid-19-impact-and-responses-bangladesh/. Accessed November 26, 2020.

———. 2020. "Covid-19 Impact and Responses: BangladeshFair Wear, 4 May." *Fair Wear*, May 4. https://www.fairwear.org/covid-19-dossier/covid-19-guidance-for-production-countries/covid-19-impact-and-responses-bangladesh/. Accessed November 26, 2020.

Frayer, L. 2020. "1 Million Bangladeshi Garment Workers Lose Jobs Amid COVID-19 Economic Fallout." *NPR*, April 3. Accessed November 26, 2020.

Gostin, L. O., E. A. Friedman, and S. A. Wetter. 2020. "Responding to COVID-19: How to Navigate a Public Health Emergency Legally and Ethically." *Hastings Cent Rep* 50, no. 2: 8–12.

Habib, M. 2009. "An Integrated Educational Supply Chain Management (ITESCM)." Ph.D. Dissertation, Graduate School of Information Technology, Assumption University of Thailand.

———. 2010. "Supply Chain Management: Theory and Its Future Perspectives." *Int. J. of Business, Management and Social Sciences (IJBMSS)* 1, no. 1.

———. 2011. *Supply Chain Management (SCM): Theory and Evolution in Supply Chain Management–Applications and Simulations*.

Habib, M., and I. Islam. 2019. "Supply Chain Management (SCM)—Is it Value Addition Towards Academia? 528." *IOP Conference Series: Materials Science and Engineering* 528: 012090.

Haque Nuruzzaman, A., and R. Azad. 2010. "Is Bangladeshi RMG Sector Fit in the Global Apparel Business? Analyses the Supply Chain Management." *The South East Asian Journal of Management* IV, no. 1.

Hasan, K. M. Faridul, et al. 2016. "Role of Textile and Clothing Industries in the Growth and Development of Trade & Business Strategies of Bangladesh in the Global Economy." *International Journal of Textile Science* 5, no. 3: 39–48. https://doi.org/10.5923/j.textile.20160503.01.

Health Bulletin. 2020. *Directorate General of Health Services, Ministry of Health and Family Welfare, Bangladesh*, July 6. https://corona.gov.bd/storage/press-releases/July2020/KDEsHotTIYV0QG3rxOpY.pdf. Accessed November 26, 2020.

Islam, M. S. 2012. "Supply Chain Management on Apparel Order Process: A Case Study in Bangladesh Garment Industry." *Asian Journal of Business and Management Sciences* 2, no. 8: 62–72.

Kathawala, Y., and K. Abdou. 2003. "Supply Chain Evaluation in the Service Industry: A Framework Development Compared to Manufacturing." *Managerial Auditing J.* 18, no. 2: 140–149.

Lango, Miriam N. 2020. "How Did We Get Here? A Short History of COVID-19 and Other Coronavirus-Related Epidemics." https://doi.org/10.22541/au.158888276.61023550.

Lau, A. K. W. 2007. "Educational Supply Chain Management: A Case Study." *On the Horizon* 15: 15–27.

Le, Jian-Bin, et al. 2020. "Self-Control Moderates the Association Between Perceived Severity of Coronavirus Disease 2019 (COVID-19) and Mental Health Problems Among the Chinese Public." *Int Journal of Environment Research and Public Health* 17, no. 13: 4820, July 4. https://pubmed.ncbi.nlm.nih.gov/32635495/. Accessed November 28, 2020.

Lin, Jesse, and Christian Lanng. 2020. "Here's How Global Supply Chains Will Change After COVID-19." *World Economic Forum*, May 6. https://www.weforum.org/agenda/2020/05/this-is-what-global-supply-chains-will-look-like-after-covid-19/. Accessed November 15, 2020.

O'Brien, E. M., and R. Kenneth. 1996. "Educational Supply Chain: A Tool for Strategic Planning in Tertiary Education?" *Marketing Intelligence & Planning* 14, no. 2: 33–40.

Pathak, B. B., and M. Habib. 2012. "Redesigned ITESCM Model: An Academic SCM for the Universities." *Int. J. of Supply Chain Management (UK: ExcelingTech Publisher)* 1, no. 1.

Pathik, B. B., M. Habib, and M. T. Chowdhury. 2012. "A Descriptive Study on Supply Chain Management Model for the Academia." *The 6th IEEE Conf. of Management of Innovation and Tech.* Indonesia.

Prothomalo. 2020. "The Closed Garment and Textile Factory Has Reopened." *The Daily Prothom Alo*, April 26. https://www.prothomalo.com/economy/article/1653215/. Accessed November 26, 2020.

Quarterly Labor Force Survey Bangladesh. 2015–16.

Ralph, R. 2020. "COVID-19 (Coronavirus): ADB's Response." *Asian Development Bank*, November 23. https://www.adb.org/what-we-do/covid19-coronavirus. Accessed November 26, 2020.

Sampson, S. E. 2000. "Customer-Supplier Duality and Bidirectional Supply Chains in Service Organization." *Int. J. of Service Industry Management* 11, no. 4: 348–364.

Tanvir, S. I., and N. Muqaddim. 2013. "Supply Chain Management Offering the New Paradigm for Bangladesh Garment Industry." *Journal of Economics and Sustainable Development* 4, no. 20.

The Daily Prothom Alo. 2020. "96 Garment Workers are Affected by Corona, The Daily Prothom Alo, May 7." *The Daily Prothom Alo*, May 7. https://www.prothomalo.com/economy/article/1655181/. Accessed November 22, 2020.

———. 2020. "Physical Distance Is Not Being Observed in Most of the Garment Factories." *The Daily Prothom Alo*, May 9. https://www.prothomalo.com/economy/article/1655466/. Accessed November 27, 2020.

The Daily Star. 2020. "RMG Workers Agitate for Full April Salary." *The Daily Star*, May 10. https://www.thedailystar.net/frontpage/news/rmg-workers-demonstrate-demanding-full-wages-1901209. Accessed November 26, 2020.

———. 2020. "Brac Rapid Survey: 47pc Garment Workers Yet to Be Paid." *The Daily Star*, April 19. https://www.thedailystar.net/frontpage/news/brac-rapid-survey-47pc-garment-workers-yet-be-paid-1894444. Accessed November 26, 2020.

———. 2020. "Factories Open in Port City with Lax Health and Safety Measures." *The Daily Star*, May 4. https://www.thedailystar.net/business/news/factories-open-port-city-lax-health-and-safety-measures-1899259. Accessed November 26, 2020.

———. 2020. "Infected RMG Workers: Half Tested Positive After Factories Reopened." *The Daily Star*, May 8. https://www.thedailystar.net/backpage/news/infected-rmg-workers-half-tested-positive-after-factories-reopened-1900540. Accessed November 24, 2020.

———. 2020. "RMG Worker with Fever and Respiratory Problem Dies in Lalmonirhat." *The Daily Star*, May 8. https://www.thedailystar.net/country/news/rmg-worker-fever-and-respiratory-problem-dies-lalmonirhat-1900720. Accessed November 27, 2020.

———. 2020. "Some RMG Factories Reopen on a Limited Scale." *The Daily Star*, April 27. https://www.thedailystar.net/frontpage/news/some-rmg-factories-reopen-limited-scale-1897177. Accessed November 26, 2020.

United Nations Development Program (UNDP). 2020. "Human Rights Due Diligence and COVID-19: Rapid Self-Assessment for Business." *UNDP*, April 10. https://www.undp.org/content/undp/en/home/librarypage/democratic-governance/human-rights-due-diligence-and-covid-19-r. Accessed November 28, 2020.

United News of Bangaldesh. 2020. "Tk 5,000cr for Workers' Pay." *The Daily Star*, March 26. https://www.thedailystar.net/frontpage/news/tk-5000cr-workers-pay-1885891. Accessed November 26, 2020.

Zanni, Tim. 2020. "Technology Supply Chain Disruption." *KPMG Blog*, April 21. https://home.kpmg/xx/en/blogs/home/posts/2020/04/technology-supply-chain-disruption.html. Accessed November 15, 2020.

CHAPTER 9

Sustainable Democracy, Economy, Youth: Leadership in Local–Global Contexts

Ziaur Rahman

INTRODUCTION

Sustainable democracy, the economy, and the youth help blend individual dreams, state mechanisms, leadership development, and the role of the economy in a rich fabric of socio-politico discourse. These form the three vital components of state leadership this chapter addresses to show that leadership through people is integral to the success of a country aspiring to lead globally. That "global" connection is not just *consequential*. It is as much *causal*: democracy may be best measured locally, but becomes a part of external "waves" and "reaches", at times the extreme of Kantian democracy, producing cosmopolitan laws and "perpetual peace".

With the term democracy originating from the Greek word *dēmokratía*, literally meaning "rule by people". The basis of a democratic state being liberty (Aristotle, *Politics*, Book VI, 1317.a40), its modern application becomes synonymous to a system of government built upon

---

Z. Rahman (✉)
Judge Court, Dhaka, Bangladesh

© The Author(s), under exclusive license to Springer Nature Singapore Pte Ltd. 2022
I. A. Hussain (eds.), *Global-Local Tradeoffs, Order-Disorder Consequences*, Global Political Transitions,
https://doi.org/10.1007/978-981-16-9419-6_9

citizen voting. It is this connection with the most micro-level agent, the individual, that becomes its strength at both macro levels, domestically, with the most legitimate government, and globally under the "perpetual peace" imperative of the cliché "democracies do not fight with each other".

In a democracy, the government which comes into power symbolizes people's participation, either through direct voting or through elected representatives. Democracy may be equated to an equilibrium: a system of "self-government" in which the distinction between the rulers and the ruled disappears, leaving the micro-level individual sovereign, and permitting a collection of individuals, as in states, or the international community to also boast a macro-level sovereignty. Through the ages, we have seen various forms of democracy ranging from a liberal direct democracy to an illiberal totalitarian democracy.

'The true notion of democracy conforms to the notion that none shall have power over the people. It is taken to mean that none shall be able to restrain or to elude its power. In a true democratic culture, none shall have power over the people and nor be able to restrain or to elude its power. Democracy offers a mechanism of safeguards against someone running away with a total decision making power. In a true democracy, one may wield a powerful influence on others but each individual is independent in 'agreeing' or 'disagreeing' with that person through secret voting, clearly casting confidence on the institution of democracy for its check and balance schema.

Through the above statement, it becomes abundantly clear that the center stage of *democracy* is held by the citizens, and the citizens decide how the state and its organs will work or in what forms of a democratic regime the state shall run. Similarly, the Constitution of Bangladesh has also made the people of the country supreme and the owner of the state, enriched in Article 7(1). If a state is run by the mandate of the people, then issues of complexity will fall, and through the values and principles embedded within a democracy, a country will function properly. The International Covenant on Civil & Political Rights (ICCPR) clearly mandates political participation, including the right to vote (Article 25); and non-discrimination, minority rights, and equality before the law (Articles 26 and 27). Bangladesh and many other countries with U.N. membership are signatories to this covenant. Many other stipulations are both incorporated within a country's legal regimes and international covenants. These systems are in place to operate as a check and balance mechanism for a country so that the state does not aspire to or move in the direction of a totalitarian state. In other words, a small democratic surge can have large global consequences, just as global norms can seep deep into every known community.

Sustainability and Sustainable Democracy

Sustainable democracy begs a definition of sustainability first. It generally means the process of effecting change in a balanced way whereby it meets the needs of the present without compromising the ability of future generations to meet their own needs. At the epicenter of sustainability is a complex web of resource allocation, reducing exploitation of resources, directing of investments, incorporating technological development, and ensuring that institutional changes harmonize while enhancing both current and future potential to meet human needs and aspirations. Weaving in with this idea of sustainability, environmental impacts add a distinct dimension as well and any definition of sustainability without environmental footprint would be inconclusive.

The concepts of *sustainability in democracy* and *sustainable democracy* are synonymous; taking the interchangeable terms further, we can extend the meaning of sustainable democracy to mean a holistic system of governance in which all the tenets of democracy remain in continuous checks and balances, if need be, through popular participation, as in voting. It is this system of governance through its various ways of operational culture that the notion of the democracy turns into 'Sustainable democracy' actually acquiring irreversible sustainability. The basis of any sustainable democracy is liberty, equality, and solidarity in the sense of unity among the people. Liberty in the broad sense extends to various freedoms and fundamental human rights; equality through the dispensation of rule or law and equity and justice at all levels. If the tenets of democracy are persistently present in the body politic of a country, then we can safely attribute that country to be a sustainable democracy.

Interacting global and local dynamics become an intrinsic and indispensable component of sustainable democracy. Most countries in the West and in the Fareast have achieved these standards, over a long phase of trials and errors, while many of the less developing countries (LDCs) and developing countries (DCs) have barely begun that trial-and-error interim, oftentimes slipping more than consolidating. In the current context of the world, we notice a trend of revivalism of dogmatic approach to running states and principled around certain issues, "isms", perspectives, and so forth, with state loyalty being pushed to accept a particular narrative. This predicament has been noticed in the United States, Russia, India, and, to some extent, in other countries that hitherto were not of much significance. Democracy in those countries also continues transforming and, whether we like it or not, some form of hegemonic ideas nurture and solidify the platform around which everyone is asked to rally. The scope of logic and reasoning is being adeptly marginalized. Distinct attempts through clever idea positioning, media management, guided by technology and catered by people resources are being used to change the mindset of the population. These crafty ways have often given dividends, and spin doctors have also played their roles, directly or indirectly, to box off full-fledged democracy in place of a tweaked version of democracy. Narrow self-interest triumphs, not realizing the fact that these twists and turns principally push back democratic institutions, while also festering frustrations in the hearts of others wanting to engage in a fair democratic practice. When one party or a few parties take disingenuous turns in managing democracy, a "belief system" gets installed in contradiction to the ideal spirit of "democracy". The dwindling of faith does not take place overnight, but each brick of frustration adds on until disbelief is firmly etched in the souls of the citizens. The public becomes disenfranchised in the system, disbelieving the people in power. Adding to this disbelief contesting parties rub on their harsh views, causing even more public grievance and grief. The philosophy of the public, being owners of the State, works to rescue the elected body in office by the public themselves. Unfortunately, with a disenfranchised larger public body, citizens lose the motive to invite a new set of elected representatives to rule over them. In addition, the incumbent regime would often hoist a structural mechanism in place that would deter the public to place an alternative person in power. Therefore, for a sustainable democracy to flourish, it becomes a necessity to ensure that the public must have an instrument to validate the performance of each representative that a constituency selects for the parliament.

Sustainable Democracy and Equity

Sustainable democracy intertwines with the principle of equity. One loses its strength without the safeguard of the other. The notion of democracy sits on the vital issues of equity. Broadly, equity focuses on dispensing justice and ensuring rule of law without regard to selectively offering justice based on family, status, gender, religion, and so forth. With a fair system, public order will be easy to manage as frustration is not being pent up simply due to the fact that all issues are reviewed with the strict principle of equity and rule of law. Countries with a better legal justice system invariably perform better in its standing as a democracy.

Democracy, Capitalism, and Socialism

The spirit of democracy attains its fullest strength when disparity between classes or between individuals and regions are not significant and allocation of resources is fairly distributed. When "resource allocation" and "fairness" principles, enshrined in the activities of a nation state is rationally decided, then runaway capitalism and individual survival perspectives of the fittest, propagated by Charles Darwin, loses its intellectual rigor. The principle of 'survival of the fittest' can be changed with the notion that capitalism championed on this spirit does not offer cohesive glue within the very fabric of a state. To take the idea forward, I propose a perspective that democracy to sprout in its majestic sense, runaway capitalism impedes that growth and stress spirals within that state, creating a chronic consequence. Socialism, in contrast to capitalism, proposes the ideas of "no person shall be left behind", and that "the state will take the responsibility of its citizens". These provide an umbrella to all human beings and addresses their aspirations, however small in degree. With an extended service base and philosophy to serve humanity, quite naturally, sustaining a democracy with a socialist bent can ideally offer a stable government within a country when other socio-economic variables, such as health, education, international cross border trading remain in reasonable standing. Scandinavian countries, where political unrest is rarely heard, illustrate the point. Bangladesh, being a heavily populated country, has also progressed in the context of economic parameters, but having similar views on dispensing justice for citizens cannot be endorsed. However, different forms of support and safety net measures have been introduced in the last few years. It may typify the next "wave" of developing countries rising through equity and sustainability into a full-fledged democracy.

Democracy and Economy

An unstable economy will virtually never have a fully functioning democracy and vice versa. However, the debate over development or democracy first is not just a debate within Bangladesh, but resonating across the globe. It is of pertinence to realize that one cannot run without the other. On the grounds of rationality, we need to blend in both. They must run side by side in any economy, fledgling or matured. Globally any country heavily focusing on development and then weaving in democracy has often turned sour with popular upsurges or international interventions. This danger threatens all those developing countries, and increasingly haunts developed countries today, as we note from the spread of populist preferences and policies. Therefore, it is predicted that a system of governance based on development while paying little or no heed to democracy may be a concoction of imminent danger accentuating future failure, the timeline of which may not be ascertained but surely brews in the horizon. All countries in this type of quicksand ought to find their way out through installing a democratic culture and democratic institutions. The democratic institutions are namely the Election monitoring commission, the office of Ombudsmen, impartial and independent Judiciary, and Government administration without the negative influence of political parties.

Youths in Democracy

Youths are the major driving force these days in socio-politico engagements, and they want to have a say in the ways a country operates. Two dynamics may be at play. First, the obvious: that all human beings, deep down, young or old, want to have a say in their lives and how things ought to work. When they see things operating not in a way to their likings, most youths, being young at heart, absorb the negative vibes and move on. Most do not want to extend time and effort to correct a system that they feel has been altered, deliberately or accidentally. It may suffice to point to the fact that a proclivity of detachment and disengagement is prevalent in countries where the governments are borderline totalitarian. However, this view may be tested against some target countries to substantiate the claim made above The second dynamic focuses on time. Time is important for the youth. The youth often do a mental math gauging how much effort to expend to correct the system or whether they will grudgingly accept and move on. States must give due importance to these youths because their pent-up demands can spiral into unruly flashes of mob violence. With an immense number of youths deciding to engage in street protests or other forms of ventilation of frustration, any movement can spiral out of control inadvertently. The scope presents for opposition parties to make an issue and add fuel to fire. While the role of any opposition party is also to bring out the gaps and infractions of the party in power, the government must also ensure through regular dialog with the youths and younger communities to voice their ideas, views and find collective efforts to manage any grievance having surfaced or simmering within. All parties wanting to come close to the public, must have regular feedback sessions to understand the public mindset and introduce or alter polices accordingly. The more opposed the government is toward a rational policy, the worse the public sentiment will brew. The issues of quota movement and "safe traffic" initiatives were two such scenarios in which organic youth engagement took place in the context of Bangladesh. There were some controversies in both movements that eventually led public sentiment to subside. Without trying to find the fault lines, it may be suggested that interactions with the youths and younger population can bring rich dividends and assist any government from trying to tackle unforeseen circumstances. The youth energy adds to any organically brewed movement and governments have to understand their mindsets, cultural perspectives, and trigger points.

Another could be the economic setting: if the economy continues spiraling downward or the competitive edge of the country has begun vanishing, finger-pointing begins, often from outsiders or from abroad. Prolonged crises like these could produce the very populism just alluded to. This may be one factor behind twenty-first Century global populism. If not just the vanishing glow, then its surrogate: immigration, which typically follows from wage differentials between countries. These can even reverse steadfast democratic principles for the youth, something Aristotle warned us about when pointing to mobocracy as the "perverted form" of "democracy by the many".

Leadership and Democracy

As Donald Trump indicated, leadership defines a country whose brand value of the country rises and/or falls based on its leadership, not just political leadership, but leadership as a whole. Having stated this, the vision for a prosperous country depends not just on technology and financial resources, but the person steering the boat. It is equally important in all facets of life. Image the body of a human being, being the total part of a state or body politic. Now, if a single component of one's body, say an arm, is not working properly, then it has dire and impacting consequences on other body parts and one's psyche as well. This same context can be extended to democracy. Any leadership component, in politics or trade, business or education, and in other arenas, the same scenario is noticed. Hence, for a country to ensure democracy runs with fluidity, it must have leadership development and national budgets for training the people within that particular country. A half-baked country can never deliver; therefore, each country may allocate a decent slab of resources to keep the able minds of the country in active work and advancement, thereby building the national fabric of the country. Here again, we see the critical role of a micro agent for a macro belief to prosper. Arab Spring of 2010 in much of the Arab world showed that distrust toward a system can evoke great potential for change. Governments around the world may take note to satisfy their youths and citizens' base otherwise get a potential farewell through organic or systematic uprisings in the guise of the Arab Spring.

Voting is the final tool for a democratic system to operate. Lord Acton, in his review of "Sir Erskine May's Democracy in Europe" in *The Quarterly Review* (January 1878), p. 75, wrote: **The one pervading evil of democracy is the tyranny of the majority, or rather of that party, not always the majority, that succeeds, by force or fraud, in carrying elections.** If the vast majority of the people's voice are not heard through guile and deception, the probability of a democratic process may backfire and stunt the growth of the country, causing irreparable consequences for a country. Such is the danger when democratic norms and aspirations of the citizens are not taken into consideration.

Conclusions

Democracy flourishes in a free and fair environment where people enjoy equal protection of law and equal freedoms, as enshrined in UN charters or documents, like the Universal Declaration of Human Rights (UDHR) or the International Covenant on Civil and Political Rights (ICCPR), in which many a stipulations abound to promote and safeguard humanity. ICCPR Article 25 deals with the notion of the right to vote; similarly,

Article 6 recognizes the individual's 'inherent right to life' and requires it to be protected by law. Similarly, Article 7 prohibits torture and cruel, inhuman, and degrading punishment. Freedom is integral to democracy. U.S. President Franklin D. Roosevelt defined "freedom" as "the supremacy of Human Rights everywhere". This freedom of human spirit works as a glue for sustaining democracy. They are inalienable freedoms of all humans, that is, a globally resonating action, belief, and right, but whose effectiveness demands local sustenance, shaping, and nourishment. The implications of these issues are profound. If left to rot or nonchalantly addressed, then democratic lapses open a fissure for greater chaos and disturbance. Each country now in an inter-related world must guard its corridors of democratic institutions with more vigor not by tyrannical energy but by championing democratic values in great proportions. Bangladesh, a country of 170 million people, with a multitude of aspirations needs to run with a democratic and pragmatic soul, ensuring sustained economic progress, rule of law, and equity in all spheres of lives. Any alternative prescription or policy may not bring rich reward to our densely populated country that we call Bangladesh. Similarly, as the current COVID-19 pandemic shows, a planet with 8 billion people can only live safely by collaborating, at first against the pandemic, then hopefully, against similar globally rampaging "isms".

Bibliography

https://www.ohchr.org/documents/publications/guidingprinciplesbusinesshr_en.pdf.
https://www.ohchr.org/documents/Professionalinterest/ccpr.pdf.
https://shodhganga.inflibnet.ac.in/bitstream/10603/148743/7/07_chapter%201.pdf.
https://carnegieendowment.org/sada/76323.
Sustaining Democracy: Localization, Globalization, and Feminist Praxis by Nancy A. Naples at https://onlinelibrary.wiley.com/doi/epdf/10.1111/socf.12054.

CHAPTER 10

Liberating Education and Awakening Refugee Consciousness: Insights from Rohingya–Syria Comparisons

Jessica Tartila Suma

INTRODUCTION

If refugee life is a borrowed and oppressed life, how can a refugee go beyond? Does awakening one's critical consciousness, which gets most provoked when routine life is destabilized, through cultural voices, particularly a persecuted such voice, contribute to the host community's objective position, while maintaining aloofness?[1] Education typically emancipates from any "normative" or "ethical framework", but for refugees a critical conscience is further stirred. Paolo Freire, who saw education as a liberating force, but through a critical Marxist pedagogy,[2] interpreted education to deliberately indoctrinate the student to

---

J. T. Suma (✉)
Department of Global Studies and Governance (GSG),
Independent University, Bangladesh (IUB), Dhaka, Bangladesh
e-mail: jessica@iub.edu.bd

© The Author(s), under exclusive license to Springer Nature Singapore Pte Ltd. 2022
I. A. Hussain (eds.), *Global-Local Tradeoffs, Order-Disorder Consequences*, Global Political Transitions,
https://doi.org/10.1007/978-981-16-9419-6_10

produce social and cultural contexts augmenting a ruling class agenda.[3] Since the objective of education is to "dominate the mind and regulate behaviour" of a certain class in society, education becomes "a murder machine".[4] Freire talked about the oppressed being liberated through education to feed an ideal based on dialogue, praxis and problem generation, in contrast to the ground realities where the oppressed (in this case, refugees) suffer from basic livelihood needs to even think of education. Contrary to conventional Marxist wisdom, best educational practices must also be dug up in the refugee camps. They must ask how a variety of necessary practices enmesh with the rational actor (such as refugees, their children, and the stakeholders) to mould their emancipation.

This chapter thrusts local practices against global contexts by examining the provisions of refugee education and the rationality dictated by their social circumstances—in this case Rohingya and Syrian refugees—to understand how access to "innovative and tailor-made" education awakens refugee consciousness, facilitating emancipation, if at all. In this *Anthropocene* era, immense and challenging Sustainable Development Goals (SDG) spiral into new global governance needs. These, in turn, get infected by fluctuating geopolitics. As the world stumbles against the coronavirus (COVID-19) pandemic presently, for instance, not only has global cooperation become perilous, such as the difficulties the World Health Organization has experienced in combating the threat, but also the additional impediments any SDG progress must now face. One front, *SDG 4: Quality Education* (ensuring inclusive and equitable quality education and promoting lifelong learning opportunities for all) illustrates the pitfalls. Humans have shown resilience against natural calamities time and again, but how do we transmute the refugee version of the plight? Will education permit these helplessly displaced persons to assimilate with host community children, especially after all the trauma they arrive with, thus liberating them from their refugee status? Even that presumes a Rohingya/Syrian refugee to cleanse one's minds from the inherent traumatic memories to concentrate on education.

According to a 2019 United Nations High Commissioner for Refugees (UNHCR) report, a global refugee population of 25 million, of which more than half remain under 18 years of age, includes 7.1 million refugee children of school age, 50% (3.7 million approximately) of whom do not have access to school.[5] The 2017 UNESCO (United Nations Educational, Scientific and Cultural Organization) report shows refugee primary education enrollment to be 63% (against the global enrolment of 91%), in secondary education 24% (against the global 84%), and in higher education only 1% (versus 37%).[6] Although the international communities, local and international non-government organizations (INGOs), and other relevant stakeholders deserve credit for bringing refugee children into classrooms, challenges remain: the "global" education imperative must meet its eviscerated "local" recipient under circumstances at best expedient for the former and too inconsequential-to-bother for the latter.

Refugee crises demand emergency responses, a complex phenomenon that requires joint efforts to address and ensure the continued financial support, international commitments, and collaboration between humanitarian actors and authorities to deliver support to the refugees and host communities.[7] Humanitarian support for Rohingyas is ensured by the Government of Bangladesh and this Joint Response Plan (JRP) instrument, in addition to Inter-Sector Coordination Group (ISCG) interventions. Syrian Refugees, on the other hand, find support from Syrian Refugee Affairs Directorate and UNHCR humanitarian responses through the Regional Refugee and Resilience Plan (3RP) which offers a strategic, coordination, planning, advocacy, and programming platform for humanitarian and development partners to respond to the Syria crisis at the regional level in host countries.[8] Here the Inter Agency Working Group (IAWG) and the host country's government (involving Egypt, Iraq, Jordan, Lebanon, and Turkey), disseminates, as with the Rohingyas, through the local NGO or INGO partners. Whether as a coordination or working group, they oversee sectoral responses, with education ranking as a major flank.

What we see is an interplay of actors and functions at all aggregation levels, ranging from the micro (individual) to the macro (state), with all permutations in between, from the micro–macro (individuals and relief organizations) to the macro–macro (state and non-state organizations). Both fragmentation (of authorities, for example) and integration (enhancing the common goal of education), mix and mingle. Such a *fragmegrative* outcome can be traced back to a variety of sources: authority crises, bifurcation of global structures (a Chinese project in Rakhine evicting the Rohingyas and Middle East religious-ethnic conflict exploding inside Syria), organizational explosion (given the onset of multiple NGO mandates), mobility upheaval (refugee exposure to *jihadis*, for example), weakening of territoriality, states, and sovereignty, as well as globalizing national economies.

EDUCATION AS BACKBONE OF RACE?

The UNHCR report states that higher level education makes leaders. It promotes creativity and brings forth energetic refugee youth and idealism by converting into role models. This they do to facilitate the critical thinking skills required for making rational choices and decisions. Not only are their voices amplified but rapid generational change also gets projected.

What do these education investments seek? Will they help the refugees to transcend persecution through people's innate capacity and working cooperatively with commitment within a framework of "Liberatory" education to transcend and change their reality?[9]

Accordingly, the chapter explores three questions: Does education accesses of vulnerable refugee children awaken their critical consciousness and facilitate their emancipation? Is identifying generative themes, the core of "Liberatory", or "liberating" education, at all possible in refugee camps? Does education (as self-actualization) liberate them of the refugee tag? In other words, does the "global" sow the seeds of a steady-state future relationship with the "local" against all odds?

Theoretical roots may be explored in *jihadi* ideology or Marxism, among others, since both forces stand poised at the perimeters to intervene. The latter is chosen for this investigation only because its relationship with education has a sturdier intellectual background. Freire's critical pedagogy explores how Marxist ideas are relevant, if at all, to the case of refugees, for whom adopting best practices in education is a challenge in itself. Refugee children suffer from both humanitarian crisis and psychological trauma/distress. Many of the refugee children around the world engage in economic activities to support their families. At a cultural, as well as post-traumatic level, refugee parents, too, do not have the aspiration to send their children, and especially girls, to school. On the contrary, extending education (infrastructure, curriculum, availability of the teachers, and so forth) to the refugee children is a subject of international investments. It calls for resource mobilization through complex emergency response. Educating the refugees, in other words, involves multiple actors in each phase of the decision-making process, including the refugee children themselves, their parents, and the community hosting them. Therefore, though the research questions project a Freirean critical pedagogy perspective, empirical evidences illustrate how refugee that the educational interventions and accesses adhere to rational choices germane to a socio-ecological model (to create a supportive environment prerequisite to interventions). Refugee education becomes inclusive enough through resilience building and a sustainable process.

EMPIRICAL BACKGROUND

In understanding the quandary of the refugees pertaining mostly to their education system, knowledge of prior experiences and refugee camp circumstances help. Accessing education does not spring from just having a school around. Other constraints intervene: holding the proper status (as refugees), and if that qualifies them (mostly Syrians in Turkey and Rohingyas in Bangladesh) for school, culture, and language; their mobility capacity; distance of schools; funds availability and the degrees of international community willingness to how much to engage and how far to go; and finally their status quo in terms of poverty as well as mental health conditions due to suffering from the trauma of violence and being driven out of their homes.

THE ROHINGYA CASE

Rohingyas represent one of the most marginalized South Asian refugee communities. Since 1978 they have been continuously denied their citizenship by the Myanmar government. A Muslim ethnic group from Rakhine state (also called Arakan) on the western Myanmar coast, Rohingyas trace their history back to the seventeenth Century, when Arab Muslims settled here. They have been targets of human rights violations in many forms, and as a result, millions of them now have fled to neighbouring Bangladesh, among other neighbouring Muslim countries. Rohingyas, right now the largest "stateless" people of the world, once occupied Rakhine for generations, but through a conundrum of identity and citizenship, the ordinary life of an entire ethnic group got ensnarled. Regardless, the new Myanmar constitution draft preserved the voting right of the Rohingyas, even though they are not acknowledged by the Myanmar government (which accepted 135 other ethnic minorities as citizens). Many Rohingyas failed to prove their citizenship according to the 1982 Citizenship Law of the then military junta. The historically rooted ethnic conflict turned into ethnic cleansing accompanied by the mass infiltration we now see along Bangladesh border areas, especially in and after August 2017. Kutupalong, in Cox's Bazaar, has become the world's largest refugee camp, hosting more than a million Rohingya refugees.

One of the strategies of the systematically discriminating Myanmar government was through educational denial. It directly prevented social growth and development. Many Rohingyas in Myanmar would avail primary education through the Muslim seminaries or the mosques, but higher education was impossible. Stateless under the 1982 citizenship law, the Rohingyas were barred from holding government jobs. Availing higher education also meant sacrificing their Rohingya identity. This was facilitated through the National Verification Cards (NVCs), which identify the Rohingyas as foreigners.[10]

Since Rohingyas are barred from attaining education in Bangladesh, and their mobility out of the camps is restricted, schooling has been provided by aid groups to small children, through largely nursery-style learning. This is because, Bangladesh as a sovereign country, strongly believes the Rohingyas will go back home, to Myanmar. Under these circumstances, the only education available to Rohingya refugees was based on lesson plans that did not provide any guidance to the inexperienced teachers—in English, Burmese, math, and "life skills".[11]

As a party to the 2020 Convention on the Rights of the Child and treatise like the 2018 Global Refugee Compact, Bangladesh has lifted restrictions established 30 years ago on education for young Rohingya children, so that a generation is not lost.[12] Children aged 11–13 years will be the first beneficiaries of such ease of restriction. Under this new initiative, humanitarian groups behind the education initiative in Cox's Bazaar piloted the Myanmar refugee camp curriculum from April, with 10,000 Rohingya students from grades six to nine, with programmes in the pipeline to offer "skills training" to youth over 14 of age.

Earlier, the Rohingyas had established their own centres to teach basic skills, like English, Mathematics, and Sciences, despite opposition from the government. Frustration intensified as no one could obtain any qualification document or achieve a status.

Bangladesh never catered to educating Rohingya children since that promoted a "refugee staying factor", helping them easily integrate with the host community when the Bangladesh Government wanted them to repatriate to Myanmar.

Education as a Sector in the Joint Response Plan 2020

The 2020 Joint Response Plan caps the Rohingya humanitarian responses efficiently. Reflecting the coordination among the sector-based approaches to address the immediate needs of the refugees and the impact on the host communities, the JRP task is to mobilize humanitarian communities to understand the needs assessment that includes provisions for consultation and strategic planning, led by the Government of Bangladesh. With JRP sharing engagement in the Strategic Executive Groups (SEG)-led IOM (International Office for Migration) under UNHCR coordination, an ISCG outcome was possible in Cox's Bazaar.

According to the 2020 JRP document, a comprehensive roadmap to meet "needs" and bridge "gaps" was built. Costing US$877 million, it mobilized 117 partners, 61 of them Bangladeshi organizations.[13]

That same document emphasized "essential knowledge" and "skills" for refugee children to prevent a lost generation. Education based on the Learning Competency Framework Approach (LCFA) under the Guidelines for Informal Education Programme (GIEP) will complement the Myanmar curriculum on a pilot basis, commencing at the middle school level before being extended to higher levels.

The Syrian Case

The Regional Refugee and Resilience Plan (3RP) supports the Syrian refugees, as did the JRP Rohingya counterpart, operating under UNHCR and UNDP auspices. Under the 3RP roadmap, over 270 partners have been mobilized to intervene and focus on "policy and programming innovation". Over the last five years, the 3RP, channelled over USD 14 billion in funding in order to meet the refugee "needs".[14] In 2020 they channelled a USD 5.5 billion comprehensive plan that would only support: (a) access to "asylum and international protection"; (b) "basic needs"; and (c) "specialized services and support".[15]

According to a 2016 UNESCO report, internally displaced persons (IDPs) within Syria number 6.6 million,[16] and those who sought refuge to five nearby countries (such as Egypt, Iraq, Jordan, Lebanon, and Turkey) amount to more than 5.6 million people,[17] including 2.5 million children,[18] who have been living as registered refugees in Egypt, Iraq, Jordan, Lebanon, and Turkey since the onset of the conflict. Since more than half of Syrian IDPs and refugees are children and youth under age 24, Irin Bakova, UNESCO Director-General, reiterated in 2016 how access to quality education had become a pertinent feature to reconstruct the region.

The continued Syrian civil war (more than 6 years now) leaves a damaging trail on the lives of not only 11 million Syrians, but also millions of people in the host countries. The war has been a major barrier to quality education for all in Syria who have been internally displaced as well as for refugees. The total number of Syrian children in dire need of support both inside Syria and host countries is 8 million. Of these, 2.6 million are internally displaced and over 2.5 million are registered children in the camps of the host countries.[19] While 3RP sector funding shows the education sector received USD 435 million (53%), in reality it requires USD 816 million.[20]

Syria had achieved universal primary enrolment in 2011, almost achieved universal enrolment in lower secondary education. One 2017 UNESCO report also mentioned that in 2011 (before the war broke out in Syria), 91% of primary school aged children were in school, and by 2015 that rate had fallen to 37%. If not engaged in the learning process, the youth would not be able to think critically and develop their conscience to liberate them in the future in the hope of a meaningful and inclusive life. Against the perilous condition, the following evidence helps understand the educational access needs of Syrian refugee children in host countries as well as within Syria.

Within Syria: Massive internal Syrian displacement led the IDP groups to abandon their homes as well as livelihoods, and the country now faces consequences in the political–economic, security, and social ramifications. Over 2 million children (one-third of Syria's child population) is out of school and many others are subject to psychological support.[21]

Host countries: The host countries bear huge costs because of the impact of the Syrian civil war on the economy, infrastructure, social services, and education. However, the five host countries have responded to the educational needs of the children with a lot of challenges. These include social discontents among the host countries, funding from international communities and all the compliance issues, as well as integration of the refugees to the mainstream education. Over 800,000 Syrian refugee children in the host countries are out of school.[22] Table 10.1 overviews the essentials.

Table 10.1 A brick in the wall: regional responses to Syrian refugee education access

Host countries	No of registered refugees/areas	Age group of children	Regional norms in terms of access to school	School/University enrollment of Syrian refugees	Challenges
Egypt	130,042 Urban dwellers	• 55,328 children (42% of the entire Syrian refugee population in Egypt) • 30% (age 5–17)	Refugees have access to Egyptian public education as per 2012 presidential decree	• 42,300 students (registered/non-registered) • 7300 receive education in Syrian Community Centers • 85% total enrollment	• 11% do not attend school • Higher education needs to be expanded
Iraq	245,421 • 99% of Syrian refugees in Iraq live in the Kurdistan Region of Iraq (KR-I), mostly in urban and peri-urban areas • 37% of all Syrian refugees reside in nine camps in KR-I	• Total number of children—154,000 • 42% (age 0–17)	Refugees have access to formal education	• 42,633 children (5–17 years,) enrolled in formal general education • 1449 children (3–5 years) enrolled in ECCE and pre-primary education • 220 Syrians received DAFI (UNHCR scholarship) for tertiary education in 2017	• Language barrier for non-camp schools (as its mostly Kurdish spoken) • Children drop out due to financial constraints at the family level • Need for reinforcement of teachers' code of conduct: Syrians are subject to bullying and discrimination • Lack of essential documents for students who wish to pursue higher education: Not having residency cards, lack of government capacity, and security too contributes to children not going to school

(continued)

Table 10.1 (continued)

Host countries	No of registered refugees/areas	Age group of children	Regional norms in terms of access to school	School/University enrollment of Syrian refugees	Challenges
Jordan	630,000 • 83% live in urban communities • 17% live in camps	359,945 children (48%) are between 0 and 17 years	Refugees have access to formal education in line with the 2018–2022 Education Strategic Plan for Jordan	• 92% of Syrian youth sit idle • 38% of children (aged 15–17) do not go to school • Some 18,338 are enrolled in schools both formal and non-formal • 173,000 Syrian and Jordanian school children were provided with developing critical life skills	• Children drop out due to financial constraints at the family level
Lebanon	914,648 Mostly live in the North and the Bakka region	488,000 are children (aged 3–18)	• Education is made free up to grade 12 for the Lebanese as well as the refugees • Lebanese Education ministry (MEHE) opened second shift of the public primary school to provide life-skills program	• 1260 public school accommodate 57% of refugee children (aged 6–14) • 376 schools operate in the second shift as 71% (aged 3–18) are enrolled in this shift	Yet 50% of the Syrian refugee children are out of school Children drop out due to economic opportunities, residency permit issues, negative perspectives by the host communities, and so forth

Host countries	No of registered refugees/areas	Age group of children	Regional norms in terms of access to school	School/University enrollment of Syrian refugees	Challenges
Turkey	3,600,000 91% live in Turkey's 81 province	44% of the total refugees are children	Syrians have access to public education in Turkey	• 640,000 Syrians have enrolled in schools in Turkey of which 80% go to public schools • Turkey also offer language training skills and successfully enrolled 75% of the targeted Syrians	• Children drop out due to economic constraints, and many of them have to choose to go to work • Language acts as a barrier as all Syrians have to adhere to Turkish language for academic success and not all children can acquire language skills

Sources UNHCR, 3RP and Turkey Chapter 2018

Egypt: Egypt hosts 130,045 (registered) Syrian refugees, of which approximately 30% belong to the 5–17 age group.[23] In Egypt, the current norm allows the Syrian refugees to access public education on an equal level to nationals. Of course, UNHCR intervention, along with its partners, supports access to primary, preparatory, and secondary educational institutions (UNHCR, *Egypt Factsheet* 2019), and UNHCR grants for some of the refugee children contributes to school fees, transportation, uniforms, and school supplies.[24] Approximately 42,300 (registered or non-registered) Syrian students enrolled in Egyptian public schools, with 7300 boys and girls receiving education in Syrian community education centres.[25]

The Egyptian approach covers all public school facilities, including access to vocational and technical schools and higher education universities and institutes. However, despite boosting enrollment to 89% (according to a 2018 UNHCR internal survey), the challenges remain. The survey findings indicate that poverty and child labour forces 11% of Syrian refugee children to not attend school, or attend less than three times per week.[26] There is no barrier to language as the medium of instruction in Egypt is Arabic, however, dialect barrier exists. Syrians, even though they have access to higher educations in Egypt, face the challenges of attending such institutions; and higher education opportunities for them in Egypt still need to expand. The Ministry of Higher Education (MoHE) in 2016 decreed (a) Syrian refugees with secondary school certificates from an Egyptian public school would be granted access to prevalent university facilities, just as the Egyptians; and (b) Syrian refugees with a Syrian secondary school certificate would have to pay 50% of the international student's fee amounting to $2500 per annum.

Iraq: The country itself is in a devastating state, needing international support to meet some of its own fundamental restructuring. Nevertheless, 62% of Syrian refugees live in urban areas outside camps and do not have much access to secondary schools. Still, 5% of youth aged 15–17 are in formal secondary education.[27] The other barriers that impact access to education in Iraq are not having residency cards, government capacity, and security.[28]

Jordan: More than 630,000 registered refugees have settled here, of which 83% live in communities, particularly in Amman and in the northern governorates, and the rest 17% live in camps.[29] With 359,945 (48%) refugees in the 0–17 age bracket,[30] though Jordan has welcomed all Syrian children into its public schools, thousands of the Syrian refugees remain out of school. Youths aspiring to vocational education were denied free access until late 2015. The government has outlined some policy shifts, where the Jordanian universities welcome Syrians eligible for higher education only if they have the required documents and can pay fees (as applicable to other international students), making the eligibility criteria unaffordable as well as luxurious for most Syrian families. Although 92% of young Syrians potentially vulnerable to radicalization are eligible for higher education, they sit idle.[31] In Jordan, 38% of Syrian children aged 15–17 years old do not go to school, due to distance, cost, lack of space, and bullying as reasons for dropping out or not enroling.[32] The two significant camps in Jordan, namely Zaatari and Azraq, host most of the Syrian refugees. The Azraq camp is home to 36,010 Syrian refugees, and almost 60% are children, with 22% under five years of age.[33] Zaatari camp under the joint administration of the Syrian Refugee Affairs Directorate (SRAD) and UNHCR is home to 76,143 refugees, and nearly 20% are under five years old. Some 18,338 children are enroled in 32 schools, with 58 community centres offering activities.[34]

Lebanon: Most of the Syrian refugees have settled in the north of Lebanon and in its Bakka region, which are already deprived regions. The registered number of Syrian refugees in Lebanon is 914,648,[35] and a total of 488,000 are school-aged children between 3 and 18 years of age.[36] The UNHCR webpage on Lebanon states that the Ministry of Education and Higher Education (MEHE) of Lebanon through its national programme called "Reaching All Children with Education" (RACE), and with the support from UNHCR, UNICEF, UNESCO, and bilateral donors, is designed to provide free education up to the 12th grade, both for the refugees as well as the Lebanese.[37] Thus, Lebanon has put forth the effort to bring back to school the Syrian refugee children and youth by opening second shifts in public primary schools and providing them with life-skills programme RACE.[38]

A 2016/17 MEHE provision in its 1260 public schools, sought to enroll Syrian children in the morning shift where roughly 57% of refugee children (age group 6–14) are enrolled.[39] It also opened 376 schools for the second shift; as out of 221,000 Syrian refugee children aged 3–18 years, 71% are enrolled in this shift for the school year 2016–2017.[40]

No matter how the data looks and despite the relentless efforts of the Lebanese government and by the support of the international community, the number of Syrian refugee children out of school is more than 50%. The reason simply is not access, but rather intertwining with the challenges the Syrian refugees face to access economic opportunities. Residency permit, mobility, closed jobs, and quotas and negative perception by the host communities play pivotal roles in whether a child can afford to go to school or not,[41] and hence determining the rational choice made by the refugee families.[42] There are also curriculum issues in the Lebanese public schools, and, for example, though the Syrians have no language problems in Lebanon, it being Arabic, however, the school curriculum requires taking foreign language. In 2017 a new community-based programme started to teach the refugee children by the "Foreign Language in English and French" option, taught by volunteering Lebanese university students, so that 4–12 graders can boost their language skills required to keep them in public schools.[43] There are also reports of 180,000 young Syrian refugees into child labour in Lebanon through a UNICEF inquiry.[44] These challenges play as the underlying factors that affect the decision-making on the education of the children and the youth, collectively from the family or at individual level.

Turkey: Of almost 3.6 million Syrian refugees over 98% live in Turkey's 81 provinces.[45] Almost 44% of the total refugee population are children. The Syrians, under the Temporary Protection Regulation (TPR) of 2014 are ensured of their access to services by the national systems through the Directorate General of Migration Management (DGMM) and other relevant government entities, such as ministries and municipalities.[46] Thus, in Turkey, the Syrian refugees, who are under temporary protection, have access to free health care and education. However, since the nature of the crisis is protracted, about 64% of the Syrian refugees living in the urban area fall below the poverty line.[47] Unemployment adds to their woeful *status quo* breeding tensions between the host communities and the refugees in regard to competition for jobs and other economic opportunities. National resources are in constraints due to the increased demand for public services by the Syrians. Increased pressure on the infrastructure and expertise prevails, and this crisis is mostly visible in the education sector. The Turkish national education system is strained due to an increase in enrollment, classrooms that are overcrowded, and of course scarce school resources. Despite these anomalies, 640,000 refugee children were enrolled in Turkish public schools and Temporary Education Centers (TECs) in the year 2018–2019, of which 80% attended public schools.

However, language barriers prevent 40% of the school-aged children from going to schools.[48] According to *Outcome Monitoring Report*

(2018), Turkey has taken initiatives to increase social inclusion through addressing language barriers. The importance of speaking Turkish for both social inclusion and access to the labour market has led both the Education and Livelihood sector partners to engage in supporting language skills training sessions with funding levels of 61 and 78%, respectively. The education sector successfully enrolled 75% of the targeted Syrians under temporary protection in language classes, while they could cover 31% of the livelihood target.[49] However, Turkey positively contributes to its resilience developing strategies towards social inclusion of the Syrian refugees.[50] The tertiary level enrollment has risen to 4% which represent just over 20,000 youths.

THEORETICAL CONTESTATION

As the empirical evidences strongly suggest, it is imperative to send the refugees back to their homes where they at least have property they can call their own. Here, too, two differing cases expose the theoretical divide: Syrians, on the one hand, can voluntarily go back (of course. there are criteria), but Rohingyas must first build a *modus operandi* with the Myanmar government for any chance to return; and on the other, as the international community reiterates, the only option left with the refugees and the host communities (both local forces) is to build social cohesion as a step towards regional resilience (an externalizing process with the globalizing instrument of education). Functioning as a catalytic medium, education is central to social cohesion. Social cohesion needs the conscience of not just the refugees, but also host communities. For host communities, the cohesion and social resilience obviously entail a top-down approach, i.e., regulations imposed by the government for its own citizen's internal/achievement refugee motivation, that is, something to do with their own concept of liberating themselves from the *status quo*. Critical refugee conscience through "liberatory" education in vulnerable situations can never be neutral.[51] Since it becomes an instrument for liberating people, arguably it is dominating and disempowering them. New relationships between teachers and students as well as with society must evolve. This does not involve the curriculum contents or the enthusiasm of the teacher, but a pedagogical approach utilizing "generative themes": people become more motivated to learn how to read and write if the experience illustrated the power networks behind their plight in other words, "the relationship between an objective situation and the perceptions held of that situation by the people involved in it".[52]

Freire defines *critical consciousness* as the ability to enter any reality in order to change it. His key to liberation is the awakening of critical awareness and the thinking process in the individual. Drawing on revolutionary scholarships that include both Marxist social thought and liberation theology, he crafted a convincing yet controversial set of arguments, not only for critical pedagogy but also for associated key cultural actions that may potentially lead to self-emancipation and a just flourishing society free from oppression (here the refugees).[53] Freire's work is based on both an appraisal of existing observed concrete realities of oppression: "a culture of silence" and a "fear of freedom" and his belief in radical dialogic education as "the practice of freedom" to contribute to personal (through self-actualization) and societal liberation through an awakening of critical consciousness and intervention.[54]

Conscientization, thus, becomes an ongoing process by which a learner moves towards critical consciousness. It is the process through which individuals and communities develop a critical understanding of their social reality, which would involve reflecting and acting on the root causes of oppression.[55]

This takes an individual beyond obtaining the technical skills of reading and writing, but to device instruments to end the culture of silence, in which oppression is not mentioned but maintained. Freire iterates that it was the role of the educator to foster a process of dialogue and liberation that would enable citizens to reach critical consciousness. This process is the heart of "liberatory" education: true education involves a pedagogy based on the practice of liberation. This pedagogy of liberation centres around the principles of social change and transformation through education, based on consciousness elevation and engagement with oppressive forces.[56] Thus "liberatory" pedagogy recognizes the politics of education and its goal is *self-actualization* or "humanization". However, is it the right kind of approach given the refugee context?

COMPARATIVE ANALYTIC INTERPRETATIONS

In order to build their self-actualization leading to their emancipation, refugees require the right environment. As the most vulnerable people, their freedom from one oppression seems to have led to another form of oppression, characterized by misery. A comparative appraisal shows the

Syrians may be better positioned politically than the Rohingyas because of the nature of the conflict, legally because legitimacy of Syrian refugees as Syrian citizens contrasts with the denials the Rohingyas face, and geographically because of the kindred sentiments and return-home capacities Syrians can depend upon that the Rohingyas cannot. Syrians can return to their country without any need to demonstrate their citizenship and civil rights, yet Rohingyas face a triple jeopardy (Benjamin Zawacki in 2013): (a) nationality and discrimination (an exclusively Myanmar problem); (b) statelessness and displacement (implying Myanmar's neighbours as well); and (c) the "responsibility to protect" (R2P) (implying the role of the international community). These are progressively causal, and they imply where efforts towards solution may be directed and prioritized. Whether they are Syrians or Rohingyas, the refugees and their identity in a foreign land do not give them freedom. Entrapped in what Freire calls, "a culture of silence" and a "fear of freedom",[57] the only way refugees can find their existence depends upon the international community's willingness and capacity to promote social cohesion initiatives through creative resilience. Refugee education is a synergy to that social cohesion otherwise, idle youth time, could ultimately breed frustration, easily degenerating into eventual terrorism, trafficking, and other unethical activities.

EDUCATION UNDER VULNERABLE CONDITIONS AND AWAKENING OF CRITICAL CONSCIOUSNESS

Through the 2013 "No Lost Generation" (NLG) initiative, the international community chose to focus attention on the Syrian refugee children plight. Real concerns about the possible "loss" of a whole generation of children, adolescents, and youth to the effects of violence and displacement emerged as areas of deep concern, placing education and child protection at the centre of any response inside Syria, and across the five refugee host countries. Informed by and under 3RP integration, reflecting the vision for protecting and educating all war-affected children, the NLG-based global accessing platform from 2019 allowed Rohingyas NLG support. Still, NLG experiences with hundreds of Rohingya refugee children exposed how front-line caregivers often lack the professional and educational backgrounds in child well-being and protection. Infrequent extant humanitarian interventions addressing these training gaps compound matters, making them inaccessible, or being hindered by communication or language barriers.

Though just one factor helped to create a psychological balance for the refugee children, thus allowing them to realize their existence, the NLG initiative must be supplemented by other factors like breaking language barriers and social cohesion and resilience within the host communities.

Evidence suggests host country initiatives, as Syrian refugee work permits, and especially in Turkey, help, particularly if augmented by language courses. Not all parts of the refugee world are so ideal; for Rohingyas mobility is much more restricted than it is for Syrians, and their educational accesses were also withheld up until 2020.

The Turkey Case

A majority of the 60,000 Syrian refugees holding work permits have been channelled into agriculture. Many of them have access to language trainings. Though employment within families is crucial, having a job for children to access education, challenges prevail. For a start, as per the Turkish education system, since Grades 1, 5, and 9 fall in the transition between school levels in Turkish Public Schools (TPS), the language of instruction in these grades is Turkish. Syrian children at these grade levels require a good level of Turkish language proficiency to be able to learn effectively, so they get off to a disadvantageous start. Current enrolment in grades 1, 5, and 9 is monitored by the Ministry of National Education (MoNE), with support from 3RP partners. MoNE management agreed to extend the target for the grade 5 Gross Enrolment Rate in 2018, but not for Grade 9.

Since 45,000 children enroll in school, community, and home-based Early Childhood Education (ECE) activities, expanding ECE access is key as it increases school readiness (particularly Turkish language proficiency) and enrollment in Grade 1, again Syrian children fall short: 90% of children benefitting from ECE summer school activities implemented by 3RP partners during the summer of 2018 are currently enroled in formal ECE and Grade 1.[58] Other hindrances also riddle the picture: economic, for example, adolescent boys (and to a lesser extent girls), being subject to contributing to the family purse; security, the school being distantly located, or transportation shortages, particularly of girls; while some adolescents do not have interest in education as they have been out of school for a long period or are not proficient enough in Turkish language, negatively affecting their school performances.

On the other hand, conditional cash transfer for education (CCTE) programmes play a key role in supporting the attendance of children and adolescents in schools (from ECE to Grade 12), with 411,000 refugee children (63.7% of those enroled), benefiting from the CCTE.[59]

However, the overall condition of access to education and a liberating education, is determined by the socio-economic model of how the humanitarian responses strategize to create the environment to foster such basic needs. While ensuring the education of Syrian refugees, other functionally interdependent strategic factors need to be considered. The 3RP strategic objectives include: (a) protecting vulnerable individuals; (b) providing public services through national systems; (c) supplying assistance to vulnerable individuals and reducing effects of poverty and displacement; and (d) expanding livelihood and job opportunities for refugees as well as the host community. The 3RP developed an "Inter-Agency Social Cohesion Framework" outlining initiatives to scale-up social cohesion. In 2018, 73 local municipalities, social service centres, and directorates of ministries were engaged in events to promote peaceful co-existence among the refugees and the host communities where the results met 50% of the target.[60] Scaling-up this programme initiative would ultimately contribute to creating a supportive educational environment of both the target groups. Table 10.2 shows the strategic objectives of 3RP which, in turn, are essential to ensure and create a holistic system through which education to the Syrian refugees could be delivered. It showcases the access to service of the Syrian refugees and the efforts of the organizations and relevant stakeholder to enhance the standard of living of the Syrian refugees that are underlying factors affecting access to education.

The Bangladesh Case

Rohingyas, residing in 34 congested camps designated by the Government of Bangladesh in Cox's Bazaar, lack formal legal status, and hence a challenge to implement policy frameworks of all the humanitarian aid and assistance remains (JRP 2020).[61] Emerging trends in rising Rohingya household debt, which was 35% in 2018 and 69% in 2019,[62] post a steep constraint. According to their 2020 response plan of the JRP target of a total of 421,771 population accessing education, 375,924 are Rohingya

Table 10.2 Underlying education conditions: impact factors and Syrian refugee response plan

Dimensions	Socio-cultural-legal	Socio-economic-legal	Economic-legal
Objectives:	Protection	Provision for public services through national system	Reduce effects of poverty and displacement
Impact factors:	Improved protective environment	Essential services	Improved living conditions through complementary and temporary services
	Social cohesion, inclusion and trust		Improved job opportunities and expanding livelihood
			Increased self-reliance both for refugees and host communities

Dimensions	Socio-cultural-legal	Socio-economic-legal	Economic-legal	
Outcomes:	(1) Awareness of access to services and their rights and obligations	(1.a) Enhanced participation in communities by vulnerable people to bring about social cohesion, prevention of Gender Based Violence (GBV), and child abuse (1.b) Inter-Agency Social Cohesion Framework facilitating initiatives to bring refugees and host communities together to a common goal (1.c) Established community centres for refugees and local populations to develop practices for co-existence and to transform society's view of refugees (1.d) Engage youths in social cohesion	(1) Access to affordable health: Health services have the highest score in terms of satisfaction that testifies for increased accessibility and quality *For example: There is a network of 178 Migrant and Refugee Health Centers across Turkey and it involves Syrian health professionals trained by Ministry of Health of Turkey*	(1) Ensure basic needs and reduce negative coping strategies	(1) Employability: *Example of best practices in Turkey- Out of total caseload of 470,000 poor active Syrians, 21% of Syrian refugees and host community members reached employability through increased vocational skills entrepreneurial and/or language skills 53,000 Syrians under temporary protection and host community members received skills training in agricultural and non-agricultural livelihoods that also includes health care*

(continued)

Table 10.2 (continued)

Dimensions	Socio-cultural-legal	Socio-economic-legal	Economic-legal
	(2) Service delivery and capacity building of government and non-government organizations (NGOs): *All material and technical supports are enhanced to provide quality protection services; for example, Ministry of justice and Turkish Bar Association facilitate legal clinics*	(2) Access to Quality formal and informal education and access to public schools: (2.a) youth empowerment, life-skills training, and enhancing efforts to enroll children in schools or youth in training or internship schemes. This also contribute to social cohesion	(2) Contingencies plan to meet potential crisis are already in place
	(2.a) Inclusion through eliminating language barrier: The importance of speaking Turkish for both social inclusion and access to education and labour market	(2.b) Implementing social cohesion programmes using schools and Public Education Centres (PECs)	(2) Income generation: *Example of best practices in Turkey: Under the Regulation on Work Permits for Foreigners under temporary protection in January 2016, the number of work permits granted to Syrians is 60,000 as of 2018 and this also includes Syrians with residence permits—not under temporary protection*
	(2.b) Turkish language courses are provided through Public Education Centres (PECs) free of cost	(2.c) The Conditional Cash Transfer for Education (CCTE) program is playing a key role in supporting the attendance of children at school	Livelihoods Sector partners fostered business start-ups for a total of 54,597 Syrians under temporary protection and host community members in 2018

Dimensions	Socio-cultural-legal	Socio-economic-legal	Economic-legal
	(3) Legitimacy of refugees under temporary protection: Directorate General of Migration Management (DGMM) issues temporary protection cards to the Syrians to access to services, including health care, education, and so forth	(3) Municipality services: there remains a funding challenge to this sector for the capacity building	

Sources UNHCR, 3RP and Turkey Chapter 2018

refugees and 45,847 from the host community. Even after the significant progress by putting intensive efforts in promoting equitable children education since 2019, 30% (youth and children aged 3–24 years) still needs access to education; and 83% of the adolescent and youth (aged 15–24) do not have access to education or any form of skill development activities.[63]

Still the 2020 JRP document lists fundamental reasons to support Rohingya refugees to build sustainable skills and capacities upon return and make reintegration more conducive. Myanmar offering improved access to education and skills development activities, as well as ensure Rohingya refugee women, men, girls, and boys access to safe, transparent, and consultative communication mechanisms regarding solutions and the situation within Myanmar.[64] Thus, access to Myanmar's national curriculum, and skills development, from 2021 is stated in order to prepare Rohingya for a future in their own country. As camp parents and students in the camp request education in the Myanmar curriculum, the piloting of 10,000 students aged between 11 and 13 under the Myanmar curriculum and those whose secondary studies were interrupted by the influx, will be an important step in this direction. At primary levels, the Learning Competency Framework (LCF) and approach under the Guidelines for Informal Education Programme (GIEP) will be the basis of instruction, in line with the Government of Bangladesh's policy framework. Rohingya refugees will also benefit from skills development programmes aimed at engaging them productively and facilitating their eventual sustainable reintegration in Myanmar. The JRP categorically points out that designs of camp-skill development programmes are to complement Myanmar's labour market experiences and cater to the need within the communities. These innovative measures remain subject to further discussions with the Bangladesh Government. The Rohingya refugees have no access to public schools in Bangladesh. Educating the children within the periphery of the camp, too, is too sensitive an issue. Since the Rakhine language and Bangla sound similar, Bangladesh authorities fear they will easily integrate with the local people. All these years, the Rohingyas had no formal access to education. Add to that the sociocultural barriers, early marriage, and children supporting families through their jobs, and we can sense the formidable barriers to accessing education opportunities. However, all the endeavours including education are through the Myanmar Curriculum Pilot.

Therefore, the Turkish and Bangladesh cases show challenging sociocultural, legal, economic, and political dimensions that must be understood when considering and creating a supportive environment for the refugee children and their education. One factor to be noted: the Syrian regional response plan has evolved over the 9-year time-span, against which the Rohingya humanitarian response is comparatively immature. Challenges for the Syrian refugees to access education has been relatively overcome through the collective effort of the Turkish MoNE, international community, and relevant stakeholders: they have been incorporated in employment, language skill development, access to public school facilities, as well as their basic needs and essential services have been ensured through a scaling-up strategy. But the Syrians are eligible to return to their own land whenever they feel comfortable as they are not stateless, they are just homeless. Rohingya refugees entering a new land do not have a safe return ticket to Myanmar, as do the Syrians; and they face more cultural identity and political challenges to integrating into mainstream Bangladesh or Myanmar.

The strategic objectives of both 3RP and JRP show the services provided to both the Syrians and the Rohingyas, as Tables 10.2 and 10.3 depict. Though the objectives of the strategic plans are to provide refugees a life of dignity and ensure their rights as refugees, we find both cases to be unique in nature, and one better off than the other, not only because of their geographic placement but also because of the socio-political and cultural aspects. Hence access to facilities for both the groups are not adherent to universal rights only, illustrating how the same globalizing force can face different local consequences; and, in the same way, different local circumstances, such as the political and economic aspiration of the refugees' country of origins and the host country's inability/unwillingness to predict identical global/external/theoretical outcomes. If we take a close look at the strategic objectives of both the response plans, we find the final objective for the Rohingya crisis response is to plan their safe repatriation. How feasible that task will be only time will say. Whereas Tables 10.2 and 10.3 briefly compare Rohingyas and the Syrian refugees underlying conditions to access to education, Table 10.4 casts some light on the differences.

On social and legal dimensions, the Syrians may be better positioned inside Turkey as they do not require living in the camps. Though this gives them the right to movement, it causes huge demands for service delivery from the government's side, including public school services to

Table 10.3 Underlying education conditions: impact factors and Rohingya refugee response plan

Dimensions:	Political-social-cultural-legal	Socio-economic-legal	Economic-legal	Political-cultural-economic
Objectives:	Protection	Deliver quality lifesaving assistance to people in need	Foster Community Well-being	Sustainable solution in Myanmar
Impact Factor:	Strengthening protection Enhancing negative coping mechanism	Sustain and improve assistance to multiple sectors Essential Service delivery Govt and NGOs	Enhance peaceful co-existence	Increased self-Reliance and voluntary and dignified repatriation of the Rohingyas

10 LIBERATING EDUCATION AND AWAKENING REFUGEE ... 253

Dimensions:	Political-social-cultural-legal	Political-cultural-legal	Socio-economic-legal	Economic-legal	Political-cultural-economic
Outcomes:	(1) Ensure registration and documentation to access the facilities in the camp and avail their rights as refugees (2) This is to support the Rohingyas in Bangladesh and will also preserve their right to return to Myanmar (in line with strategy 4 of JRP)	(1) Providing Quality child protection, GBV, psychological support, and legal service	(1) Ensure access to food assistance (2) Improved WASH facilities across camps and provision for chlorinated safe water Inclusive facilities for women and children (3) Health facilities will continue to be free (4) The JRP aims to prevent "Lost Generation" through providing education under LCF starting on a pilot basis this year (2020)	(1) Plans to improve the layout of the camp with help from the Bangladesh Government and the humanitarian response to ensure that refugees can get optimal access to services (2) National and local disaster response to support first responders to prepare for a major disaster	(1) Ensuring the host community in Ukhiya and Teknaf does not have to bear the undue burden of the refugees (2) Facilitate training/campaigns/dialogues that would bring the host communities and the Rohingyas together (3) Environment and eco-system rehabilitation is made a priority	(1) Access to Myanmar's national curriculum and skill development to prepare the Rohingyas for a future in Myanmar and their sustainable integration in Myanmar (2) Cross-sectoral planning will expand access to skill development to youth and women (3) Registration and documentation will preserve the refugee's right to return to Myanmar

Sources JOINT RESPONSE PLAN 2020 and 2019

Table 10.4 Refugee access to education: comparative determinants

	Factors determining access to education	Turkey	Bangladesh
1	Legality	Registration and documentation allow the Syrians stay out of camps	Registration and documentation do not allow Rohingyas to stay out of the camp, they are confined
2	Employment and economic barriers	Syrians have right to employment in Turkey	Rohingyas are not allowed work permits
3	Access to education through the national curriculum of host countries	Accommodating school-going refugees into national curriculum and providing access to public schools	Rohingyas for all the past years had no access to education and are not allowed to integrate into public schools. New initiative only this year (2020) will cater to pilot 10,000 Rohingya refugees access to education under a given framework
4	Language issues	Language barriers are addressed through MoNE and are facilitated among the Syrian refugee communities	Since Rohingyas cannot avail national curriculum for their education and they do not have work permit, learning language remained a salient feature because systematically they were not entitled to learn Bengali

Factors determining access to education		Turkey	Bangladesh
5	Social cohesion to promote integration of the refugees with the mainstream	Social cohesion through events with host community is a routine activity more so because the Syrians live outside the camps and have access to the job market and education	There are no refugees outside the camp, as Rohingyas are confined to one area. Therefore, systematically acculturation does not occur and Rohingyas are identified as outsiders though there exist peaceful co-existence

Sources 3RP, JRP (2020) and Turkey Chapter (2018)

the refugee children. They are allowed to acculturate into the Turkish society through language learning and social cohesion. For the Syrians inside Turkey, language is a barrier, yet the evidence suggests both communities strive to incorporate each other and participation in social cohesion activities have become routine activities of both the refugees and the host communities. Therefore, for the Syrian refugees, it is just a matter of refugee consciousness, how hard they will push themselves to achieve those opportunities and attain their desired goals.

Rohingyas, on the other hand, are not allowed to live outside their camps and there are no means to acculturate with their Bangla-speaking hosts. They are not allowed work permits in Bangladesh, and hitherto several organizational and international communities did not even have access to teach the refugees to learn Bangla. Adhering to such educational rigidities ensured the refugee future would only be possible inside Myanmar. Even though the pilot sampling of educating the Rohingyas in Burmese language has started, we do not know if the Rohingyas will be repatriated at all, and if not, what will happen to this "lost generation" due to the time lapse remains an open question.

Then there are issues with education infrastructures, educational accessories, and most importantly funding from the international communities which are often contested. The resilience development efforts most of the time falls back due to these funds' constraints.

Thus, critical conscience becomes a luxury for those who have identity, language, and citizenship, and hence civil rights. For refugees, it is one of the needs only after fulfilling their basic needs. Other questions arise further ask: who and how will one imbed those radical thoughts of emancipation and in what forms when basic education itself is in question. Generative themes creating critical conscience may have an answer.

IDENTIFYING GENERATIVE THEMES: THE "LIBERATORY" EDUCATION CORE

Generative themes consist of the relationship between an objective situation and the perceptions held of that situation by the people involved in it.[65] Teachers and educators are sources of such emancipation,[66] but teaching refugees involve a more constrained and monitored environment. Education through generative themes then requires multi-lateral cooperation from the host government, international communities, and implementing partners.

Bangladesh Rural Advancement Committee (BRAC), the world's largest NGO, helps Rohingyas through camp schools. Since knowledge is enhanced for Rohingya children under the Learning Competency Framework and Approach under the Guidelines for Informal Education Programme (GIEP), the NGO scope to look for generative themes, which is a full-scale interdisciplinary ethnographic study of the students' community to understand their beliefs and themes, diminishes or vanishes. These generative themes incorporate usages of charged words by the educator to initiate action for social change. Therefore, through an exchange of dialogue and an understanding of the culture, the educator is to create awareness of the realities of the refugees and entrench them towards self-actualization, an outcome not facilitated by camp culture and constraints.

Calls for "humanization", or what Freire calls a pedagogical approach, carry three axioms: (a) problem posing-dialogue, (b) dialogue-praxis, and (c) praxis-problem posing. Refugees understanding the problem and its empirical realities, and designing action to resolve it can help the most appropriate plan of action through analysis. This process will be continued until that goal is reached. Experience awakens a critical attitude among learners, producing self-actualization. Evidence shows there is no scope for such dialogue and praxis among the infrastructural set-up of the education system to be provided (for the Rohingyas), or already provided (for the Syrians) education system.

Table 10.5 outlines the difference between the Frerian critical pedagogy and Rational Actor Theory.

Refugees hardly get enrolled in secondary education. UNHCR data show only 23% of refugee children attain secondary education against the backdrop of 84% global enrollment, and only 1% of the refugees enroll in higher education against the backdrop of 37% globally. Critical thinking capacities expand with age, and so too the wisdom to utilize it. When a refugee cannot avail higher levels of education, how would one implement such learning? And how would one gain experience of those learnings when one has a restriction for mobility, resident permits, work permits, and so forth. One obvious question suffices to conclude the paper: Does conscientization through education (meant for self-actualization) shed the refugee "tag"?

Table 10.5 Freirean critical pedagogy V. Rational actor theory: comparisons

	Thematic differentiation	Freirean and refugee context	Rational Action and refugee context
1	Generative theme *Vis-à-vis* Supportive environment	• Critical conscience is produced by generative themes and its prerequisite is an ideal environment. In any refugee camp which in its very nature is situated in foreign lands, it is not possible to cater generative theme within the refugee reality • The camp context is controlled	• The Response plans (JRP and 3RP) both cater to create a supportive environment that facilitates basic humanitarian protection and essential services (Tables 10.3 and 10.4) for the Syrian and Rohingya refugees • Hence the rational choice making is done within the options provided
2	Critical conscience *Vis-à-vis* Resilience	• Critical conscience is a luxury for those who have citizenship, identity, language, and hence civil rights • Refugee realities do not adhere to their self-actualize when they cannot meet their basic needs: food, shelter, and so forth	• The landless/displaced people are already traumatized and are enveloped in the grief of their loss. Hence, they require developing resiliencies first • For critical conscience to develop, resilience and adaptation are prerequisite

Thematic differentiation	Freirean and refugee context	Rational Action and refugee context
3 Tripartite model *Vis-a-vis* Socio-ecological model	• The axiom of critical pedagogy is: (a) problem posing-dialogue, (b) dialogue-praxis and; (c) praxis-problem posing • When refugees do not adhere to the environment that will facilitate practicing through the tripartite model of critical thinking, the axiom is inefficacious	• Since the humanitarian response is a complete human rights-based approach, the circumstances of refugees adhere to best practices only • Therefore, rational choice-making by the individuals, community, organization, and policymaking ensures best practices through a socio-ecological model
4 Macro level *Vis-a-vis* Micro level	• Refugees are not in a situation to bring about their own social stability and change	• Small-scale interactions between and within community enables social changes • Socialization through resilience helps in the penetration of values and norms, leading to trust and confidence between refugees and the host communities
5 Teachers as co-researcher and developer of knowledge *Vis-a-vis* Teachers as trained personnel to promote needs-based approach	• In a refugee's camp—Who is the teacher? The teacher's training is a top-down approach in the refugee camps hence no scope for developing knowledge in the class	• Teachers are trained to ensure best practices and make students aware of their needs and how those could be achieved through best practices available from few options in the camp

(continued)

Table 10.5 (continued)

Thematic differentiation	Freirean and refugee context	Rational Action and refugee context
6 Revolutionary *Vis-a-vis* Functional and evolutionary	• It is likely not possible for refugees to bring about fundamental changes in their situation as they are controlled and observed and are subject to global governance • Deprivation may affect revolution but not necessarily initiate conscientization process to bring about social changes and break free of their situations	• The Syrian case is a good example of how the scale-up approach is helping refugees integrate to the mainstream, if not completely into education sector. This is a functional approach and any humanitarian endeavour is both functional and evolutionary in its nature • The JRP plan 2020 states a similar approach of scaling-up services; however, the evolutionary approaches are towards the repatriation of the Rohingyas

CONCLUSIONS

There is no end to the discussion of refugee emancipation, yet the answer to the above question is a big "No". How many of the refugees have regained their status as a citizen of the world. Yusra Mardini is just one in thousands of the refugees to find the liberation through her swimming skills. Restrictions imposed on the refugees are themselves the biggest obstacles for their emancipation; yet, though education is important, it remains a trifling issue to those who need such basics as food, sleep, shelter, clothing, health; psychological support and love in the form of acceptance, social interaction intimacy; security in the form of employment and education, only when they can develop self-esteem in the form of human dignity, self-confidence, and being respected by others; and finally achieve self-actualization, will they become critical thinkers. Yet will that remove their refugee "tag"?

Education: Revolution or Rational Choice Making? Education itself is a "brick in the wall" for the refugees. An overview of education access shows how the Rohingya case differs from the Syrians. The latter meet opportunities, but availing those, become subject to rational choice-making, choosing from the given options loaded with other priorities. The former, encounters no educational opportunities, up until now, and when the opportunities do take shape, only a handful are allowed to enjoy education, though on a pilot basis. Therefore, social cohesion and trust-building are a priority between the refugees and the host communities.

The underlying factors or dimensions, social, economic, cultural, and legal that impact access to education are being revised in the respective JRP or 2RP regional plans, so that education may be prioritized. For Syrians, social cohesion through events with host community is a routine activity, more so because the Syrians live outside the camps and have access to job market and education. Rohingyas, alternatively, remain confined to one area. Therefore, systematic acculturation does not occur, with Rohingyas identified as outsiders, though under a precarious peaceful co-existence mindset. For all the past years, Rohingyas had no access to education and were not allowed to integrate into public schools or hold a work permit. Politically, the idle Rohingyan or Syrian youth or adolescent refugee may relapse into frustration and anger, thus more prone to becoming radicalized. The proximity of the Syrians to the ISIS (Islamic State of Iraq and Syria) concept and the Rohingyas to drug trafficking, or even ARSA (Arakan Rohingya Salvation Army) fighters, opens opportunities for explosions of sorts. It is not *deprivation* affecting revolution, but neither will conscientization bring about social changes and breaking free from their situations begin. Thus, there may be possibilities that the sociopsychological aspect of revolution is likely to play out, if at all, but not a revolution through critical conscientization.

Critical conscience is a luxury for those who have citizenship, identity, language, and hence civil rights. Refugee realities do not adhere to raising their critical conscience when they cannot meet their basic needs: food, shelter, and so forth. The landless and displaced people are already traumatized and enveloped in the grief of their loss. Hence, they require developing resiliencies first. For critical conscience to develop, resilience and adaptation are prerequisites. Since refugees are not in a situation to bring about their own social stability and change, small-scale interactions between communities and within each community enable social changes and socialization through resilience. This helps in the penetration of values and norms, leading to trust and confidence between the refugees and the host communities. The Syrian case is a good example of how the scale-up approach is helping the refugees integrate to the mainstream, if not completely into the education sector. Consequently, JRP 2020 states a similar approach of scaling-up services; however, efforts to repatriate Rohingyas invert the scale-up approach. "Liberatory" education lacks a generic space, making "education" only a subject of rational choice-making by the oppressed.

Notes

1. Donaldo Macedo, "Introduction to the Anniversary Edition," *Pedagogy of the Oppressed*, ed. Paulo Freire (New York: The Continuum International Publishing Group Inc., 2005).
2. Paulo Freire, "*Pedagogy of the Oppressed*," Thirtieth Anniversary Edition (New York: The Continuum International Publishing Group Inc., 2000).
3. Criostoir MacCionnaith, "Paolo Friers's 'Pedagogy of the Oppressed': A Personal Review," Academia.edu. n.d., https://www.academia.edu/17064856/Paulo_Freire_s_Pedagogy_of_the_Oppressed_A_Personal_Review, accessed May 6, 2020.

4. P. H. Pearse, "A Murder Machine," *Connoly Youth Movement*, 1916.
5. UNHCR, "Stepping Up: Refugee Education in Crisis," 2019, https://www.unhcr.org/steppingup/wp-content/uploads/sites/76/2019/09/Education-Report-2019-Final-web-9.pdf, accessed May 7, 2020.
6. UNESCO, "Regional Education Response Strategy for the Syria Crisis," 2016–17, https://unesdoc.unesco.org/ark:/48223/pf0000244333, accessed May 4, 2020.
7. JRP—For the Rohingya Humanitarian Crisis, March–December 2018, https://reliefweb.int/sites/reliefweb.int/files/resources/JRP%20for%20Rohingya%20Humanitarian%20Crisis%20-%20FOR%20DISTRIBUTION.PDF, accessed May 10, 2020.
8. 3RP. n.d., http://www.3rpsyriacrisis.org/, accessed May 5, 2020.
9. Criostoir MacCionnaith, n.d.
10. Sorwar Alam and Md. Kamruzzaman, "The Rohingya and Their Fight for Education," February 24, 2020, https://www.aa.com.tr/en/asia-pacific/the-rohingya-and-their-fight-for-education/1743113, accessed May 1, 2020.
11. Human Rights Watch, "'Are We Not Humans?' Denial of Education for Rohingya Refugee Children in Bangladesh," December 3, 2019, https://www.hrw.org/report/2019/12/03/are-we-not-human/denial-education-rohingya-refugee-children-bangladesh, accessed August 7, 2020.
12. Kaamil Ahmed, "Bangladesh Grants Rohingya Refugee Children Access to Education," *The Guardian*, January 29, 2020, https://www.theguardian.com/global-development/2020/jan/29/bangladesh-grants-rohingya-refugee-children-access-to-education, accessed May 2, 2020).
13. JRP, January–December 2020, https://reliefweb.int/files/resources/jrp_2020_final_in-design_280220.2mb_0.pdf, accessed May 1, 2020.
14. 3RP, *Regional Strategic Overview*, 2020–21, https://data2.unhcr.org/en/documents/download/73116, accessed May 2, 2020.
15. Ibid.
16. United Nations Office for the Coordination of Humanitarian Affairs (OCHA), March 2016, http://www.unocha.org/syria, accessed May 17, 2020.

17. UNICEF, "At A Glance: Syrian Arab Republi," 2018, https://www.unicef.org/emergencies/syria_102805.html, accessed May 1, 2020.
18. UNICEF, "Syria Crisis Fact Sheet. August 2019," https://www.unicef.org/mena/reports/syria-crisis-fast-facts, accessed May 5, 2020.
19. Ibid.
20. 3RP, "Sector Funding," April 2020, http://www.3rpsyriacrisis.org, accessed May 21, 2020.
21. UNICEF, "Syria Crisis Fact Sheet," August 2019, https://www.unicef.org/mena/reports/syria-crisis-fast-facts, accessed May 5, 2020.
22. Ibid.
23. Syrian Regional Refugee Response: Egypt, 2020, https://data2.unhcr.org/en/situations/syria/location/1, accessed May 7, 2020.
24. UNHCR, "Egypt Factsheet," July 2019, https://reliefweb.int/sites/reliefweb.int/files/resources/2019-07_UNHCR-Egypt_Fact-Sheet_July_2019_FINAL-1.pdf, accessed April 30, 2020.
25. Syrian Regional Refugee Response: Egypt, 2020, https://data2.unhcr.org/en/situations/syria/location/1, accessed May 7, 2020.
26. Ibid.
27. UNESCO, "Regional Education Response Strategy for the Syria Crisis," 2016–17.
28. 3RP, "Regional strategic overview," 2020–21.
29. UNESCO, "Regional Education Response Strategy for the Syria Crisis," 2016–17.
30. UNHCR, "Education Activities for Refugees: Jordan," August 2019. https://reliefweb.int/sites/reliefweb.int/files/resources/70537.pdf, accessed May 8, 2020.
31. UNHCR, " Egypt Factsheet," July 2019, https://reliefweb.int/sites/reliefweb.int/files/resources/2019-07_UNHCR-Egypt_Fact-Sheet_July_2019_FINAL-1.pdf, accessed April 30, 2020.
32. UNICEF, "Syria Crisis Fact Sheet," August 2019.
33. UNHCR, "Zaatari Refugee Camp—Factsheet," January 2020. https://reliefweb.int/report/jordan/zaatari-refugee-camp-factsheet-January-2020, accessed May 3, 2020.
34. Ibid.
35. 3RP, "Regional Strategic Overview," 2020–21.

36. 3RP, "2019: Annual Report," April 2020, http://www.3rpsyr iacrisis.org/wp-content/uploads/2020/05/annual_report.pdf, accessed May 6, 2020.
37. UNHCR, "Lebanon 2020," https://www.unhcr.org/lb/education, accessed on June 7, 2020.
38. UNESCO, *Regional Education Response Strategy for the Syria Crisis*," 2016–17.
39. UNHCR, "Lebanon 2020," https://www.unhcr.org/lb/education, accessed June 7, 2020.
40. Ibid.
41. 3RP, "Regional Strategic Overview," 2020–21.
42. Ibid.
43. UNHCR, "Lebanon 2020".
44. Lisa Khoury, "Special Report: 180,000 Young Syrian Refugees Are Being Forced into Child Labor in Lebanon," July 2017, https://www.vox.com/world/2017/7/24/15991466/syria-refugees-child-labor-lebanon, accessed May 20, 2020.
45. UNHCR, "Turkey Operational Mandate," March 2020, https://www.unhcr.org/tr/wp-content/uploads/sites/14/2020/05/UNHCR-Turkey-Operational-Update-March-2020.pdf, accessed May 6, 2020.
46. 3RP Turkey Chapter, "Outcome Monitoring Report," 2018, https://reliefweb.int/sites/reliefweb.int/files/resources/70022.pdf, accessed May 3, 2020.
47. Omer Karasapan, "Turkey's Syrian Refugees—The Welcome Fades," November 2019, https://www.brookings.edu/blog/future-development/2019/11/25/turkeys-syrian-refugees-the-welcome-fades/, accessed May 10, 2020.
48. Ibid.
49. *3RP Turkey Chapter*, "Outcome Monitoring Report," 2018.
50. International Crisis Group, "Turkey's Syrian Refugees: Defusing Metropolitan Tensions," January 2018, https://www.crisisgroup.org/europe-central-asia/western-europemediterranean/turkey/248-turkeys-syrian-refugees-defusing-metropolitan-tensions, accessed May 11, 2020.
51. Freire, 2000.
52. History of Social Work, 2009, https://historyofsocialwork.org/eng/details.php?cps=23&canon_id=157, accessed May 2, 2020.
53. Criostoir MacCionnaith, n.d.

54. Ibid.
55. History of Social Work, 2009.
56. Liberatory Education, "Education for Freedom or "Critical Education": Libertarian, Liberation, Liberating or 'Libratory' Pedagogy," n.d., https://www.holisticeducator.com/libratorypedagogy.htm, accessed May 3, 2020.
57. Freire, 2000.
58. *3RP Turkey Chapter*, "Outcome Monitoring Report," 2018.
59. Ibid.
60. Ibid.
61. JRP. January–December 2020. https://reliefweb.int/sites/reliefweb.int/files/resources/jrp_2020_final_in-design_280220.2mb_0.pdf, accessed May 1, 2020.
62. Ibid.
63. Ibid.
64. Ibid.
65. Ellen Joanne Millard, "The Investigation of Generative Themes in ESL Needs Assessment," 1986, https://open.library.ubc.ca/media/download/pdf/831/1.0078361/2, accessed April 27, 2020.
66. Freire, 2000.

Bibliography

3RP. n.d. http://www.3rpsyriacrisis.org/. Accessed on May 5, 2020.

———. 2020. 2019: Annual Report. April 2020. http://www.3rpsyriacrisis.org/wp-content/uploads/2020/05/annual_report.pdf. Accessed on May 6, 2020.

———. 2020–21. *Regional Strategic Overview.* https://data2.unhcr.org/en/documents/download/73116. Accessed on May 2, 2020.

———. 2020. *Sector Funding.* April 27, 2020. http://www.3rpsyriacrisis.org/. Accessed on May 21, 2020.

3RP Turkey Chapter. 2018. *Outcome Monitoring Report.* https://reliefweb.int/sites/reliefweb.int/files/resources/70022.pdf. Accessed on May 3, 2020.

Ahmed, Kaamil. 2020. "Bangladesh Grants Rohingya Refugee Children Access to Education." *The Guardian.* Januray 29. https://www.theguardian.com/global-development/2020/jan/29/bangladesh-grants-rohingya-refugee-children-access-to-education. Accessed on May 2, 2020.

Arche-Nova. n.d. *LEBANON: Syrian Refugee Children Receive the Basic Right to Education in Lebanon.* https://arche-nova.org/en/project/syrian-refugee-children-receive-basic-right-education-lebanon. Accessed on May 3, 2020.
Freire, Paulo. 2000. *Pedagogy of the Opressed.* Thirtieth Anniversary Edition. New York: The Continuum International Publishing Group Inc.
History of Social Work. 2009. https://historyofsocialwork.org/eng/details.php?cps=23&canon_id=157. Accessed on May 2, 2020.
Human Rights Watch. 2019. *"Are We Not Humans?" Denial of Education for Rohingya Refugee Children in Bangladesh.* December 3. https://www.hrw.org/report/2019/12/03/are-we-not-human/denial-education-rohingya-refugee-children-bangladesh. Accessed on August 7, 2020.
Information, Syria Regional Refugee Response: Inter-Agency. n.d. http://data.unhcr.org/syrianrefugees/regional.php. Accessed on May 17, 2020.
International Crisis Group. 2018. *Turkey's Syrian Refugees: Defusing Metropolitan Tensions.* January 2018. https://www.crisisgroup.org/europe-central-asia/western-europemediterranean/turkey/248-turkeys-syrian-refugees-defusing-metropolitan-tensions. Accessed on May 11, 2020.
JRP. 2018. *JRP—For the Rohingya Humanitarian Crisis.* March–December 2018. https://reliefweb.int/sites/reliefweb.int/files/resources/JRP%20for%20Rohingya%20Humanitarian%20Crisis%20-%20FOR%20DISTRIBUTION.PDF. Accessed on May 10, 2020.
———. January–December 2020. https://reliefweb.int/sites/reliefweb.int/files/resources/jrp_2020_final_in-design_280220.2mb_0.pdf. Accessed on May 1, 2020.
Karasapan, Omer. 2019. *Turkey's Syrian Refugees—The Welcome Fades.* November 2019. https://www.brookings.edu/blog/future-development/2019/11/25/turkeys-syrian-refugees-the-welcome-fades/. Accessed on May 10, 2020.
Khoury, Lisa. 2017. *Special Report: 180,000 Young Syrian Refugees Are Being Forced into Child Labor in Lebanon.* July 26. https://www.vox.com/world/2017/7/24/15991466/syria-refugees-child-labor-lebanon. Accessed on May 20, 2020.
Liberatory Education. n.d. *Education for Freedom or 'Critical Education': Libertarian, Liberation, Liberating or 'Libratory' Pedagogy.* https://www.holisticeducator.com/libratorypedagogy.htm. Accessed on May 3, 2020.
MacCionnaith, Criostoir. n.d. "Paolo Friers's 'Pedagogy of the Oppressed': A Personal Review." *Academia.edu.* https://www.academia.edu/17064856/Paulo_Freire_s_Pedagogy_of_the_Oppressed_A_Personal_Review. Accessed on May 6, 2020.
Macedo, Donaldo. 2005. "Introduction to Teh Anniversary Edition." Paulo Freire, ed., *Pedagogy of the Opressed.* New York: The Continuum International Publishing Group Inc., 11.

Marx, Karl. 1845. *The German Ideology. Part I: Feuerbach. Opposition of the Materialist and Idealist Outlook. B. The Illusion of the Epoch.* Available at: https://www.marxists.org/archive/marx/works/1845/german-ideology/ch01b.htm. Accessed on May 11, 2020.

Millard, Ellen Joanne. 1986. "The Investigation of Generative Themes in ESL Needs Assessment." https://open.library.ubc.ca/media/download/pdf/831/1.0078361/2. Accessed on April 27, 2020.

OCHA. 2016. *United Nations Office for the Coordination of Humanitarian Affairs.* March 2016. http://www.unocha.org/syria. Accessed on May 17, 2020.

Pearse, P.H. 1916. "A Murder Machine." *Connoly Youth Movement.* https://www.cym.ie/documents/themurdermachine.pdf. Accessed on May 6, 2020.

Regoinal Refugee and Resilience Plan (3RP). 2016–17. http://www.3rpsyriacrisis.org/. Accessed on May 14, 2020.

Response, Syrian Regioanl Refugee. n.d. *Situation Analysis of Youth in Lebanon Affected by the Syrian Crisis.* 2014. https://reliefweb.int/report/lebanon/situation-analysis-youth-lebanon-affected-syrian-crisis. Accessed on May 3, 2020.

Sorwar Alam, Md. Kamruzzaman. 2020. *The Rohingya and Their Fight for Education.* February 24. https://www.aa.com.tr/en/asia-pacific/the-rohingya-and-their-fight-for-education/1743113. Accessed on May 1, 2020.

Syrian Refugee Regional Response. portal. http://data.unhcr.org/syrianrefugees/regional.php. Accessed on May 8, 2020.

Syrian Regional Refugee Response: Egypt. 2020. https://data2.unhcr.org/en/situations/syria/location/1. Accessed on May 7, 2020.

UNESCO. 2016–17. *Regional Education Response Strategy for the Syria Crisis.* https://unesdoc.unesco.org/ark:/48223/pf0000244333. Accessed on May 4, 2020.

UNHCR. 2019. *Egypt Factsheet.* July 2019. https://reliefweb.int/sites/reliefweb.int/files/resources/2019-07_UNHCR-Egypt_Fact-Sheet_July_2019_FINAL-1.pdf. Accessed on April 30, 2020.

———. 2019. *Stepping Up: Refugee Education in Crisis.* https://www.unhcr.org/steppingup/wp-content/uploads/sites/76/2019/09/Education-Report-2019-Final-web-9.pdf. Accessed on May 7, 2020.

———. 2020. *Lebanon.* https://www.unhcr.org/lb/education. Accessed on June 7, 2020.

———. 2020. *Turkey Operational Mandate.* March 2020. https://www.unhcr.org/tr/wp-content/uploads/sites/14/2020/05/UNHCR-Turkey-Operational-Update-March-2020.pdf. Accessed on May 6, 2020.

———. 2020. *Zaatari Refugee Camp—Factsheet.* January 2020. https://reliefweb.int/report/jordan/zaatari-refugee-camp-factsheet-january-2020. Accessed on May 3, 2020.

UNHCR: Education Activites for Refugees: Jordan. August 2019. https://relief web.int/sites/reliefweb.int/files/resources/70537.pdf. Accessed on May 8, 2020.

UNHCR Jordan Factsheet: Azraq Refugee Camp. Januray 2020. https://relief web.int/report/jordan/unhcr-jordan-factsheet-azraq-refugee-camp-january-2020Releg. Accessed on May 3, 2020.

UNICEF. 2018. *At A Glance: Syrian Arab Republic.* https://www.unicef.org/emergencies/syria_102805.html. Accessed on May 1, 2020.

UNICEF: Syria Crisis Fact Sheet. August 2019. https://www.unicef.org/mena/reports/syria-crisis-fast-facts. Accessed on May 5, 2020.

CHAPTER 11

Globalization, Localization, and the 1990s: "Liberal" Hour Knocking on Mexico's Door

Imtiaz A. Hussain and Galia Rosemberg

INTRODUCTION: REVISITING "SOVEREIGNTY AT BAY" THESIS?

A popular refrain from the late 1960s, that *state sovereignty was at bay*,[1] revisited the 1990s. The multinational corporation emerged again as the chief threat, with new pressures from regionalization,[2] globalization,[3] and fragmentation.[4] With the *state* of the state under the microscope, how would it deliver domestic demands in an age of increasingly desired

I. A. Hussain (✉)
Global Studies & Governance Department, Independent University, Bangladesh (IUB),
Dhaka, Bangladesh
e-mail: imtiaz.hussain@iub.edu.bd

G. Rosemberg
LDV Research Partners, Mexico City, Mexico

© The Author(s), under exclusive license to Springer Nature Singapore Pte Ltd. 2022
I. A. Hussain (eds.), *Global-Local Tradeoffs, Order-Disorder Consequences*, Global Political Transitions,
https://doi.org/10.1007/978-981-16-9419-6_11

democratization and individualism amid ethnic, racial, or religious polarization? Could *swords* be turned into *plowshares* now that the Cold War was over and the laws of the market dominated?[5] Could the states continue remaining a global island?

Applying old questions to new circumstances merely thickens analytical darkness. With time, tide, events, and developments chipping away many explanatory frameworks (*realism*,[6] *liberalism*,[7] or *idealism*,[8] as well as their offshoots, *neo-realism*,[9] *neo-liberalism*,[10] or *dependency*[11]), James N. Rosenau's theory of turbulence begs attention by at least supplying us the necessary vocabulary[12]: *fragmegration* to capture both integration and fragmentation,[13] *glocalization*, likewise from admixing globalization and localization forces,[14] and *chaord*, from chaos and order.[15] How they helped understand Mexico's 1990s sheds light if a new theory informs us more.

Puzzle

Many have looked upon the 1990s as "the best decade ever,"[16] not only for the spectacular economic performances attained, but also for the unfolding *neo-liberal* economy, itself presuming democracy. What was the "roaring nineties" to Joseph Stiglitz,[17] saw the United States emerge as the springboard of *neo-liberal* philosophy and performances, riding on its longest expansionary spell in the entire twentieth century, from 1991 to 2001 (120 months). What Marina N. Whitman dubbed "America's decade, economically speaking,"[18] boasted an annual gross domestic product (GDP) growth-rate of 3.6% (which it has not as yet managed in the entire twenty-first century); unemployment collapsed to a friction-level 4%, employment grew by 2%, and over 1.7 million jobs were created annually. These meshed with the emergence of 48 new (though not perfect, nor irreversible) democracies: 22 throughout Africa, 10 across Asia, and 16 in Latin America.[19] To conclude these were not correlated may be too blindsighted, but whether it was only post-Cold War euphoria aligning them in the 1990s is a key question. Another is why that alignment did not go deep enough since with one-quarter of the twenty-first century over, relations remain prickly.

Nowhere else was that attention more riveted than on the United States, winner of the 40-year Cold War and proponent of the New World Order in triumph.[20] It contributed, in the 1990s, about 41.6% of the nominal global economic growth, far ahead of Japan's 15.7% and the

European Community's/Union's 14.6%, among the top-three contributors (even in GDP PPP terms, its 19.5% was ahead of the European Union's 19.1% and China's 11.4%, in the top-three).[21] Through the MacSharry Reforms,[22] it helped partly break the Uruguay Round multilateral trade jam (from 1986), with the European Community, so as to fuel the 1994 emergence of the World Trade Organization. It also paradoxically pushed Canada, through the 1986 Shamrock Summit, into a bilateral compact.[23] Whetted, no doubt, by Mexico's proposal to join at the 1990 Davos World Economic Forum Summit,[24] even before that, the 1989 Enterprise for the Americas Initiative (EAI) parley with 33 relatively youthful Latin leaders, the United States would host the first Summit of the Americas, in Miami during December 1994. As this turned into the Free Trade Area of the Americas (FTAA) from 1997, the emergent pattern toward a multilateral outcome was through bilateral pacts creating multilateral "regional" groups. A continent too luckless over regional arrangements in the past, the "Americas" actually outpaced the United States.[25]

Home of the then "perfect dictatorship," Latin America was not only most suitable for both liberalization and democratization, but also too hooked to the United States for the United States not to remain a partner from the outset (North American integration would reverse Mexican trade deficits with the United States for good). It was beginning to exit the "lost decade," the 1980s, with U.S.-led Baker and Brady bailout plans for a string of top-notch countries.[26] Pervasive burdens from costly military regimes,[27] and the incremental failure of import-substitution industrialization (ISI),[28] left no choice but to embrace the liberal Washington Consensus, a non-governmental campaign.[29] At least the transformation of the 1988 Canada-U.S. Free Trade Agreement (CUFTA) into the North American Free Trade Agreement (NAFTA), the December 1994 Summit of the Americas evolving into the Free Trade Area of the Americas (FTAA) from 1997, and the southern initiative of the MERCOSUR ("market of the south"), bloc, from 1989, suggested the 1990s "roar" would continue far beyond the United States and longer into the future, with Central America playing a big part in that transformation.

As agents of externalizing relations, liberalization and democratization can restructure a country's fate and fortune through policy reformation and resource reallocation. For historically introverted Latin America, the pivotal question was if externalization would ease internal problems, both at state and societal levels.

Scholars were alerted to the globalization-localization tension from the 1990s,[30] the puzzle behind this study: was this a wedge or bridge for Mexico? Mexico's highly flouted 15-year NAFTA association was itself premised upon democratization after the 1994 election. Would Mexico join the still-flowing global "third democratic wave"? How would its ISI instincts and substructure handle NAFTA *neo-liberalism*? Similar questions haunt many countries today against "fifth" democratic wave possibilities and a paradoxical populist surge.

Mexico at the Crossroads

If anything, Mexico's 1990s was like Luxembourg's "echternach waltz": three steps forward, two steps backward. After embracing multilateralism in the mid-1980s (as a precondition to receiving bailouts), and, like its northern neighbors, also regional free trade agreements, Mexico found itself crashing head-on with a deepening U.S. dependence, though its trade balance shifted from the negative into positive territory and foreign direct investment spiraled.[31] Internally, democratization began running into resilient traditional practices and structures,[32] and a motley of other features[33]: the 1994 *peso* crisis; an embedded apprehension of its giant northern neighbor,[34] and state legitimacy being challenged violently in Chiapas.[35] How could the state corral an overflowing barrage of demands, threats, and new imperatives?

Our preliminary stab at that larger puzzle dissects just a few slices for a first-cut view. We explore the changing 1990s Mexican political mindset, then turn to NAFTA's dispute settlement obligations to survey its externalizing capacities. State "strength" is measured as successful resistance to pressures, whether from below or abroad. How this measurement is made is explained within each section. We argue, the more state-strength (with the historical "perfect dictatorship" representing the máximum possible), the less its freedom to adjust to changing circumstances.

Internal Changes: Context of 2000 Elections

Trade liberalism spiked democratic demands and domestic threats, paradoxically boosting state empowerment. Old recipients of state resources and social power felt provoked, as new claimants arose. An obviously more burdened state is examined through the role of the media during the newly-instituted presidential *primary* election in 1999, as well as the Chiapas and *Barzón* movements.

Emerging from the Constitution of 1917, modern Mexico was governed by a single party, the *Partido Revolucionario Institucional* (PRI), originally the *Partido Nacional Revolucionario* (PNR), under the decisive initial leadership of Plutarco Elías Calles, Álvaro Obregón, and Lázaro Cárdenas from 1929. Created explicitly to *administer* the country, it bequeathed a top-down approach to governance in which *mass mobilization, political participation*, and *policy legitimacy* became secondary and subsequent tasks. Of course, the primary and immediate purpose was to unite the country. PRI's all-inclusive goal was a "superior synthesis"—of liberalism and conservativism, Christianity and secularity, revolution and reform, traditionalism and modernization, interventionism and laissez-faire. Carlos Fuentes argues how centralizing power made the PRI outfit "a servant of the state virtually indistinguishable from the government."[36] PRI statehood was the outcome.[37]

External developments helped. The depression of the 1930s and World War II gave nationalization and import-substitution pride of place in policymaking. Both admirably fueled the country's progress through what a later generation would call the "take-off stage of economic development."[38] As these strategies yielded diminishing returns by the 1970s, Mexico was not only caught off-guard, but had no viable policy alternative to immediately turn to. Fluctuating oil prices and indebtedness took the country on a roller-coaster ride until Miguel de la Madrid (1982–1988) reluctantly agreed to swallow the bitter pill of liberalization.[39] At first with the economy, then politically, Mexico's restructuring continues deep into the twenty-first century: no more is the PRI the symbolic *state extraordinaire*,[40] but nor has the *neo-liberal* nirvana been crossed.[41] Two issues demand attention: the increasingly variegated democratic demands; and the role of the media.

DEMANDS: DEMOCRATIZATION PROCESS

Primaries were first introduced into the 6-year, non-renewable presidency term from 1999.[42] Only the party-in-power went through the necessary motions, using the slogan of a "new PRI for a new millenium:" it alone had the wherewithals and manipulated the instruments. Hypothetically, the primaries loosened state centrality, since every presidential candidate now had to court the *people* rather than be selected by the *incumbent president* (a process called *dedazo*). Adding to the primary election reaffirming PRI controls as the *official party* was a democracy "torch-bearer" PRI claim. This simply reinforced PRI strength and legitimacy before a wider audience, yet to little or no avail.

The strength of the central apparatus showed in the primaries; only the unofficially supported candidate, Francisco Labastida Ochoa, found institutional support. This did not make the election a hoax, but alleged support from President Ernesto Zedillo, and differences in the funding, budget, and disposable resources made Labastida stand over the other three PRI candidates (Manuel Bartlett, Roberto Madrazo, and Humberto Roque). All losing candidates accused Labastida of using "official resources," such as a federal government building for his official campaign house,[43] and assistance from state governors, party leaders, and public officials in Chiapas, Chihuahua, Colima, Michoacan, Oaxaca, Quintana Roo, Sinaloa, and Yucatan.[44] In the final analysis, these did not matter. Evaporating *dedazo* (note how its vibes still lingered), may have strengthened presidential, party, and state-strength generically by exposing each to intra-party, intra-politics, and intra-state differences and diversities, but the costs of a diminished PRI presence would be minimized further through the evolving *neo-liberal* euphoria. Mexico's historically least popular PRI president, Salinas, institutionalized *dedazo* by 1994, but another party and another president, the PAN rival's Vicente Fox Quesada, took home the 2000 laurels. Nothing in the 1999 PRI primaries predicted this see-saw change.

Media Utilization

Nowhere is asymmetrical resource allocation more notable than in the media, our second democratic demand variable. Media's immense role in global twenty-first century politics includes influencing public opinion like no other political resource can, reaching millions regardless of borders, frontiers, or any other barriers, and, whether in the form of a radio, newspaper, television set, or social media dictating any candidate's agenda and relative weight by allocating access.[45] Ultimately influencing electoral outcomes, how presidential candidates handle the media becomes central to organizing their campaign.[46]

"A Nation-State without communication capabilities is a weak State," according to conventional political thinking, but as Enrique Leon

Martinez once insisted, it can also be "permanently subject to political and mercantile pressures of the elites that control the media."[47] Mexico illustrated this. State influenced the media (be it in written form, or through television and radio), epitomized by *Televisa*, Mexico's largest and most important broadcasting network, and a strong PRI supporter, and *Hechos*, a less strident pro-PRI channel (by the time of the 2000 presidential election, *Azteca*, would dilute the PRI-dominated media atmosphere).

In the 1994 presidential election, the PRI candidate received more media time than any other candidate. Tables 11.1 and 11.2 show *air-time* distribution for political parties and presidential candidates in the two main prime-time newscasts, both government influenced, between January and April 1994.

Numbers alone indicate the uneven playing field. Both Luis Donaldo Colosio and Ernesto Zedillo, the 1994 PRI presidential candidates,[48] received more *air time* than PRI/PRD contenders: each opposition

Table 11.1 Political parties: television time allocation

Newscast subject	24 Horas (Televisa)	Channel 13 (Hechos)	Total
PRI	1:24:01 (h:m:s)	2:20:34	3:44:35
PAN	43:56	53:36	1:37:32
PRD	54:58	34:33	1:29:31

Source Miguel Acosta Valverde and Luz Paula Parra, *Los procesos electorales en los medios de comunicación* (México, D.F.: Universidad Iberoamericana, 1994)

Table 11.2 Presidential candidates: television time allocation

Newscast subject	24 Horas (Televisa)	Channel 13 (Hechos)	Total
Luis Donaldo Colosio (PRI)	2:11:54	1:38:18	3:50:12
Ernesto Zedillo (PRI)	1:55:30	1:27:41	3:23:11
Diego Fernández C. (PAN)	58:53	53:32	1:52:25
Cuauhutemoc Cárdenas (PRD)	54:06	54:10	1:48:16

Source Miguel Acosta Valverde and Luz Paula Parra, *Los procesos electorales en los medios de comunicación* (México, D.F.: Universidad Iberoamericana, 1994)

candidate received less time than his PRI counterpart, and even together, the three opposition candidates commanded less than 2 h, the PRI candidate over 4 h on *Televisa*; similarly, *Hechos* time-coverage carried a 3:2 PRI ratio tilt. State both controlled the media and utilized this to further its coverage strength at the expense of other political parties. Even though it vouched giving all candidates the same rights to campaign, the *official* PRI candidate enjoyed a huge comparative advantage, reflecting the historical favoritism. Francisco Labastida continued the tradition of getting greater media access than any of his PRI opponents, as Tables 11.3 and 11.4 show: more than one-third of total air-time was devoted to Labastida, both on television (35.7%) and radio (37.9%), with Madrazo a distant second in both television (26.3%) and radio (27.6%). Television dedicated 5 hours and 46 minutes to Labastida, the radio 35 hours and 52 minutes. Still the three opposition candidates commanded a higher media time-allocation against the official PRI candidate in 1999 than in 1994, but that the chosen one still enjoyed asymmetrical attention continued to reaffirm past practices. Without raising the ante, Mexican politics could no longer continue as usual. This is the net global impact on something as local as an election: how democratic vigilance carries a global check-and-balance flair under both state and non-state referees, whereas voting itself being the most local of practices, must now mend idioysyncratic tendencies to avoid international black-listing. Among the state's

Table 11.3 Television time dedicated to primary election presidential candidate

Candidate	August 16–November 3 1999 (hours:minutes), %
Francisco Labastida	5:46 or 35.7
Roberto Madrazo	4:34 or 26.3
Manuel Bartlett	2:36 or 16.1
Humberto Roque	3:12 or 19.8

Table 11.4 Radio time dedicated to primary election of presidential candidates 1999 (%)

Candidate	August 16–November 3 1999 (%)
Francisco Labastida	37.9
Roberto Madrazo	27.6
Manuel Bartlett	17.6
Humberto Roque	17.0

Table 11.5 Time paid for televisa and channel 13 advertisement by primary election candidates

Candidate	August 16–November 3, 1999 (hours:minutes), %
Francisco Labastida	1:43 or 22.3
Roberto Madrazo	3:26 or 44.7
Manuel Bartlett	2:16 or 29.5
Humberto Roque	0:13 or 3.6

Source Reforma, November 6, 1999, A6. This is Mexico's leading daily newspaper

benefit: fully responding to the democratic demands for greater political liberalization; and strengthening its own capacity to control outcomes. As democratic exercises become more common, the state can only become stronger through corporatist relations with the media amid opposition size-growth.

Table 11.5 reveals asymmetry of a different sort. Although Roberto Madrazo paid more for advertisement on television and radio, Francisco Labastida got more media attention. In fact, Madrazo paid twice as much as Labastida for advertisements, but still received only two-thirds of the total time allocated Labastida.

Our observations resonate well against others in the literature evaluating public *trust* in the electoral process: whereas Mexico's 1990s political liberalization curbed the perceived fraudulent methods of the 1988 elections, new seeds of both doubts and distrust were sown.[49] This tallies with democratic transitions: expressed opposition grows as the legitimate windows of expression increase. For Mexico, in spite of benefiting from an uneven playing field in terms of media access and exposure, the PRI capacity to boost public confidence was not enhanced. The long-term PRI popularity decline and the historically second lowest voter turnout in 1988 left distaste in the air. "Taking on Goliath," an euphemistic PRI-dubbing cliché attributed to Kathleen Bruhn, no longer seemed a threat.[50] If trust in the political process diminishes because of electoral fraud and an uneven playing field, declining legitimacy cannot be far behind (Table 11.6).

Mexico also exemplified how democratic disparities altered the nature of politics. Again, harsh criticism of trade liberalism bred social unrest (the 1995 *Barzón* movement), turmoil, and finally, armed insurrection

Table 11.6 Voting in presidential elections, 1934–1994

Year	Votes for P.R.I.	Votes for P.A.N.	Votes for P.R.D.	Turnout
1934	98.2			53.6
1940	93.9			57.5
1946	77.9			42.6
1952	74.3	7.8		57.9
1958	90.4	9.4		49.4
1964	88.8	11.1		54.1
1970	88.3	13.9		63.9
1976	93.6			59.6
1982	71.0	15.7		66.1
1988	50.7	16.8	31.1	49.4
1994	50.1	26.0	16.8	

Source Merilee S. Grindle, *Challenging the State: Crisis and Innovation in Latin America and Africa* (Cambridge, UK: Cambridge University Press, 1996), 61

(the 1994 Chiapas uprising). Although the shift to free trade fundamentally transformed Mexico's economy immediately, costs were borne largely on Main Street: small businesses and entrepreneurs, the middle class, the indigenous population, and the 40 bypassed millions at the poverty level. At the same time, the rich–poor gap only widened, exacerbating social/class differences. Both the Chiapas uprising and the *Barzón* movement symbolized these unequal consequences, with corporatism their chief institutional villain.[51]

Even with public opinion mobilized, it is truly amazing how so many Mexican citadels fell in the 2000 presidential election. The growing glowing *neo-liberal* component catapulted the conservative, free-market PAN (*Partido Acción Nacional*) outfit above all else, and at the surprising cost of the left-anchored PRD (*Partido Revolucionario Democrático*) counterpart (whose leader Cuauhtemoc Cardenas, son of Mexico's most revered president, Lazaro, in 1934, had just been Mexico City's first elected mayor). Its leader, Vicente Fox, fitted the 1990s tempo: a former head of *Cocoa Cola* in Mexico, he wanted to push the NAFTA marriage into a Mexico-U.S. marriage, so trade and investment flows could be matched by human flows—that, too, at a time of surging Mexican emigration to the United States. His magic of matching the local with the global over human, product, and service flows set him far apart from the relatively stoic Labastida—and five percentage points clear as winner:

42.5%, as opposed to 36.10% for the PRI candidate (while Cardenas mustered 16.6%), with 20 of the 32 provinces in his kitty, as against 11 for Labastida.[52]

Analysts, resoundingly reaffirm media effects: these were not as "massive" as John S. Faller had euphorically predicted at the start of the 1990s,[53] but Chappel Lawson and James A. McCann reported "substantial" media effects from examining the 2000 election.[54] They further observed how the more liberal atmosphere permitted one new television channel, *Televisión Azteca*, to nibble into the monopolistic PRI media control: its net positive coverage of Fox was measured at 46%, for Labastida 36%, and Cardenas 44%, whereas for *Televisa* the corresponding figures were 36, 59, and 42%. Of course, channel biases and the public not necessarily tip-toeing media preferences intervene in actual voting, but at least we get an impression or two of the different Mexican electoral atmosphere and dynamics appearing after the *dedazo* eclipse.

Inserting both the public desires for change, a new found option, and the enormous mindset change of the United States shifting from being the "northern colossus" to an "*amigo*" by virtue of the NAFTA adoption, we can picture how enormous the sea-change. This is what Mexico's "liberal hour" represented: the local and global not only closer to one another than ever before, but also relishing a constant upbeat that could not but permeate public attitudes, mindsets, and perceptions.

Yet, behind these glossy snapshots of cross-border integration by way of elections, there were more sinister developments. Fragmentative dynamics both threatened the state and dangled as a future threat. Two expose what was at stake: the 1994 January Chiapas uprising, and the 1995 *vox populi* reaction through *Barzón*.

CHIAPAS AND THE EZLN UPRISING

On January 1, 1994, the very day of NAFTA implementation, the *Zapatista* army revolted against the government as a result of continued social injustice. Alan M. Rugman, the Canadian scholar of multinational enterprises, identified NAFTA as the explicit product of *globalization*.[55] On the other hand, the Chiapas uprising was a clear case of *localization*. Rosenau's *glocalization* captures the occasion. As the December 1993 Declaration of Selva Lacandona indicated, the segregated peoples of Chiapas were fighting for "work, land, roof, food, health, education, independence, liberty, democracy, justice, and peace." More importantly, the leader of the movement, Subcomandante Marcos, stated that the *Zapatista* movement was "a war against NAFTA, the death certificate of the indigenous people."[56] It also asked for the PRI "dictatorship" to end, and for President Carlos Salinas de Gortari (1988–1994) to resign. Stating democratization as an irreplaceable pre-requisite, the *Zapatistas* proved to be one of Mexico's biggest state threats.

This movement started, not with the NAFTA advent, but many years before. Ever since the 1950s, the Selva Lacandona had been the stage of numerous social movements, but until the uprising of January 1, 1994, remained *in crescendo*. Social differences between a typical Mexican and an indigenous individual were stark.[57] "It is beyond any doubt," asserted Nora Lustig, a scholar of the Mexican economy, "that poverty, lack of political freedom, and discrimination by the local elite (in particular) is at the root of the Chiapas uprising."[58] These were only compounded by Salinas de Gortari's late 1994 land reforms. In a nutshell, Article 27 of the Constitution governing land tenure was modified to allow collective lands, or *ejidos*, be replaced by private property, rekindling the historically discredited *latifundos* pattern,[59] but in contemporary *neo-liberal* outfit.

The military EZLN (*Ejército Zapatista de Liberación Nacional*: Zapatista Army of National Liberation) movement threatened the Mexican state the most. Yet, although the existence of the movement was not a secret, why didn't the state take precautionary steps? Miscalculation partly explains why: the state overlooked EZLN emergence and strength. Long segregating those communities, in particular Chiapas province, the government had forgotten about the subject. NAFTA negotiations may have temporarily blinded the state to the needs of these communities: signing the free trade agreement would be postponed or even threatened altogether, or so the Salinas administration feared, if *guerrilla* presence in Mexico's southeast became known.

Lighting a fire where ashes exist is much easier than lighting a fire on virgin territory. Six years after the initial *shot*, the government could not afford to look at the *Zapatista* forces just as an armed movement. By reducing the situation to a simple military conflict, the state ignored its economic and social undercurrents, and thereby a permanent solution. Although the movement largely petered out, and although certain negotiations have taken place within a controlled dialogue framework, socio-economic imbalances remain stark, unnecessarily stretching state resources and institutional capacities through high troop mobilization and fruitless diplomatic maneuvers. The *Zapatista* uprising seems to be more than the "minor incident in Mexico's history" that President Ernesto Zedillo believed it to be in his February 2000 visit peech in Spain.[60] Still, here we see the strength of local dynamics and mindset: though born of alienation, in this case, aloofness, adding globalizing forces ignites the cauldron.[61]

Metropolitan Uprising, Countryside Discontent: Barzón and the Debt

Similar cries also had metropolitan outlets and countryside echoes. Mexico's *Barzón* rallied citizens, regardless of profession, wishing to renegotiate debts incurred during the 1995 devaluation. Although the individual debt ranged from U.S.$50 to U.S.$500,000, the point of the matter is the sheer inability to pay. An exact number of *Barzón* followers is difficult to discern, but their leaders, Maximiano Barbosa and Juan José Quirino, estimated up to 1 million across the whole country.[62]

The initial *Barzón* members were small, middle-class entrepreneurs blaming surging interest rates. Somehow the movement also became the flagship or shield of Mexican farmers, who were the most affected by the *peso* devaluation, NAFTA implementation, and the loss of communal land.[63] Numerous farmers and agricultural organizations joined the *Barzón* bandwagon, including the Union of Democratic Farmers, the National Farmers Confederation, the National Union of Agricultural Workers, the National Union of Regional Autonomous Farmer Organizations, and many more.

Barzón sought a NAFTA renegotiation, and for farmers to continue receiving state support and subsidies. Farm problems compound urban credit woes. As debt repayments ate a larger share of disposable income and savings diminished, climbing food prices marginalized what seemed to have been in 1994 a durable, even robust, middle class. By simply reaching these groups, the perceived NAFTA benefits not only polarized society, but also wiped out many corporatist support networks.

Civic movements becoming militarized can no longer be taken lightly in Mexico. Public protests and demonstrations have become more and more recurrent, even reaching the point of *barzonistas* taking the streets by horse, car, on foot, and any other means available. More than 1000 people rode horses, for example, from Ciudad Juárez to Mexico City, staging numerous protests in front of the Secretary of the Treasury, the Senate, the House of Representatives and the Internal Revenue Service, in some instances even resorting to violence. José Quirino spoke of two clear-cut steps to strengthening the movement further: divide the movement by sectors, for example, the farmer section, the small entrepreneur section, the hotelkeepers, the restaurant keepers, the dairy workers, and so forth; and more importantly, take to the streets to force the state into negotiations through civil resistance. Restlessness replaced seven decades of stability under various PRI governments.

Since the movement reflects both socio-economic and politico-military tensions, the state faced a dilemma: it could clamp down to restore order, thereby preferring short-term gains at the expense of long-term socio-economic costs; or it could tackle those underlying problems, but in the process loosen its overpowering mechanisms of control. Unfortunately, and especially in an atmosphere charged with liberal and democratic thinking, short-term benefits usually override their long-term counterparts. Ultimately, a return to the stability under a corporatist past might itself prove difficult now that so many unpredictable factors float aimlessly[64]: integration abroad and restlessness within; and obsolescence of stable policy responses and the suddenness of shifting to the individual initiatives democracy depends on. *Fragmegration, glocalization,* and *chaord* have clearly described Mexico's domestic climate since.

Philippe Schmitter's provocative, prescient, and premature query if the twentieth century was still the century of corporatism,[65] seems more pertinent for Mexico in the twenty-first: state corporatism, based as it is on a strong state, was not only a dominant characteristic of twentieth-century Mexican politics, but also arguably critical to the development of the country—economically through import substitution, politically through a single-party system. What the country faces in the twenty-first century are the fruits of that development: higher mass awareness, mobilization, and demand for participation in the political processes; but also the loss of union bargaining power over wages and trade liberalism,[66] and the neglect of the traditionally staunch PRI supporters, the rural sector.[67] To address these, irrespective of external pressures, a more flexible political system and trade-offs with an empowered state demand attention. Yet, even with external pressures entering the playing field, as the next section shows, the outcome does not change much.

EXTERNAL CHANGES: NAFTA, DISPUTE SETTLEMENT ARRANGEMENTS, AND STATE OBLIGATIONS

Over NAFTA commitments, the Mexican state, though more porous than ever, still played a necessary *neo-liberal* role. Initiated from the mid-1980s for a variety of reasons,[68] and institutionalized multi-dimensionally, North American regional efforts reaffirmed one Rosenau observation: that "the paths to governance will lead in many directions, some emerging into sunlit clearings and others descending into dense jungles."[69]

Of several such behavior types, we examine NAFTA's pivotal dispute settlement arrangements. Clearly the core dispute settlement mechanism was the binational panel addressing antidumping and countervailing duties (ADDs and CVDs, respectively). Gilbert R. Winham saw it as being the *linchpin* of the Canadian-U.S. Free Trade Agreement (CUFTA), the NAFTA parent body.[70] Its methods and procedures offer an innovative approach; and by virtue of the sheer number of cases handled since 1989, it stands out. But three other NAFTA arenas of similarly institutionalized economy-related conflicts exist: investment, through Chapter 11; and the environment and labor, both through their side-agreements. Building upon their designs and preliminary outcomes,[71] Tables 11.7 and 11.8 illustrate the rules of the game.

Addressing institutional design, Table 11.7 presents the key provisions (row 1),[72] and dimensions of comparative value (from the second row downwards): the roles of state, societal groups, supranational tendencies, and the relative place of the state (rows 8–11).

Row 2 succinctly captures the central observation. The very institutions mandated by the dispute settlement arrangements convey a case of *splitsville*—one leg of the state rooted in traditional domestic structures, the other merely experimenting, not grounded in, supranational complements. The former represents national administrative agencies, such as SECOFI in Mexico, or the U.S. International Trade Authority of the Department of Commerce or the International Trade Commission in the United States for antidumping and countervailing duties, and the appropriate ministers/secretaries for environmental and labor disputes. Involving inter-governmental liaison of this kind facilitates the supranational pursuit of establishing a binational panel, and in the extreme case, the Extraordinary Challenge Committee (ECC) for trade, and the arbitral

Table 11.7 NAFTA's dispute settlement mechanisms: institutional designs

Parameters	Trade	Investment	Environment	Labor
1. Key provisions	Chapter 19: • Article 1901: scope: only goods, not services • 1902: use of domestic trade relief laws • 1903: review of domestic rulings by partners possible • 1904: appeal to binational panel or ECC • 1905: authority to review domestic legislation	Chapter 11: • Articles 1116, 1117: eligibility to file claims • 1120: supranational sources identify • 1121, 1122: waiver of right to domestic law • 1123–25: constitution of tribunals • 1134: nature of rulings, criteria for invoking Chapter 20	Side Agreement: • Article 22: Consultations when domestic laws are not enforced • 23: Procedures • 24–27: Arbitral panel formation, Roster, panelists • 28: Rules of procedures • 29: Third party participation • 30: Role of experts • 31–34: Report and its Implementation	Side Agreement: • Article 27: Probe failure by any party to enforce ECE report • 28: Procedures • 29: Arbitral panel created • 30: Roster for panel • 31–35: Procedures of panel, selection of panelists • 41: Suspension of benefits
2. Relevant institutions	• National administrative agencies • Binational panel • ECC	• Tribunals	• Council of Ministers • JPAC • Arbitral Panel	• Council of Ministers • ECE • Arbitral Panel
3. Subject of adjudication	• ADD/CVD	• Portfolio & direct foreign investment	• Complaints by public	• ECE Report

Parameters	Trade	Investment	Environment	Labor
4. Types of resolution prescribed	• Binational or ECC panel review	• Direct consultation/negotiation • Arbitration	• Consultation, good offices, conciliation, mediation, recommendations, arbitral panels, mutual solution, monetary penalty, suspension of benefits	• Consultation, good offices, conciliation, mediation, recommendations, arbitral panels, mutual solution, monetary penalty, suspension of benefits
5. Nature of rulings (or determinations)	Binding	Binding	Non-binding, but with penalties	Non-binding, but with penalties
6. Exit option?	Yes: 60-day notice	No	Yes	Yes
7. Sources of legitimacy	• Domestic trade relief laws • Precedents of binational panel rulings	• ICSID Convention (additional facility rules too) • UNCITRAL	• Domestic laws (Mexico's 1971, 1982, 1988) • Consistency with external agreements	• Member country labor laws • Consistency with ILO
8. Role of State	• Critical conduit	• Important conduit	• Critical conduit	• Critical conduit
9. Role of societal actors	• File complaints	• File complaints	• File complaints	• File complaints
10. Role of supra-national rules	• Set rules	• Set rules	• Set rules	• Set rules
	• Arbitrate	• Arbitrate	• Arbitrate	• Arbitrate
11. Relative place of the State	• Critical link in dispute chain	• Important link in dispute chain	• Decisive, determining	• Decisive, determining

panels for environmental and labor disputes.[73] The investment mechanism also involves overlap, but with a more supranational center of gravity of actions and determinations.

From the adjudication subject of each dispute settlement mechanism, shown in the third row, we get a preview of the complicated process and institutional linkages. Since disputes stem from a state policy measure, the number of institutions invoked prior to adjudication varies, from the minimal (investment), to the maximal (all other mechanisms). One reason why is that Chapter 11 of NAFTA obtains its legitimacy from supranational sources, such as the International Convention for the Settlement of Investment Dispute (ICSID) and the U.N. Conference on International Trade Law (UNCITRAL), thus requiring the plaintiff to first waive any recourse to domestic law; yet, all other disputes begin with the application of domestic law as the first step toward internationalizing them.[74] Thus, for example, the arbitral panel to review a labor dispute is created to review an Evaluation Committee of Experts (ECE) report reflecting a stalemate between member countries (that is, any ECE invocation conveys how the Council of Ministers is itself deadlocked over any of a variety of complaints). Triggering these complaints would be a domestic policy action falling short of domestic labor laws, or domestic labor law being inconsistent with ILO conventions. If it is the former, domestic legislations face external review; if the latter, invoking external agreements become a domestic legislation standard. Under both circumstances, the state must adapt and take adjustment responsibilities. Similar processes intertwine state policies with both societal complaints and external reviews under the environmental side-agreement and NAFTA Chapter 19 ADD and CVD tussles. In effect, NAFTA plucks Mexico out of its own corporatist, protectionist cocoon to socialize with external rules, norms, principles, and decision-making procedures.[75] The remaining question (how sovereign rights fare under the circumstances?) exposes an "external obligation"—"internal legislation" overlap pressuring a much-needed state.

Regardless of the number of intervening institutions prior to adjudication, all four dispute settlement mechanisms encourage a variety of resolutions. These escalate in the degree of formality and stakes, from consultations, which involve minimal formalcy, to arbitration, the most formal. The fourth row illustrates the many options available, while the fifth underscores the importance of a solution: escalation is possible from the informal confines, such as from a failed consultation, to the formal confines, such as a binational or arbitration panel. Non-compliance leads to monetary penalties or a benefit suspension under the side-agreements, and ADD/CVD consequences. Only under trade is there an exit option: the state can withdraw from NAFTA membership. To do so, hypothetically, opens up a number of questions as to the capacity of the state to adjust to the not insubstantial pressures of regional integration or globalization, the worst-case outcome from which is greater isolation and enhanced turmoil. For the environmental and labor mechanisms, no such exit option formally exists, since both were *side* agreements for NAFTA facilitation rather than prioritized procedures. Yet, both elevated negotiations: private settlements get encouraged, but the state remained central to the entire process regardless.

Already alluded to, only the investment dispute settlement mechanism escaped domestic adjudication legitimacy. By virtue of NAFTA membership, all dispute settlement mechanisms rely on regional-level sources of legitimacy, in many cases multilateral-level too, for example, the ICSID or UNCITRAL platforms for investment, binational panel precedents or consistency with WTO provisions for trade, the ILO counterpart for labor, and a variety of bilateral, international, or multilateral environmental principles and/or provisions. With all but investment inextricably linked to domestic sources, the roles of state, societal actors, and supranational tendencies also differed.

With the state as a central player, how autonomous it was from societal groups and external rules remained a question mark. Eric Nordlinger makes the case for state autonomy,[76] implying its unambiguous stand against external pressures. Yet, Peter Katzenstein and others show how democracy weakens states in their ability to formulate and implement coherent policies precisely because of the multiple and competitive influences of domestic societal groups,[77] leaving them more space to function in vis-a-vis foreign interests, especially economic. In terms of the four NAFTA dispute settlement mechanisms, we already see the pitfalls of a stereotypical state: its investment dispute behavior differs from ADD, CVD, labor, and environmental dispute responses.

In the post-Cold War era, we argue, there were many clusters of state responses as there were policies. Further, since several types of disputes directly involve societal groups, in fact originated from their preferences being threatened, we do not find the state to be as autonomous as Nordlinger would have us believe, nor as ambiguous over foreign policy responses as Katzenstein's weak states thesis suggests. True to the dictates of democracy, we find the state constantly interacting with societal groups, and not always in a deterministic, dominant capacity: not doing so erodes the essence of economic liberalization, which promoted Mexico's actual NAFTA proposal. We also find the state committed to its external obligations, whether domestically popular or not, and whether the state endeavored to defect from them or not in the process. With the opportunity costs of democratization and liberalization sufficiently high, state fully regressing into its own nationalistic cocoon, and specifically for Mexico, returning to its corporatist and protectionist webs again, may be too steep a mountain to climb.

Societal actors were among the biggest post-Cold War beneficiaries, as the outburst of several non-military issues to the forefront indicated. Indeed, the consolidation and proliferation of dispute settlement mechanisms exemplified this—and responses to the burgeoning societal demands. If the NAFTA passage in the U.S. Congress depended upon the adoption of the two side-agreements, then the proverbial can of worms was opened: myriad issues related directly or indirectly to trade and investment entered the dispute equation, as the *Metalclad* waste disposal project in San Luis Potosi, or the fate of migratory birds from Canada, indicated. This potentially spiraling function of associating environmental and labor issues to a trade agreement is likely to burden all three NAFTA members, with Mexico bearing the brunt: since Mexico's more relaxed approach to environmental protection and lower wages sparked the demand for the two side-agreements, the Mexican state faced more pressures from both domestic and transnational groups, placing a true test on the maturity of its political institutions.[78] As previously noted, as those institutions attenuated considerably, local societal demands outpaced the supply of adequate policies, constraining the full range of expected regional integration benefits, economic liberalization, democratization, and ultimately externalization.

Like societal pressures, supranational influences upon the Mexican state also represented an increasing function. It cannot be otherwise for a country largely insulated from external economic developments for most of the twentieth century and caught irretrievably within the gravitational pull of the U.S. economy for all of it. From that perspective, mixed NAFTA consequences awaited Mexico: if it is in fact a temporary arrangement in true GATT Article XXIV spirit, Mexico's benefit would be to liberalize its economy, thereby completing the pre-requisite of diversifying partners elsewhere; but if in turn liberalization deepens dependency on the United States, as was the unraveling NAFTA story, Mexican exposure and vulnerability only grow.

Finally, the relative place of the state against these societal and supranational forces makes the Mexican state a central dispute settlement player, but whether in that capacity it maximizes opportunities or vulnerabilities is the more interesting, perhaps critical, question to ponder. If it is the latter, there will always be the reassurance that the Mexican state is not alone in succumbing to those pressures: not only will a large number of economically weaker countries go the same way, probably faster, but the reverberations of a sinking economy might also pull the relatively stronger economies with them, at least to some degree. If it is the former, societal and supranational pressures will at least have been tamed, albeit at a cost: regional integrative efforts would automatically slow, delaying adjustment to liberalization, globalization, and democratization in the process. Any U.S. NAFTA withdrawal beckons similar consequences, only with greater costs. Whichever way, the dispute settlement mechanisms already released the bug that afflicted the continued strength and viability of the Mexican state.

Table 11.8 confirms how the state becomes part of an entire chain of events beginning with a complaint against a policy inconsistency or lapse, to its final resolution.[79] For both side-agreements, the disputes were restricted only to the state not fulfilling its own laws, but several domestic labor and environmental legislations, certainly in Canada, Mexico, and the United States, merely fulfilled obligations of external agreements. State policies thus were not islands of sovereign rights, even though hitherto they were.

It is not mysterious why antidumping, countervailing, environmental, and labor dispute settlement arrangements involved more disputes than investment. Investment is more trade-creating and job-creating, whereas all the others impose constraints of sorts: an antidumping or countervailing duty diverts trade or imbalances the playing field; and a labor or environmental law not fully implemented adds costs to ongoing trade or imposes a future societal burden. Table 11.9 lists the NAFTA cases periodically filed, and how they were treated by the various dispute settlement mechanisms.[80] From the state-strength view, a number of features stand out.[81]

First, the high degree of private settlement suggests the state, by nipping disputes in their bud, performed a very useful task, and in the process directly engaged with societal actors filing the complaints and

Table 11.8 Process of NAFTA dispute settlement mechanisms

Trade	Investment
Preliminary duty determination: administrative review of petition by affected group (90–135 days) ▼ Final duty determination: judicial review culminates in duty imposition ▼ Affected party asks for review under Article 1903; private settlement possible ▼ Appeal to binational panel if no prior settlement ▼ Appeal to Extraordinary Challenge Committee to review binational panel ruling (ECC also authorized to review domestic legislation) ▼ Final ruling: compliance, private settlement, or 60-day notice of desire to suspend agreement	Notice of intent to submit a claim to arbitration (90 days before filing claim) ▼ Waiver of the right to domestic law ▼ Submission of claim to arbitration (six months subsequently) ▼ Notice of submission of a claim to other parties (30 days after claim is submitted) ▼ Constitution of a tribunal with 3 members ▼ Final award ▼ Possibility of revision upon request of party ▼ Option to appeal to Chapter 20 of NAFTA ▼ Determination of inconsistency/ Recommendation to comply

Environment	Labor
Submission of complaint to Secretariat or JPAC ▼ Council of Environmental Ministers: If deadlocked, panel created based on two-thirds vote (must convene within 20 days, resolve case within 60 days) ▼ Arbitral panel of 5 from Roster of 45 experts in environmental law (15-day selection limit, 60-day limit for Report) ▼ Panel Report (60–120 days for implementation, failing which panel reconvened after 180 days) ▼ Reconvened Panel Report (60 days limit) ▼ Monetary enforcement ▼ Suspension of benefits	Submission of complaint to Secretariat ▼ Council of Labor Ministers: If deadlocked, panel created based on two-thirds vote (must convene within 20 days, resolve case within 60 days) ▼ Arbitral panel of 5 from Roster of 45 experts in labor law (15-day selection limit, 60-day limit for Report) ▼ Panel Report (60–120 days for implementation, failing which panel reconvened after 180 days) ▼ Reconvened Panel Report (60 days limit) ▼ Monetary enforcement ▼ Suspension of benefits

Table 11.9 Summary of NAFTA disputes

Years	Trade	Investment	Environment	Labor
1989–1993	43:27			
1994	9:8			4:1
1995	10:7	1:1	2:0	1:1
1996	5:2		4:1	2:1
1997	11:0		7:1	3:3
1998	3:0		7:0	5:0
1999			2:0	
Total	81:44	1:1	22:2	15:6

a: b, where a = number of cases filed, b = number of cases accepted for action

shielding the supranational mechanisms from undue pressures. Secondly, in spite of occasional disagreements or frustrations, the state complied with supranational rulings even when they chipped away at state policy preferences. Third, although domestic legislations were not being collectivized across North America, several common procedures and institutions developed roots, suggesting the willingness of the three countries to negotiate sovereign rights in selected policy areas. Finally, the evolving society–state–supranational nexus gave credence to rules, norms, principles, and decision-making procedures befitting post-Cold War democratization, liberalization, and regional integration without abandoning their state-dominant Cold War counterparts.

From Table 11.9 we get the impression of the NAFTA dispute settlement mechanisms fulfilling their stated purposes: generating and adjudicating complaints. Of the 81 antidumping and countervailing complaints filed, only 44 necessitated further binational panel action; and similarly, of the 22 cases of environmental complaints filed, only two reached the Council of Environmental Ministers, while of the 15 labor complaints, only 6 were heard by the Council of Labor Ministers. Several factors explain the shortfall: First, an overexuberance in trying out the various mechanisms, resulting in submitting either incomplete or inappropriate complaints. Second, in some cases, the various secretariats receiving the complaints needed more information to register the cases. Finally, informal methods, such as consultation or conciliation, were usefully intervened.

Of the 44 antidumping and countervailing cases necessitating further binational panel action, 14 were affirmed, 7 were remanded, and 23 involved partial affirmation and partial remand. Interestingly, only 3 went to the Extraordinary Challenge Committee: pork, swine, and lumber, all involving CUFTA cases from 1991, 1992, 1993, respectively. Of the 2 environmental cases heard by the Council, one was against the Canadian government for not protecting fishing rights (1996), the other against the Mexican government's approval of a harbor terminal in Cozumel (1997). Although Mexico challenged the Council of Environmental Commission jurisdiction in evaluating the complaint, the case was dismissed in October after the Factual Report was published. In the same way, out of the 6 cases heard by the Council of Labor Ministers, 5 involved freedom of association and/or right to organize cases, the other gender discrimination. Mexico was the target on 4 occasions, all involving freedom of association and/or right to organize–once by Canada (1998), and thrice by the United States (1994, 1995, 1996). In all cases, joint conferences were prescribed by the Council, involving relevant officials from the disputing parties, which produced mutually satisfactory solutions. No penalties or suspension of benefits were adopted, indicating how Mexico, the most vulnerable NAFTA partner over issues of labor rights, managed to preserve its own sovereign rights, abide with external rules, and adjust to the remedial measures. We note the growth of the domestic audience, and the state fidgeting in its new gatekeeping role.

Such an accommodative late 1990s Mexican state contrasted its steadfast corporatist twentieth century counterpart. State now responded to (a) domestic societal groups from outside of the corporatist framework, as in the instance of the environmental case; (b) foreign societal groups in spite of its nationalistic tendencies, as in the four labor cases; and (c) external panel rulings, as in trade cases, against its northern "colossal" neighbor. Compared to the increasingly intensive 1980s trade skirmishes with the United States,[82] the Mexican state, even amid greater post-1994 trade flows, developed a *modus operandi* with its U.S. counterpart. Highlighting it was a more relaxed treatment of public demands domestically and a willingness to barter some sovereign rights for supranational rules abroad.

Conclusions

We make three empirical observations, and conclude with a theoretical reprise. First, although several political, economic, and societal characteristics of corporatism continue to characterize Mexico in the early twenty-first century, we also find extensive networks of state engagement with other independent actors, both domestic and foreign, to permit a full-fledged corporatist return. In fact, too many linkages existed with autonomous societal actors, arrangements with external actors, and political representativeness for liberalized, democratized, and regionally integrative rules to be reversed. That we did not find ample signs of these policy pursuits attaining fulfillment or maturity prompts a second comment.

Mexico muddling through this transition (or any other) is more likely rather than flowing through fluently, or discovering an efficient or consistent pathway. Political prudence might slow down the speed of that transition rather than stop it. This was already evident in the reciprocal embrace of Labastida and Madrazo, the ideological opponents of the maiden PRI primaries, and in President Zedillo's paradoxical 2000 comments at the World Economic Forum in Davos, Switzerland (unflinching support for the broad principles of globalization, yet explicit postponement of the specific policy of privatizing the electricity sector, as required under the NAFTA phase-out plan).[83] The response was consistent with the emergent pattern of roundabout approaches to and explanations of democratization, liberalization, and regional integration until more policy options become available to the beleaguered state, or until new institutional innovations help compensate the losses of a passing order for the benefits of the new.

Finally, the *critical* agents of change stemmed as much from outside the country as from within. The 2000 PRI presidential loss exposed how critical the need for structural changes in the national economy, politics, or society: this would be less compelling and more costly to fulfill than to continue adjusting only to external demands and pressures. Yet, since regional integration necessitated political liberalization, a mobilized public either awaits the expected economic nirvana, or has given up hope it will ever come. Even though President Zedillo dubbed the 1997 midterm elections a "great democratic fiesta," to the PRI surprise, containing pressures proved the better strategy than resolution after losing its lower house majority for the first time.[84] Mexico's locked-in position amidst these cross-currents constrains policy initiatives or innovations to respond to external stimuli.

Theoretical Reprise

Two theoretical comments detain us: fragmegration in Mexico, and the prospects of generalizing from Mexico's experiences.

Lying at the interface of three flows,[85] *fragmegration* offers a more comprehensible picture of the "organic crisis" befalling Mexico than theories of nationalism, relative power, interdependence, or dependency.[86] The first flow of globalization, based on innovative technologies such as neofordist manufacture,[87] led to Mexico's NAFTA proposal, then as a member, to innovate collective policy-frameworks, such as dispute settlement, to adjust to a new setting. In response, a second flow localized these dynamics, at times accentuating existing discontinuities, as in Chiapas, at other times creating new ones, such as the *Barzón* movement. By fragmenting the domestic milieu, globalization weakened the capacities of the state; but through exposure and involvement abroad, retained a clear, concrete, often critical role for it. In performing this role, the state engaged in a third flow, managing connections between the first and second, for example, facilitating the democratization process to sustain regional integration and appease external scrutinizers, but clearly stipulating its length, breadth, and depth.[88] In the process, subnational and supranational, national and transnational, unilateral and multilateral, as well as cooperative and conflictual actors and behaviors had to pool together.

Corporatism became the sacrificial lamb, suggesting that other countries with similar structural traditions, and simultaneously engaged in implementing a free trade agreement, would undergo identical *fragmegrative* tendencies. Latin America is often seen as the playground of state corporatism,[89] and regional trading partnerships. We suggest a *fragmegrative* future for Argentina, Bolivia, Brazil, Chile, Colombia, Ecuador, Paraguay, and Uruguay, among others, no different in its fundamentals than Mexico's. In that sense, the superior synthesis of bilateral forces Carlos Fuentes observed as being critical to Mexico's development in the twentieth century, is predicated to becoming more trilateral in the twenty-first through exposure to external influences of all sorts–regional, multilateral, business, communications, and so forth. And Latin America is fated to follow.

NOTES

1. Among the earlier works to generate ripples over state irrelevance is Raymond Vernon, *Sovereignty at Bay: The Global Spread of Multinational Corporations* (New York: Basic Books, 1971). He relives the failed forecast in "Sovereignty at Bay: Twenty Years After," *Millennium* 20, no. 1 (1991): 191–195. J. P. Nettl was one to disagree with this threat. See "The State as a Conceptual Variable," *World Politics* 20 (July 1968). Others later elaborated similar themes. See Peter Evans, Dietrich Reuschemeyer, and Theda Skocpol, *Bringing the State Back In* (New York: Cambridge University Press, 1985).
2. A succinct overview in Richard S. Belous and Rebecca S. Hartley, eds., *The Growth of Regional Trading Blocs in the Global Economy* (Washington, DC: National Planning Association, 1990).
3. *Globalization* is an imprecise term, and the random references below highlight the variety of dimensions or meanings. On its meaning, see Charles P. Oman, *Globalization and Regionalization: The Challenge for Developing Countries* (Paris: O.E.C.D., 1994), ch. 1. For a flavor of that variety, see Thomas Risse-Kappen, ed., *Bringing Transnational Relations Back In: Non-State Actors, Domestic Structures and International Institutions* (Cambridge, UK: Cambridge University Press, 1995); Benjamin Barber *Jihad vs. McWorld* (New York: Times Books, 1995); and Martin Libicki, "Rethinking War: The Mouse's Roar," *Foreign Policy*, no. 117 (Winter 1999–2000): 30–43.
4. Without adopting *jargon* from the international relations literature, such as *fragmegration*, historian John L. Gaddis nevertheless presents a contemporary cartography based on simultaneous fragmentation and intergration. See "Toward the Post-Cold War World," *The Future of American Foreign Policy*, ed. Eugene R. Wittkopf (New York: St. Martin's Press, 1994), 16–36.
5. Title of Inis L. Claude's study of international organizations. *Swords Into Plowshares* (New York: Random House, 1964).
6. Among the classic works include E. H. Carr, *The Twenty Years' Crisis, 1919–1939* (London: Macmillan and Company, 1939); and Hans J. Morgenthau, *Politics Among Nations: The Struggle for Power and Peace* (New York: Knopf, 1948).

7. Unlike realism, liberalism is not a singular theory deducible to any specific text or author. It is multifaceted, and has several sources dating many centuries back. See discussions by Michael Doyle, "Liberalism and World Politics," *American Political Science Review* 80 (1986): 1151–1169. One variant of this school is neofunctionalism. See Ernst B. Haas, *The Uniting of Europe: Political, Economical and Social Forces, 1950–1957* (Stanford, CA: Stanford University Press, 1958).
8. Among the many advocates, though with different prescriptions, see David Mitrany, "The Functional Approach to World Organization," *International Affairs* 24 (1948): 350–363.
9. Kenneth N. Waltz, *The Theory of International Politics* (Reading, MA: Addison-Wesley, 1979).
10. Boils down to a study of international institutions or regimes, treating them as having an autonomous presence. See, among others, the collection of articles, both for and against them, edited by Stephen D. Krasner, *International Regimes* (Ithaca, NY: Cornell University Press, 1982).
11. Traced back to Albert O. Hirschman's, *National Power and the Structure of Foreign Trade* (Berkeley, CA: University of California Press, 1945).
12. *Turbulence in World Politics: A Theory of Change and Continuity* (Princeton, NJ: Princeton University Press, 1990).
13. Rosenau, "Fragmegrative Challenges to National Security," *Understanding U.S. Strategy: A Reader*, ed. Terry Heyns (Washington, DC: National Defense University, 1983), 65–82.
14. Term traced back to Dee W. Hock, "Institutions in the Age of Mindcrafting," paper presented at the Bionomics Annual Conference, San Francisco, 1994.
15. From Roland Robertson, "Glocalization: Time-Space and Homogeneity-Heterogeneity," *Global Modernities*, eds. Mike Featherstone, Scott Lash, and Robertson (Thousand Oaks, CA: Sage, 1995), 25–44.
16. Kurt Anderson, "The Best Decade Ever? The 1990s, Obviously," *New York Times*, February 6, 2015, www.nytimes.com/2015/08/opinión/Sunday/the-best-decade-ever-the-1990s-obviously.html, last accessed May 8, 2021.

17. Joseph Stiglitz, "The Roaring Nineties," *The Atlantic*, October 2002, www.theatlantic.com/magazine/srchive/2002/10/the-roaring-nineties/302604/, last accessed May 8, 2021.
18. Marina v. N. Whitman, "American Capitalism and Global Convergence: After the Bubble," Research Seminar in International Economy, Gerald R. Ford School off Public Policy, Discussion Paper, #549, University of Michigan, Lansing, Michigan.
19. Jeffrey Haynes, *Democracy and Political Change in the Third World* (London: Routledge, 2006); and *Democracy in the Developing World* (Cambridge, UK: Polity Press and Blackwell, 2001).
20. On "New World Order", see Will Jannace and Paul Tiffany, "A New World Order: The Rule of Law of Law of Rules?" *Fordham International Law Journal* 42, Issue 5, Article 2 (2019): 1379–1417; and Majid Tehranian, "Where is the New World Order: At the End of History or Clash of CIvilizations?" *The Journal of International Communications* 18, no. 2 (2012). https://doi.org/10.1080/13216597.2012.709926.
21. Contribution to global economic growth, in nominal GDP, 1990–2000: United States: 41.6%, China: 11.4%, India: 5.1%, Japan 15.7%, European Community/Union: 14.6%, and Mexico: 3.7%. In GDP (PPP): United States: 19.5%, European Community/Union: 19.1, China: 11.4%, India 5.1%, Japan: 4.0%, and Mexico: 2.3%.

    Similarly for 1980–1990 in nominal terms: European Community: 29.7%; United States: 27.1%; Japan: 6.3%, Germany: 5.4%. In GDP (PPP) terms: European Community: 24.8%, United States: 22.7%, Japan: 9.9%, China: 5.8%, and West Germany: 5.4%.

    Source: www.wikipedia.org/wiki/List_of_countries_by_GDP_growth_1980-2010, last accessed Mary 8, 2021.
22. See H. Wayne Moyer, "The European Community and the GATT Uruguay Round: Preserving the Common Agricultural Policy at all costs," *World Agriculture and the GATT*, ed. William P. Avery (Boulder, CO: Lynne Rienner, 1993), 95–120; H. Wayne Moyer, "The MacSharry reforms of the CAP: their politics, and their implications for the Maastricht Treaty and the GATT Uruguay Round," Paper, *International Studies Association, Annual Convention* (Acapulco, Mexico, March 1994); and Timothy E. Josling, *Agricultural Policy Reform: Politics and Process in the EC and the USA* (Ames, IO: Iowa State University Press, 1990), 59–60.

23. Gilbert R. Winham, *Trading with Canada: The Canada-U.S. Free Trade Agreement* (New York: Priority Press, 1988); Gilbert R. Winham and Heather Grant. 1994. "Antidumping and Countervailing Duties in Regional Trade Agreements: Canada-U.S. FTA, NAFTA, and Beyond," *Minnesota Journal of Global Trade* 3, no. 1 (Spring 1994): 1–34.
24. Morton Kondracke, "Mexico and the Politics of Free Trade," *The National Interest* 25 (Fall 1991): 36–43.
25. On MERCOSUR, see Hem C. Basnet and Gyan Pradhan, "Resional Economic Integration in Mexico: The role of Real and Financial Sector," *Review of Development Finance* 7, no. 2 (December 2017): 107–119. https://doi.org/10.1016/j/rdf.2017.05.001; and Council of Foreign Relations, Editors, "Mercosur: South America's Fractious Trade Bloc: Backgrounder," December 17, 2021, cfr.org/backgrounder/mercosur-south-americas-fractious-trade-bloc, Last Consulted February 1, 2022.
26. On Baker/Brady plans, see Manuel Monteagudo, "The Debt Problem: The Baker Plan and the Brady Initiative: A Latin American Perspective," *The International Lawyer* 28, no. 1 (Spring 1994): 59–81; and Ian Vasquez, "The Brady Plan and Market-based Solutions to Debt Crises," *CATO Journal* 16, no. 2 (Fall 1996): 233–243.
27. On democratic transitions in Latin America, see Terri Lynn Karl, "Dilemmas of Democratization in Latin America," *Comparative Politics* 23, no. 1 (October 1990): 1–21; and Marcelo Covarozzi, "Beyond transitions to democracy in Latin America," *Journal of Latin American Studies* 24, Issue 3 (October 1992): 665–684, https://doi.org/10.1017/s0022216X00024317, Last Consulted February 1, 2022.
28. On Latin ISI, see Sebastian Edwards, *Crisis and Reform in Latin America: From Despair to Hope* (New York, NY: Oxford University Press, for IBRD, 1995).
29. John Williamson coined the term. See his, "Did the Washington Consensus Fail?" *Presented at Center for Strategic and International Studies*, Washington, DC, November 6, 2002. Available at: http://www.iie.com/publications/papers/paper.cfm?ResearchID=488; and "From Reform Agenda to Damaged Brand

Name: A Short History of the Washington Consensus and Suggestions For What to do Next," *Finance and Development* (September 2003): 10–13.
30. See Rosenau, *Along the Domestic-Foreign Frontier: Exploring Governance in a Turbulent World* (Cambridge, UK: Cambridge University Press, 1997), among others.
31. Guadalupe González and Jorge Chabat, "Mexico's Hemispheric Options in the Post-Cold War Era," *Foreign Policy and Regionalism in the Americas*, eds. Gordon Mace and Jean-Philippe Thérien (Boulder, CO: Lynne Rienner, 1995), 39–52.
32. Peter H. Smith, "Political Dimensions of the Peso Crisis," *Mexico 1994: Anatomy of an Emerging Market Crash*, eds. Sebastian Edwards and Moisés Náim (Washington, DC: Carnegie Endowment for Peace, 1997), 31–53.
33. Denise Dresser, "Falling from the Tight Rope: The Political Economy of the Mexican Crisis," *Mexico 1994*, 55–79.
34. Robert A. Pastor, *Whirlpool: U.S. Foreign Policy Towards Latin America and the Caribbean* (Princeton, NJ: Princeton University Press, 1992).
35. Juan D. Lindau, "Technocrats and Mexico's Political Elite," *Political Science Quarterly* 111, no. 2 (1996): 295–322.
36. *A New Time for Mexico*, trans. Marina Gutman Castañeda and Fuentes (New York: Farrar, Straus and Giroux, 1996), 69, but see 68–85.
37. Roderic Ai Camp, *Politics in Mexico* (New York: Oxford University Press, 1996), chaps. 1, 6.
38. Walt Whitman Rostow, *The Stages of Economic Development: A Non-Communist Manifesto* (Cambridge, UK: Cambridge University Press, 1960).
39. Quick overview by Sidney Weintraub, "Mexico's Foreign Economic Policy: From Admiration to Disappointment," *Changing Structure of Mexico: Political, Social, and Economic Prospects*, ed. Laura Randall (Armonk, NY: M.E. Sharpe, 1996), 43–54.
40. Even the national colors are trademarks of the P.R.I. flag, as other party members often complain!
41. Wayne A. Cornelius, "Mexico: Salinas and the PRI at the Crossroads," *Journal of Democracy* 1, no. 3 (Summer 1990): 61–70.

42. Marios Vargas Llosa, the Peruvian poet, once dubbed the Mexican single-party system "a perfect dictatorship."
43. *Reforma*, November 3, 1999, A6.
44. "Documentado, el uso recurso oficiales en la campaña de Labastida," *Proceso*, October 2, 1999, 9–12.
45. See, for instance, Noam Chomsky *Manufacturing Consent: The Political Economy of the Mass Media* (Barcelona: Crítica, 1988); Marshall McLuhan, *La Aldea Global* (Mexico: Gedisa, 1997); and Giovani Sartori, *Homo Videns* (Madrid: Taurus, 1998).
46. See Sartori, *op cit.;* and John Downing and Ali Mohammadi, *Questioning the Media* (Thousand Oaks, CA: Sage Publications, 1995).
47. Enrique Leon Martinez, *Los medios de comunicación en el proceso político de México* (México: IPN, 1998), 57.
48. Donaldo Colosio was murdered during his campaign in Tijuana, Baja California, during March 1994, and Zedello replaced him.
49. See Andreas Schedler, "Civil Society and Political Elections: A Culture of Distrust?" *Annals of the American Academy of Political and Social Science*, no. 565 (September 1999): 126–141.
50. Kathleen Bruhn, *Taking on Goliath: The Emergence of a New Left Party and the Struggle for Democracy in Mexico* (University Park, PA: Penn State University Press, 1997). Quote from title.
51. Francisco Zapata, "Mexican Labor in a Context of Political and Economic Crisis," *Changing Structure of Mexico*, 127–136.
52. Congressional Research Center, "Mexico's Presidential, Legislative, and Local Elections of July 2, 2000," *CRS Report for Congress*, September 28, 2000, Order Code # RS20611.
53. John S. Zaller, *The Nature and Origins of Public Opinion* (Cambridge, UK: Cambridge University Press, 1992).
54. Chappell Lawson and James A. McCann, "Television News, Mexico's 2000 Elections and Media Effects in Emerging Democracies," *British Journal of Political Science* 35 (2004): 1–30.
55. "North American economic integration and Canadian sovereignty," no further publication information of this mimeograph presently available. But similar themes pervade his other works on the subject. See, for instance, Rugman and Michael Gestrin, "NAFTA's Treatment of Foreign Investment," *Foreign Investment and NAFTA*, ed. Rugman (Columbia, SC: University of South Carolina Press, 1994), 47–79.

56. Primer Comunicado del Subcomandante Marcos, *EZLN, Documentos y Comunicados* (Mexico: Ediciones Era, 1994), 35.
57. Appendix 1 lists such groups.
58. "The 1982 Debt Crisis, Chiapas, NAFTA, and Mexico's Poor," *Changing Structure of Mexico*, 164, but see 157–165.
59. Neil Harvey, "The Reshaping of Agrarian Policy in Mexico," ibid., 106–107.
60. "Zedello Catches Flak for Dismissing Zapatistas," *The News*, February 3, 2000, 2. This is a Mexico City English daily.
61. A similar conclusion is drawn, among others, by José L. García-Aguilar, "The Autonomy and Democracy of Indigenous Peoples in Canada and Mexico," *Annals of the American Academy of Political and Social Sciences*, no. 565 (September 1999): 82–87.
62. Guillermo Correa and Ismael Bojorquez, "La cabalgata contra el olvido," *Proceso*, November 21, 1999, 15.
63. Denise Dresser, *Neopolitical Solutions to Neoliberal Problems: Mexico's National Solidarity Program* (La Jolla, CA: Center for U.S.-Mexico Studies, University of California, San Diego, 1991).
64. Robert E. Blum does not agree. Believing Mexico has not experienced any radical breaks for 400 years, he traces revolutions to periods of economic growth during which institutions adapt. See "The Weight of the Past," *Journal of Democracy* 8, no. 4 (October 1997): 29–30, but also 28–42.
65. Philippe C. Schmitter, "Still the Century of Corporatism?" *The Review of Politics* 36, no. 1 (January 1977): 85–131.
66. Fascinating recent study by Katrina Burgess shows this in "Loyalty Dilemma and Market Reform: Party-Union Alliances Under Stress in Mexico, Spain, and Venezuela," *World Politics* 52, no. 1 (October 1999): 105–134.
67. Merilee S. Grindle, *Challenging the State: Crisis and Innovation in Latin America and Africa* (Cambridge, UK: Cambridge University Press, 1996), 59–61, but see 50–61.
68. From a bulging, broader literature, see Andrew Cooper, "Overcoming Ambivalence: Canada as a Nation of the Americas," Paper presented at the International Studies Association annual convention, Chicago, February 1995; Louis Bélanger, "U.S. Foreign Policy and the Regionalist Option in the Americas," *The Americas in Transition: The Contours of Regionalism*, eds. Gordon Mace, Bélanger, et al. (Boulder, CO: Lynne Rienner, 1999), 95–110; and

Frederick W. Meyer, *Interpreting NAFTA: The Science and Art of Political Analysis* (New York: Columbia University Press, 1998), 31–50.

69. From *Along the Domestic-Foreign Frontier: Exploring Governance in a Turbulent World* (Cambridge, UK: Cambridge University Press, 1997), 449. Parallel themes also found in Rosenau, *Turbulence in World Politics*.
70. See *Trading with Canada: The Canada-U.S. Free Trade Agreement* (New York: Priority Press, 1988), 35, but see 35–42.
71. On the specific provisions of each, see the original agreements. For analysis, see, among others, Winham and Heather Grant, "Antidumping and Countervailing Duties in Regional Trade Agreements: Canada,-U.S. FTA, NAFTA, and Beyond," *Minnesota Journal of Global Trade* 3, no. 1 (Spring 1994): 1–34; Robert E. Herzstein, "The Labor Cooperation Agreement Among Mexico, Canada and the United States: Its Negotiation and Prospects," *U.S.-Mexico Law Journal* 3 (1995): 121–131; Jorge F. Pérez-López, "The Institutional Framework of the North American Agreement on Labor Cooperation," ibid., 132–147; Joaquin F. Ortero, "The North American Agreement on Labor Cooperation: An Assessment of Its First Year's Implementation," *Columbia Journal of International Law* 33 (1995): 637–662; and Pierre Marc Johnson and André Beaulieu, *The Environment and NAFTA: Understanding and Implementing the New Continental Law* (Washington, DC: Island Press, 1996), Part IV.
72. Obtained from the original agreements.
73. Andrew Moravscik shows that such an arrangement works well in the European Union, although he finds the center of gravity more with the inter-governmental than with the supranational institutions. See "Negotiating the Single European Act: National Interests and Conventional Statecraft in the European Community," *International Organization* 45, no. 1 (Winter 1991): 19–56.
74. Judith Goldstein elaborates the *internationalization* of domestic trade laws. See "International Law and Domestic Institutions: Reconciling North American *unfair* Trade Laws," *International Organization* 50, no. 4 (Autumn 1996): 541–564.
75. These are the standard terms used to define a regime in the literature. See Stephen D. Krasner, "Structural Causes and Regime Consequences," *International Regimes*, chapter 1.

76. Nordlinger, op cit.
77. Various articles in Katzenstein, *Between Power and Plenty* show this.
78. In the case of environmental protection, as Barbara Hogenboom shows, pressure groups sprouted almost overnight, some created by the state, others more independently, some purely domestic in concerns, others transnational. The impact on the state was strong, but the state was itself then (1992–1993) in a robust phase, and could absorb the costs effectively. Since the peso crisis of 1995, however, one does not see the state as much concerned about environmental issues. See *Mexico and the Environmental Debate: The Transnational Politics of Economic Integration* (Utretch, Netherlands: International Books, 1996), 141–250.
79. Asking a different question and utilizing other dimensions of the dispute settlement mechanisms of N.A.F.T.A., Isidro Morales draws similar conclusions. See "NAFTA: The Governance of Economic Openness," *Annals of the American Academy of Political and Social Sciences*, no. 565 (September 1999): 35–65.
80. Cases are tabulated up to the most recent year for which we have information; and this time period also varies, with only environmental cases available upto 1999, trade and labor upto 1998, and investment upto 1995. We understand a handful of other investment cases have been filed, but at present we do not have their details.
81. Several other studies discuss the cases in greater details, and we refer the readers to them. For instance, see the selection of articles in Beatriz Leycegui, William P. Robson, and S. Dahlia Stein, *Trading Punches: Trade Remedy Law and Disputes Under NAFTA* (Washington, DC: National Planning Association, 1995).
82. Ably shown by Jorge Miranda, "An Economic Analysis of Mexico's Use of Trade Remedy Laws from 1987 to 1995," *Trading Punches*, 137–160.
83. "Zedello: NGOs Cannot Speak for Poor," *The News*, January 31, 2000, 2; and "President Gives Up on Privatization," ibid., 34.
84. From Chappell Lawson, "The Elections of 1997," *Journal of Democracy* 8, no. 4 (October 1997): 13, but see 13–26.
85. Rosenau, *Domestic-Foreign Frontier*, chaps. 3, 6.
86. Stephen Gill uses an appropriate Gramscian term *organic crisis* to describe almost similar circumstances. See "Globalisation, Market

Civilisation, and Disciplinary Neoliberalism," *Millennium* 24, no. 3 (1995): 399–423, esp. 399–402.
87. Robert Kreklewich, "North American Integration and Industrial Relations: Neoconservatism and Neo-Fordism?" *The Political Economy of North American Free Trade*, eds. Ricardo Grinspun and Maxwell Cameron (New York: New York: St. Martin's Press, 1993), 261–270.
88. This is not to say democracy invariably increases trade openness. See Daniel Verdier, "Democratic Convergence and Free Trade," *International Studies Quarterly* 42, no. 1 (March 1998): 1–24.
89. James M. Malloy, *Authoritarianism and Corporatism in Latin America* (Pittsburgh, PA: University of Pittsburgh, 1977); and Ruth B. Collier and David Collier, *Shaping the Political Arena: Critical Junctures, the Labor Movement, and Regime Dynamics* (Princeton, NJ: Princeton University Press, 1991).

Bibliography

Anderson, Kurt. 2015. "The Best Decade Ever? The 1990s, Obviously." *New York Times*, February 6. www.nytimes.com/2015/08/opinión/Sunday/the-best-decade-ever-the-1990s-obviously.html. Last accessed on May 8, 2021.

Barber, Benjamin. 1995. *Jihad vs. McWorld*. New York: Times Books.

Basnet, Hem C., and Gyan Pradhan. 2017. "Resional Economic Integration in Mexico: The role of Real and Financial Sector," *Review of Development Finance* 7, no. 2 (December): 107–119. https://doi.org/10.1016/j/rdf.2017.05.001

Bélanger, Louis. 1999."U.S. Foreign Policy and the Regionalist Option in the Americas." Gordon Mace, Bélanger, et al., eds., *The Americas in Transition: The Contours of Regionalism*. Boulder, CO: Lynne Rienner, 95–110.

Belous, Richard S., and Rebecca S. Hartley. 1990. Eds., *The Growth of Regional Trading Blocs in the Global Economy*. Washington, DC: National Planning Association.

Blum, Robert E. 1997. "The Weight of the Past." *Journal of Democracy* 8, no. 4 (October): 28–42.

Bruhn, Kathleen. 1997. *Taking on Goliath: The Emergence of a New Left Party and the Struggle for Democracy in Mexico*. University Park, PA: Penn State University Press.

Burgess, Katrina. 1999. "Loyalty Dilemma and Market Reform: Party-Union Alliances Under Stress in Mexico, Spain, and Venezuela." *World Politics* 52, no. 1 (October): 105–134.
Camp, Roderic Ai. 1996. *Politics in Mexico*. New York: Oxford University Press.
Claude, Inis L. 1964. *Swords Into Plowshares*. New York: Random House.
Carr, E. H. 1939. *The Twenty Years' Crisis, 1919–1939*. London: Macmillan and Company.
Chomsky, Noam. 1988. *Manufacturing Consent: The Political Economy of the Mass Media*. Barcelona: Crítica.
Collier, Ruth B., and David Collier. 1991. *Shaping the Political Arena: Critical Junctures, the Labor Movement, and Regime Dynamics*. Princeton, NJ: Princeton University Press.
Cooper, Andrew. 1995. "Overcoming Ambivalence: Canada as a Nation of the Americas." Paper presented at the International Studies Association annual convention, Chicago, February.
Cornelius, Wayne A. 1990. "Mexico: Salinas and the PRI at the Crossroads." *Journal of Democracy* 1, no. 3 (Summer): 61–70.
Correa, Guillermo, and Ismael Bojorquez. 1999. "La cabalgata contra el olvido." *Proceso*, November 21, 1999, 15.
Council of Foreign Relations, Editors. 2017, December 17. *Mercosur: South America's Fractious Trade Bloc: Backgrounder*. cfr.org/backgrounder/mercosur-south-americas-fractious-trade-bloc. Last Consulted February 1, 2022.
Covarozzi, Marcelo. 1992. "Beyond Transitions to Democracy in Latin America," *Journal of Latin American Studies* 24, no.3 (October): 665–684, https://doi.org/10.1017/s0022216X00024317. Last Consulted February 1, 2022.
"Documentado, el uso recurso oficiales en la campaña de Labastida." *Proceso*, October 2, 1999, 9–12.
Downing, John, and Ali Mohammadi. 1995. *Questioning the Media*. Thousand Oaks, CA: Sage Publications.
Doyle, Michael. 1986. "Liberalism and World Politics." *American Political Science Review* 80: 1151–1169.
Dresser, Denise. 1991. *Neopolitical Solutions to Neoliberal Problems: Mexico's National Solidarity Program*. La Jolla, CA: Center for U.S.-Mexico Studies, University of California, San Diego.
———. 1994. "Falling from the Tight Rope: The Political Economy of the Mexican Crisis." In *Mexico 1994*, 55–79.
Edwards, Sebastian. 1995. *Crisis and Reform in Latin America: From Despair to Hope*. New York, NY: Oxford University Press, for IBRD.
Evans, Peter, Dietrich Reuschemeyer, and Theda Skocpol. 1985. *Bringing the State Back In*. New York: Cambridge University Press.

Fuentes, Carlos. 1996. *A New Time for Mexico*. Trans., Marina Gutman Castañeda and Fuentes. New York: Farrar, Straus and Giroux.

Gaddis, John L. 1994. "Toward the Post-Cold War World." *The Future of American Foreign Policy*, ed., Eugene R. Wittkopf. New York: St. Martin's Press, 16–36.

García-Aguilar, José L. 1999. "The Autonomy and Democracy of Indigenous Peoples in Canada and Mexico." *Annals of the American Academy of Political and Social Sciences*, no. 565 (September): 82–87

Gill, Stephen. 1995. "Globalisation, Market Civilisation, and Disciplinary Neoliberalism." *Millennium* 24, no. 3: 399–423, esp. 399–402.

Goldstein, Judith. 1995. "International Law and Domestic Institutions: Reconciling North American *Unfair* Trade Laws." *International Organization* 50, no. 4 (Autumn): 541–564.

González, Guadalupe, and Jorge Chabat. 1995. "Mexico's Hemispheric Options in the Post-Cold War Era." Gordon Mace and Jean-Philippe Thérien, eds., *Foreign Policy and Regionalism in the Americas*. Boulder, CO: Lynne Rienner, 39–52.

Grindle, Merilee S. 1996. *Challenging the State: Crisis and Innovation in Latin America and Africa*. Cambridge, UK: Cambridge University Press.

Haas, Ernst B. 1958. *The Uniting of Europe: Political, Economical and Social Forces, 1950-1957*. Stanford, CA: Stanford University Press.

Harvey, Neil. "The Reshaping of Agrarian Policy in Mexico." *Changing Structure of Mexico*, 106–107.

Haynes, Jeffrey. 2001. *Democracy in the Developing World: Africa, Asia, Latin America, and the Middle East*. Cambridge, UK: Polity Press and Blackwell.

———. 2006. *Democracy and Political Change in the Third World*. London: Routledge.

Herzstein, Robert E. 1995. "The Labor Cooperation Agreement Among Mexico, Canada and the United States: Its Negotiation and Prospects." *U.S.-Mexico Law Journal* 3: 121–131.

Hirschman, Albert O. 1945. *National Power and the Structure of Foreign Trade*. Berkeley, CA: University of California Press.

Hock, Dee W. 1994. "Institutions in the Age of Mindcrafting." Paper presented at the Bionomics Annual Conference. San Francisco.

Hogenboom, Barbara. 1996. *Mexico and the Environmental Debate: The Transnational Politics of Economic Integration*. Utretch, Netherlands: International Books.

Johnson, Pierre Marc, and André Beaulieu. 1996. *The Environment and NAFTA: Understanding and Implementing the New Continental Law*. Washington, DC: Island Press, 1996.

Jannace, Will, and Paul Tiffany. 2019. "A New World Order: The Rule of Law of Law of Rules?" *Fordham International Law Journal* 42, no. 5, Article 2: 1379–1417.
Josling, Timothy E. 1990. *Agricultural Policy Reform: Politics and Process in the EC and the USA*. Ames, IO: Iowa State University Press. 59–60
Katzenstein, Peter. 1978. Ed., *Power and Plenty: Foreign Economic Policies of Advanced Industrialized States*. Madison, WI: University of Wisconsin Press.
Karl, Terri Lynn. 1990. "Dilemmas of Democratization in Latin America," *Comparative Politics* 23, no. 1 (October): 1–21.
Krasner, Stephen D. "Structural Causes and Regime Consequences." *International Regimes*. Ithaca, NY: Cornell University Press, chapter 1.
———. 1982. *International Regimes*. Ithaca, NY: Cornell University Press.
Kreklewich, Robert. 1993. "North American Integration and Industrial Relations: Neo-Conservatism and Neo-Fordism?" Ricardo Grinspun and Maxwell Cameron, eds., *The Political Economy of North American Free Trade*. New York: New York: St. Martin's Press, 261–270.
Lawson, Chappell. 1997. "The Elections of 1997." *Journal of Democracy* 8, no. 4 (October): 13–26.
Leycegui, Beatriz, William P. Robson, and S. Dahlia Stein. 1995. *Trading Punches: Trade Remedy Law and Disputes Under NAFTA*. Washington, DC: National Planning Association.
Libicki, Martin. 1999–2000. "Rethinking War: The Mouse's Roar." *Foreign Policy*, no. 117 (Winter): 30–43.
Lindau, Juan D. 1996. "Technocrats and Mexico's Political Elite." *Political Science Quarterly* 111, no. 2: 295–322.
Lustig, Nora. 1995. "The 1982 Debt Crisis, Chiapas, NAFTA, and Mexico's Poor." *Challenge* 38, no. 2 (March–April): 45–50.
Malloy, James M. 1977. *Authoritarianism and Corporatism in Latin America*. Pittsburgh, PA: University of Pittsburgh.
Martinez, Enrique Leon. 1998. *Los medios de comunicación en el proceso político de México*. México: IPN.
Moyer, H. Wayne. 1993. "The European Community and the GATT Uruguay Round: Preserving the Common Agricultural Policy at all costs," William P. Avery ed. *World Agriculture and the GATT*. Boulder, CO: Lynne Rienner, 95–120.
Moyer, H. Wayne. 1994 March. "The MacSharry Reforms of the CAP: Their Politics, and their Implications for the Maastricht Treaty and the GATT Uruguay Round," Paper, *International Studies Association, Annual Convention*. Acapulco, Mexico.
McLuhan, Marshall. 1997. *La Aldea Global/* Mexico: Gedisa.
Meyer, Frederick W. 1998. *Interpreting NAFTA: The Science and Art of Political Analysis*. New York: Columbia University Press.

Miranda, Jorge. 1995. "An Economic Analysis of Mexico's Use of Trade Remedy Laws from 1987 to 1995." B. Leycegui, W. P. B. Robson, and S. Stein. *Trading Punches: Trade Remedy Laws and Disputes Under NAFTA*. Washington, DC: National Planing Associatioon, 137–160.

Mitrany, David. 1948. "The Functional Approach to World Organization." *International Affairs*, no. 24: 350–363.

Morales, Isidro. 1999. "NAFTA: The Governance of Economic Openness." *Annals of the American Academy of Political and Social Sciences*, no. 565 (September): 35–65.

Moravscik, Andrew. 1991. "Negotiating the Single European Act: National Interests and Conventional Statecraft in the European Community." *International Organization* 45, no. 1 (Winter): 19–56.

Morgenthau, Han J. 1948. *Politics Among Nations: The Struggle for Power and Peace*. New York: Knopf.

Monteagudo, Manuel. 1994. "The Debt Problem: The Baker Plan and the Brady Initiative: A Latin American Perspective," *The International Lawyer* 28, no. 1 (Spring): 59–81.

Nettl, J. P. 1968. "The State as a Conceptual Variable." *World Politics* 20, no. 4 (July): 559–592.

Nordlinger, Eric. 1981. *On the Autonomy of the Democratic State*. Cambridge, MA: Harvard University Press.

Oman, Charles P. 1994. *Globalization and Regionalization: The Challenge for Developing Countries*. Paris: O.E.C.D.

Ortero, Joaquin F. 1995. "The North American Agreement on Labor Cooperation: An Assessment of Its First Year's Implementation." *Columbia Journal of International Law* 33: 637–662.

Pastor, Robert A. 1992. *Whirlpool: U.S. Foreign Policy Towards Latin America and the Caribbean*. Princeton, NJ: Princeton University Press.

Pérez-López, Jorge F. 1995. "The Institutional Framework of the North American Agreement on Labor Cooperation." *U.S.-Mexico Law Journal* 3: 132–147.

"President Gives Up on Privatization." *The News*. January 31, 2000 34.

Primer Comunicado del Subcomandante Marcos. 1994. *EZLN, Documentos y Comunicados/* Mexico: Ediciones Era.

Reforma, November 3, 1999, A6. Mexican daily.

Risse-Kappen, Thomas. 1995. Ed., *Bringing Transnational Relations Back In: Non-State Actors, Domestic Structures and International Institutions*. Cambridge, UK: Cambridge University Press.

Robertson, Roland, 1995. "Glocalization: Time-Space and Homogeneity-Heterogeneity." Mike Featherstone, Scott Lash, and Robertson, eds., *Global Modernities*. Thousand Oaks, CA: Sage, 25–44.

Rosenau, James N. 1983. "Fragmegrative Challenges to National Security." Terry Heyns, ed., *Understanding U.S. Strategy: A Reader*. Washington, DC: National Defense University, 65–82.

———. 1990. *Turbulence in World Politics: A Theory of Change and Continuity*. Princeton, NJ: Princeton University Press.

———. 1997. *Along the Domestic-Foreign Frontier: Exploring Governance in a Turbulent World*. Cambridge, UK: Cambridge University Press.

Rostow, Walt Whitman. 1960. *The Stages of Economic Development: A Non-Communist Manifesto*. Cambridge, UK: Cambridge University Press.

Rugman, Alan, and Michael Gestrin. 1994. "NAFTA's Treatment of Foreign Investment." Rugman, ed., *Foreign Investment and NAFTA*. Columbia, SC: University of South Carolina Press, 47–79.

Sartori, Giovani. 1998. *Homo Videns*. Madrid: Taurus.

Schedler, Andreas. 1999. "Civil Society and Political Elections: A Culture of Distrust?" *Annals of the American Academy of Political and Social Science*, no. 565 (September): 126–141.

Schmitter, Philppe. 1977. "Still the Century of Corporatism?" *The Review of Politics* 36, no. 1 (January): 85–131.

Smith, Peter H. 1997. "Political Dimensions of the Peso Crisis." Sebastian Edwards and Moisés Náim, eds., *Mexico 1994: Anatomy of an Emerging Market Crash*. Washington, DC: Carnegie Endowment for Peace, 31–53.

Stiglitz, Joseph. 2021. "The roaring Nineties." *The Atlantic*, October 2002. www.theatlantic.com/magazine/srchive/2002/10/the-roaring-nineties/302 604/. Last accessed on May 8, 2021.

Tehranian, Majid. 2012. "Where is the New World Order: At the End of History or Clash of CIvilizations?" *The Journal of International Communications* 18, no. 2. https://doi.org/10.1080/13216597.2012.709926

Vasquez, Ian. 1996. "The Brady Plan and Market-based Solutions to Debt Crises," *CATO Journal* 16, no. 2 (Fall): 233–243.

Verdier, Daniel. 1998. "Democratic Convergence and Free Trade." *International Studies Quarterly* 42, no. 1 (March): 1–24.

Vernon, Raymond. 1971. *Sovereignty at Bay: The Global Spread of Multinational Corporations*. New York: Basic Books.

———. 1991. "Sovereignty at Bay: Twenty Years After." *Millennium* 20, no. 1: 191–195.

Waltz, Kenneth N. 1979. *The Theory of International Politics*. Reading, MA: Addison-Wesley.

Weintraub, Sidney. 1996. "Mexico's Foreign Economic Policy: From Admiration to Disappointment." Laura Randall, ed., *Changing Structure of Mexico: Political, Social, and Economic Prospects*. Armonk, NY: M.E. Sharpe, 43–54.

Whitman, Marina v. N. 2003. "American Capitalism and Global Convergence: After the Bubble." Research Seminar in International Economy, Gerald

R. Ford School off Public Policy, Discussion Paper, #549, University of Michigan, Lansing, Michigan.

Winham, Gilbert. 1988. *Trading with Canada: The Canada-U.S. Free Trade Agreement*. New York: Priority Press.

Williamson, John. 2002, November 6. Did the Washington Consensus Fail?" *Presented at Center for Strategic and International Studies*, Washington, DC. Available at: http://www.iie.com/publications/papers/paper.cfm?ResearchID=488.

Williamson, John. 2003, September. "From Reform Agenda to Damaged Brand Name: A Short History of the Washington Consensus and Suggestions For What to do Next," *Finance and Development* (September 2003): 10–13.

Winham, Gilbert, and Heather Grant. 1994. "Antidumping and Countervailing Duties in Regional Trade Agreements: Canada-U.S. FTA, NAFTA, and Beyond." *Minnesota Journal of Global Trade* 3, no. 1 (Spring): 1–34.

www.wikipedia.org/wiki/List_of_countries_by_GDP_growth_1980-2010. Last accessed on May 8, 2021.

Zapata, Francisco. 1996. "Mexican Labor in a Context of Political and Economic Crisis." Laura Randall, ed., *Changing Structure of Mexico: Political, Social, and Economic Prospects*. Armonk, NY: M.E. Sharpe, 127–136.

"Zedello Catches Flak for Dismissing Zapatistas." *The News*, February 3, 2000, 2. Mexico City English daily.

"Zedello: NGOs Cannot Speak for Poor." *The News*. January 31, 2000, 2.

CHAPTER 12

Floating Frameworks and Precipitous Posturings: Post-Cold War Anarchy?

Imtiaz A. Hussain

INTRODUCTION: SMALL STEPS, LARGE CONSEQUENCES

Generalizing from a single case study is too foot-loose for merit, but seeking common conclusions from ten of them, as with this volume, seems at least as precarious. Yet in the post-Cold War world we may not have other options: every single case seems to be unravelling somewhere else in the world almost constantly, perhaps more or less assertively than found here. It remains up to the policy-makers, as much as the analytical scholars to draw a line somewhere, if only to get to the next base. We can find relief the Cold War mindset of "better dead than red" mindset and atmosphere no longer leaves us at the Manichean end of the string; but if having too many options poses problems of promptness, unanimity, or

I. A. Hussain (✉)
Global Studies & Governance Department, Independent University, Bangladesh (IUB), Dhaka, Bangladesh
e-mail: imtiaz.hussain@iub.edu.bd

© The Author(s), under exclusive license to Springer Nature Singapore Pte Ltd. 2022
I. A. Hussain (eds.), *Global-Local Tradeoffs, Order-Disorder Consequences*, Global Political Transitions,
https://doi.org/10.1007/978-981-16-9419-6_12

efficacy for anyone of us as a decision-maker, negotiating our own preferences with those of others can easily leave us, the policy prescriber, on the threshold of despair.

No better place to anchor the generalizations than *fragmegration*, the worldview under the microscope. More concretely, James N. Rosenau, who made mileage of this proposition (standing, as he admits, upon the shoulders of others), offered us some measurement yardsticks: the *fragmegrative* sources, all eight of them; and a number of aggregation levels. These suffice to get the ball rolling so some comparative theoretical conclusions can also be formulated from the 10 case studies.

Table 12.1 plots the sources against the key takeaways from each chapter; and Table 12.2 places those 10 chapters against the aggregation levels. Caveats pave the way. In Table 12.1, whether each source has had a high, medium, or low impact is registered as "H", "M", or "L", with "N" denoting "no impact", "O" for "opposite impact, and "Mx" for mixed impact (typically when actors from 2 or more aggregation levels coexist). Subjectivity will inevitably enter the purpose, even by default, but the most emphatic observations will be those at the extreme: "H",

Table 12.1 Collapsing constructs and half-baked substitutes: post-cold war brinkmanship

Substantive chapters	Key puzzle addressed	Emergent worldview
2	International institutions and new governance	Neo-liberalism (NL)
3	Populism	Fragmegration (F)
4	Peace operations	NL → F
5	Espionage (Bangladesh)	Realism (R)/Neo-realism (NR) → F
6	Climate-change displacing persons	Neo-liberalism (NL) → F
7	Land-reforms (Rwandan)	NL → F
8	Bangladesh RMG (ready-made-garments) and pandemic impact	F
9	Democracy (Bangladesh)	F
10	Refugee-camp education (Rohingyan-Syrian)	F
11	Neo-liberal and democratizing 1990s transitions (Mexico, 1990s)	F

Table 12.2 Fragmegration sources, aggregation levels, and a ten-chapter overview

Sources of fragmegration	Ch. 2	Ch. 3	Ch. 4	Ch. 5	Ch. 6	Ch. 7	Ch. 8	Ch. 9	Ch. 10	Ch. 11
1. Skill revolution	N	O	L	M	N	N	L	N	L	M
2. Authority crises	M	H	H	L	H	L	M	L	H	M
3. Bifurcation of global structures	H	H	H	N	L	L	M	N	L	H
4. Organizational explosion	H	O	L	L	L	N	N	N	N	M
5. Mobility upheaval	H	H	L	L	H	M	L	L	H	M
6. Micro-level technological dynamic	N	O	N	M	L	L	L	N	N	Mx
7. Weakening of territorialities, states, and sovereignty	M	O	H	M	M	N	L	L	H	H
8. Globalization of national economies	M	O	L	L	N	H	H	N	L	H
Aggregation levels of fragmegration										
Micro	L	H	M	L	H	H	H	H	H	H
Micro-macro	M	M	M	M	H	H	M	H	H	H
Macro	H	L	H	M	M	L	L	L	H	L
Macro-macro	H	L	H	H	H	M	H	M	H	L

Legend:
H: high impact
L: low impact
M: medium impact
Mx: mixed impact
N: no impact
O: opposite impact

"N", or "O". Others could swing this way or that with any observer, therefore play a lesser part in drawing conclusions. Table 12.2 depicts a similar portraiture, with the micro, representing people/individuals, clearly distinguishable from the macro, denoting the state (and the macro-macro accounting for state-state or state-international organization). Crucial in this analysis will be the micro–macro level so that a "H" observation highlights tension worth attention.

As other case studies will reaffirm, skill revolution and micro-level technology, as sources of *fragmegration*, have been profound and growing, particularly with the Fourth Industrial Revolution's artificial intelligence unfolding in mind-boggling ways. For the 10 cases here, though, no "H" label could be assigned to either of these sources: both register, at best, a "M" label in espionage (Chapter 7), and *neo-liberalism*/democratization (Chapter 11). Yet, the "H" presence in all other chapters may convey a message or two: the corresponding *fragmegrative* source is valid, viable, and potentially significant to understanding why a *fragmegrative* explanatory framework cannot be dismissed. Half of the remaining 6 *fragmegrative* sources registered "H" in 4 chapters: authority crises, bifurcation of global structures, and mobility upheaval. In the same vein, 2 other sources, weakening of territorialities, states, and sovereignty as well as globalization of national economies received a "H" labeling in 3 chapters, with the organizational explosion source similarly highlighted in one chapter (Chapter 2).

If anything, extant institutions and structures have been at bay this century, as we know from news media, scholarly analyses, and the cases in this volume. Not only that, but the cases in this volume show (that other scholarly analyses and news media can confirm), how two of the *fragmegrative* causes for this institutional/structural weakening have been the neo-liberal driven globalization of national economies and the weakening of territorialities, states, and sovereign rights, themselves also vulnerable to the force and fury of neo-liberal and democratic competitiveness and comparisons. These two *fragmegrative* sources need not be the dominant destabilizing dynamics, but since both launched themselves vigorously in the 1990s, we can see a generation later much of the damage wrought: they have provoked local groups or indigenous peoples in some areas, aggravated climate-change concerns in others, and widened inequalities such that low-wage producing countries constitute a far different and much more circumscribed ballpark than high-wage or high-tech countries. Steps to narrow that income development gap, such as Bangladesh still prioritizing the RMG sector for foreign-exchange earnings than climbing the value-chain to produce other low-wage products of a higher value, or Rwanda's land reforms, carry destabilizing forces in and of themselves, mostly at the social level or in migration-triggered urbanization, both capable of capturing environmental hazards of climate-change proportions. In other words, one *fragmegrative* source can easily combine with others, and together shake whatever edifices we have: these are the very institutions/structures.

Outside the "H" compass, the other generalizable observation related to "O" being monopolized by Chapter 3, on populism. Given its anti-establishment, science-repressing, value-ranking, and, at the extreme, nihilist outlook, populism may become the scourge of the next twenty-first-century generation. With its popularity spiraling faster than any other commensurate ideology, populism carries the potential to carry the critical veto power of global integration. This strengthens the *fragmegrative* forces more than, say, climate-change, or mobility upheaval, sources, and clamping down drastically on yet other sources, like globalization of national economies, micro-level technological dissemination, or skill revolution.

In other words, the unstable tapestry caught within this volume from developments of the last thirty-odd years, that is, since the Cold War ended, could be poised to destabilize further in the forthcoming years. Are there any countervailing forces? While a generalizable cure appears whimsical, certain stop-gap measures may buy time. With institutions and structures at stake, decentralizing them could be useful. Controlling how rampant the globalizing forces, both human and transactional, could be another, while easing transitions (whether skill-based or technology-triggered) should leave plenty on the table to work on: they dilute the populist cry, bring governance where perhaps none previously prevailed, and deploy citizens in productive directions to thwart extremist pulls.

Decentralizing international institutions to regional levels, as proposed in this volume (for peace-keeping purposes) should get the ball rolling, in addition to formulating pre-emptive measures against cyber-insecurity, as also proposed (in espionage discussions), and building/strengthening existing laws by giving them teeth, as a third string of climate-control measures. Then it becomes a question of how not to protect an industry as much as retraining the workers. This can be done by decentralizing job-opportunities domestically, and, in general, not through wholesale reform without having fallback options. Prioritizing new jobs for migrating farmers over how much more to export and where to send those exports exemplifies these proposals.

None of these palliatives will bring short-term solutions, pointing to the critical and secular control variable: how to instill long-term thinking in place of the short-term in vogue. Policies can do that better than markets, in turn suggesting how even the free-market needs control, if not for environmental or egalitarian reasons, then to stabilize society. Extending that to the free political market, that is, democratic rights, becomes easier if the voting is unfettered: the assumption being just that, that political parties play by certain common rules, make that the fundamental task, and amply represent the micro-level. It is to the aggregation levels where we must turn now.

Given the institutional/structural instability, as Table 12.1 portrayed, attention shifts primarily to the micro-level as a threat springboard. Understanding Table 12.2 begins with this premise: robust attention where the micro-level demands "H" intensity of impact and the macro counterpart elicits only a "L" impact intensity, but soft attention if the macro reading generates "M" impact intensity. That "H"–"L" gap matters, since many of the sources sprang from that (like authority crises, bifurcation of global structures, organizational explosion, and mobility upheaval). In other words, how to manage that gap remains the policy-maker's challenge in just about every country, and perhaps one reason why there is so much disarray on the analytical/theoretical front.

Table 12.2 shows us 4 of the cases with a "H"–"L" gap favoring the "H" side of the equation, and 3 others with a narrower gap. Obviously populism, a true kernel of unrest, leads the former list (Chapter 3), with the Mexican *neo-liberal*/democratic 1990s transformation (an established case of an unstable 1990s), standing next. That gap was much narrower with Rwandan land reform (Chapter 7), and Bangladesh democratization (Chapter 9): much needs to be done to iron out the gap to thwart further destabilization, a message for all countries implementing land reforms or democracy, meaning, a large part of the world.

On the other hand, with identical "H"-impact intensity, as with climate-change, RMG networking, and educating refugees (Chapters 6, 8, and 10), one must literally hold one's breath. They are not present fissure-points, but climate-change pressures intensify constantly, and not avoiding some disaster somewhere becomes less wishful thinking each day. So too with RMG networking since, as the pandemic revealed, RMG owners have the option to automate at the expense of low-wage workers, but those low-wage workers remain flat-footed without the same monotonous assembly-line tasks. Educating refugees also cannot be an end in itself, depending almost exclusively on how refugee repatriation unfolds since remaining a refugee only fuels the precarious situation.

Contrariwise, where a macro "H" reading pairs with a "L" micro-reading, chances of smoothening wrinkles may be the most. These include reorganizing extant international institutions, in particular decentralizing functions somewhat. This may be the only pathway of retaining Cold War structures in this post-Cold War era, though in changed form.

THEORETICAL TALK

When we take the necessary next step into theoretical observations, we cannot but find the *fragmegrative* worldview offering more complete explanations than its two rivals. Let us not, first of all, belittle the *neo-realist* view: when push turns to shove, any country will shift to this prism for interpretation and action, and if we academics do likewise, we understand more. It serves as the *necessary condition* for just about every case studied[1]: to turn to when vital interests get threatened, but otherwise silently observe other variables of little or no interest (or that neo-realists/*neo-realism* can satisfactorily explain). *Neo-liberalism* holds a similar proclivity: when optimism prevails, countries seem more inclined to collaborate abroad than under hard times. That becomes the golden moment to nurture international institutions. Much dirty water has flown since that last happened, in the 1990s. Clearly it was absent during the entire Cold War, except for the very brief euphoric moment just as World War II was ending. The end result may be that sticky negative reputation may simply hinder even the most serious nurturing exercise.

In the final analysis, we are left with *fragmegrative* views: this is unlikely to terminate directly in conflict, but too many skirmishes over a long period of time in reconciling the *fragmegrative* sources, or aggregation levels, or both, may unwittingly trigger a military showdown. With China-India, Iran-Israel, North Korea-South Korea, among others, we have come close to that point. At some future point, we may not be able to pull back.

Transitions as Global Mainstay?

It is difficult to conclude about transitions in a volume that has been about nothing else. Whether it is any of the *fragmegrative* sources, how it produces its end-products, fragmentation or integration, or even both, is hard to fathom without acknowledging the transition from one to the other (and back perhaps). This is equally emphatic with aggregation levels, indeed, why the two polar ends, micro and macro, had to spawn micro–macro or macro-macro without wanting to compromise with transitions, behooves comprehension if transition dynamics do not get fitted into the explanatory equation.

In a nutshell, the post-Cold War has been one of far more transitions than any since World War II, and perhaps more emphatically, than at any historical period. On the one hand are the number of countries and international organizations, corporations, and non-government entities, industrial revolutions coexisting on this planet, and the highest number of democratic countries, which fuels transitions much more than authoritarian governments. On the other are more disposable income in individual hands, material goods to whet appetites, and more education to open the human mind to new possibilities. Whichever way we look at, the puzzles in this volume, and many others not touched, transitions have become a sixth sense, a third foot, or, at the least, a second option where there was only one before.

That may be the most troubling optimism to conclude with: we have, sort of, "been there" and "done that", and all that jazz, for far too long to think an alternative exists. Yet, it is in the cumulative civilizational effect of all this open-endedness where the rainbow or silver lining lies. In an age of far longer "rising expectations" than ever before, simply because we have too many units at both micro and macro levels, those end-points look farther and farther away. And that is not a pretty juncture for sustaining stability.

Note

1. Robert Gilpin makes the most of the variable *necessary condition*. See *U.S. Power and the Multinational Corporation: The Political Economy of Foreign Direct Investment* (New York, NY: Basic Books, 1975, Chapter 1).

Index

A
ACSA (Acquisition and Cross Servicing Agreement), between Bangladesh and United States, 123, 130, 138
Acton, Lord, 17, 224
ADB (Asian Development Bank), 40, 41, 54, 205, 207
Ahmed Taufiq, Hossain, 14
AL (*Awami League*), Bangladesh political party, 112, 113
Aldrich, Richard, 113, 118, 133–137
Al-Mourabitoun (a branch of AQIM), 101
Al Shabab, 100, 115
AMISOM (African Union Mission in Somalia), 114, 115
Angelov, Angel, 100, 107
Ansar Dine (a branch of AQIM), 101
anti-dumping duties (ADDs), 285, 286, 288, 289
AOEI (ASEAN Our Eyes Initiative), 114
AQIM (Al-Qaeda in the Islamic Mahgreb), 101
AQIS (*Al Qaeda in Indian Sub-Continent*), 128
Arab Spring, in 2010, 72, 77, 224
Aristotle, 73, 217, 223
ARSA (Arakan Rohingya Salvation Army), Myanmar rebel group, 262
ASEAN (Association of South East Asian Nations), 53, 114, 115
Ashraf, A.S.M. Ali, 13, 133, 136, 138, 139
Asian Four Tigers, 3
ATU (Anti-Terrorism Unit), 120, 137
AU (African Union), 96, 99, 105, 115
Azad, A., 196, 208
Azraq, refugee camp for Syrians in Jordan, 239
Azteca, Mexico's television channel, 277, 281

B

Baker Plan, U.S. bailout plan for Mexico, 1984, 273
Bakka region, refugee camps in Lebanon for Syrians, 236, 239
Bangladesh, 13, 14, 73, 76, 112, 113, 120–133, 139, 142, 193, 194, 196, 197, 199, 201, 206–208, 218, 221–223, 225, 229, 231, 232, 250, 251, 253–256, 263, 314, 316, 318
Bangladesh Garment Shramik Sanghati, 202
Barbosa, Maximiano, Mexican political commentator, 283
Barzonistas, followers of *Barzón*, 283
Barzón, Mexican social group, 275, 279–281, 283, 296
BDT (Bangladesh Taka), 200
Berger, Suzanne, 27, 50, 51
Bernstein, Steven, 32, 52
BFIU (Bangladesh Financial Intelligence Unit), 121, 126
BGMEA (Bangladesh Garment Manufacturers and Exporters Association), 199, 201, 208, 209
Bhardwaj, Arjun, 32, 34, 49, 51–53
BIMSTEC (Bay of Bengal Multi-Sectoral Technical and Economic Cooperation), 124, 128, 132, 142
Biswas, Niloy Anjan, 13
BNP (Bangladesh Nationalist Party), 112, 113
Bosnia, 95
BRAC (Bangladesh Rural Advancement Committee), 201, 257
Brady Plan, U.S. bailout plan for Mexico, 1988, 273
BREXIT, 65
BRI (Belt Road Initiative), China's pre eminent global investment project, from 2013, 119, 132

C

Calles, Plutarco Elías, Mexico president from 1924, *Partido Nacional Revolucionario*, 275
candidate, Mayor of Mexico City, 1997–99, founder of *Partida Democratica Revolucionario*, 276, 278, 281
Cárdenas, Lázaro, Mexican president. 1934–40, *Partido Revolucionario Institucional*, 275
Cárdenas Solórzano, Cuauhtemoc, son of President Cárdenas, Lázaro, failed presidential candidate, Mayor of Mexico City, 1997–99, founder of *Partida Democratica Revolucionario*, 277
Cardoso, Fernando Henrique, 16, 30, 51
Cashore, Benjamin, 32, 52
CBDR (Common but Differentiated Responsibilities), 150, 151
CCID (Climate Change Induced Displacement), 149
CCTE (conditional cash transfer for education), a Turkish program, 245, 248
CDP (climate change-displaced person), 149–157
Chambers, Robert, 25, 33, 50, 52
chaord, 6, 272, 284
Chiapas, Mexico's rebellious province, 274–276, 280–282, 296, 303
China, 3, 62, 113, 119, 122, 124, 127, 132, 134, 194, 197, 198, 204, 273
China-bashing, 5
Chomsky, Naom, 24, 302

Chowdhury, Tamim (Holey Artisan Bakery attack leader Dhaka, Bangladesh, 2016), 124, 127
CIC (Central Intelligence Cell), Bangladesh, 121
CIID (Customs Intelligence and Investigation Directorate), Bangladesh, 121, 126
Ciompi Revolt, 14th Century, 64
CIS (Commonwealth of Independent States, a Soviet Union successor), 100
CISSA (Committee of Intelligence and Security Services of Africa), 115
Cold War, 1947–89, 3–5, 7, 10, 12, 24, 25, 35, 37, 50, 64, 67, 71, 90–92, 118, 272, 293, 313, 317, 319
Colosio, Luis Donaldo, assassinated presidential candidate, 1993, *Partido Revolucionario Institucional*, 277, 302
constructivism, a theoretical paradigm in International Relations, 117
coronavirus, 61, 62, 82, 83, 194, 198, 199, 201, 205, 209, 211
corporatism, form of interest intermediation, popular in Latin America and Mediterranean Europe, 280, 284, 296
Council of Environmental Ministers, NAFTA, 292, 293
Council of Labor Ministers, NAFTA, 292–294
countervailing duties (CVDs), 285, 291, 304
COVID-19, 1, 68, 73, 74, 76, 78, 84, 191, 194, 198–207, 211, 225. *See also* coronavirus; and pandemic

Cox's Bazaar, Bangladesh, home of over 1m, Rohingya refugees, 245
CSOs (civil society organizations), 31, 33, 38, 40
CTED (Counter Terrorism Committee Executive Directorate), 125
CTTC (Counter Terrorism and Transnational Crime) Unit, 120, 122, 128
CUFTA (Canada-U.S. Free Trade Agreement), 1989–1993, 273, 285, 294
Curato, Nicole, 65, 72, 78, 81
CVE (countering violent extremism), 90, 97, 100–103

D

Darwin, Charles, 221
Davos World Economic Forum, an annual Retreat for leaders, in Switzerland, 273
DDR (disarmament, demobilization and reintegration), 92
De as Gortari, Carlos, President of Mexico, 1988–94, *Partido Revolucionario Institucional*, 282
dedazo, finger-pointing, Mexican tradition of presidential successor selection, 276, 281
de-globalization, 62, 65, 67, 68
de la Madrid, Miguel, 275
dēmokratía (Greek for democracy), 217
Depression Era, 1929–39, 69, 70
descamisados (shirtless), 64
de Soto, Hernando, a political commentator, 167, 180, 184, 187
DGIF (Directorate General of Forces Intelligence), Bangladesh, 120

DGMM (Directorate General of Migration Management), Turkey, 240, 249
DNA (deoxyribonucleic acid, hereditary material in humans), 112
DRC (Democratic Republic of Congo), 90, 98, 100, 102, 104
Duterte, Rodrigo, President The Philippines, 65

E
EAI (Enterprise of the Americas Initiative), 1989, 273
East Asia, 47, 138
ECC (Extraordinary Challenge Committee), dispute settlement body in NAFTA, 285–287, 292, 294
ECE (Early Childhood Education) a Turkish program, 244, 245, 286, 288
ECOWAS (Economic Community of West African States), 99
Egypt, 229, 233, 235, 238
ENIAC (Electronic Numerical Integrator and Computer), Moore School, University of Pennsylvania, 1958, 4, 17
European Community, 1967–91, 5, 273
European Union (EU), 1992–, 5, 10, 11, 61, 113–115, 119, 194, 273, 304
Export-led growth strategies, 34
EZLN *(Ejército Zapatista de Liberación Nacional*: Zapatista Army of National Liberation), secessionist indigenous group led by mainstream leader, 282, 303

F
Faletto, Enzo, 16, 30, 51
Faller, John S., political commentator, 281
FAO (Food and Agricultural Organization), 166, 167, 179, 183
Farage, Neil, 65
FGD (focused group discussion), a form of interview, 179
FIB (Force Intervention Brigade), United Nations, 95
Five Eyes (FVEY) Defence Pact, 115
"flying geese", 17
Fourth Industrial Revolution, 316
Fox Channel, television, 75
Fox Quesada, Vicente, Mexican President, Partido Acción Nacional, 2000–2006, 276
fragmegration, 6, 7, 13, 14, 272, 284, 296, 297, 314, 316
fragmegrative, 7, 10, 12–14, 16, 117, 119, 229, 296, 314, 316, 317, 319, 320
France, 28, 63, 65, 71, 75
Freedom House, 14
free-trade agreements (FTAs), 4, 10
Freire, Paolo, 227
French Revolution, 1789, 63, 64
FSU (Former Soviet Union), 24, 26, 114
Fuentes, Carlos, proposed Mexico to be a "perfect dictatorship", 275, 296
Fukuyama, Francis, 25

G
Gandhi, Mahatma, 11
GATT (General Agreement on Tariffs and Trade), 1947–1993, 4, 290
Gellner, Ernest, 64, 78
Germany, 28, 44, 66, 299

GHG (greenhouse gases), 151
GIEP (Guidelines for Informal Education Program), refugee-camp related, 233, 250, 257
Gill, Stephen, 30, 51, 305
globalization, 1, 3, 5–7, 9, 11, 12, 14, 16, 18, 23–38, 40, 43–53, 62, 63, 65–68, 72, 74–77, 112, 113, 271, 272, 274, 281, 289, 291, 295, 296, 315–317
global South, 13, 37, 67, 111–113, 116, 117, 119, 122, 132, 133, 136
glocalization, 6, 272, 281, 284
Goethe, 73
Goodwin, Robert, 42, 54
governance, 2, 3, 8, 11, 12, 19, 23–25, 30, 33, 36, 38–49, 90, 219, 222, 228, 260, 275, 285, 314, 317
Gramscian, 30, 31
Granovetter, Mark, 43
Greenback Party, the, 70
GSOMIA (General Security of Military Information Agreement), a Bangladesh-U.S. agreement, 123, 130, 138

H
Habib, Mamun, 14, 206–208
Hasan, Ikram, 14
Hasina, Sheikh, Prime Minister Bangladesh, 1996–2000; 2009–, 201
Hechos, Mexico's television channel, 277, 278
Heck, Dee W., 6, 18
Held, David, 28, 51, 52
HIPPO (UN High Level Independent Panel on Peace Operations), 95, 102

historical structuralism, 24, 29
Hitler, Adolf, 2
Hobsbawm, Eric, 68, 79
Hofstadter, Richard, 70
Holey Artisan Bakery attack in Dhaka, 2016, 124
Hossain, Delwar, 12, 13, 32, 34, 49, 51–53, 134
Human Development Report 1999, 32, 37, 52
HUMINT (human intelligence), 116, 130, 131
Hussain, Imtiaz A., 138, 141

I
IAWG (Inter Agency Working Group), 229
ICCPR (International Covenant on Civil & Political Rights), 218, 224
ICSID (International Convention for the Settlement of Investment Disputes), a U.N. body, 288, 289
ICT (information and communications technologies), 32, 36, 37, 53
IDC (International Donors Community), 40, 41, 47
IDP (internally displaced person), 92, 233, 234
ILO (International Labor Organization), 205, 287–289
IMF (International Monetary Fund), 26, 48
INCB (International Narcotics Control Board), 115
India, 66, 93, 113, 122–132, 134, 138, 140, 154, 185, 204, 220
INGO (international non-governmental organizations), 229
Ingram, James D., 64, 78

institutionalism, 118
interdependence, 26, 27, 29, 30, 50, 66, 67, 296
International Trade Authority, U.S., 285
Interpol (International Police), an organization, 115, 126, 136
IOM (International Office for Migration), 233
Ionescu, Ghita, 64
IPE (International political economy), 23, 24, 29
Iraq, 68, 229, 233, 235, 238, 261
IR (International Relations), 23, 24, 27, 62, 112, 117, 119, 132
ISI (import substitution industrialization), 2, 129, 273, 274
ISIS (Islamic State of Iraq and Syria), 123, 124, 128, 140, 261
IS (Islamic State), 100, 123, 261
ITESCM (Integrated Tertiary Educational Supply Chain Management), 196, 206

J
Japan, 3, 5, 28, 44, 272, 299
Japan-bashing, 5
jihadis, 229
JISD (Joint Intelligence and Security Division), a NATO unit, 115
JMB (*Jama'at ul Mujahideen Bangladesh*), 122, 128, 129
Jordan, 114, 229, 233, 236, 238, 239
JP (*Jatiya* Party), Bangladesh, 112, 113

K
Kaltwasser, Cristóbal Rovira, 65, 71, 78, 81
Kapstein, Ethan, 35, 52

Katzenstein, Peter, U.S. political scientist, 289, 305
Keohane, Robert O., 18, 24, 26, 49, 50
Keyman, Fuat, 30, 51
Khan, Md. Abdul Awal Khan, 13
Know Nothing Party, the, 70
Kutupalong, refugee camp for Rohingyas in Cox's Bazaar, Bangladesh, 231
kybernetes, 38

L
Labastida Ochoa, Francisco, Mexican presidential contender, 1994, *Partido Revolucionario Institucional*, 276
Lake, David, 43, 55
land reforms, 14, 168, 282, 317, 318
Lanng, Christian, 204, 211
Latin America, 2, 26, 40, 47, 62, 64, 69, 71, 111, 114, 115, 272, 273, 296, 300
Law, David, 30
Lawson, Chappel, political commentator, 281, 302, 305
LCF (Learning Competency Framework), Myanmar, 250, 253
LCFA (Learning Competency Framework Approach), refugee-camp related, 233
LDC (less developed country), 14, 29–31, 151, 166, 219
Lebanon, 229, 233, 236, 239, 240
liberalism, 6, 25, 63, 64, 69, 117, 272, 274, 275, 279, 284
liberalization, Mexican, 279, 290, 291
"Liberatory", 230, 241, 242, 262
Lin, Jesse Lin, 204, 211
localization, 1, 3, 5, 6, 11, 12, 62, 65, 67, 72, 112–114, 272, 274, 281

LTRP (Land Tenure Regularization Programme), Rwanda, 166–169, 171, 172, 175, 176, 178, 180–182

M
MacSharry Reforms, European Union, 1993, on agriculture, 273
Madrazo, Roberto, Mexican presidential Candidate, 1994, *Partido Revolucionario Institucional*, 278, 279, 295
Manuel Bartlett, Mexican presidential Candidate, 1994, *Partido Revolucionario Institucional*, 276, 278, 279
Martinez, Enrique Leon, political Commentator, 277, 302
Marx, Karl, 73
McCann, James A., political commentator, 281, 302
McCarthyism, 64
Mearsheimer, John, 132, 142
Mercosur (Market of the south in Latin America), from 1989, 273, 300
Merkel, Angela, German Chancellor 2005–21, 77
Middle East, 229
MINUSCA (U.N. Mission in Central African Republic), 95
MINUSMA (U.N. Multidimensional Integrated Stabilization Mission in Mali), 94, 95, 101
Mitrany, David, 6, 18, 298
MONUSCO (U.N. Stabilization Mission to the Democratic Republic of the Congo), 95
Morgenthau, Hans J., 27, 50, 297
Mother Teresa, 11
Mudde, Cas, 78

N
NAFTA (North American Free Trade Agreement), 1994, 17, 273, 274, 280–283, 285, 288–291, 293–296, 302–304
narodnichestvo (populism), 64
NATO (North Atlantic Treaty Organization), 4, 100, 115
Nazism, 71
NBR (National Board of Revenue), Bangladesh, 121
neo-liberalism, a theoretical paradigm in International Relations, 13, 15, 16, 26, 27, 72, 272, 274, 316, 319
neo-populism, 69
neo-realism, a theoretical paradigm in International Relations, 5, 13–16, 27, 113, 119, 272, 319
new institutionalism, 24, 25, 42, 43
NGOs (non-governmental organizations), 12, 37, 40, 41, 49, 53, 152, 155, 175, 187, 229, 248, 252, 257, 305
NLG ("No Lost Generation"), a global Initiative, 243, 244
NPO (non-profit organizations), 37, 40, 192
Nuruzzaman, A.H., 196, 208

O
OAS (Organization of American States), 99
Obama, Barack, U.S. President, 2009–16, 70, 80
Obregón, Álvaro, Mexican president, 1920–24, 275
OECD (Organization for Economic Cooperation and Development), 36, 53
OLL (Organic Land Law), Rwanda, 166

Oman, Charles, 24, 49, 297

P

pandemic, 1, 12, 61, 68, 73, 74, 76–78, 191, 194, 198, 201–203, 205, 209, 225, 228, 314, 318
PAN (*Partido Acción Nacional*), Mexican political party, 277, 280
peacekeeping v. peace enforcement, 89, 103
Pearson, Lester, 91
"perfect dictatorship," reference to Mexico by Carlos Fuentes, 15, 273, 274, 302
Pieterse, Nederveen, 30, 51
PIF (Pacific Islands Forum), 100
pluralists, 43
PNR (*Partido Nacional Revolucionario*), predecessor of PRI political party in Mexico, 275
populism, 5, 10, 12, 16, 62–65, 67–73, 75, 77, 80, 81, 84, 223, 314, 317, 318
Populist Party, the, 70
"populist public", 12, 62, 63, 65, 68, 69, 72–77
PPE (personal protective equipment), paraphernalia popularized during Covid-19 pandemic, 2019–, 204
PRI (*Partido Revolucionario Institucional*), Mexican political party, 275–279, 281, 282, 284, 295
Putnam, Robert, 44, 55

Q

Quirino, Juan José, Mexican political Commentator, 283, 284

R

RAB (Rapid Action Battalion), Bangladesh, 120, 122, 123, 129
RACE (Reaching All Children with Education), children programme in Turkey, 239
Rahman, Ziaur, 14
Rakhine, Myanmar, 229, 231, 250
Refugees, 15, 91, 92, 115, 155, 156, 227–234, 236–247, 251, 253–263, 318, 319
Rohingyan, 15, 228, 243, 251, 261, 314
Syrian, 15, 75, 228, 229, 233, 234, 238–241, 243–245, 251, 254, 256, 261, 262
refugees, Syrian, 75, 228, 229, 233–241, 243–245, 251, 254, 256
education for, 234, 240, 245, 251
Rohingyan, 228, 243, 251, 261
Regional Refugee and Resilience Plan (3RP), 229, 233, 234, 243–245, 251, 258, 261, 263–265
Rhodes, R.A.W., 38, 53
RMG (ready-made-garments), 14, 192–194, 196, 197, 199–203, 205, 206, 210, 314, 317, 318
Robertson, Robert, 6, 18
Roque, Humberto, Mexican presidential Candidate, 1994, *Partido Revolucionario Institucional*, 276–279
Rose, General Sir Michael, Chief, 95
Rosenau, James N., 5–7, 10, 12, 13, 18, 19, 272, 281, 285, 298, 304, 305, 314
Rwanda, 14, 95, 165, 168, 171, 178, 180–183, 314, 317, 318
Rwanda's Economic Development and Poverty Reduction Strategy, 166

RWF (Rwandan Franc), 169–173, 180

S
SAARC (South Asian Association for Regional Cooperation), 117, 124–126, 128, 132
Sanders, Bernie, 65
SARPCCO (South African Regional Police Chiefs Cooperation Organization), 115
SARS (severe acute respiratory syndrome), 194, 197
SAVAK, Iran's secret police, 116
SCM (supply chain management), 191–193, 195, 196, 198, 205–208
SC (supply chain), 192, 194, 196–199, 203–207
SDCD (*Summary of Deliberations of Climate Change and Displacement*), UNHCR document, 153
SDOMD (SAARC Drug Offenses Monitoring Desk), 125
SECOFI, Mexican Secretary of Commerce and Industrial Development, 285
Security Council, U.N., 2, 10, 91–93, 95, 96
SEG (Strategic Executive Groups), 233
Shamrock Summit, Canada and the United States, 1986, 273
SIGINT (signal intelligence), 116, 118, 122, 123, 130, 131
Smith, Adam, 66
Somalia, 93, 95
SRAD (Syrian Refugee Affairs Directorate), 229, 239
STOMD (SAARC Terrorism Offenses Monitoring Desk), 125
Summit of the Americas, Florida, 1994, 273
sustainable democracy, 217, 219, 220
Swadhin Bangla Betar Kendra (Independent Bangladesh Radio Station, a 1971 Liberation War unit), 122

T
Tandon, Rajesh, 38, 53
Tartila Suma, Jessica, 15
TCE (transactional cost economics), 43
TECs (Temporary Education Centers), Turkey, 240
Televisa, Mexico's largest television channel, 277, 278, 281
Thucydides, 27, 50
Thunberg, Greta, 11
Toffler, Alvin, 36
TPR (Temporary Protection Regulation), refugee related, in Turkey, 240
Trotsky, Leon, 73, 81
Trump, Donald, 65, 70, 74–76, 82, 97, 223
Turkey, 229, 233, 237, 240, 241, 244, 251, 254–256

U
UAVs (unmanned aerial vehicles), 98
UBUDEHE, a Rwandan poverty-alleviating program, 178
UDHR (Universal Declaration of Human Rights), 224
UKUSA Agreement, 115
UNAMSIL (U.N. Mission in Sierra Leone), 95
U.N. Chapter VII, 90, 91, 93, 95
U.N. Charter, 91, 94, 95, 99, 100

UNCITRAL (United National Commission for International Trade Law), 287–289
U.N. Congo peacekeeping mission, 91
UNDP (United Nations Development Programme), 37, 40, 52, 53, 178, 187, 211, 233
UNEF (United Nations Emergency Force), 91, 93
UNESCO (United Nations Educational, Scientific, and Cultural Organization), 66, 228, 233, 234, 239, 263–265
UNFCCC (United Nations Framework Convention on Climate Change), 150–152, 156, 157
UNHCR (United Nations High Commissioner for Refugees), 153, 155, 156, 159, 228–230, 233, 235, 238, 239, 257, 263–265
United Kingdom (U.K.), 63, 65, 66, 114–118, 123, 127
United Nations (U.N.), 2, 11, 15, 90–107, 125, 126, 132, 149, 151–154, 156, 157, 218
United States (U.S.), 3–5, 10, 24, 25, 63–65, 68–70, 74–76, 80, 97, 113–116, 118, 119, 122–124, 127, 129–132, 194, 198, 205, 220, 272–274, 280, 281, 285, 290, 291, 294, 299, 304
U.N. Peacekeeping, 89, 90
UNPROFOR (United Nations Protection Force), 95
UNSC (United Nations Security Force), 91–93, 95, 99
Uruguay Round (of GATT), 1986–1993, 273

W
Waltz, Kenneth N., 17, 27, 50, 298
Warsaw Pact, 1955, 4
WB (World Bank), 26, 40, 41, 48, 166, 198, 200
Webb, Adele, 65, 72, 78, 81
Weiss, Linda, 28
Whitman, Marina N, proponent of "American decade" idea in 1990s, 272, 299
Williamson, Oliver, 43, 55, 300
WTO (World Trade Organization), 4, 26, 34, 67, 273, 289

Y
Yasmin, Lailufar, 12, 134
Yousafzai, Malala, 11

Z
Zaatari camp, for Syrian refugees, in Jordan, 239
Zakaria, Fareed, 74, 82
Zaman, Rashed Uz, 13, 104
Zapatistas, followers of EZLN, 282
Zawacki, Benjamin, 243
Zedillo, Ernesto de Ponce, Mexican President, *Partido Revolucionario Institucional* 1994–2000, 276, 283, 295

Printed by Printforce, United Kingdom